No Day in Court

Studies in Postwar American Political Development

Steven Teles, *Series Editor*

No Day in Court

Access to Justice and the Politics of Judicial Retrenchment

SARAH STASZAK

OXFORD
UNIVERSITY PRESS

OXFORD
UNIVERSITY PRESS

Oxford University Press is a department of the University of
Oxford. It furthers the University's objective of excellence in research,
scholarship, and education by publishing worldwide.

Oxford   New York
Auckland   Cape Town   Dar es Salaam   Hong Kong   Karachi
Kuala Lumpur   Madrid   Melbourne   Mexico City   Nairobi
New Delhi   Shanghai   Taipei   Toronto

With offices in
Argentina   Austria   Brazil   Chile   Czech Republic   France   Greece
Guatemala   Hungary   Italy   Japan   Poland   Portugal   Singapore
South Korea   Switzerland   Thailand   Turkey   Ukraine   Vietnam

Oxford is a registered trademark of Oxford University Press
in the UK and certain other countries.

Published in the United States of America by
Oxford University Press
198 Madison Avenue, New York, NY 10016

Library of Congress Cataloging-in-Publication Data
Staszak, Sarah L., author.
No day in court : access to justice and the politics of judicial retrenchment / Sarah Staszak.
pages cm
Revision of author's disseration (doctoral—Brandeis University, 2010), issued under title: The politics of
judicial retrenchment.
ISBN 978–0–19–939903–1 (hardback : alk. paper) — ISBN 978–0–19–939904–8 (pbk. : alk. paper)
1. Political questions and judicial power—United States.   I. Title.   II. Title: Politics of judicial
retrenchment.
KF8748.S825 2015
347.73′052—dc23
2014019304

For My Family

Contents

Acknowledgments

MARLENE BENJAMIN HAS indelibly shaped how I think about politics and law, and she in many ways inspired this project. The process of moving through graduate school, a dissertation, and onto a book has led me to accumulate many debts, and I could not be more grateful for the sheer number that I have accumulated along the way. First and foremost, I cannot possibly say enough about the role that Steve Teles has played at all stages. I am so thankful to have had the opportunity to work with him, and I am forever grateful for him not only in his role as dissertation advisor, but also especially for his continued support as my all-around life's guide and friend. In my time at Brandeis, Dan Kryder was an invaluable source of support and intellectual guidance, particularly in helping me to shape the theoretical contours of this project. I am also incredibly lucky that Tom Burke and Shep Melnick were each willing to take me under their wing. Without them, I can't imagine how I would have tackled a project on public law.

Chapter Four is a revised version of "Institutions, Rulemaking, and the Politics of Judicial Retrenchment," *Studies in American Political Development* (October 2010), which was a product of support that I received from both Brandeis University and Princeton University. The CUNY Research Foundation also provided generous funding for this project through a PSC-CUNY grant, and I am so thankful for my wonderfully supportive group of colleagues and inspiring students at The City College of New York—CUNY as well. While writing my dissertation, I was a research fellow in Governance Studies at the Brookings Institution, where Sarah Binder, Amy Widestrom, and Benjamin Wittes were wonderfully supportive in that process. I am also exceptionally grateful to be Robert Wood Johnson Scholar in Health Policy Research at Harvard University, and to have amazing colleagues like Joanna Veazey Brooks, Daniel Carpenter, Sage Kochavi, Daniel Gillion, Daniel Navon, Katherine Swartz, and Robert Vargas.

A variety of individuals have been incredibly generous with their time in reading and commenting on portions of this manuscript, including Stephen Burbank, Charles Epp, Sean Farhang, Paul Frymer, George Lovell, Judith Resnik, and John Skrentny. I have also benefited greatly over the years from conversations, comments, and cheerful encouragement from Jack Balkin, Jeb Barnes, Pam Brandwein, Daniel Carpenter, Stuart Chinn, Elisabeth Clemens, Daniel DiSalvo, Lynda Dodd, Heather Elliot, Steve Engel, Malcolm Feeley, Robert George, Leslie Gerwin, Daniel Gillion, Mark Graber, Michael Greve, Paul Herron, Robert Kagan, Stuart Kane, Tom Keck, Kip Kendall, Ken Kersch, Daniel LaChance, Catherine Lee, Michael McCann, Timothy McCarty, Robert Mickey, Quinn Mulroy, Naomi Murakawa, Chuck Myers, Herschel Nachlis, Eric Patashnik, Karen Orren, Devah Pager, Adam Sheingate, and Gordon Silverstein. David McBride has been phenomenal in his support and guidance as well, and the two anonymous reviewers for Oxford University Press provided invaluable feedback and insight, to which I hope I have done justice. I am also particularly grateful to Sarah Paige for her top-notch research support, Michael Shohl for his expertise in editing, Derek Gottlieb as a wonderful great indexer, and Sarah Rosenthal for her wisdom and kindness.

I am no doubt underserving of the wonderful support community that has cheered me through this process. I have no idea how I could have done this without Sarah Ambrose, John Blake, Joanna Veazey Brooks, Tom Clark, Jen and Pierce Cole, Julianna Cook, Erica Czaja, Romeo Giron, Lynn Horan, Chris Kendall, Christine Kiernan, Laura LeDuc, Kelly Mailly, Christine and Tim Wyman McCarty, David and Karen Nathan, Dan Navon, and Andrea Runstadler, who have been so generous in their support, each in their unique ways. I am eternally grateful to you all. And it is without the slightest bit of embarrassment or shame that I thank my cats, who—after all—spent the most time with me while I worked on this book, no doubt creating a vast array of typos in their attempts to "help" by distracting their anxious friend.

Most of all, I thank my family. I am so lucky to have inherited Patrick Carroll and Murry, Barbara, Ben, and Carrie Frymer into that family. The role that David, Sharon, Meredith, and Emily Staszak have played in all aspects of my life is so extensive as to elude a simple summary. Their love, support, and laughter have always been the greatest gifts. Finally, thank you for everything, Paul; for so many reasons, I am just ridiculously lucky to have you in my life. You are my favorite thing.

Sarah Staszak
Somerville, MA
August 10, 2014

I

Introduction

THE SUPREME COURT'S 2011 decision in favor of Wal-Mart was hardly a surprise. After all, now more than four decades removed from the height of the rights revolution—an era defined by a series of foundational courtroom victories for activists of civil rights and liberties—it was far from unexpected that a sex discrimination case against a major corporation would gain little traction with the nation's highest court. As the Warren and Burger courts of the 1950s, 60s, and 70s gave way to the antilitigation spirit that would characterize those led by Justices William Rehnquist and John Roberts, by 2011 it was perhaps less a question of whether the 1.6 million women seeking back pay for years of unequal wages and treatment by the company would win and more a question of on what legal grounds they would fail.

For a Court that had recently undercut the ability of taxpayers to challenge government programs in court, of the wrongfully convicted to hold errant district attorneys responsible for prosecutorial misconduct, of states and groups to compel the federal government to regulate polluting power plants, and of consumers to sue to have their grievances against powerful corporations heard by a judge, the more relevant question was just how hard a blow large-scale civil rights cases would take.[1] As far as the national media was concerned, at issue was whether the company's practices ran afoul of a key provision of the nation's most acclaimed rights statute—the Civil Rights Act of 1964—and specifically of Title VII, which prohibits discrimination in the work place on the basis of sex. But close followers of the Roberts Court had other suspicions as to what might influence the outcome of the case; as Stanford law professor Richard Thompson Ford wrote on the eve of the *Wal-Mart* decision, at issue was not only whether the women's constitutional or statutory claims would be denied, but also whether class action lawsuits—so integral for many of the landmark gains of the Civil Rights era—would "continue to be a way to address pervasive discrimination, or whether America's battle against prejudice will have to be fought on a case-by-case basis."[2]

For legal scholars, this question was hardly a new one. Legal innovations like the class action were created at the height of the Civil Rights era to help individuals otherwise lacking the necessary resources to tackle the legal system and to get their day in court. But in the context of a national political climate increasingly hostile to massive legal actions aimed at solving broad societal and political problems, the fate of their continued availability became "the central question in many of the most important civil rights disputes of the last 30 years." And the answer, Ford noted, has become consistently clear; "in almost every case since the early 1980s, the Supreme Court has come down on the side of individualism against social justice."[3]

The position taken by the Court in *Wal-Mart*, then, ultimately fulfilled what was widely feared, but also widely expected: the Court threw out the case filed jointly by Wal-Mart's female employees who claimed that the company's nationwide policies led to systemic and systematic gender discrimination in both wages and opportunities for promotion. But the decision did not turn on a constitutional claim, nor did it resolve a question of law or statute. And although the litigants alleged that the company's practices violated the Civil Rights Act, the Court never even addressed the question of whether the women suffered discrimination in their years with the company. Instead, the pivotal question, as far as the Roberts Court majority saw it, was whether this massive group of litigants—which included all women employed by Wal-Mart stores nationwide since late 1998—could be properly certified as a "class"; that is, whether they could bring their like-grievances together in one case, or whether they would have to do so individually, in separate cases. And because they lacked sufficient "commonality" under the relevant procedural rules, the Court said that they could not.[4]

As the media scurried to explain the decision, and the public to understand it—a case otherwise so reminiscent in its details of the many successful civil rights cases from decades prior—the nation received a basic primer on the previously obscure Federal Rules of Civil Procedure, under which the Court had denied the women's claim. These rules, first promulgated in 1938, govern everything about a civil legal proceeding: they provide the standards for determining what constitutes a case or legal controversy, how it must be filed by a potential plaintiff, how the case will be adjudicated, and what remedies are available for the winners. The women in the *Wal-Mart* case, the

Court argued, failed to meet the criteria for a specific subsection of one such rule: Rule 23(a), which requires (among other things), that "there are questions of law or fact common to the class," and that "the claims or defense of the representative parties are typical of the claims or defenses of the class."[5] As far as the majority was concerned, Wal-Mart's female employees failed to show that the facts of their individual experiences were sufficiently similar to bring a lawsuit together as a group, and thus would have to file approximately 1.6 million individual cases, each at their own individual expense. Although some of the justices suggested that perhaps under another rule the women might have succeeded in being certified as a class, just like that, the merits of their discrimination claim went unexamined—seemingly on a purely procedural technicality—and therefore unaddressed by the Court.[6] Subsequently, the question quickly became how these procedural rules had largely flown under the public's radar for so long, when they clearly stood to have such profound and practical legal importance.

Prominent legal analyst Dahlia Lithwick has noted that there are two types of stories that the media tells us about the Supreme Court.[7] The vast majority of the time, we comb through newspapers and blogs, and turn to social media in search of the "Type A" stories; those that explain the exciting, contentious, and closely divided 5-4 decisions, usually on the fate of a major constitutional right, and that seem to hinge on the ideologies and political and policy preferences of the individual justices. Sometimes there are surprises—Chief Justice Roberts' support of the Affordable Care Act is one notable example—but more often than not this is a partisan story, and one that rightfully keeps us cognizant of just how important it is to know *who* exactly is on the Court, and therefore whether we have a Democratic or Republican president in the position to fill vacancies should they occur.

But there is also another story. Each year there are many cases that defy the intense partisan divide that so often characterizes the membership of the Court, and that also—much like the *Wal-Mart* decision—are not decided on the basis of a constitutional question at all. While our default position may be to think that we hear less about these cases because they simply address the mundane, benign "housekeeping" aspects of the law that are ultimately irrelevant to the day-to-day experience of individuals, the *Wal-Mart* case makes clear that these "Type B" stories can and do have a tremendous impact on the protection of rights and access to justice in the United States.[8]

This book is inspired by the "Type B" stories. It seeks to weigh in on an issue that receives much "Type A" attention: the degree to which the access that Americans have to courts to resolve their rights claims has been constricted in the decades since it was dramatically expanded during the rights revolution of the 1950s and 60s. But it does so in a different way. We are now intimately familiar with the story of how, in recent decades, an increasingly conservative Supreme Court has used its authority in an attempt to scale back the developments of the New Deal and Civil Rights eras, and of conservative activists regularly lobbying Congress to do the same. This movement is in many ways part of a broader backlash to the rights revolution in America, a time when the federal government significantly increased legal protection for disadvantaged individuals and groups, leading in the process to a dramatic expansion of judicial authority to oversee these protections. The extension of civil rights, privacy rights, consumer rights, defendant and prisoner rights, voting rights, immigrant rights, environmental rights, and religious freedoms constituted a revolutionary period in U.S. political and legal history as activists, lawmakers, bureaucrats, and judges combined efforts to fundamentally remake the contours of the nation's government and democracy. And in response, conservatives have since mobilized in an effort to constrain its key features and effects.

This conservative backlash has manifested itself in a variety of ways. The justices that once sat on Earl Warren's Supreme Court were long ago replaced by those of the Rehnquist and Roberts Courts, who each brought with them a profoundly different jurisprudential perspective. As the Court moved from its decision in *Roe v. Wade* to its narrower position on the legality of abortion in *Planned Parenthood v. Casey*, for example, or as it invalidated a central provision of the historic Voting Rights Act, conservative justices have slowly and surely chipped away at many of the Civil Rights era precedents.[9] Groups like the Federalist Society formed in the aftermath of the rights revolution to bring together judges, lawyers, law professors, and students with the shared goal of promoting a return to greater judicial restraint.[10] Republican presidents from Ronald Reagan to George W. Bush touted tort reform as a central part of their executive agenda, and attacks on judicial activism, "legislating from the bench," and the overly litigious nature of an American public increasingly comfortable with looking to juries to compensate their every injury have become the standard rhetoric of Republican stump speeches. Campaigns for policies aimed to ensure "law and order" (including the now controversial "stand your ground" laws) have largely replaced demands for defendant and prisoner rights, and Congress has constricted the rights of immigrants to challenge the outcomes of their deportation hearings.

But there is another important element to the story, in which these very same goals—scaling back the reach of the rights revolution—have come through less readily visible and often less overtly partisan efforts that target the "rules of the game": those institutional and legal procedures that, while seemingly benign at first glance, determine in practice what constitutes a valid legal dispute; who you can sue and for what; in what venue a dispute is handled; what tools lawyers and judges have at their disposal for arguing and adjudicating cases; what remedies are available for particular types of claims; whether further judicial review of a contested outcome is available; and perhaps most importantly, what incentives and resources we have to bring a case to court to begin with.[11] The reformers who target these mechanisms are pursuing a different form of countermobilization: they seek to diminish the effects of the rights revolution by *constricting access to courts* for those individuals asking that judges and juries hear and remedy their rights claims. This phenomenon—which I call *judicial retrenchment*—is an essential part of the larger narrative.

Contentious, ideologically driven Supreme Court decisions can certainly affect these considerations; the conservatism of the Roberts Court was no doubt an impetus for narrowing the availability of class actions in the *Wal-Mart* decision, a trend that the majority of conservative justices have continued in recent years.[12] But the Court is just one actor in a much broader, more complicated story. As an institution, the judiciary's influence and authority in American politics stems not only from its judges and their decisions, but also from a wide array of rules, procedures, and incentives, as well as a variety of actors with the power to shape them. At times these rules have been written so as to enhance the capacity of courts to take on more cases and thus be a more active player in promoting and enforcing political and policy goals. So during the rights revolution, for example, judges gained new powers to interpret statutes, and they used these powers to expand rights. At the same time, judges also became active administrators, implementing public policy and managing government institutions in areas as diverse as environmental protection, welfare administration, prison reform, medical care, and education and housing policy.[13] Congress further created judicial administrative bodies that were empowered to write and oversee rules of practice and procedure so as to manage the flood of litigants knocking at the courthouse door. And as demand for legal redress skyrocketed, so too did supply; during the rights revolution era, the number of lawyers, mediators, and administrative law judges grew exponentially, and all three branches of government strove to deepen funding and incentives for legal services.[14] The result—a vastly broadened and empowered institutional judiciary—has led many scholars to argue that the judiciary is now a centerpiece of the modern American state, essential for resolving issues of politics and policy when the elected branches fail to address them.[15]

It is unsurprising, then, that as opponents of the rights revolution mobilized, they also focused their attention on these very same institutional components. Constricting access to the judiciary has no doubt been a goal of the Republican Party since their political reemergence in the 1970s, often taking form in campaigns to relocate matters of policy and political importance back to the realm of politics and out of the hands of "activist judges."[16] But judicial retrenchment is not the singular project of conservatives in the Republican Party; it is a product of multiple coalitions, promoting different goals and interests, which have changed over time. Efforts to streamline the adjudicative process date back well into the nineteenth century as reformers, including a diverse set of politicians, activists, and judges, worked to close courtroom doors to certain types of disputes in order to ease judicial caseloads and therefore maintain a functioning legal system. Even in the modern era of conservative retrenchment, bipartisan coalitions in Congress have passed laws like the Private Securities Litigation Reform Act (1995) and the Class Action Fairness Act (2005), coalescing in their interest of reducing litigation rates by narrowing opportunities for potential plaintiffs to reach the courtroom. The Supreme Court has made a series of rulings, often unanimously, that limit its own institutional reach and discretion, particularly by constricting standing and (at times strategically) providing greater "Chevron deference" to administrative adjudication and rulemaking.[17] Further, the Court, Congress, and states have fought over who has the ultimate authority to shape legal remedies such as punitive damages, immunities, and attorney's fees in order to limit the possibility of and incentives for litigation. As a result of the alternative dispute resolution movement and the growth and entrenchment of the New Deal administrative state, certain types of claims traditionally heard by courts have been moved outside of traditional legal institutions, arguably at the expense of due process rights. Courts, Congress, and judicial administrators have also changed an array of procedural and institutional rules in response to the perceived explosion of litigation cases and expenses. Over time, these activities have changed the power dynamics of the judicial branch, as well as access to its institutions and remedies.

However, these changes to rules and procedures are not merely examples of simple institutional maintenance and housekeeping; they have real consequences on the ground, as certain groups of litigants now find themselves with limited legal redress for infringements upon their rights. Whereas litigation rates skyrocketed during the 1950s and 60s as landmark civil rights legislation provided new causes of action for the "have-nots" to have their day in court, lit-igation rates decreased dramatically in the 1990s and 2000s, as more cases now settle outside of court—and therefore prior to a legal proceeding and deter-mination made by a judge or jury—than ever before.[18] These trends are often to the disproportionate disadvantage of the very groups who are intended to benefit most from expanded access, namely potential civil rights plaintiffs, consumers, and other disadvantaged groups.[19] In total, only 1 to 2 percent of federal civil cases are decided by trial today, down 60 percent from 1985.[20] In short—depending on who you are, as well as the nature of your claim—one's right to a day in court has clearly been constricted in recent years.[21]

In this book, I argue that judicial retrenchment is as much—if not much more—about Congress, bureaucrats, legal organizations, business, interest group politics, and judicial administrators acting with a variety of both politi-cal and institutional goals in mind as it is about conservative judges on the nation's courts. The goal of scaling back access to courts comes from a mul-titude of actors both within and outside of the government. Sometimes it is a partisan project, motivated by ideological opposition to particular public policies, but sometimes it isn't. It *can* stem from the jurisprudential goals of legal conservatives, but it is often the product of intense, interbranch negotia-tions where various groups and institutions struggle for control over the rules that govern access to courts: that is, for the power to define which disputes must legitimately be handled by judges rather than being sorted out through the political process, the discretion of administrators, or intervention from the private sector. Capturing and understanding this institutional battle, then, means that we must recognize what has proven historically to be a cross-party appeal of reducing access to courts. It requires that we expand our view of the judicial branch beyond judges to include lawyers, legislators, administrators, and other interest groups. More broadly, it necessitates that we situate the judi-ciary in the broader landscape of American politics as we seek to understand the politics and processes of efforts to constrict access to a legal hearing.

Perhaps most importantly, it is essential to recognize that change in the more "subterranean," hidden realm of procedural rules is where actual con-striction in the availability of access to courts frequently occurs.[22] Political scientists focused more narrowly on jurisdiction stripping and other attempts to constrain the role of judges and litigation tend to look solely at "grand acts of politics"—landmark legislation or precedent-setting Supreme Court decisions—for evidence of retrenchment. These scholars have found that overt proposals aimed at altering judicial power—particularly those coming from Congress—have been overwhelmingly unsuccessful, and many were

simply grandstanding efforts by members of minority parties with no influence on outcomes.[23] But when we expand our institutional lens, it is in this
world of quiet, procedural reform where *actual* changes have, in fact, had a
demonstrable effect on access to the courts. As I will argue, retrenchers tend
to find the most success in arenas where they can maintain significant discretion over malleable, institutional rules and can successfully insulate their
work from partisan scrutiny and political contestation.

The Politics of Judicial Retrenchment

In this book, I take a historical institutional approach to examining the politics and processes of judicial retrenchment, which involves the activities of a
wide-ranging group of actors engaged in a series of efforts to scale back access
to courts in the decades since it was dramatically expanded in the service of
the rights revolution. In response to these developments, I ask two interrelated questions: First, what explains the politics of institutional retrenchment
in the judiciary? Second, what does it look like, and when and why is it more
likely to occur? I address these questions in the chapters that follow through
detailed case studies of four principal strategies that those interested in
retrenchment, whatever their varied motivations, have employed over time:

1. *Changing the Decision Makers* The development, professionalization,
   and proliferation of alternative dispute resolution practices that have frequently empowered nonjudicial actors to resolve legal grievances in the
   place of judges.
2. *Changing the Rules* The struggle between the three branches of government, interest groups, and professional associations over the authority to
   craft and amend the Federal Rules of Civil Procedure and to better position themselves to shape what constitutes a valid legal proceeding, how it
   must be adjudicated, and what remedies will be available through courts.
3. *Changing the Venue* The growth of the administrative state, and particularly agency adjudication, as a mechanism for moving the resolution of
   political, legal, and policy disputes away from the courts.
4. *Changing the Incentives* The efforts aimed at either protecting groups of
   individuals or government actors from being sued or limiting the remedies
   that incentivize the pursuit of a legal proceeding.

Within these four broad strategies for constricting access to the courts, numerous tactics and institutional targets have been especially prominent, among

them the promotion of increased deference to agency adjudication and decision making; the proliferation of binding arbitration contracts; changes to the rules governing class actions, discovery, pleading, summary judgment, and settlement; the development of qualified immunity for state and federal officials; the use of the Eleventh Amendment to protect states from being sued in their own courts; constrictions on attorney's fees, punitive damages, and what it takes to establish legal standing; and attempts to constrict the jurisdiction of courts to hear cases or establish new remedies under the law. This list is far from exhaustive. For example, I focus on matters of civil and not criminal law, which has its own meaningfully different politics.[24] I also focus primarily on federal courts and law, while recognizing that similar struggles occur in the states. But this list does encompass the predominant strategies that surface when we turn our attention to the mechanisms that most deeply affect the phases of a legal proceeding: filing a claim, the process of adjudication, and remedies. My focus on these subterranean mechanisms is also meant to complement and complicate the relevant topics already well addressed by legal scholars and social scientists who also seek to explain the rise of legal conservatism in the post–rights revolution era.[25]

While I devote substantial attention to the most recent period of partisan backlash, in which conservatives have made their goal of decreasing access to courts for particular types of litigants and claims most explicit, the project of judicial retrenchment dates back much further. Disenchantment with judges and the judicial process was a consistent theme in nineteenth-century American state building, and as early as the first decades of the twentieth century legislators, judges, lawyers, activists, and other groups regularly expressed a growing concern that the increased ease with which litigants could reach the courts was causing a crisis in court capacity. In order to address these concerns, actors on both sides of the partisan aisle proposed and fought for various measures that began to constrict access to courts. These reforms were critical not only for this early period of retrenchment, but also in establishing the institutional parameters in which the more familiar partisan battle we observe today is fought. Retrenchment politics are importantly "path dependent" in that early reform of the legal process established policies, procedures, and rules that would shape and confine the courses of actions available for future reformers.[26] In order to understand this sometimes counterintuitive period of retrenchment, as well as how it enabled the more familiar partisan politics that we see today, a historical approach is therefore essential. As such, I examine retrenchment efforts over the course of three time periods: (1) the development and entrenchment of the above legal practices and procedures (beginning as early as the mid- to late 1800s) that would later be used as mechanisms for decreasing access to courts; (2) the seeds of the "institutional maintenance" imperative for retrenchment in the first half of the twentieth century and its relationship to the politics and developments of the rights revolution era; and finally (3) the expansion and politicization of the "zones of conflict" that led to increased partisan conflict and, later, conservative backlash against judicial activism, largely beginning in the 1970s and 80s.

Through this historical inquiry, three possible explanations, or explanatory variables, become readily apparent: these include the important roles that *insularity, ideology,* and *temporality* play in explaining the politics and processes of judicial retrenchment. First, it is not only clear that there are a vast array of actors interested in constricting access to courts, who often run up against a variety of veto points that can impede their efforts; but it is also the case that the degree of autonomy and insularity enjoyed by those in a position to control institutional and procedural rules are crucial factors in determining the possibility of success for would-be retrenchers.[27] Success varies in many cases with the degree to which reformers can avoid having their reform efforts subject to political contestation. Second, retrenchment is neither solely driven nor fully explained by partisan politics; rather, there is variation in the ideologies of those seeking judicial retrenchment. This does not diminish the political salience and practical effects of their efforts, of course. On the one hand, both conservatives and liberals have an incentive to ensure access to courts for causes that they deem relevant and to try to shut their competitors out of court. On the other hand, however, what emerges from these case studies is the importance of an ideology of "institutional maintenance" wherein both conservatives and liberals have consistently—and with significant success—promoted constricting access to the courts for the "greater good" of keeping an increasingly overworked judiciary functional. Third and finally, it is clear that the strategies and mechanisms employed for limiting access to the courts must be understood in terms of institutional change over time. At any given historical moment, the particular constellation of actors and entrenched institutions may importantly shape what these efforts look like, as well as their potential for success or failure. In this regard, recognizing the sequence and timing of retrenchment efforts is critical, as some succeed because of their ability to co-opt existing institutional mechanisms—some of which were put in place for entirely different political and functional reasons—for the purpose of restricting access to courts.[28]

By examining these variables in the context of my four cases studies, I find that the groups involved in judicial retrenchment change over time and are motivated by more than mere partisan backlash; that the processes of retrenchment are distinctive but not static, unfolding in a series of methods for attempted institutional change according to factors such as the presence of veto players, levels of discretion, insularity, and overreach; and that the availability of malleable institutional "rules" that are less subject to political contestation enhance the likelihood of effective change. Finally—and often ironically—I find that the process of state development itself sows the seeds for subsequent retrenchment, as reformers have successfully usurped those legal practices put in place for expanding access to courts for the opposite purpose. The institutional mechanisms developed to promote rights revolution-era policies are not only components of an ever-growing American "litigation state", for these very same mechanisms have also been used to scale it back. Retrenchment, then, must be understood in the context of broader theories for how institutional change and reform occur.

Plan of the Book

In Chapter Two, I review the ways in which retrenchment and institutional change in the courts have been treated by social scientists and legal scholars and propose a detailed theory of judicial retrenchment. Given that this phenomenon is often viewed through the lens of partisan politics, is considered at its core a question of judicial discretion, and is therefore viewed primarily as a product of fluctuations in legal doctrine, I suggest that we broaden the context in which we view retrenchment. This involves viewing the judiciary as an *institution*, composed of more than just courts and judges, that has developed its own institutional incentives over time; recognizing that the judicial branch is also an autonomous institution in American politics, not simply an agent of the elected branches; embracing that the population pursuing retrenchment, as well as their motivations, change over time; and valuing that discerning who has control over the subterranean "rules of the game" is essential to understanding when retrenchment efforts are likely to succeed or fail. In so doing, I suggest that we study this legal phenomenon much in the way that historical and institutionally minded social scientists study the processes of change in other political institutions.

Chapters Three through Six form the empirical core of the book. In Chapter Three, "Changing the Decision Makers," I examine the development of Alternative Dispute Resolution (ADR) procedures in the United States. In terms of their ability to detract from access to courts, practices such as arbitration and mediation empower both private individuals (often—but certainly not always—lawyers trained in the field) and nonjudicial actors within the government to resolve disputes that would otherwise be adjudicated by judges and juries. ADR has a long history in the United States and has at times been promoted by both liberals and conservatives. In the years following the passage of the Federal Arbitration Act (FAA) of 1925, liberals (often relying heavily on private donors) strived to make ADR widely available in order to ensure access to justice for those struggling to find it in traditional courts. ADR's broad appeal inspired the American Bar Association (ABA) to jump onboard and work to professionalize the field, particularly when it embraced certain forms of ADR in the mid-twentieth century. But although progressives and supporters of the New Deal originally developed ADR, conservatives began to promote it in the latter part of the century as a way to keep what they considered "lesser" cases out of court, and to better protect the interests of business. The Supreme Court has facilitated this by interpreting the FAA to preempt state laws designed to promote litigation and instead to compel mandatory arbitration in lieu of traditional legal hearings, often even in the case of constitutional claims.

In Chapter Four, "Changing the Rules," I examine the strategies aimed to constrict access to courts through changes to the Federal Rules of Civil Procedure. These rules were first put into place by Congress in 1938 and are largely controlled by the Judicial Conference of the United States, a body of experts appointed by the Chief Justice of the Supreme Court. For the first thirty-five years of their existence, these rulemakers benefitted from the widely held belief that the rules were "purely procedural" and therefore not of particular interest to elected officials or to the public. As such, rulemakers had great success in exercising a vast amount of discretion, even as they used the rules to fuel the substantive, political, and policy goals of the Civil Rights era. But once these actors seemingly overreached in the early 1970s, exposing the degree to which the rules could change the substance of policy and rights protections, legislators and interest groups aligned with the Democratic Party began to strive for greater influence over the rulemaking process. In the 1980s these actors continued to push for further changes, but were joined by legal reformers internal to the rulemaking process who wanted—for largely nonpartisan reasons—to find ways to address what they deemed a litigation crisis that was overwhelming court capacity. Only after 1994 has rule reform been dominated by Republican legislators and business lobbyists interested in reducing tort and public interest litigation, through class action reform in particular.

In Chapter Five, "Changing the Venue," I examine the growth of the administrative state, and especially the practice of agency adjudication, as a mechanism for moving and insulating disputes from the courts. The growth and development of administrative agencies with their own internal apparatus for dispute resolution has, in effect, led to a change in venue for individuals and groups pursuing various would-be legal claims. As groups like the ABA and New Deal opponents in Congress began to fear that agencies were in essence performing core judicial functions without providing basic due process guarantees, reformers sought to codify rules of administrative procedure to protect aggrieved individuals from powerful and potentially politically-biased federal agencies. But while Congress passed the Administrative Procedure Act in 1946 with the goal of establishing guidelines for agency rulemaking and adjudication, agencies were nonetheless left with appreciable discretion. And although courts served in an important watchdog role over agency adjudication for much of the 1950s and 60s, increased deference to quasi-judicial administrative rulings and diminished opportunity for judicial review have left many wary about the quality of rights protection that agencies provide.

Finally, in Chapter Six, "Changing the Incentives," I examine the ways in which reformers have prioritized (1) creating immunities to protect government officials and states from suit in court, and (2) reducing the monetary remedies available for successful plaintiffs, both as strategies for de-incentivizing individuals who would otherwise take their grievances to court. These strategies have been described as the most "insidious" of ways to constrict access to courts: leaving rights in place, but removing the remedies for those rights.[29] This fairly straightforward project has taken a variety of forms. In terms of immunities, the courts have at once created doctrines (like state sovereign immunity) and weakened others (such as Section 1983 of the Civil Rights Act of 1871, which allows for suits against state officials) in an effort to constrain who can be subject to a lawsuit and for what. As far as judicial remedies are concerned, both the courts and the elected branches have alternatively expanded and attempted to constrict the monetary incentives for bringing a case to court, most prominently in the form of attorney's fees and punitive damages. Over time, Congress and the courts have also gone back and forth over who ultimately has proper authority to address questions of remedy, thereby creating an institutional battle that has, at times, served to mask the extent and depth of these efforts.

I conclude by reflecting on what the politics of judicial retrenchment helps us to understand about the ideologies that drive reform, the importance of rules as levers for change in the American legal and political landscape, and—more broadly—the processes of institutional change in American political development. I also address the ways in which the politics of judicial retrenchment intersect with foundational questions of political power, as well as the political salience of these reform efforts. Finally, now more than three decades into a period of sustained efforts to retrench many of the hallmark achievements of the rights revolution, I discuss how the growth and development of state authority in the middle of the twentieth century continues to have implications during the attack on such authority in the early years of the new millennium.

The Politics of Judicial Retrenchment

Institutional Rules and the "Vanishing Trial"

Wal-Mart v. Dukes is an apt starting point for examining the broader institutional struggles that encapsulate the politics of judicial retrenchment—although it is, in fact, only a start. It is not at all surprising that opponents to Wal-Mart's labor practices chose the legal route for their attack. Although Wal-Mart's opponents exercise a range of political tactics in an effort to change the corporation's employment policies, for more than a half century litigation has been a strategy of choice for aggrieved individuals seeking to resolve a dispute or change a policy or practice of broad import.[1] From the NAACP Legal Defense Fund's litigation against racial segregation to defense attorneys arguing on behalf of defendant and prisoner rights to tort lawyers using targeted litigation to prompt requiring seatbelts in cars and warning labels on cigarettes, it was through the legal process that many of the biggest political battles of the mid- to late twentieth century were fought. This "rights revolution," as it is commonly labeled, greatly expanded legal protections for disadvantaged individuals and groups, as well as dramatically enhanced of the power of judges to shape matters of politics and policy.

The facts of *Wal-Mart* fit comfortably in the classic mold of civil rights cases from the previous era, pitting a group of working class women against the nation's largest private company, which represents 2 percent of the national economy with profits of $6 billion in 2011 alone, and which employs nearly 2 million workers—more than triple the nation's second largest private company.[2] In its more than 4,000 enormously sized discount merchandise stores across the country, consumers can buy everything from groceries to guns to prescription medications. The company name has become ubiquitous in the

American cultural landscape, not only for its incredible economic success, but also for the controversy it has generated with many of its business practices. Just over the last decade, Wal-Mart has been the site of several fiercely fought civil rights and labor battles, resulting in a series of high-profile lawsuits, and culminating (for the moment) with the Supreme Court.

The case began in 2001 when Betty Dukes, a Wal-Mart employee in Pittsburg, California, filed suit against the company in the U.S. District Court in San Francisco on the grounds that she had been directly injured by acts of sex discrimination. In the seven years that Dukes had worked at Wal-Mart, she was continually passed over for promotion and raises while such opportunities were regularly offered to her male colleagues, some with far less experience. She also discovered that men with less experience working the same position as her earned higher salaries for the same job. Furthermore, after complaining about these gender-based discrepancies, company management arguably retaliated by demoting her from customer service manager to cashier.[3]

But as with many of the notable civil rights cases of the twentieth century, Dukes' case was not just about her. She initially joined with five other women to file a class action lawsuit alleging that Wal-Mart's policies resulted in lower pay and a longer wait for promotions for women *nationwide*. Although women represent more than 70 percent of the national Wal-Mart workforce, they represent less than a third of management, a percentage that continues to drop the higher one climbs up the corporate ladder. The women argued that because local managers in the company have significant discretion over pay and promotions, and because this discretion had led to a disproportionate benefit of men over women, Wal-Mart was acting in violation of Title VII of the Civil Rights Act of 1964 for failing to supervise the disparate treatment of female employees by its managers. Wal-Mart, they argued, had a strong and uniform "corporate culture" that permitted bias against women to infect a range of employment-related decision making. Eventually, the six women were joined by approximately 1.6 million others, and together they sought legal judgment against the company for injunctive and declaratory relief, punitive damages, and back pay.

The class action lawsuit has been a long-standing vehicle for rights activism in the courts, leading to major victories aimed at rooting out discrimination in a range of different settings, from schools to police departments to corporations like AT&T, Denny's, and United Steel. Historically, class actions have proven to be a potent mechanism for changing practices related to hiring and firing, pay, workplace culture, and diversity in the workforce, and have also at times required companies to dole out large sums of back pay and damages to compensate for their discriminatory practices. Perhaps unsurprisingly, then, prior to reaching the Supreme Court, Dukes and her co-plaintiffs found repeated successes in the courtroom. The district court judge approved of their class action—"certifying" them as a class, a necessary step for the merits of their case to be heard—and the Ninth Circuit Court did the same on three separate occasions. But even while most of the Civil Rights era precedents shaping the rights of women subject to sex discrimination have remained on the books, it was unclear at best whether a conservative-leaning Supreme Court would reach the same conclusion.

As we know, the Supreme Court threw out their claim on procedural grounds, holding that the women could not be certified as a class because their injuries were not sufficiently consistent to warrant the filing of a single claim. As such, the Court never reached a decision on the merits of whether Wal-Mart engaged in discrimination on the basis of sex. The Court did not overturn a legal precedent, and it did not revise its understanding of Title VII of the Civil Rights Act or weigh in on the Fourteenth Amendment's Equal Protection Clause. In this way, the case was not only notable for what it meant to the plaintiffs; it just plain looked different as well. As legal scholars explained in the *New York Times*, "The Supreme Court's decision today in the case of *Wal-Mart v. Dukes* is ostensibly focused on a narrow procedural issue but is in fact the latest installment in a long running debate about equality, in the workplace and beyond." How are the two tied together? In this case, what do procedural rules have to do with equality? Consistent with what I will argue, "As is often the case with legal rulings, procedural questions are informed by substantive concerns."[4]

Yet among journalists, law professors, and social scientists alike, there is a strong tendency to separate the two, if not to ignore matters of procedure altogether when considering the rights of Americans before the law. Even among political scientists who pay close attention to the politics and inner workings of governing institutions, where it is widely recognized that procedural rules absolutely stand to shape the substance of policy (think of the importance of the filibuster in Congress, for example), there is a tendency to divorce matters of "pure procedure" from substantive, on-the-ground ramifications when we study law. This characterization, as well as a preference for studying grand acts of politics, such as the passage of landmark jurisdiction stripping legislation, executive orders, and high-profile Supreme Court decisions, is of course far from uniform; but it *is* particularly dangerous when it comes to understanding the antilitigation agenda. If we focus solely on moments where the rights and abilities of Americans to access the justice system are constricted on a grand scale, and if we divorce procedural concerns from substance, we miss the more "subterranean" realm where so much of the politics of retrench-ment takes place, and where actual changes have had a demonstrable effect on access to the courts.[5]

For example, federal judicial caseload statistics indicate a dramatic decline in the use of class actions for employment-based civil rights cases. As John Donahue and Peter Siegelman describe, by 1990, "class actions, once a main-stay in the efforts to enforce civil rights in the workplace ... virtually vanished from the scene." Just over fifty requests for class certification in employment discrimination cases (the type of case brought by the plaintiffs in *Wal-Mart*) were filed that year, a number down by over 95 percent from its peak of 1106 in 1975.[6] Data from the Administrative Office of the U.S. Courts indicates that class action requests for other nonemployment civil rights cases declined similarly, from a peak of nearly 2,000 in 1978 to 195 in 2003 (See Figure 2.1).[7]

While the class action is just one example of a procedural device affecting access to courts, the constriction of its use is undoubtedly reflected in the broader decline of the rate at which civil rights claims reach a decision on the merits. As a result, access to the courtroom for those seeking resolution of rights claims under the provisions of the Civil Rights Act of 1964 has been dramatically restricted. While 17 percent of all civil rights cases reached trial in federal district courts in 1976, only 3 percent did in 2012. Importantly, this decline—as well as the decline in overall civil rights cases that reached trial—has occurred despite the fact that the only statutory changes to the law itself have largely been geared toward *expanding* opportunities for litigation, pri-marily through increased attorney's fee awards and other monetary incentives

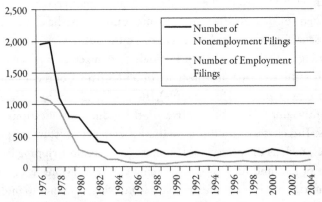

FIGURE 2.1 Number of Civil Rights Class Actions Filed, 1976–2004.

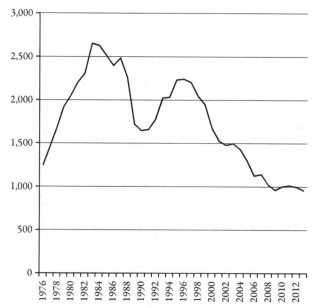

FIGURE 2.2 Number of Civil Rights Cases that Reach Trial in Federal District Courts, 1976–2013.

for lawyers to take on civil rights cases; the Civil Rights Act of 1991 did reverse downward trends, but only temporarily (see Figure 2.2).[8]

These trends in civil rights litigation are part and parcel of what Marc Galanter calls the phenomenon of the "vanishing trial." In his work on trends in litigation rates, Galanter finds a 60 percent decrease in the absolute number of federal civil trials between 1985 and 2002, and the portion of cases reaching trial dropped from 4.7 percent to 1.8 percent during the same time period.[9] Extending Galanter's data another decade, these trends have continued. There were 3,132 civil trials completed in federal courts in 2013, down from a high of more than 12,000 in 1985 (See Figure 2.3). The number of jury trials has also continued its decline, from 3,006 trials in 2002 to 2,182 in 2013, from a high of over 6,000 in the mid-1980s (See Figure 2.4).[10] The percentage of all court actions resulting in trial has also continued its decades' long decline, from 1.8 percent in 2002 to 1.1 percent in 2012 (See Figure 2.5).[11]

That 96 percent of civil rights cases and 99 percent of all civil cases fail to reach a trial in court today is striking. And it suggests that much of the important activity in determining whether Americans have suffered a legal injury takes place just *outside* the courtroom door, before plaintiffs are able

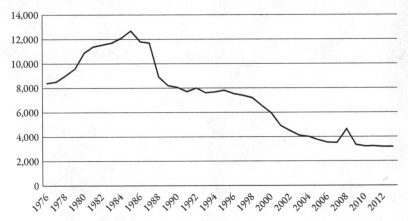

FIGURE 2.3 Number of Civil Cases that Reach Trial in Federal District Courts, 1976–2013.

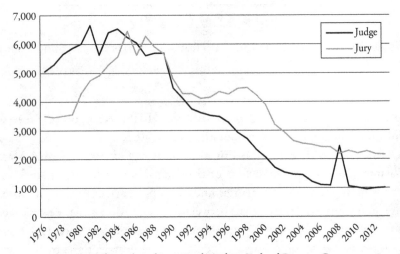

FIGURE 2.4 Number of Bench and Jury Civil Trials in Federal District Courts, 1976–2013

to make their case in a traditional proceeding, with all the practical and rights-based benefits a trial can afford. As we will see, there are a variety of developments that contribute to this trend. In some instances, the right to sue has been waived by contractual agreements designed to mandate private arbitration. In others, Congress precludes judicial review as a matter of statute. Still further, the right to sue is constrained by a variety of legal procedures. For example, expansions in the use of pretrial determinations like settlement and summary judgment, as well as heightened pleading standards, lead an increasing number of cases to be dismissed or settled prior to a hearing.

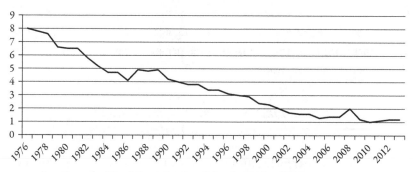

FIGURE 2.5 Percent of Civil Cases that Reach Trial in Federal District Courts, 1976–2013.

Further, these procedural hurdles are often costly and difficult to navigate for individuals and groups who are not "repeat players" in court, and failing to succeed in these early stages often means that injured parties are deprived of the crucial opportunity to gain further information about those they are accusing through the process of discovery.[12] And without that opportunity, the chances of being able to mount a case compelling enough to command a trial by judge and jury are slim. What this state of affairs makes clear is that changes to rules and procedures constitute a critical realm in which battles over access to courts are fought.

As we know, however, this realm tends not to be at the center of public attention. Importantly, it often evades the academic eye as well. While today's anticourt, antilitigation agenda has many moving parts, much of the scholarly attention—particularly from political scientists—has focused either on efforts by elected officials to pass legislation designed to strip the courts of jurisdiction or efforts to change the ideological composition of courts in hopes of empowering judges who will interpret laws in a manner that better reflects their political interests. These accounts are essential, but they are not sufficient. By focusing on the broader phenomenon of judicial retrenchment, a process by which a range of actors both exogenous and endogenous to the courts and Congress work to scale back access to the courts by targeting the institutional and procedural rules that govern political institutions, I argue that we are better able to understand the politics behind the phenomenon of the "vanishing trial."

I proceed by examining in detail the ways in which questions of access to courts have been treated by social scientists, as well as the literature in political science that guides the analysis in this book. I suggest that we must broaden our conception of what constitutes the judiciary, the role that it plays in American politics, and the context in which we study retrenchment.

To this end, I detail the difficulties inherent in defining retrenchment when it comes to strategies aimed at constricting access to courts and propose a theory that brings a historical institutional perspective to bear on the study of the judiciary as an institution.

Institutional Change and the Judiciary
in American Politics

I examine judicial retrenchment in a manner that both dovetails with and is distinct from conventional approaches to the study of judicial politics and public law. In part, this analysis follows in the spirit of an extensive literature in political science on the subject of law and courts, ranging from attitudinal and rational choice scholars to historical institutionalists to those who study constitutional development, all of whom have increasingly highlighted the importance of nonjudicial actors such as members of Congress, the executive branch, and national party leaders for understanding judicial politics and power. Given that the judicial branch arguably lacks a clear, constitutional grant of independent authority to intervene in public policy, those who study law in the field of political science have increasingly argued that the study of court behavior must include the role that elected officials play in enabling or constraining judicial activism.[13]

I am particularly influenced by scholarship from the fields of historical institutionalism and American Political Development (APD). Borrowing from the broader work in these subfields, two theoretical precepts guide this analysis: *path dependence* and *intercurrence*. In recent years, historical institutional scholars have transformed the idea of path dependence—loosely understood as the idea that "what happened at an earlier point in time will affect the possible outcomes of a sequence of events occurring at a later point in time"—into a rigorous concept for guiding studies of institutional change.[14] Starting from the recognition that "history matters" when studying how political and policy change occurs, historical institutionalists have stressed that path dependence is "a social process grounded in a dynamic of 'increasing returns.'" As Paul Pierson describes, when political institutions develop over time, "particular courses of action, once introduced, can be almost impossible to reverse; and consequently, political development is punctuated by critical moments of junctures that shape the basic contours of social life."[15] In short, timing and sequence matter, and taking path dependence seriously means paying special attention to how the processes, politics, and outcomes of institutional development over time shape and limit later options for reform.

Given this, to understand the scope and extent of judicial retrenchment we must look for more than just grand acts of court curbing, as these are only snapshot moments in what is a far more complex trajectory of institutional change. This is especially true in light of the growing literature on gradual institutional change, which emphasizes the degree to which the cumulative effects of *incremental* change, and not just critical junctures, can transform institutions over time.[16]

Theories of gradual institutional change are also intimately intertwined with the second precept that guides this analysis: "intercurrence", or the idea of "multiple orders in action." The term, as Karen Orren and Stephen Skowronek describe, encapsulates the reality that political institutions do not simply come and go as a functional response to fluctuating societal demands and political coalitions; instead, the historical construction of politics operates amidst both older and newer operating structures—each with their own distinctive institutional goals—that in turn leads to a political landscape with multiple orderings of authority that are often problematic in relation to each other. Only by paying attention to political development and the ways in which institutions both evolve and change over time, they argue, can we understand the significance of multiple political institutions that operate together and often clash at any given historical moment. Orren and Skowronek describe intercurrence as, at once, "a descriptive statement of the normal state of the political universe—of multiple orders arranged uncertainly in relationship to one another; a statement of *the* historical institutional problem—the operation of asymmetric standards of control and incongruous rules of action; and a standard template from which the familiar themes of historical institutional research—the contingencies of order, the multiplicity of authorities, the particularity of path trajectories, the significance of redirecting junctures from which our current political experience can be derived."[17]

Drawing substantially from these precepts, I diverge from conventional accounts of judicial development in three ways. Two are interrelated. First, I conceptualize and examine the realm of judicial politics as a state of intercurrence, one built of an expansive group of institutions and actors, consisting of far more than just courts and judges, with multifaceted interests that often coexist awkwardly. This stands in contrast to much of the scholarship on law and APD that devotes its attention primarily to the Supreme Court and its interaction with political branches. Second, I argue that broadening our conception of the judiciary reveals that negotiations about the power of courts, the development of judicial institutions, and access to their services frequently defy straightforwardly partisan explanations. This complex

arrangement challenges accounts that emphasize a "regime politics" approach
to understanding law and courts, which largely provides a partisan story of
doctrinal change that tends to minimize the broader range of rules, procedures, incentives, and actors that constitute the judiciary as an institution and
are often critical for institutional change.[18]

Third, I argue that retrenchment in the judiciary must be understood
as a distinctive form of institutional change. This utilizes historical institutional scholarship that examines the causal mechanisms that make retrenchment unique but contrasts with a tendency in the APD literature to subsume
moments of retrenchment within a trajectory of continued institutional growth
and expansion. The contributions of this literature have been indispensable to
the study of political development over time, particularly in detailing how the
entrenchment and layering of institutions create significant barriers to future
change. However, it can obscure the ways in which politics can also promote
genuine constrictions in the capacity of our political institutions and our ability to access them, as well as the ways in which retrenchment uniquely shapes
gradual institutional change over time. Further, it leaves imprecise a conception of the political and institutional processes that constitute retrenchment,
and therefore the variables that affect both its success and failure.

I address each of these claims at length in the next section. In total, I argue
that explaining judicial institutional change requires a richer conception of
the judiciary as an institution and a greater recognition of the distinctive
politics and processes of retrenchment. Whatever else the U.S. judiciary may
be, it is a complex body of rules, procedures, incentives, and actors. And as
it evolves over time, little is more fundamental to its politics than recurrent
efforts to change its institutions.[19] Actors motivated to change and protect
judicial institutions are multiple, and come from inside and outside of the
judiciary. Their relationships to it are multifaceted, and their interests often
transcend traditional partisan and ideological lines. Perhaps most importantly, judicial institutional change exists in a broad temporal context. As barriers to authoritative change rise and fall, and as support for judicial authority
ebbs and flows, the processes of institutional retrenchment and the groups
driving them fluctuate as well.

Understanding Courts in American
Political Development

With the rights revolution came the development of a support structure
that successfully expanded opportunities for individuals and groups to

access the courts, also entrenching the legal strategy for enforcing policy.[20] In light of this transformation—which had the effect of entrenching a system of "adversarial legalism"[21] where "law and politics cannot be disentangled in the United States[22]—political scientists increasingly focused on the conditions under which elected officials find it in their best interest to grant or delegate policy making authority to the judiciary. Law and APD scholars in particular have examined how party leaders seek to entrench their policy agendas through court appointments[23]; how political parties actively encourage courts to engage in judicial review when they wish to avoid a controversial issue that might upset their coalition[24]; how the Supreme Court is most powerful when elites across governmental institutions share a commitment to policy making[25]; and how judicial authority is itself a product of our democratic system, where presidents have also found it expedient to legitimate and even expand judicial power for their own interests.[26] Subsequently, scholars have also explored the relationship between the elected branches and judicial activism in specific areas of policy.[27]

The emphasis on the partisan roots of judicial authority also figures prominently in the growing literature on court curbing, in which scholars interested specifically in attacks on judicial independence and hostility to courts and judges have focused on similar dynamics, looking to the interaction between courts and elected officials in order to explain the success or failure of these efforts. These approaches examine a variety of overt attacks on the authority of the courts—usually stemming from Congress—which take the form of statutory proposals or constitutional amendments that strip the courts of their jurisdiction to hear cases in particular areas of policy, constrain the judicial review powers of courts more broadly, or restructure the judiciary in order to reign in its review power, among others.[28] Often driven by public hostility to controversial court decisions or a similar discontent on the part of lawmakers, these scholars address a similar question: When, and for what ends, do lawmakers seek to harness the power of the courts, and how much success do they have?

Emphasizing the partisan dimension of the relationship between elected officials and judicial power has been important to explaining why an institution with relatively few formal powers has at times leveraged vast authority, dramatically influencing politics. But this regime politics approach has been countered, or at least supplemented, by scholars studying judicial institutional development and reform who demonstrate that electoral dynamics do not fully explain the range of institutional change observed in the judiciary over time. This is true in two regards. First, although political parties have undoubtedly sought to entrench and enable their ideological positions and policy interests (through court appointments and by legitimating broad "warrants" for judicial activity and power, respectively), such expansions in judicial authority have often stemmed from cross-party coalitions as well. Robert Kagan, for example, has written extensively about the bipartisan appeal of "adversarial legalism," ascribing the phenomenon to cultural and structural features of American democracy.[29] In his study of antilitigation legislation, Thomas Burke finds that certain types of legislative proposals garner bipartisan support, or can even be characterized as *non*-partisan in nature.[30] Sean Farhang has illustrated how, due to their intense suspicion of bureaucracy, the Republican Party established a system of private litigation to handle the problem of job discrimination around the time of the 1964 Civil Rights Act, despite the fact that such a system would ultimately aid litigation for causes near and dear to the Democratic Party, and Shep Melnick has explored how the threat of unfunded judicial mandates in special education policy gave rise to effectual alliances among parents, lawyers, and states, as opposed to coalitions along party lines.[31] In short, conservatives at times have reasons to support expansive judicial power, and liberals have, at times, supported constraining it. As I will describe, there is considerable evidence that some areas of judicial retrenchment are driven primarily by concerns for the systemic integrity and efficient functioning of the court system, evidencing a different type of ideology altogether.[32]

Second, unlike historical institutional scholars who stress the importance of rules, practices, and procedures when studying institutions such as the legislative branch, administrative agencies, and political parties, historically-minded legal scholars tend to operationalize a more narrow conception of judicial institutions by limiting their focus to the Supreme Court, with a special emphasis on how ideology affects both its decision making and negotiations with political actors. But the judiciary is a far more complex institution, built not only of judges, but also of lawyers, professional associations, administrators, judicial policy making bodies, mediators, and a vast array of interest groups. This universe of actors directly influences judicial activities that bear on state authority and the implementation of national policy, often by controlling the rules and procedures critical to courtroom access. For example, judicial administrators are empowered to shape rules that bear on whether lawyers will be incentivized to file certain types of cases (such as class actions or those involving attorney's fees or punitive damages) and can therefore enhance or detract from the capacity of courts to carry out policy goals. Interest groups pursuing legal change frequently employ "stealth" insider strategies that skirt the courtroom entirely.[33] Institutions like the Judicial Conference (the primary policy-setting body for the U.S. courts) are often overlooked, despite the critical role that they play in negotiations with members of Congress and interest groups seeking judicial reform.[34] Losing sight of the ways in which the development of *other* political institutions, like administrative agencies, can cause a shift in venue for where legal determinations are made significantly detracts from our analyses of access to courts,[35] as does ignoring the range of private foundations and donors that fueled, professionalized, and sustained the growth of alternative dispute resolution movement, for example. In short, a focus on partisan politics and judges misses much of the action in legal politics. A more robust conception of the judiciary as an institution, then, is essential for both a true historical institutional treatment of law and courts and an understanding of how the "vanishing trial" has come to be.

Assessing Institutional Change

Most APD accounts of institutional change emphasize development, reconstitutions of political authority, and the layering of political and institutional orders.[36] APD scholars emphasize path dependence,[37] argue that state institutions "thicken,"[38] political actors are "entrenched,"[39] and policies and agencies take on lives independent from their initial purpose, often leading to a "disjointed" polity where the layering of new institutions over old leads to conflicts that stunt reform movements.[40] They view the potential for changes in judicial authority similarly; once legal reforms are enacted, interests mobilize and defend the new laws and institutions from which they benefit.[41] APD scholars grapple with the relationship between institutional durability and change; but too often, even when institutions are confronted and dislodged, individual instances of retrenchment tend to be subsumed within a broader narrative of state development. For example, perhaps the most dramatic instance of judicial retrenchment—the New Deal "switch in time that saved nine"—is *most* remembered for its pivotal role in the growth and development of the twentieth century American state.[42]

Entrenchment is a historical reality, but it is not the whole story. Retrenchment efforts, after all, do sometimes succeed. From Andrew Jackson's war against the national bank onward, retrenchment examples range from the successful elements of the New Deal and Reagan Revolution to legislative constriction of court jurisdiction and informal changes to interpretations of statutes that limit the range of their application. As these examples show, even when institutional orders break down, authority is not always simply transferred to other sectors of the state. Reforms often seek to fundamentally reduce state capacity as a whole—even if informally, through chipping away at the margins, or by gradually unearthing and transforming the purpose and operation of a governing institution—or to transfer state power to nongovernmental actors. Further, some institutions may be subject to retrenchment while we continue to see broader growth in others, and even the same institution can at once constrict in one regard and expand in another.

But subsuming examples of retrenchment within a broader narrative of growth hinders our understanding of institutional reform; and given the recent anticourt, anti-activist judge political and legal movement, it is increasingly essential that we account for judicial retrenchment within broader theories of institutional change. If we focus only on the fact that growth and expansion have continued, in broad strokes, to characterize institutional change in the judiciary (whether evidenced by the proliferation of courts themselves, the "judicialization" of politics, or the ambitious exercise of judicial authority), we obscure effectual instances of retrenchment. We run the risk, for example, of missing the reality that certain groups of citizens find access to justice increasingly difficult or even absent. As innumerable legal scholars have noted, the jurisprudence of the Rehnquist and Roberts Courts has been defined by an antilitigation sentiment; and whether or not that sentiment has definitively turned the tides away from judicial development is in many ways irrelevant to the practical consequences that it has had for the protection of rights and access to courts.[43]

Recent work on institutional change, however, has focused on how retrenchment fits into debates about the relationship between order and change. While this literature has been primarily devoted to retrenchment in the welfare state, it has much to offer our understanding of constricted access to courts. These scholars argue that the process of development fundamentally changes politics; through the process of "policy feedback," it alters both the political context and goals of policy makers, thereby creating a distinctive politics of and strategies for countermobilization. As Paul Pierson describes, policy feedback—how previous policy choices influence the present political landscape—shapes the distribution of political resources, broadens the range of pertinent actors interested in a particular policy or legal development, and creates incentives for both further reform (often due to unintended consequences) and for defending the status quo. Given this, there are persuasive reasons to believe that retrenchment is a meaningfully different enterprise than state building, in need of its own analytical tools.[44]

Because retrenchment generally requires imposing concentrated costs for diffuse gains, authoritative acts of retrenchment can be hard to come by. Retrenchment necessarily follows development or entrenchment—whether of a policy, procedure, or precedent—which often leads individuals and groups to adapt and make extensive commitments to a new institutional arrangement, thereby increasing the costs of future change.[45] Where judicial retrenchment is concerned, the creation of a "legal state" or "litigation state" (much like the welfare state) effectively restructured the political landscape and created dense networks of interest groups for whom imposing losses for diffuse gains (namely a more efficient judiciary) can be a difficult enterprise. Because of this, and as historical institutional scholars have described, we should expect that retrenchment is more likely to occur through subtle, incremental change over time. Whether by strategically redeploying existing legal procedures for new purposes, layering new institutions upon old, or by quietly allowing the ground-level operation of a policy to adapt to shifts in the political environment, the most successful instances of judicial retrenchment have involved efforts that occur largely outside of the public eye. As I will describe, by attempting to maneuver within venues fairly insulated from the political process, those who target procedural mechanisms ultimately benefit from our propensity to view matters of procedure as distinct from substantive rights, where changes must be subject to the democratic process in order to be considered legitimate. In short, with insularity comes substantial discretion, making it essential to delve into the subterranean realm where these subtler forms of retrenchment take place.

However, it is important to note that retrenchment is *both* a distinctive form of institutional change *and* an essential component of our understanding of longer trajectories of development over time. That is, with regard to judicial retrenchment specifically, the politics and processes of constricting access to courts are unique, and should be recognized for the profound consequences that they can have for individuals and groups at any one historical moment. But at the same time, it is essential to recognize that the cumulative effects of retrenchment can have a transformative effect on political and legal institutions and their further development.

Defining Judicial Retrenchment

Viewed through this lens, there are a variety of strategies employed in an attempt to scale back access to courts. First, retrenchment may result from changes in who has the authority to hear and settle a dispute, by shifting adjudicative authority from judges to other actors. Second, changes to the rules of adjudication can make it more difficult for a potential plaintiff to initiate a claim in court, build a case, or successfully navigate the legal process through to a trial; the phenomenon of the vanishing trial is in many ways the result of changes like moving from looser to heightened pleading standards, for example. Third, changes in where a grievance is heard—by shifting the venue from a court to another institution—can remove an individual or group's ability to have their dispute heard by a judge and jury, with the potential of sacrificing many of the constitutional guarantees that protect plaintiffs in a courtroom as well (such as the right to due process and the right to a lawyer). Fourth, retrenchment may occur by decreasing or removing the remedies and resources that are in place to incentivize litigation. All four of these strategies aim to make it more difficult to resolve disputes in the traditional courtroom. This has the effect of diminishing the role that courts can play in protecting individual and group rights and liberties, enforcing or implementing national policy, and punishing those individuals, groups, and institutions that infringe upon rights or fail to deliver the benefits required of them by law.

While these strategies are relatively clear, retrenchment itself can be difficult to define and identify for several reasons. First, there is often an inverse relationship between changes in judicial authority and changes in access to courts. In contrast to those who see the process of retrenchment through the lens of "court curbing" or "jurisdiction stripping," many attempts to constrict access to courts do not involve an attack on court authority at all. When a judge acts, for example, to narrowly circumscribe his or her understanding of a right, or to declare someone immune from a lawsuit, or to decrease the remedies available to a plaintiff, or to use doctrinal innovation to create higher barriers of entry to the courtroom, it is clear that these actions rest upon the *exercise* of judicial authority, not the restraint of it. How and why, then, should we consider these to be acts of judicial retrenchment?

In the most basic sense, there are two major targets available for those seeking to attack the function of the modern judiciary: the discretion and power of judges and redress to courts for the assertion of rights claims. Focusing on attacks on judicial independence as evidence of retrenchment is a potentially distinct project all its own. But even though this book focuses on access—and even though judicial authority and access to courts are conceptually distinct—the relationship between them is complex. It is rare, in fact, that any one change will decrease both, as I will describe below. It is more often the case that (1) increasing the scope of judicial authority can enable a reduction of access to the courts, if a court chooses to use its authority to limit access, or (2) reducing the scope of judicial authority may increase access, such as by the legislative imposition of more procedural rules, statutory causes of action, or incentives for litigation.

Take, for example, one of the most famous and important cases in Supreme Court history, and the first to which most students of constitutional law are exposed. In *Marbury v. Madison*, the Court struck down an act of Congress (the Judiciary Act of 1789) that intended to expand the powers of the Supreme Court by granting it original jurisdiction over petitions for writs of mandamus. In so doing, Chief Justice John Marshall ingeniously broadened the Court's authority by establishing the power of judicial review, or the ability to strike down acts of Congress and the executive branch for violating the Constitution.[46] As such, *Marbury* is considered a classic case of judicial activism, wherein the Supreme Court vastly expanded its own powers beyond those formally granted to it by the nation's founders.

This is usually where the story of *Marbury* ends. But for William Marbury, who had petitioned the Supreme Court to compel the acting attorney general to deliver the commission entitling him to become a justice of the peace, the story of this case was very different. In arguing that Marbury did not have the right to appear before the Court in order to receive his commission, Chief Justice Marshall not only established the fundamental and far-reaching power of the courts to assert judicial review; he also opted *not* to hear Marbury's case. Even though the Court did make clear that the failure to deliver Marbury's commission was "clearly violative of a vested legal right" for which there must be a remedy, he ultimately did not have his day in court, and he never became justice of the peace.

Because of moments such as these, where the authority of courts is expanded in a way that simultaneously narrows opportunities for a potential litigant to have his or her day in court, it is hard to imagine an analysis that focuses on only authority or access while still effectively capturing the complicated project that is retrenchment. I am hardly alone in making this claim, joining other legal scholars who study antilitigation efforts and conservative judicial activism.[47] The fact that a plethora of legal scholarship on the fiercely antilitigation sentiment of the Rehnquist Court exists alongside proclamations that, at the same time, it was also "The Most Activist Supreme Court in History" captures what is often the inverse relationship between broad judicial power and access to courts.[48] I follow the lead of these scholars in attempting to distinguish and balance these concepts in hopes of providing a more complete picture of judicial retrenchment.

Second, while my goal here is to explain the politics of judicial retrenchment and not to quantify "degrees" of it, it is important to bear in mind the various barriers to the overt, successful acts of retrenchment often studied by those interested in court curbing. Retrenchment of any kind is a difficult political project, and scaling back access to the courts is no different. Even if, at a particular moment, there is a widely perceived "greater good" in easing the caseload of the federal judiciary so that it can continue to perform its core functions, no person is likely to relinquish his or her own day in court without a fight—especially when the right to a trial is so deeply ensconced in American political culture.[49] In this way, we should not expect the politics of judicial retrenchment to be any different from the politics of scaling back *any* policy that offers significant benefits to a group, whether it be Social Security, pension plans, tax breaks, or regulation.

Further, successful countermobilization in any policy arena is far from guaranteed, as actors face roadblocks such as veto points, coordination problems, and the various resistive forces of policy feedback. Steven Teles has examined why mobilizing against the deeply entrenched and well-defended liberal legal network—a force to be reckoned with when it comes to scaling back access to courts—is especially problematic. The professional domain that has developed around the law is difficult to penetrate due to many well-defined barriers to entry. Because the leadership in law schools and groups like the American Bar Association are typically controlled by incumbents, reformers find themselves at a significant disadvantage, not only because of exclusion based on their interests, but also because they lack access to the information necessary to infiltrate professional networks. This is true of any entrenched institution, as members tend to alter rules and processes to advantage their resources in a durable way. And as a result, Teles rightly focuses on how organizations like the Federalist Society struggle to unearth those values, practices, and procedures guarded by entrenched institutions.[50]

Those mobilizing to decrease access to the courtroom face substantial ideational entrenchment as well. As mentioned above, by the mid-twentieth century, courts were widely considered—both by the public and by the legal community itself—as the primary, legitimate protectors of the rights of individuals and groups disadvantaged by majoritarian electoral politics. Because historically so much of the expansion of court authority was based on the entrenchment of "rights," a concept that is premised and legitimated on the denial of moderation or infringement by any political group, it is difficult to wrest this authority away from them, even when there are empirical concerns regarding the practical sustainability of such a system, as has often been the case in light of the recent "litigation crisis."[51] Given this, most grand attempts to retrench access to the courts (like legislation designed to strip courts of jurisdiction in a policy arena) or efforts to reverse a legal precedent (such as the right under the First Amendment to burn a flag or the right under the Fourteenth Amendment to choose whether to have an abortion) have typically failed. Once a right has been granted, it is extremely hard and politically dangerous to take it away, at least directly.

Retrenchment can be difficult to identify for a third reason as well. In many instances, efforts at reducing access to courts have required the interested parties to actively create a new policy or rule aimed at raising the threshold for reaching the courtroom, or to get rid of a practice or procedure that previously expanded access. In recent years, for example, the Supreme Court has built a doctrine of "state sovereign immunity," based on a novel (and controversial) interpretation of the Eleventh Amendment, in order to protect states from being sued in their own courts. They also famously created a doctrine of "Chevron deference" whereby judges broadly defer to agency adjudication instead of engaging in more judicial review. During this same time period, several state legislatures capped the amount of punitive damages that successful plaintiffs can recover in a case (which otherwise serve to incentivize litigation) and, as we have seen, the Supreme Court has interpreted the civil procedural rules to make it more difficult to certify as a class action.

But reformers looking to scale back access to courts have also found significant success by pursuing yet another tactic: usurping judicial institutional practices and procedures historically employed by liberals. In areas as wide-ranging as crime policy, class actions, changes to the Federal Rules of Civil Procedure, and the use of the binding arbitration, conservatives have transformed institutional mechanisms originally put in place by liberals motivated to expand access to a just hearing for precisely the opposite goal. This tactic has proven particularly effective in the area of alternative dispute resolution (ADR), where conservative judges have arguably reinterpreted the foundational legislation for arbitration with the goal of keeping certain types of plaintiffs and cases out of court. A major reason why ADR, and the increasing use of arbitration procedures by conservatives in particular, has gone overlooked as a potent mechanism for constricting access to courts is because activists neither had to create an "arbitration state" nor scale it back in order to achieve their desired ends. Here too, we need to expand our historical time frame in order to capture this gradual retrenchment that, as in this example, took the form of co-option and displacement over time.

As such, the actors engaging with the judiciary on questions of access may not at first look like classic "retrenchers" at all. To use E. E. Schattschneider's famous language, increases and decreases in judicial power and fluctuations in the availability of legal redress have often been the product of "expanding the zone of conflict"; that is, as interested parties pursue retrenchment, they engage with other political actors who may also be drawn into the fray.[52] In practice, this has meant that individuals and groups have often unwittingly instigated or furthered retrenchment efforts by waging their own (often unrelated) political battles in which they seek to increase or decrease judicial authority for other reasons—most notably by exposing the "rules of the game" to the political process.

Toward a Theory of Judicial Retrenchment

In the analysis that follows, I hope to add to the debates detailed above by focusing on the roles that that *insularity, ideology*, and *temporality* play in the project of judicial retrenchment. While meaningfully different, the strategies for scaling back access to courts that I examine—which involve changing who is empowered to adjudicate legal disputes, the rules by which cases may or may not proceed, the venue in which disputes are heard, and the availability of remedies—have some overlap between them. To evaluate the role that these variables play, I employ the method of a "structured, focused comparison" by asking and evaluating the same questions of each case study.[53] First, who are the actors pursuing retrenchment, and what organizational/structural challenges do they face? Are these actors in the position to assert a high degree of autonomy over the institutional mechanisms that they are attempting to change, and do they enjoy insularity from the political process in their activities? Second, are the relevant actors driven primarily by classic partisan politics, or do they ascribe to an ideology of institutional maintenance? If both, how do they negotiate the potential conflicts? Third, what does the trajectory of institutional change look like over time? How do retrenchment strategies change in response to earlier developments, and how does this shape their effects, or lack thereof? Out of this analysis, I make three claims:

Claim 1: *The availability of malleable institutional "rules" enhances the likelihood of successful institutional change.* With regard to insularity, I find that when actors enjoy significant discretion over malleable, institutional rules and are successful in insulating their work from the political arena, there is a greater chance that their retrenchment strategies will succeed. As with any institution, rules govern a wide variety of activity within the judiciary, with dramatic consequences for incentivizing lawyers and litigants to seek justice through the courts. In the first half of the twentieth century in particular, the rules relevant to the judiciary—whether affecting the standards for filing a claim, the processes of discovery, the discretion of judges, administrative adjudication, or arbitration (to name a few)—were widely accepted as "purely procedural" and therefore irrelevant to the concerns of elected officials. Institutional rules of this sort tend to be considered the province of "experts" and subsequently do not draw much political or partisan attention. They therefore afford those who control them a high degree of discretion and insularity in reforming them. Under these conditions, rules of any kind are highly mutable; and as "actors relate to institutional rules as a repertoire or tool kit,"[54] individuals and groups are often able to leverage their control of rules for numerous goals, from entrepreneurial to procedural, to substantive political and policy making ends.[55] Accordingly, during that time, various groups and individuals found themselves relatively insulated from the political process and therefore able to assert a great effect on the availability of litigation. Even as we entered the more recent period of partisan conflict over the role of the courts, the power inherent in controlling the rules persists; and for that very reason, groups and institutions struggle mightily over that power.

Claim 2: *The groups and political cleavages that pursue retrenchment have multifaceted interests that transcend partisan lines and change over time.* Retrenchers have success when they can build support across or even transcend partisan and ideological lines. Where the role of ideology is concerned, the "who" and the "why" of judicial retrenchment are not as straightforward as we might expect. At times, efforts to scale back access to courts are waged by conservatives; but not all retrenchers are pursuing a conservative political platform. For example, in his study of antilitigation reform Thomas Burke identifies several different versions: discouragement reforms (that make it harder or less profitable to bring lawsuits); management reforms (that streamline the litigation process), and replacement reforms (that provide alternatives to litigation). Crucially, he argues that each type of reform engenders its own politics, which may be partisan, but may also not be. So while discouragement reforms tend to spawn partisan battles between trial lawyers and their Democratic allies and business groups and their Republican allies, replacement reforms involve complex, cross-partisan dynamics, and management reforms tend not to be partisan at all. While he finds this in the realm of formal legislative reforms, his analysis suggests that the story of retrenchment is more complicated than the partisan politics approach suggests—an insight that also holds true in the realm of institutional reform.[56]

Although the more recent period of retrenchment (in the context of the political resurgence of the Republican Party and a burgeoning conservative legal movement) looks more like the partisan battle we are most accustomed to—with conservatives bemoaning the work of activist judges and lawsuit-happy citizens, and liberals maintaining the value of the legal process, even with all its flaws—the politics of previous periods looked different. Retrenchment has often been pursued by administrators, experts, and other interested parties primarily concerned with protecting or bettering the practical function of the judiciary. I characterize this as the "institutional maintenance" ideology that precedes (and in some cases, persists throughout) the largely partisan battles that we observe from the 1970s onward. In many ways my characterization of this particular impetus for constricting access to courts draws from Daniel Carpenter's illustration of the role that "uniqueness" and "multiplicity" play in creating bureaucratic legitimacy. That individuals and groups voice significant concern for the upkeep of our judicial system over time (and put forth proposals to that end) is illustrative of the unique value that we assign to the idea of procedural justice. This is further evidenced by the degree to which these values cross partisan lines; in this way, the legitimacy of the legal process is grounded—as Carpenter describes with regard to administrative agencies—"not among the voters of one party or one section, not in a single class or interest group, but in multiple and diverse political affiliations."[57] The "institutional maintenance" imperative is grounded in a similar multiplicity of interests, often irreducible to party lines.

Claim 3: *The processes of retrenchment are distinctive but not static, often unfolding in a series of methods for attempted institutional change.* More often than not, successful retrenchment involves multiple modes of institutional change that evolve over time. While studies of court curbing focus mostly on authoritative legislative change, retrenchment of that kind is rare in practice. As Jacob Hacker argues, "By looking only at affirmative choices on predefined issues, retrenchment analyses tend to downplay the important ways in which actors may shape and restrict the agenda of debate and prevent some kinds of collective debate altogether."[58] Because the ground-level operation of policies can shift without formal revision through "decentralized and semiautonomous processes of alteration within existing policy bounds," analysts have largely missed much of the retrenchment that occurs. Because retrenchment is a difficult political project, especially in cases where policies are embedded in ways that insulate them from authoritative reform, actors seeking change often find it best not to attack institutions directly. By pursuing "drift, conversion, and layering," actors engage in what Hacker calls "everyday" forms of retrenchment; they seek to "to shift those institutions' ground level operation, prevent their adaptation to shifting external circumstances, or build new institutions on top of them." By pinpointing these institutional mechanisms, Hacker allows us to identify retrenchment where it occurs most; in the "subterranean" realm of informal institutional change.[59]

Jeb Barnes has recently operationalized Hacker's typology in order to explain "court-based tort reform" in the case of asbestos policy. What he found, however, is that identifying the dominant form of retrenchment—in this case, administrative "drift"—had explanatory value only when placed within a longer trajectory of change over time. In order to better explain institutional change, he concludes that "these concepts must be fit together to identify recurring patterns of development that encompass the multiple forums, access points, and exit strategies inherent in the striated American state."[60] I follow his lead in applying Hacker's "modes of retrenchment" typology to the judiciary, concluding that—just as political environments and cleavages change over time—so do modes of retrenchment. In order for this typology to have any explanatory value, then, it must be placed in a broader temporal context. This is consistent with the importance that both the institutional change and APD literatures give to historical development as an independent variable and the forces of path dependence.

In sum, I find that the groups involved in judicial retrenchment change over time and are, at times, motivated not only by partisan concerns or ideological backlash to the rights revolution, but also by an "institutional maintenance" imperative; that the politics and processes of retrenchment as a form of institutional change are distinctive, but can (and often do) unfold in a series of different methods in response to the institutional constraints and political pressures that reformers face; and that the availability of insulated, institutional rules that are less subject to political contestation enhance the likelihood of effective change. But the complications, as always, lie in the details.

3

Changing the Decision Makers: From Litigation to Arbitration

Introduction

To obtain a credit card today, one has to sign a lengthy and detailed contractual agreement with a bank provider. Most people sign their name or click the relevant online box without reading the fine print and paragraph upon paragraph of legalese. Were they to do so, they would typically find a clause buried in the contract stating that should the cardholder wish to dispute fees at any point with the provider, he or she must do so through a process of arbitration. This means that consumers are not able to resolve their complaint in court, regardless of the nature and severity of their dispute with the bank.

In the first decade of the new millennium, millions of credit card users in the United States have become bound by this process of mandatory arbitration to resolve disputes with their banks. As of 2006, more than 200,000 cases a year were handled by the National Arbitration Forum (NAF), a for-profit company that specializes in resolving disputes where a consumer, or group of consumers, believes that a bank, credit card company, or major retailer owes them money.[1] A 2007 Public Citizen report found that arbitrators in California working for the NAF had ruled against consumers 94 percent of the time; a subsequent lawsuit filed by the City of San Francisco provided data showing that the NAF won 99.8 percent of the time.[2] In 2009 Public Citizen found that 80 percent of credit card companies (including all ten of the nation's largest), 70 percent of banks, and 90 percent of cell phone companies currently have mandatory arbitration clauses in their contracts with consumers,[3] and a report issued by the Consumer Financial Protection Bureau at the end of 2013 determined that more than half of outstanding credit card loans are subject to arbitration clauses, a number that could soon reach as high as 94 percent if some of the prominent banks that agreed to remove the clause from their contracts temporarily decide to reimplement it.[4]

These reports, and the trend that they reflect, sparked a flurry of intensely partisan congressional hearings on the practice of mandatory arbitration, where consumers are required to sign away their right to legal redress as part of the terms of service.[5] The titles of the majority and minority reports published from the hearings illustrate the fundamentally different understandings of the nature of the problem that has given rise to this trend. The title of one House majority report, written by Dennis Kucinich, the Democratic chairman of the Domestic Policy Subcommittee, was "Arbitration Abuse: an Examination of Claims Files of the National Arbitration Forum"; the minority report, authored by Jim Jordan, the Republican ranking subcommittee member, was alternatively entitled, "Justice or Avarice: The Misuse of Litigation to Harm Consumers."[6] The Democrats' report focused on harms to consumers with regard to debt collection arbitration, claiming that consumers' due process rights were denied by the NAF's debt collection processes, and it promoted legislative action to end mandatory arbitration in the industry. The Republican report, by contrast, criticized the cost, excess, and greed of trial lawyers who promote and potentially benefit from traditional litigation, defending mandatory arbitration as a process that is therefore to the consumer's advantage.[7]

Credit cards and loan agreements are not the only areas of American life pervaded by mandatory arbitration agreements. Increasingly, working Americans have to sign contracts with employers specifying that they must enter into similar binding arbitration to resolve any workplace-related claims that may arise, and students are increasingly bound to arbitration when they obtain student loans or enroll at for-profit colleges. One study of twenty-one major corporations found provisions for mandatory arbitration in 93 percent of their employment contracts, and another estimated that at least one-third of nonunionized employees in America are bound by mandatory arbitration clauses.[8] Individual workers fare only slightly better with their employers than they do in disputes with credit card companies; a study of nearly 4,000 employment arbitration cases found that arbitrators found in favor of employees only 21 percent of the time, significantly lower than rates of success in litigation proceedings.[9] Members of Congress have responded to this phenomenon in the same partisan manner that reflected the split on the use of arbitration in banking. When the Commercial and Administrative Law subcommittee of the House Judiciary Committee held hearings entitled

"Mandatory Binding Arbitration: Is It Fair and Voluntary?," Republicans on the committee praised arbitration as "a critical tool in our society because it makes justice prompt and accessible for millions of Americans, and without it too many citizens would be left out in the cold by overburdened courts and overpriced lawyers."[10] By contrast, Democrats such as John Conyers and Loretta Sanchez expressed concern that mandatory arbitration denied proper legal redress for consumers and employees, forcing them to go through a biased and unequal bargaining process designed to protect big business at the expense of civil and legal rights.[11] Cliff Palefsky, co-founder of the National Employment Lawyer's Association, argued to House members that while arbitration is a dispute resolution system, it is "not a justice system." Instead, he stressed that "what is going on is do-it-yourself tort reform."[12]

The Supreme Court has decided various cases in the last few years in which it clearly adopted the position that businesses may use mandatory, binding arbitration to deny consumers and students the opportunity to litigate disputes and that individuals are bound by those agreements. In 2011 the Court held that AT&T Mobility could force customers to settle their disputes through arbitration and to waive their right to participate in any future class action lawsuits (notwithstanding a California law prohibiting contracts that disallow class action litigation), a decision that Andrew Cohen, writing in the *Atlantic*, called "as big a pro-business, pro-corporate ruling as we've ever seen from the Roberts Court."[13] Lower courts extended the holding to students seeking damages from both their universities and the financial institutions handling their student loans as well.[14] The next year, the Court again upheld the use of mandatory, binding arbitration (with only Justice Ruth Bader Ginsburg dissenting), holding that consumers who sign credit card agreements with arbitration clauses do not have the option to dispute any charges or fees in court—despite specific provisions in the Credit Repair Organizations Act that provided for precisely that.[15] And in 2013, the Court held that courts were not permitted to invalidate a contractual waiver requiring class arbitration for antitrust claims against a restaurant, effectively prohibiting merchants from pursuing a class action. This, too, occurred despite the fact that the maximum limits of an arbitration award as designated in the contract at hand would not allow the individuals to recover enough to afford arbitrating their claim.[16]

The majority defended each of these cases on the grounds that Congress has had a long-standing "liberal federal policy favoring arbitration agreements"[17] dating back to the Federal Arbitration Act (FAA) of 1925, and that the act was explicitly designed to curb "widespread judicial hostility to arbitration agreements." The Court's interpretation of the FAA as forcing individuals into arbitration and prohibiting groups with similar claims from asserting their rights by filing class action law suits, however, may well have surprised those who crafted the law in 1925. The interpretation certainly prompted skepticism from liberals as to what might be motivating a conservative Court to so fervently defend arbitration clauses, an innovation that was initially championed more than a century ago as a development geared toward giving workers in labor disputes greater access to justice. As Vermont Senator Patrick Leahy commented, "Congress never intended the law to become a hammer for corporations to use against their employees."[18]

The increasing use of mandatory arbitration to settle disputes without the option of going to federal courts is part of a broader trend toward the use of "alternative dispute resolution," a term that encompasses a number of conflict resolution techniques that fall outside of the traditional legal process. These techniques, which include not only arbitration but also mediation, settlement, and negotiation, typically involve the use of a nonjudicial third party actor to facilitate a resolution outside of court.[19] Because ADR consists of dispute resolution techniques that fall outside of the traditional judicial process, it by nature lessens judicial authority and access to courts. This has always raised the question of whether or not it relegates certain categories of claims to a system of second-rate justice—and over time, the ADR infrastructure has, in fact, arguably moved from being a form of justice enhancement for those unable to represent themselves adequately in court to one co-opted by groups less concerned with matters of justice and more concerned with defining certain types of legal claims as not warranting a hearing by judge and jury.[20] Moreover, the normative and practical impacts of these developments are, in many ways, continually controversial, raising questions about how well the judicial system is suited to meeting its goals, and whether these alternative mechanisms address the shortcomings of our justice system or just complicate them further.

The use of ADR to constrict access to courts has been a strikingly successful retrenchment strategy for conservatives, who seem to have co-opted these resolution procedures in order to impose binding mechanisms that reduce access to courts. Both national and state-level studies have found that the expansion and availability of arbitration and other forms of ADR has clearly resulted in a significant number of cases being "diverted" away from traditional court proceedings. One study found that nearly one-seventh of the cases filed in federal courts in 2001 were channeled to some form of

ADR.[21] According to the American Arbitration Association's Department
of Case Administration, the caseload of ADR practitioners nationwide grew
from 63,171 cases in 1993 to 95,143 cases in 1998, and dramatically increased
again (arguably due to the Alternative Dispute Resolution Act passed that
year) to 140,188 cases in 1999, reaching all the way to 230,258 cases in 2002.[22]
State-level data suggest that these numbers may even underestimate the magnitude of the shift toward ADR, given that the state of Florida alone reports
that its state courts referred 120,000 disputes to mediation in 1998 (compared
to 34,000 in 1989), and courts in Los Angeles, California, referred 28,000
to mediation in 2003.[23] While such litigation and arbitration data remain
piecemeal, it is clear that a significant number of litigants either choose or
otherwise find themselves in the realm of alternative dispute resolution in lieu
of their day in court. As such, this trend is now considered a leading cause
of what Marc Galanter has called the phenomenon of the vanishing trial.[24]
As Stephen Subrin and Thomas Main describe, "The jurisprudence of binding arbitration is now redirecting cases from courthouses to suburban office
parks."[25]

But while liberals such as Senator Leahy frequently condemn its use—
particularly mandatory arbitration clauses, in which disputes are resolved
without judges, juries, or guarantees of due process—the idea of creating
alternatives to traditional litigation actually received extensive bipartisan support over time and has been described as "so universal across both time and
space ... that we can discover almost no society that fails to employ it."[26] In
fact, despite the unique "juridification"[27] and "litigiousness"[28] that arguably
define American political culture, ADR also has a long and vibrant history
in the United States, particularly at the state and local level. Many ADR procedures were entrenched decades prior to the beginnings of the conservative
legal movement, and the fact that these procedures were well established
made co-opting them for purposes of retrenchment even easier, as reformers did not need to dismantle the "litigation state" nor create an "arbitration
state" to pursue their goals. The initial impetus for ADR stemmed from a
liberal desire to address the problems of an overloaded judiciary and sub-par
justice by giving litigants the option to handle their dispute in a less adversarial, expensive, and time-consuming way. Early arguments in its favor centered around (1) a desire to give more citizens better access to justice than
were found in the courts (often coinciding with time periods when courts
and lawyers were under attack by political interests that saw themselves as
ill-represented by the judicial branch), (2) creating an incentive to avoid the
costs of the adversarial legal process, and (3) providing individuals and groups

the opportunity to avoid using lawyers in an effort to more directly and easily participate in the resolution of their disputes.

Although proponents of ADR have been strikingly consistent in their arguments over time, far less consistent has been *who* has invoked these arguments. From its earliest stages, much of the support for ADR came from business interests who saw arbitration as a cost-effective and efficient way of handling daily disputes involving commercial transactions. In the Progressive era, they were frequently joined by liberals in the Democratic Party who saw arbitration and conciliatory courts as ways of responding to the perceived crisis that the adversarial litigation model was creating for overburdened dockets.[29] ADR became increasingly mainstream once it was embraced by the federal government in the 1920s and 30s (beginning with the passage of the Federal Arbitration Act in 1925 and incorporated into foundational New Deal statutes such as the National Labor Relations Act of 1935), and as it gained further support in the 1960s and 70s through the consistent efforts of a coalition of liberal rights activists, private donors and foundations, law schools, and the American Bar Association (ABA).

When Congress passed further legislation codifying its use in the 1980s and 90s, it was the professional organizations that had developed to promote, expand, and train individual practitioners in ADR techniques (largely funded by liberal donors like the Ford Foundation) that provided them with the substance needed to pass relevant laws: namely an established, entrenched body of battle-tested ADR procedures. These organizations also trained thousands of professionals to carry out ADR in practice, and these professionals, in turn, worked closely with judicial administrators from within government, themselves authoring procedural innovations to alleviate the overburdened judicial system. Once it became clear that ADR was here to stay, the ABA helped to entrench it further, establishing an organized section devoted to promoting ADR practices in 1993. This translated over time into the development of legal journals devoted to the topic, inclusion in law school curriculum, and the establishment of masters and doctoral programs in the field.

However, as the infrastructure for ADR grew and developed, other actors were gradually able to utilize these institutional mechanisms for their own purposes. Although liberals concerned with the rights protections of workers, the poor, and other less powerful plaintiff groups were critical to the creation and entrenchment of ADR, conservatives were rarely active in their opposition to it and, in fact, grew to support it increasingly over time. The reasons for their support, however, do not track with those of Democrats; instead, conservatives have arguably supported ADR as a device for keeping less profitable claims by less wealthy litigants out of the courts, and as a way of preventing management and corporate interests from facing costly litigation in labor, employment, commercial, and consumer disputes. In recent years, businesses and corporations also realized that they have clear incentives to create an "alternative procedural universe" for themselves in which they can use arbitration clauses to shorten statutes of limitations, restrict discovery, require confidentiality, waive plaintiffs' rights to recovering a variety of remedies, and contract with arbitrators sympathetic to their position as businesses. Arguably the most "advantageous aspect of their control over arbitral procedures" has been in avoiding class action lawsuits, which are particularly costly for corporations.[30]

Much of this has been enabled by a conservative Supreme Court, which has succeeded in "converting" the FAA into a modern device for relegating certain individuals and groups to a system of quasi-judicial dispute resolution in which sophisticated legal actors rewrite the procedural rules that govern the proceedings—very often to their advantage. When enacted in 1925, the act provided for judicial facilitation of private dispute resolution through contractually-based compulsory and binding arbitration and, as such, serves as the foundational legislation for arbitration in the United States. However, starting in the late 1980s, and subsequently through a series of approximately twenty decisions, the Supreme Court has given the FAA an increasingly prominent role in shaping dispute resolution, applying it to a wide range of disputes, and in a manner that is arguably far beyond what the FAA was initially intended to do. This has included considering arbitration sufficient for protecting most statutory rights, including major civil rights provisions,[31] limiting judicial review of arbitration outcomes, determining that the FAA preempts state law,[32] and allowing corporations to prohibit class action lawsuits against them.[33] These outcomes represent successes for legal and political conservatives, who seem to have co-opted the ADR infrastructure in order to pursue these goals. Yet at the same time, many Democrats continue to promote the virtues of ADR as well, further complicating the prognosis.

Part I: Origins of the Arbitration State
Ousting the Courts of Jurisdiction

The idea of using alternative dispute resolution to lesson the "delay, expense, and formality of a lawsuit" percolated throughout American communities as early as the late 1700s.[34] Some saw ADR as simply a benign matter of efficiency and ensuring proper access to justice; as a legislator in the Pennsylvania House of Representatives argued in 1791, "The idea that we are lessening the jurisdiction of the courts of law, and curtailing the benefits of young lawyers" is absurd. Defending a proposal to extend the jurisdiction of justices of the peace to small monetary disputes, he argued that "a physician should not envy his neighbors good state of health; neither ought a lawyer to be unhappy by feeling the causes of litigation done away with."[35] A decade later, the Pennsylvania legislature passed a law establishing that arbitration, rather than courts of law, would be used for *all* civil cases. The law was praised for lessening the expense of and time spent on litigation ("that unwieldy machinery of a jury trial is necessarily promotive of a great waste of time and money, compared with this simple principles of arbitration")[36] and alternatively attacked by those who believed that the law would violate the constitutional right to a jury and empower an arbitrator, as opposed to a judge, as the sole determinant of law. If arbitration courts supplant the function of lawyers, opponents argued, "then in all cases in which fact is mixed with the law, and many are the cases of this description, the judges must grope for the meaning of an intricate statute, or for the nature and extent of a custom, with what Rights they may"; if judges fail to find a specific law to apply, "the law will have the same measure as the arbitrator's floor."[37]

In the mid-nineteenth century, there was a flurry of legislative activity at the state level to create "courts of conciliation." In 1846 the state of New York amended its constitution to include conciliation tribunals in order to regulate costs and "carry out in Christian rule, that before you turned your adversary over to be dealt with by the judge, you should make a reasonable effort to conciliate and settle the difficulty before the arbitrators—who, without the aid of counsel, heard the parties, and sought to bring them to a settlement."[38] Conciliation courts were designed to "go very far to repress litigation, and speedily to arrange those controversies that sometimes spring up between very honest and well meaning men, without the costs and delays attending upon a litigation in our courts."[39] An editorial in the *Baltimore Sun* at the time believed these courts to be "among the interesting and excellent propositions of reform," the "desirable effect which is promised by such a benevolent project, cannot be too highly estimated, for it is those of our fellow citizens less favored in pecuniary means, who experience the greatest amount of oppression, from the burdensome and costly legal system in operation amongst us."[40] The narrative was convincing, as numerous other East Coast states and cities followed suit and established similar courts. Prominent newspapers like the *Boston Herald* bemoaned rising litigation rates and speculated that "the root of the mischief lies in the temper of the litigants and their abettors, and deeper than courts, juries or counsel can reach; perhaps, if it cannot be eradicated, its propagation may be shocked by legislation."[41] As the *Massachusetts Spy* put it, we do "not expect that either courts or lawyers are to be annihilated; but every sensible man will agree with us that very much of the ordinary litigation could be dispensed with, at a great advantage to all classes."[42]

As such, courts of conciliation became a popular innovation, backed by a range of supporters. In the years before widespread industrial strife and labor organization became national news, much of the support came from local business and railroad leaders who saw arbitration as a quick and cheap way of resolving conflicts with other railroads.[43] Even Colonel Thomas Benton, speaking before the new "Americans" in territory claimed in the Mexican-American War, recommended to the new citizens that they create courts of conciliation that can "terminate disputes without litigation, by means of a Judge; they can be easily engrafted on the Roman law, which you already have." Such a process, he argued, was "founded on the declarations of Scripture—'Agree quickly with your opponent, whilst he is ready to do so.'"[44]

The legal community, however, was never of one mind about these proposed courts of conciliation. Many lawyers and judges believed such courts could play an important role in keeping more "trivial" matters from cluttering their dockets, and some envisioned that they might have a role to play in these new courts as less adversarial administrators of justice.[45] But others saw arbitration schemes as a direct attack on judicial authority and jurisdiction. A significant swath of federal and state judges in the early nineteenth century were consistently skeptical of arbitration proceedings, embracing Lord Coke's 1609 sentiment that such proceedings must not "oust" the courts of their jurisdiction and deprive the parties of the right to an appeal on a matter of law.[46] Judges interpreted arbitration agreements as only pertaining to fact finding and in no way legitimately barring parties in a dispute from pursuing civil litigation in the future. Supreme Court Justice Joseph Story, for instance, argued that the "policy of the common law" prohibits people from giving up their rights and interests to an arbitration policy. "Nay, the common law goes farther," he argued, "and even if a submission has been made to arbitrators, who are named, by deed or otherwise, with an express stipulation, that the submission shall be irrevocable, it still is revocable and countermandable, by either party, before the award is actually made."[47] Relying entirely on English common law precedent, Story further argued "that a man cannot, by his act, make such authority, power, or warrant not countermandable, which is by law, and of its own nature, countermandable; as if a man should, by express words, declare his testament to be irrevocable, yet he may revoke it, for his acts or words cannot alter the judgment of law, to make that irrevocable, which is of its own nature revocable."[48]

Justice Story was also particularly suspicious of the use of a professional arbitrator—as opposed to a judge—as a finder of law. Arbitrators, he said, "at the common law, possess no authority whatsoever, even to administer an oath, or to compel the attendance of witnesses. They cannot compel the production of documents, and papers and books of account, or insist upon a discovery of facts from the parties under oath. They are not ordinarily well enough acquainted with the principles of law or equity, to administer either effectually, in complicated cases."[49] In 1874 the Supreme Court took a similar position when it struck down a Wisconsin state law that attempted to deny a disputing corporation the right to appeal to the federal courts. Justice Ward Hunt, writing for the majority, referenced both Justice Story's skepticism and English common law when arguing that no entity could legitimately divest a court of its jurisdiction by binding himself "in advance by an agreement, which may be specifically enforced, thus to forfeit his rights at all times and on all occasions, whenever the case may be presented."[50]

But the momentum behind ADR continued to build, particularly in the last decades of the century. Alternative dispute mechanisms were even proposed in the aftermath of the Civil War as a better way of reconciling international conflict.[51] The same year that Congress was debating its use in interstate commerce, the Senate Committee on Foreign Relations listened to the likes of Andrew Carnegie and respected judges who stressed the virtues of arbitration for settling differences between the United States and Great Britain. The Honorable David Dudley Field, also a member of the New York City committee for international arbitration, called upon Congress to "negotiate, talk, think, reason about the dispute rather than fight. Fight is vulgar. Fight is old. Let us have a new era."[52]

The growing conflict over the Industrial Revolution and the broader creation of a federal administrative state created a prominent forum for discussing the virtues of ADR and its expanded use.[53] Labor disputes between unionizing workers and numerous industries, most notably the railroads, were at the center of what would become an outpouring of the first notable arbitration legislation at both the state and federal level.[54] The first legislative enactments related to the railroad industry came in an attempt to stop workplace strikes from so frequently shutting down commerce. In 1888 Congress passed the Arbitration Act, providing for voluntary arbitration and ad hoc commissions for investigating the cause of railway labor disputes. While the railroad industry typically opposed compulsory arbitration and federal intrusion, railroad brotherhoods supported arbitration as a way of making owners accountable by, at the very least, bringing them to the bargaining table. Other groups, like the Anti-Monopoly League, saw arbitration as a way of addressing and balancing the desires of what they perceived to be radicals on both sides: economic individualists on the right, and socialists and activist unions on the left. It was thought that the use of arbitration, particularly when consensual, would enable fair outcomes for both sides, mediated by state regulation.[55] As such, the act promoted a middle ground, authorizing voluntary but not compulsory arbitration, and providing little by way of enforcement provisions beyond requiring that arbitrator findings and conclusions were to be published and submitted to the president and commissioner of labor.[56]

The most ambitious legislative effort, however—the inclusion of ADR provisions in the Interstate Commerce Act of 1887 in order to ensure that railroads complied with the act's antimonopolistic regulations—was ultimately struck down by a resistant Supreme Court. Justice David Brewer led the charge against the ICC and broader efforts at establishing and regularizing ADR, arguing that would-be administrative reformers were "mischief makers who ever strive to get away from courts and judges" and opposing "the demand for arbitrators to settle all disputes between employees and employers and for commissions to fix all tariffs for common carriers."[57] During the same time period, the Court also struck down state-level commissions aimed at arbitrating interstate commerce disputes; for example, it held that a Minnesota railway commission "deprives the company of its right to a judicial investigation, by due process of law, under the forms and with the machinery provided by the wisdom of successive ages for the investigation judicially of the truth of a matter in controversy, and substitutes therefor, as an absolute finality, the action of a railroad commission which, in view of the powers conceded to it by the state court, cannot be regarded as clothed with judicial functions or possessing the machinery of a court of justice."[58]

Despite this continued resistance from the Supreme Court, by the turn of the century, half of the nation's state legislatures had created arbitration schemes designed to handle a range of disputes, primarily in the railroad industry and other labor matters.[59] Most of these state arbitration boards were appointed by governors, and participation was again largely voluntary in nature, although some states authorized arbitrators to compel witnesses and force decisions if both sides previously agreed to be bound by the outcome. A report commissioned by Congress in 1901, however, found that many of these state arbitration boards were still in their infancy, with some states (notably Michigan) having failed to appoint board members, let alone take on any business. Illinois, Indiana, Massachusetts, and New York were notable exceptions, with their arbitration boards participating meaningfully in a number of major labor strikes, particularly in the coal mining industry. States typically created three-person arbitration boards, with one member selected by each party and a third from an outside source, and the boards were given the power of a final determination. But even in these states, compliance with the arbitration outcome was rare, and the inability of arbitrators to mandate participation or enforce agreements left them largely playing the role of mediator.[60] The New York board, for instance, found that "more is accomplished through mediation than by arbitration" because while at least one party was "disinclined to submit the matter in dispute to arbitration" the parties could sometimes nonetheless be compelled to make mutual concessions in conference meetings with the board.[61] As Herbert Schreiber has well pointed out, the significance of these state arbitration laws came less from their success on the ground (they were frequently ignored, as labor insisted on maintaining a right to strike and as management was unwilling to formally recognize union organizations through an arbitration hearing) than in establishing a model for future legislation at the federal level.[62]

Many judges also continued to reject arbitration schemes in these years, even in the midst of state-level legislation, claiming that such practices unconstitutionally ousted the courts of jurisdiction. Especially when faced with the question of whether and under what conditions arbitration could be considered a valid stand-in for litigation, many courts asserted that judges alone retained broad authority over questions of law. An early decision by Justice Benjamin Cardozo in New York was emblematic:

> Jurisdiction exists that rights may be maintained. Rights are not maintained that jurisdiction may exist. ... Power lodged in the Supreme Court is not to be withdrawn merely that it may be transferred and established somewhere else. Power, though not transferred, is still not to be withdrawn, if fundamental or inherent in the conception of a court with general jurisdiction in equity and law. Changes, we may assume, will be condemned if subversive of historic traditions of dignity and power. Such is not the change effected by this statute. The Supreme Court does not lose a power inherent in its very being when it loses power to give aid in the repudiation of a contract, concluded without fraud or error, whereby differences are to be settled without resort to litigation. For the right to nullify is substituted the duty to enforce.[63]

Despite the push and pull between state legislatures and courts, and in the face of the rampant unenforceability of arbitration outcomes, the federal legislature continued to build a slow but steady accumulation of laws supporting ADR procedures. In response to the Pullman Strike, Congress passed the Erdman Act of 1898, which made available arbitration procedures that could be used as an alternative to judicial intervention when resolving railroad disputes. The Newlands Act of 1913 created a permanent arbitration board for these purposes.[64] And during the Wilson administration, the Department of Labor used the National War Labor Board as an arbitration tribunal, resolving over 1,200 industrial disputes in the short sixteen months of its existence (from 1918 to 1919.)[65] The creation of the Department of Labor in 1913 in particular, however, was a groundbreaking development for ADR. In its establishment, the new bureau was given "the power to act as mediator and to appoint commissioners of conciliation in labor disputes whenever in his judgment the interests of industrial peace may require it to be done." The Department immediately began mediating labor disputes, an effort led by the department's head, William B. Wilson. By 1917 Wilson had pushed Congress to approve the United States Conciliation Service, the oldest continuing mediation institution in the United States. The House Committee on Interstate and Foreign Commerce promoted further expansion as well, suggesting broadening the Erdman Act to provide for more mediators and establishing a permanent board of mediation and conciliation. More controversially, it also suggested removing the availability of judicial review, arguing that court review simply encourages parties to evade arbitration decisions and creates obstructions to the primary goals of the process.[66] But in all of this activity, arbitration remained voluntary, altering but not getting rid of court jurisdiction by allowing judges to use injunctions to enforce arbitration awards.[67]

In the early 1900s support for ADR, and particularly arbitration, came from a diverse set of individuals whose ideological and political interests favored expanding arbitration as a worthy alternative to litigation. Amidst the popular sense that the courts were primarily defending the interests of capital, business support for ADR was actually more widespread and far more enthusiastic than was the response from the labor community, for whom ADR was purported to benefit.[68] Indeed, a range of local chambers of commerce had long provided arbitration as an attractive alternative to its members seeking to resolve commercial disputes in a quicker, less costly, and less formal way.[69] In the early 1900s, the National Civic Federation promoted mediation and arbitration in labor disputes, much as prominent ADR groups like the

American Arbitration Association (AAA) would in later years. This privately funded group was composed primarily of corporate businessmen, although on the record it claimed support from union officials like Samuel Gompers, president of the AFL, and John Mitchell, president of the Mineworkers union.[70] The federation worked to promote a body where "industrial decisions could be jointly made," and where "the large and the largest employers of labor can meet with representatives of organized labor to discuss their relative interests and try to find a way out where mutual interests of both may best be conserved."[71]

By contrast, labor activists seemed ambivalent as to the likelihood that arbitration would produce truly fair agreements, particularly in situations where the two parties were unequal in bargaining power. On the one hand, they expressed a marked preference for union recognition over a reliance on third party arbitration.[72] Given that judges consistently used a range of constitutional and common law doctrines to break strikes with injunctions, arrest union members on conspiracy charges, deny union members standing, and prohibit government regulatory innovations on grounds of employer freedoms of due process, their hesitance to rely on *any* method of dispute resolution was unsurprising.[73] But on the other hand, many labor leaders saw arbitration as a way to at least bring employers to the bargaining table. The appeal of collective bargaining outside of the courtroom began to spread in many unions across the country, becoming an especially prominent feature of railroad and coal miner labor disputes. As Gompers said in an arbitration ratification meeting in New York City in 1897, "Labor has always been in favor of arbitration. … [W]e want to settle these questions of controversy that arise and can be settled by an appeal to reason and an appeal to our judgment, an appeal to our sense of honor, an appeal to our interests; they can and should be settled around the table where discussion and judgment and truth and justice shall decide."[74]

With so much activity occurring both in government and the private sector, members of the organized bar began to see it as in their best interest to get involved in the conversation. The Pound Conference of 1916 brought together lawyers and legal academics concerned that the current civil litigation system made it difficult for ordinary citizens with relatively minor, less profitable cases to find lawyers willing to represent them. The dean of Harvard Law School, Roscoe Pound, was himself a leading critic of the legal system, suggesting in a famous 1906 speech to the ABA that the adversarial system of justice was on the verge of collapse under mounting pressures coming from industrial society, and that the way forward was a new form of "administrative justice" that heavily involved ADR.[75] Some even feared that, because of these pressures, clients would stop using lawyers if these problems were not urgently addressed.[76] Like other Progressive reformers from both within and outside the legal community, Pound believed that the judicial system needed to adapt to the increasing complexity of an industrial America.[77] The promotion of ADR by those in the legal profession stemmed from many of the same concerns that fueled reforms of the Federal Rules of Civil Procedure, small claims courts, and legal aid societies: namely a fusion of ideological Progressivism concerned with addressing increasing inequality in society and in the law and an administrative pragmatism designed to deal with the problems of expense and delay by fostering greater efficiency in the judicial system. While there were concerns expressed at the conference about the potential consequences of the increasing use of ADR—as one lawyer wrote, "When arbitrators step in, lawyers step out. They are not essential to the arbitration process and are sometimes expressly barred"[78]—others focused on the rapidly growing criminal caseload that was squeezing out much civil litigation, making reform of some kind a necessity.

Arbitration's Triumph: The Federal Arbitration Act and the New Deal

The perceived need for federal legislation establishing arbitration came to the fore in the 1920s, benefiting from the support of business interests and the organized bar. Early in the decade, shortly after the passage of the New York arbitration statute, a New York lawyer named Moses Grossman created the Arbitration Society of America, which sought to promote arbitration by conducting conferences, disseminating pamphlets and information, and holding training sessions for would-be arbitrators. A year later, the state of New Jersey followed with a similar statute, and Congress began to hold hearings about the possibility of a similar federal law. At the same time, New York businessman and member of the New York Chamber of Commerce, Charles Bernheimer, wrote a series of articles and books promoting the merits of commercial arbitration.[79] "To litigate," he wrote, is "the most wasteful procedure to which a business man can resort, means strife, expense, annoyance, and the rupture of business friendship, sapping the very lifeblood of commerce. The application of some other less wasteful method for the settlement of such differences and disputes becomes imperative."[80] Arbitration, to Bernheimer, was comparatively "sane, speedy, and inexpensive"; it freed up what were otherwise "congested court calendars," relieved "the law office of the many irksome litigious commercial matters that never pay," and helped the "small man or the poor man who cannot stand the stress and expense of protracted litigation."[81] After creating the Arbitration Foundation, Bernheimer quickly joined forces with Grossman and four others to form the American Arbitration Association (AAA), arguably the most influential and prominent source of support for ADR to the present.

Bernheimer teamed up with other leaders from regional chambers of commerce and leading members of the ABA to help promote and write what would become the Federal Arbitration Act (FAA) of 1925. The act provided for judicial facilitation of private dispute resolution through contractually-based compulsory and binding arbitration. Relying on its power to "prescribe the jurisdiction and duties of the Federal courts," the act mandated that courts uphold and enforce arbitration agreements unless such agreements were produced as the result of corruption, fraud, or prejudice. In drafting the legislation, Congress was explicit in its purpose; it sought to put arbitration agreements "upon the same footing as other contracts, where [they] belong."[82] This language was undoubtedly in response to the fact that, at the time, courts viewed arbitration agreements with hostility, perhaps because—as a Senate report on the bill hypothesized—it required them to surrender jurisdiction over particular issue areas: "The jealousy of their rights as courts, coupled with the fear that if arbitration agreements were to prevail and be enforced, the courts would be ousted of much of their jurisdiction."[83] In the congressional hearings, Bernheimer defended the interests of business, claiming litigation as the "most unprofitable thing" that can confront "anyone engaged in buying and selling."[84] Julius Henry Cohen of the ABA backed Bernheimer's endorsement, claiming that no one opposed the bill; he also downplayed fear on the part of judges that they were losing jurisdiction ("We oust the courts of jurisdiction everyday") and argued that lawyers "can handle an ordinary arbitration case in our offices and make more money out of it than we can if the case goes into litigation."[85]

The ABA's Commerce Committee ultimately drafted the language of the act and defended its proposal against those within the legal community who feared that the law constituted Congress attacking the authority of the courts. The committee accomplished this largely by downplaying court hostility, claiming that pushback was more "due to an adherence to precedent."[86] As Cohen argued before Congress, fear among judges that arbitration would enable the stronger to "take advantage of the weaker" was largely unfounded in the cases of commercial litigation to be addressed by the law because "people are protected today as never before" due to government regulation.[87]

Secretary of Commerce Herbert Hoover also endorsed the legislation, arguing that it would unclog the courts, speed up mercantilist transactions,
and promote commerce. As he put it, "Next to war, the greatest source of
economic waste in our national life is needless litigation."[88]

Business interests remained at least cautiously supportive of the use of
ADR in certain contexts as a way of promoting labor peace and, as such,
promoted the Railway Labor Act (RLA), which established a new board of
mediation.[89] In order to avoid the violence and long-standing strikes that had
dominated the national news during the 1920s, the board worked to resolve
claims by promoting mediation first and arbitration second, should mediation fail. The RLA provided the board with the power to compel mediation
before a union could strike, as well as to work with the president to create an
emergency board to intervene with injunctions against recalcitrant parties.[90]
The spirit of the act prompted dramatic proclamations that we had entered
a new era of industrial democracy. The *New York Times* editorialist Evans
Clark wrote that a "new government" was forming, one that was "the sum of
a large number of separate and unrelated agreements between self governing
economic groups to regulate their own concerns, to make rules for their own
conduct and that of their members, and even to punish those who violate
them. It will be a government of voluntary cooperation, of self-determination
along natural economic lines."[91]

By the 1930s, arbitration provisions appeared frequently in federal legislation, coming at different times from Republican and Democratic majorities
in Congress and the White House. The Norris-La Guardia Act was a particularly prominent example of jurisdiction stripping by Congress, largely prohibiting federal courts from issuing injunctions against labor unions, legitimating
the authority of unions as economic actors, and expanding the availability
of ADR practices for labor conflicts.[92] The National Labor Relations Act
(NLRA) of 1935 further codified the availability of ADR and in important
ways protected it from erosion by courts and other sources. The act, among
other things, gave employees the right "to bargain collectively through representatives of their own choosing, and to engage in concerted activities, for
the purpose of collective bargaining or other mutual aid protections." The
law also made it illegal for employers to refuse to bargain with union representatives selected by a majority of employees, institutionalizing negotiation
through collective bargaining as national policy practice. The quasi-judicial
body charged with handling disputes under the NLRA, the National Labor
Relations Board (NLRB), consisted of a three-person panel that established
policy and rendered decisions on unfair labor charges and issues of union

representation. The board's agents would investigate the parties' charges, oversee representation elections, require good faith bargaining by both employers and employees, and enforce collective bargaining agreements. If either side failed to bargain in good faith, or violated labor law by participating in illegal acts, the NLRB was authorized to prosecute and remedy the matter, whether through injunctions or mandating the enforcement of a collective bargaining agreement without the consent of the violating party.

These laws created a larger swath of policies in which arbitration could be used, but they often did not explicitly enforce arbitration outcomes. Over the next few decades, through executive orders, legislation, and court decisions, ADR continued to proliferate; but enforceability still largely relied on the "good faith" of the participants.[93] In response to the unprecedented number of labor strikes that occurred in 1945 and 1946, the Taft-Hartley Act (though better known for its extensive amendments to the NLRA) further expanded the use of ADR in labor disputes. Although continuing to reject compulsory arbitration, the "National Emergency Dispute" section of the law established mediation for national emergency disputes. Specifically, the law authorized the president to obtain a court injunction against a strike for eighty days if it was deemed a threat to the national interest, with the ability to then command participants to go before a newly created agency, the Federal Mediation and Conciliation Service (FMCS). The FMCS was to be used whenever labor or management wished to renegotiate an expiring contract and required that they give notice to the other side and to FMCS, which would assist in mediating.

One way to bookend the early development of ADR is when the judiciary switched its perspective. Especially in the area of labor, the courts were highly unsympathetic to unions and workers, and opportunities for ADR were crucial for protecting their rights in particular. In 1962, however, the Supreme Court decided several cases (known as the "Steel Trilogy") that evidenced a new willingness on its part to protect labor's interests. In *United Steelworkers v. American Manufacturing Co.*,[94] *United Steelworkers v. Warrior & Gulf Navigating Co.*,[95] and *United Steelworkers v. Enterprise Wheel & Car Corp.*,[96] the Court for the first time established a presumption in favor of arbitration of disputes stemming from collective bargaining agreements. In each of the cases, the employers had refused to enter into arbitration with employees and brought their case to the Court in hopes that they might rule on the legal merits of the dispute. The Court, however, refused to do so, instead enforcing the arbitration agreement and deferring to the expertise of the chosen arbitrators. Deference to arbitrators was not to be unlimited;

while "an arbitrator is confined to interpretation and application of the collective bargaining agreement; he does not sit to dispense his own brand of
justice," the decision must draw "its essence from the collective bargaining
agreement. When the arbitrator's words manifest an infidelity to this obligation, courts have no choice but to refuse enforcement of the award."[97] But
the Court nonetheless did hold that the arbitrator has the final word on the
interpretation of a collective bargaining agreement. "So far as the arbitrator's
decision concerns construction of a contract," the Court wrote, "the courts
have no business overruling him."[98]

Thus, although the initial development of ADR did stem from a desire
to make pursuing rights claims easier, more efficient, and less costly, it also
fundamentally began as part of a deeply politicized process of shifting matters traditionally adjudicated by judges to other decision makers. Early in its
development, however, this did not present much trouble as far as access to
justice is concerned, as ADR practices were aimed to help those least apt to
reach or succeed in court to have a fair hearing, and judicial review was rarely
eliminated. This motivation persisted into the Civil Rights era, as judicial,
congressional, and popular support led to its further development.

But at its seeming height in the mid-twentieth century, support for ADR
began to crack under the weight of a diverse, growing, and mobilizing array
of critics. Much of this opposition came from within the legal community,
whose opposition had not disappeared during the height of the New Deal,
but lingered importantly at the margins. A divided ABA never fully embraced
the New Deal regulatory apparatus and the ADR procedures housed within
it. The ABA's Special Committee on Administrative Law, chaired by Roscoe
Pound, had argued in 1938 that the newly created agency model of regulatory enforcement was ineffective, unable to enforce decisions, and too easily
captured by special interests. Pound wrote that unless "the bar takes upon
itself to act, there is nothing to check the tendency of administrative bureaus
to extend the scope of their operations indefinitely even to the extent of supplanting our traditional judicial regime by an administrative regime."[99] Many
New Deal policy makers also became disenchanted with the administrative
regulatory model, similarly finding it too vulnerable to interest group capture, as well as criticizing public commissions for their inability to plan, coor-
dinate, or enforce policy agendas.[100] McCarthyism only furthered the fears
of rights activists, as government-based administrative proceduralism was
perceived as contributing to the denial of individual due process rights and
civil liberties.[101]

In the rights revolution era, ADR would come under further attack for denying access to courts for those left out of the insider world of interest groups and regulatory politics. Labor unions were no longer on the outside being denied access by the courts; they were now seen as dominating arbitration procedures, not just in relation to business, but also in relation to individual workers.[102] The rights revolution, with its focus on those denied access to the political process—whether groups who were denied the right to vote, or individuals unable to form effective coalitions because of irrational prejudice in society against them—seemingly turned the legal tide away from ADR-type administrative procedures and back toward valuing traditional court proceedings and the legitimacy they provide. This was especially true when constitutional rights were at issue, with the Supreme Court taking the position that arbitration clauses could not prevent individuals from going to federal court to seek enforcement of their constitutional rights.[103]

These themes also struck a chord with organizations such as the Legal Defense Fund, the legal arm of the NAACP, which would eventually turn more aggressively toward litigation as a strategy for political change.[104] Landmark judicial victories in the Supreme Court in the areas of educational and public desegregation, employment discrimination, and voting rights only furthered the enthusiasm of legal activists. Prominent law professors were equally influenced by these developments, both embracing litigation as the most powerful way for disadvantaged groups to achieve justice and understanding ADR procedures as dangerously enabling powerful interests to dominate disadvantaged communities.[105] Owen Fiss, for instance, famously likened ADR to plea bargaining, characterizing it as an institutional device employed by the state to regulate and control disadvantaged populations: "We turn to the courts because we need to, not because of some quirk in our personalities. We train our students in the tougher arts so that they may help secure all that the law promises, not because we want them to become gladiators."[106]

In this way, the achievements of the rights revolution dampened what had been a seemingly triumphant moment for ADR as the primary method for enforcing rights policies. But as we will see, this was by no means the end of the regulatory state and ADR model; although the rights-based legislation of the 1960s created a strongly private litigation-based model of legislative enforcement, this new so-called "litigation state" would not supplant the "arbitration state."[107] In fact, ADR continued to expand, even if bruised and a bit removed from the limelight. Although many liberals embraced the litigation-based approach, many did not. This split among liberals regarding ADR's ability to protect rights both provided a narrative palatable to conservatives and created an opening to use ADR as a strategy for judicial retrenchment.

Part II: Arbitration and Retrenchment
Liberals Divide, Conservatives Conquer

The passage of the Civil Rights Act in 1964, among many other things, marked yet another milestone for ADR. By creating the Equal Employment Opportunity Commission (EEOC), the act provided that violations identified by the commission would be assigned to mediation for resolution, going to the courts only if mediation failed. The act also created the more controversial Community Relations Service, designed to mediate interracial disputes. Given the compromises in the passage of the Civil Rights Act that ultimately denied the EEOC greater enforcement powers, scholars have tended to overlook these mediation provisions in favor of examining how private litigation came to the fore in enforcing the statute.[108] But at the same time, the continued centrality of mediation served to expand the infrastructure built for ADR, prompting entities like the Ford Foundation (which importantly funded many rights revolution–era efforts) to invest in its further growth. Notably, in the 1968 report issued by the National Advisory Commission on Civil Disorders in response to the widespread race riots of 1967, the Ford Foundation responded to the Kerner Commission by creating and funding the National Center for Dispute Resolution and the Center for Mediation and Conflict Resolution. These two organizations became the first to use ADR for community and racial disputes. Since the government's organization (the FMCS) was restricted to private sector labor management cases as a matter of statute, these new organizations provided an institutional infrastructure through which ADR could be expanded to other policy areas in the years to come.

In the 1970s, Congress passed new laws creating rights and benefits for environmentalists, prisoners, and the aged, and subsequently created more government agencies that used ADR procedures prior to court action.[109] Entire specialties of ADR developed around complicated environmental disputes, prisoner grievance arbitration, age discrimination, public employee disputes (including postal workers), health and safety issues, and Native American mediation. While much of this activity necessarily premised itself on new rights created by the government, the activity of private groups and organizations provided the support necessary to make ADR in these new areas a reality, fueling the maturation of ADR as a profession. In 1972 yet another major organization—the Society of Professionals in Dispute Resolution—was founded in order to help expand ADR beyond the realm of labor management in order to address these new areas of rights. While the group's membership started with a majority of labor specialists, within ten years it gained an additional 1,000 members, with a majority specializing in policy areas other than labor. The group importantly contributed not only to expanding ADR into new policy areas, but also in terms of creating and training individuals in new ADR methods. Practitioners expanded their skills in terms of ADR techniques, ranging from mediation and arbitration to specialized training in the process of fact-finding and serving as ombudsmen.

In addition to these more longstanding sources of support, ADR also began to attract new advocates, including both liberal legal academics and the mainstream legal profession itself. Many academics and activists, increasingly frustrated with the perceived ineffectiveness of litigation, turned toward ADR as a way to provide justice to those who struggled in the traditional, adversarial legal process. Lawrence Friedman's influential 1967 law review article importantly echoed many of these concerns: "The cost of using the judicial process, especially if an appeal is made, is so high that it acts as a significant barrier against litigation that does not measure its outcome in thousands of dollars. ... [T]he high price of litigation comes with its own high price: the denial, in some areas, of justice to the poor. A middle-class democratic society may consider such a situation inherently evil."[110] Many scholars subsequently devoted increased attention to the limits of law and its inability to address important societal issues.[111] ADR was seen by some legal academics on the left as an "outgrowth of the participatory model of effecting change represented by direct action, and a response to the movement's critique of the legal model of civil rights advocacy."[112]

Public interest activists adopted a similar stance. Alan Houseman, the director of the Research Institute of Legal Services, argued that the government-sponsored Legal Services Corporation needed to find more non-adversarial means to reach out to broader populations of poor who were yet still being neglected by their services.[113] It was clear that litigation, they argued, was not helping to solve the problems of the poor. The perceived advantage of ADR mechanisms was predicated upon the assumption that litigants, and not their lawyers, would be the key actors engaged in dispute resolution. In contrast to the continued developments in the Federal Rules of Civil Procedure, which made the role of the lawyer even more central in the courtroom, many ADR procedures were designed to foster direct participation by litigants.

In this respect, some ADR mechanisms do not reject the adversarial mode but rather question the faith implicit in the lawyer–client relationship. Yet other ADR procedures confront the assumption of the desirability of adversarial approaches and seek to develop a range of more cooperative responses beyond those typically employed in and by courts.[114]

In 1976 the ABA addressed these claims with another "Pound Conference," called this time by Chief Justice Burger, with a similar goal of addressing how to improve the efficacy of the courts and the administration of justice more generally. The Chief Justice himself spoke in support of integrating ADR thoroughly into the justice system; without it, he argued, "we may well be on our way to a society overrun by hoards of lawyers, hungry as locusts, and brigades of judges in numbers never before contemplated" and "we have reached the point where our systems of justice—both state and federal—may literally break down before the end of the century."[115] Harvard University law professor Frank Sander also gave a speech entitled "Varieties of Dispute Processing," in which he proposed a "multidoor" courthouse where litigants would have a choice of not only formal dispute resolution (leading to trial), but also a range of other less formal possibilities, including arbitration and mediation.[116] The Pound Conference produced several other important recommendations as well, among them the idea of creating "neighborhood justice centers" for accessible dispute resolution, as well as stressing the continued importance of experimentation and innovation in developing and fine-tuning new ADR techniques.

Participants in the conference also addressed more "lawyer friendly" versions of ADR. The discussion reflected the intuition that lawyers might well fear losing their jobs due to the expansion of these "outside of the courtroom" dispute resolution techniques. They discussed these proposed innovations in tandem with Rule 16 of the Federal Rules of Civil Procedure, which itself encourages judges to use pretrial conferences to figure out ahead of time how best to move a given case through the legal process. As part of the pretrial conference, judges can also urge parties to consider and use ADR. In all, these methods would allow for the use of discovery and more "typical" legal procedures in cases where mediation was insufficient.

Since the livelihood of lawyers is potentially threatened by moving dispute resolution out of the courtroom, one might expect that groups like the ABA would have strongly opposed ADR. But instead, the profession started to embrace it, albeit while making sure that it had an enduring role to play in this arena. Introducing a variety of techniques—many discussed at the Pound Conference—in which lawyers would be ensured a central role in ADR was crucial to this. As such, ADR grew to encompass practices such as moderated settlement conferences, which involve each side presenting a summary of its case to a panel of attorneys; summary jury trials, which involve each side presenting a case to both a jury and a judge, facilitated by lawyers; and early neutral evaluation, which involves the presentation of case summaries to an evaluator (often a lawyer) who asks questions, challenges evidence, and provides a written evaluation of each side's chances for success in litigation. As a sign of its intent to remain involved in the realm of ADR, in the aftermath of the Pound Conference, the ABA formed its first committee on the subject—the Special Committee on the Resolution of Minor Disputes—to maintain professional prominence in the field.

As with other areas of legal reform, the perceived crisis and the rising costs associated with litigation spurred yet another movement for reform, manifesting itself in a flurry of congressional activity in the late 1970s.[117] Notably, however, a split between two factions of the Democratic Party became apparent when it came to the question of whether arbitration and not litigation (with all the guarantees of due process) was actually ideal for resolving all types of disputes. Arbitration was the primary solution in the proposed "Federal Medical Malpractice Insurance Act of 1975," sponsored by Democratic Senator Gaylord Nelson of Wisconsin; it was also at the center of a similar bill proposed by Edward Kennedy and Daniel Inouye that promoted the use of arbitration for medical malpractice disputes.[118] In the introduction to his testimony in support of the bill, Senator Kennedy praised arbitration as a long-standing approach used for labor-management and commercial disputes, and one that would effectively improve health care while greatly cutting costs. He did concede, in a bow to critics, that such a bill must keep open the possibility that a plaintiff may have a day in court; but he took the position that judicial review should only be available *after* arbitration and with the arbitration panel's decision admissible as evidence.[119]

Trial lawyers were split on the matter. Richard Paulson, representing the Association of Plaintiffs and Trial Attorneys, took issue with the idea that individuals must use arbitration before going to court because "if he wins, he gets nothing in that he must give his entire recovery in court to the Secretary of HEW. The problem here is that in reality a freedom of choice is denied him by requiring arbitration as the first and only meaningful step, thus posing problems under the 7th and 14th Amendments."[120] But even the Association of Trial Lawyers of America (ATLA), which opposed federal regulation of medical malpractice remedies in 1974, nonetheless supported mandatory binding arbitration for medical malpractice suits involving less than $25,000.

Although recognizing that it lacks many of the safeguards provided by a full judicial proceeding, ATLA argued that "arbitration can often provide greater speed and economy through the more informal procedures which are utilized there."[121] The Senate also followed the Pound Conference with hearings of its own on the "Causes of Popular Dissatisfaction with the Administration of Justice," in which it was receptive to alternative dispute resolution as a way of increasing judicial access. The Senate did reject a proposal from Solicitor General Robert Bork, however, who argued that litigation arising from social welfare legislation was "legal trivia" and should be removed from federal court jurisdiction altogether.[122]

In 1977 hearings in the House of Representatives on the "State of the Judiciary and Access to Justice," conducted by Wisconsin Representative Robert Kastenmeier, began by referring to President Jimmy Carter's goal to expand the justice system, broaden standing to initiate suits against the government, and expand access to class actions.[123] But these goals were at odds with continued fears that federal courts were overwhelmed by litigation, especially in light of the fact that the number of cases in federal courts doubled between 1960 and 1975. This also meant spiraling legal costs: "Access to justice means access to the courts with legal counsel," Kastenmeier argued; "thus, for a large segment of our society, unable to pay the costs of legal representation, there is limited access to justice," rendering courts effectively unavailable for resolving minor disputes. This was especially problematic, he pressed, in light of a "growing perception that several recent Supreme Court decisions have had the effect of closing the courthouse doors to many citizens because of the Federal courts' rising workload."[124] Kastenmeier went on: "In return for aiding the Federal courts and reducing congested dockets by passing the judgeship bill and by legislating several of the proposals pending in this subcommittee, we will consider passing legislation to reopen threshold doors that the court has closed. Or, in the alternative, we ought to investigate the creation of other adequate forums—and I emphasize 'adequate'—to resolve the disputes that have been taken from the jurisdiction of the Federal courts."[125]

On the one hand, then, a strong contingent of the Democratic Party embraced arbitration and other methods of ADR as both a means for addressing the litigation crisis and providing access to justice for a broader array of citizens, most notably the poor. However, in the hearings on the "State of the Judiciary and Access to Justice," another liberal, rights revolution–era position emerged. The first two speakers—consumer advocate Ralph Nader and the president of Legal Services, Thomas Ehrlich—supported legislation that would provide for larger attorney's fee awards and broader availability of class actions as a way of opening the courthouse doors in order to solve these problems.[126] Nader complained that the Burger Court was closing the courthouse to individuals, with great consequence: "It is one thing to tell citizens their legal claims are without merit, but it is an entirely different matter to tell them that their claims will not even be heard. If a sheriff stood at the courthouse door and prevented citizens from entering to present their grievances, the public outcry would generate page one headlines all across the nation." Ehrlich addressed the idea of expanding ADR in order to address these issues, but he ultimately feared that doing so would provide limited remedies and that "the new forums will become institutionalized 'screening mechanisms' for moving cases out of the court system instead of attempts to deliver justice with better results and greater access by the public."[127] As a result, he argued that—in the spirit of the rights revolution—a hearing in federal court was essential for maintaining rights, lest ADR become the venue for whatever constituted the "lesser" legal disputes of the day.

In many ways, those speaking in favor of ADR legitimated Nader and Ehrlich's fears. Attorney General Griffin Bell, for example, characterized the expansion of ADR as ideal for dealing with cases involving monetary and not injunctive relief, and also for cases in which the legal fees would outweigh the remedies. Notably, Bell also championed ADR for cases where there is not an "important" legal question at issue. Robert Bork, then a professor at Yale Law School, largely agreed with Bell, arguing that Congress should set up administrative agencies to deal with disputes regarding its statutory entitlement programs. In response to an alternative request to increase the size of the judiciary, Bork replied, "The Federal judiciary is now too large as it stands" and preferred restricting jurisdiction in a range of cases.[128] Clearly, differentiating between "important" legal questions as opposed to those dealing with statutory entitlement programs had the potential to make it difficult for certain categories of claims or litigants to have their day in court, which strongly contrasted with what liberal rights revolution activists set out to achieve.

Attention to these issues continued in Congress the following year. The Senate unanimously passed the Dispute Resolution Act, an act that Senator Edward Kennedy called "an incentive program" designed to encourage experimentation with alternative dispute mechanisms that are expeditious and inexpensive, and to create a Dispute Resolution Resource Center in the Department of Justice, as an initial response to the perceived litigation crisis that the ABA argued left two-thirds of citizens without "easy access" to the courts.[129] This special committee, chaired by Talbot D'Alemberte, soon became a central player in a wave of congressional action promoting ADR. In August 1978 the Committee on the Judiciary in the Senate held hearings on the "Court-Annexed Arbitration Act," legislation designed to promote nonbinding arbitration as an alternative to litigation to "encourage prompt, informal, and inexpensive resolution of civil cases."[130] The proposal came in response to "widespread concern" that the federal judicial system was overloaded. On February 13, 1979, Senator Kennedy opened a Senate hearing on "Equal Access" by asserting that "equal access is more than just a hallmark of justice—it's a definition of justice, and no system merits that description if access is the privilege of a few and not the right of all. That principle is the foundation of our legal system, but the reality is that more than two-thirds of the American people lack easy access to the courts."[131] In response to these hearings, and in tandem with support from the ABA Special Committee, legislators sought to find ways to address this access deficit. Relying on examples of alternative dispute programs from different urban areas of the country, Kennedy proposed new legislation, the Dispute Resolution Act of 1979, with the intent of creating a dispute resolution resource center and providing federal seed money to states to experiment with ADR programs.

Prominent organizations in the business and legal communities supported the bill. Jeffry Perlman of the U.S. Chamber of Commerce argued in the hearings that ADR would help business resolve consumer disputes in "effective, expeditious, fair and inexpensive manner."[132] Speakers representing the ABA were also supportive, but with a much different emphasis. Shepherd Tate, the president of the ABA, focused on the need to expand legal services to help the poor, arguing that the ABA could only do so much with a private bar in this area. "There can be no doubt," wrote Mr. Tate, "that we must find ways to improve the settlement of small, personal or monetary disputes without the formalities or prohibitive costs of court action."[133] Tate embraced the concerns of public interest advocates like Nader and Ehrlich when he contrasted the legal needs of the poor, for whom the ABA recommended the expansion of opportunities for litigation through enhanced legal services programs and attorney's fee awards, with those issues that "ought" to be handled without lawyers and judges. "Minor disputes," he argued, could be handled by "neighborhood justice centers and other techniques."[134] As D'Alemberte described it:

> Consider the neighborhood dispute about a loud stereo: Is this really
> a matter for police, prosecutors and judges? Today it is, and the results

are astonishingly poor: In court, the State says the defendant broke the law by x decibels. He will either be fined, or jailed, or both if proved guilty: neither if not. Yet there is no resolution of the underlying dispute between neighbors. A finding of guilty as well as a finding of not guilty can heighten the animosity between the disputants. Soon (estimates run to about 90 days), the parties will be back with the same problem, or one which has escalated, perhaps, into a serious criminal matter.[135]

While D'Alemberte's example was palatable and relatively benign—and therefore especially effective for making clear the value in dealing with issues like noise disturbances in places other than the courts—this narrative differentiating between "minor" and otherwise legitimate disputes would be furthered in more problematic ways in years to come.

But in the years following the passage of the 1980 Dispute Resolution Act, the use of ADR in nontraditional fields boomed; new organizations continued to spring up, such as the Academy of Family Mediators, the Conflict Resolution Education Network, and the U.S. Association of Ombudsmen; legal and other academics embraced it; and the approach itself subsequently began to change. Academic interest played an especially important role in these developments. In 1981 George Mason University became the first to offer a master's degree in conflict management, and in 1989 the school established the Institute for Conflict Analysis and Resolution, which also offers a doctorate. Harvard followed suit, forming its Program on Negotiation in 1983, which drew enrollment from several other Boston area schools. Law schools also began taking ADR seriously, and by the mid-1980s, most schools offered courses or clinics on the subject.[136] Further, as ADR became a permanent fixture in the law and in legal education, law schools also began to establish ADR-specific journals.[137]

These developments in academia were undoubtedly fueled by the ABA's highly public embrace of ADR. In 1987 the ABA expanded its interest in the topic even further by establishing a Standing Committee on Dispute Resolution, making it a regular ABA section in 1993. The section's mission—"to provide its members and the public with creative leadership in the dispute resolution field by fostering diversity, developing and offering educational programs, technical assistance and publications that promote problem solving and encourage excellence in the provision of dispute resolution services"—led to its rapid growth, reaching 6,000 members by the late 1990s.

Federal administrative policy making bodies became involved as well.[138] The Administrative Conference of the United States (ACUS) first entered the discussion in 1982 when it recommended procedures by which agencies could negotiate proposed regulations. It also offered itself as a support infrastructure for those agencies interested in implementing ADR procedures. In 1986 the ACUS issued the first of its recommendations for using ADR procedures in agency adjudication. These two series of recommendations would become the basis for major legislation involving ADR in years to come, namely the Negotiated Rulemaking Act and the Administrative Dispute Resolution Acts of 1990.

Congress continued to embrace the practice of arbitration and ADR in the 1980s as well, debating expanding its use in everything from civil cases to mediating disputes between the elderly to using administrative judges to handle civil rights housing matters to ADR for FOIA requests.[139] In the early 1980s, Republican Senator Robert Dole led hearings investigating the continued problem of case backlogs, beginning the hearings by arguing that Congress could not continue to simply expand the numbers of judges, but must instead look to alternative ways of handling civil matters.[140] The Alternative Dispute Resolution Promotion Act was proposed in the Senate in 1986 to "require attorneys to certify that clients have been apprised of alternatives to court action," with many Democrats and Republican supporting it. Democrats considered the act a necessary means for reducing courtroom backlogs, and Republicans viewed it as a means of tort reform.[141] In October 1988 Congress passed the Judicial Improvements and Access to Justice Act that, among other things, marked the first time that Congress empowered federal district courts to authorize the use of arbitration. Together, the statutes provided for a range of legal matters where judges could compel parties to participate in arbitration; but the laws also stipulated that participants would have the right to dispute the outcome of the proceedings and ask for a new trial. In providing the basic structure for court-annexed ADR programs, the act permitted courts to (1) allow arbitration when the parties consent, and (2) require arbitration when the relief sought consists only of money damages of $100,000 or less. In such cases, so long as the alleged conduct is not in violation of a constitutional right, arbitrators are empowered to conduct arbitration hearings, administer oaths and affirmations, and make awards. In practice, hearings take place before a single arbitrator or panel of three 80 to 180 days after filing, and parties have up to thirty days to request a trial after the arbitrator(s) renders an award.

During the same time period, many federal courts established mediation programs to handle major public policy–oriented and complex cases. These programs were enabled by the Supreme Court, which—over the course of approximately twenty decisions in the past twenty years—has given the FAA an increasingly prominent role in shaping the contours of dispute resolution. The Court began this process with its decision in *Southland Corporation v. Keating* in 1984, where the Court concluded that the FAA preempts state law on the basis that the Congress that drafted the original act would not have wanted state and federal courts to reach different outcomes on the validity of arbitration in like-cases. In the years that followed, the Court continued to apply the FAA to a wide range of disputes—arguably *far* beyond what the FAA was intended to do. This has included considering arbitration sufficient for protecting most statutory rights, including major civil rights provisions, as well as limiting judicial review and allowing businesses to disallow class actions as a matter of contract. These decisions mark the beginnings of a conservative championing of ADR as a remedy for unclogging the burdened judicial system—but with a very different idea of what constituted a "minor" dispute than those who promoted ADR at its origins.

Conservatives "Co-opt" Alternative Dispute Resolution

With the 1990s came more activity from Congress than had characterized previous years. Congress unanimously passed two major statutes that promoted the use of ADR by the federal government: the Administrative Dispute Resolution Act (ADRA) and the Negotiated Rulemaking Act, both enacted in 1990. In addition to having broad bipartisan support in Congress, both laws enjoyed support from the ACUS and the ABA, the latter of which, in fact, had listed ADR as one of its top ten legislative priorities for the 101st Congress.[142] As far as the ACUS was concerned, the impetus for further legislation was clear; as Marshall Breger, chairman of the conference, argued at the Senate Judiciary hearings for ADRA, "The Federal Government has lagged behind the states and the private sector in simplifying the procedures and lowering the cost of participating in litigation and policy making. While Congress has occasionally encouraged agency use of ADR, it has more often mandated slow, multi-layered procedures having great transaction costs."[143]

The ADRA gave federal agencies additional authority to use ADR in most types of administrative disputes. It also directed federal agencies to put ADR requirements in all of their standard contracts for goods and services, and expanded the FMCS's jurisdiction to offer mediation training to federal agencies. Importantly, it also gave the ACUS the principal role for coordinating and promoting ADR in the federal government.[144] The Bush administration was clear in its support of the bill as well, considering it necessary in response to the "judicialization of the administrative process."[145] At the hearings, William Barr, Deputy Attorney General under President George H.W. Bush, made clear that the Department of Justice "has encouraged and continues to support the use of ADR techniques in those cases where ADR can reduce time and expense devoted to litigation."[146]

The second piece of legislation, the Negotiated Rulemaking Act, directed regulatory agencies to use negotiation to facilitate consensus building when developing federal rules, naming the FMCS as the facilitator when needed. In effect, the law signified Congress giving its blessing to regulatory negotiation. This technique brings agency representatives together with various affected interest groups to negotiate the text of a proposed rule, and facilitators help them to reach a consensus. The act itself drew widespread support for its potential to cut down on the number of agency regulations that often become the object of protracted litigation, on the basis that "in certain cases, agencies could make rules more fairly and efficiently through direct negotiations between the various interested parties."[147]

While each act had five-year sunset provisions, both pieces of legislation were renewed—and somewhat expanded—in 1996, alongside an executive order from President Bill Clinton directing federal litigation counsel to suggest and use ADR in "appropriate circumstances."[148] Notably, the ADRA officially added the use of "ombudsmen" to the definition of what constituted ADR practices, removed the authority of agency heads to vacate arbitration awards, and directed agencies to allow non-lawyers to act as representatives in ADR proceedings. The expansions are unsurprising given the amount of institutions employing ADR; by 1994, 52 percent of private companies reported using ADR for discrimination complaints. According to an EEOC survey in 1996, 31 percent of federal agencies used ADR, which increased to 49 percent just two years later.[149]

Congress also passed the Civil Justice Reform Act (CJRA) in 1990, which required all district courts to develop plans for reducing cost and delay. One of the primary methods for addressing these issues was to expand ADR. After the CJRA expired, Congress passed the Alternative Dispute Resolution Act of 1998, which not only requires federal courts to devise and implement ADR programs, but also authorizes them to order mandatory mediation or early neutral evaluations, and to ensure that the preexisting ADR programs conform to the ADRA's requirements. But unlike with earlier ADR legislation, the ABA and the Judicial Conference of the United States initially opposed the 1998 statute because of the possibility that arbitration programs could be made *mandatory* for each district court. Mitchell Dolin of the ABA argued that mandatory arbitration denied citizens their Seventh Amendment rights to a jury trial, stressing that while arbitration "can be a useful, cost-effective way to resolve many legal disputes," it must be a party's own decision.[150] The Honorable D. Brock Hornby argued on behalf of the Judicial Conference that requiring courts to implement this one narrow form of ADR would be "unnecessary and duplicative," given that "80 districts have already got some form of ADR," and given that "what we've discovered as the years have passed, as more forms of ADR have developed, is that arbitration is not the most pre-ferred method. In fact, it's one of the less preferred methods."[151] Instead, the Judicial Conference promoted the use of mediation, summary jury trials, and early neutral evaluations, the first and last of which were agreed upon in the final bill—and both of which were *voluntary*, not compulsory.

The nature of the debate over ADRA in 1998 reflected a reinvigoration of the debate over whether mandatory arbitration that would not be subject to review by courts posed insurmountable problems for the administration of justice. Arguably as part of the tort reform debate, in the 1980s numer-ous states had passed laws imposing ADR procedures as a precondition for trial in cases involving potential medical malpractice suits in particular. The Pennsylvania Health Care Services Malpractice Act, for example, mandated compulsory arbitration before a trial, only to be struck down by the state Supreme Court for infringing on the constitutional right to trial by jury. When Republicans became a majority in the House in 1995, its new speaker, Newt Gingrich, led the charge for furthering ADR, demanding that agen-cies like the EEOC increase its use in place of litigation as a condition of its congressional funding.[152] Democrats were themselves divided on the matter. In 1992 Democratic House member Barney Frank held hearings encourag-ing the use of ADR in lieu of medical malpractice litigation. Stuart Gerson, Assistant Attorney General in the Justice Department under the Bush administration, argued that "ultimately, I suggest we need to migrate toward a system where choice is allowed and ADR not only becomes an option, but becomes an option which, when selected, is binding."[153] Gerson criticized the organized bar and many politicians for emphasizing the expense of litiga-tion, and Frank agreed: "The stress of an adversarial lawsuit would not always be, I think, medically indicated. So that having this done in a more relaxed fashion probably has something to be said for (ADR) as well."[154] At the same time, Frank defended lawyers: "Lawyer bashing obviously is out of hand, and

I think what we have is a systemic problem rather than, obviously, a series of personal failings—let's be very clear: If we're talking about alternative dispute resolution, we are talking about not excluding lawyers, but having lawyers work in different roles."[155]

In this instance, there was bipartisan support for reducing litigation by requiring ADR instead. Frank did, however, "forget" to invite ATLA to the hearings, but "regard[ed] them as important participants in this process" who would be involved in future hearings.[156] The American Medical Association, undoubtedly in favor of avoiding litigation, promoted ADR as a way of getting justice to more people, as "arbitration is the only adjudicatory mechanism available to most litigants with ordinary civil cases."[157] But Robert Raven, chair of the ABA's Standing Committee on Dispute Resolution, cautioned that while he had supported the expansion of ADR, particularly as a way to ease congested courts that were denying access in other arenas because of the backlog of civil trials, it "should be voluntary, shouldn't be brought about by other forces" and certainly should not interfere with "every disputant's constitutional and other legal rights and remedies."[158]

In the mid-1990s, while some Democrats were content that ADR procedures were as adequate as courts in protecting individual civil rights and liberties (evidenced, for example, in the proposed Voluntary Alternative Dispute Resolution Act, which would have permitted federal courts to establish ADR to resolve litigation for controversies involving up to $150,000), other Democrats seriously questioned its adequacy. A contingent of the Democratic Party sought to balance this concern with the growing antilitigation sentiment in its proposed Federal Employee Fairness Act,[159] which sought to ease what the Party considered federal administrative burdens that emphasized conciliation at the expense of civil liberties and rights for employees who claimed that they were the subjects of employment discrimination. Liberals rallied against mandatory arbitration clauses in a range of industries, particularly where they were seen as prohibiting individuals from filing civil rights claims in court.[160] EEOC officials and employee advocacy groups testified that federal administrative review of alleged discrimination was, among other criticisms, "unduly time-consuming, [and] fraught with procedural obstacles."[161] The Washington Council of Lawyers criticized existing conciliatory procedures as "representing the interests of the agencies that employ them" and for frequently attempting to "discourage the filing of complaints."[162] They proposed changes stipulating that ADR "shall always be voluntary on the part of the employee" and that employees must be notified that *both* ADR and civil litigation are available to them, especially where ADR procedures fail to produce an acceptable outcome.[163] The congressional report both recommended improving the existing voluntary ADR processes so that they "are not used as a means of frustrating the protection the legislation seeks to extend to employees," and making sure that "substantive rights" are not "forfeited on procedural grounds" by providing the employee with the opportunity to forgo ADR and move forward in federal court.[164] Proponents of the bill also presented amendments to a number of civil rights laws, ranging from Title VII of the Civil Rights Act of 1964 to the Americans with Disability Act, which would have prevented employers from requiring arbitration of employment discrimination claims.

The Judicial Conference was also opposed to efforts to make ADR mandatory, especially in the realm of arbitration. While the Conference did not say much about it, complaining only that mandatory arbitration "would allow a district court to require all litigants to go through the extra step of arbitration," and "that could actually add to the cost in some cases, and add to the delay, and can also impinge upon the constitutional right to jury trial by that cost and delay," this was the first instance of judges opposing mandatory ADR for the very reasons that many of its proponents initially sought to remedy.[165] The ABA took a similar position; in its written statement in response to the Alternative Dispute Resolution and Settlement Encouragement Act of 1997, the association stated that it "strongly objects to the mandatory arbitration provisions … but it does support those provisions that requires each federal district court to authorize by local rule the use of voluntary arbitration in civil actions."[166] Given that the ABA dispute resolution section has grown to 18,000 members to date, is supported by fifty specialized committees, holds annual and midyear conferences and training sessions, and provides its own publication, it is unlikely that ABA opposition stemmed from a concern about intrusions onto its professional turf. As the largest group of practitioners for ADR, then, its opposition—arguably like that of the Judicial Conference—is centered on the "mandatory" aspect. The 1997 hearings, in fact, prompted the ABA to clarify its official position on dispute resolution, which was revised to say that the group "support[s] legislation and programs that authorize any federal, state, territorial or tribal court … in its discretion, to utilize systems of alternative dispute resolution such as early neutral evaluation, mediation, settlement conference and voluntary, *but not mandatory*, arbitration."[167]

Meanwhile, throughout the 1990s, the Supreme Court continued to apply the FAA to a wider and wider range of disputes, pursuing the ideologically conservative goal of allowing corporations to compel arbitration and to eliminate the potential for judicial review for the individuals and groups suing them. This included wielding the FAA in cases such as *Gilmer v. Interstate/ Johnson Lane Corp.* (1991),[168] in which the Court held that employers could require new employees to arbitrate any potential claims arising under the Age Discrimination in Employment Act as a condition of their employment; *Allied-Bruce Terminix Co. v. Dobson* (1995),[169] holding that the FAA applies to all disputes involving commerce; and *Doctor's Associates v. Casarotto* (1996),[170] holding that the FAA preempts any state law regarding arbitration provisions, in this case a Montana statute requiring that an arbitration clause be indicated on the first page of a contract, in prominent font. The Court continued this trend into the 2000s, most prominently with *Green Tree Financial Corporation-Alabama v. Randolph* (2000),[171] which treats agreements between individual citizens and large entities (such as those involved in employment contracts, school enrollment, and home finance loan agreements) as if they were fully bargained private contracts, and *Circuit City Stores, Inc. v. Adams* (2001),[172] which applies the FAA to disputes between employers and employees and addresses the scope of exclusions from the FAA of certain categories of employment contracts. More recently, the Court held in *Preston v. Ferrer* (2008)[173] that the FAA also overrules state laws declaring that certain types of disputes must be resolved by a state administrative agency (going further in stipulating that the FAA "supersedes state laws lodging primary jurisdiction in another forum, whether judicial or administrative"), and in *Hall Street Associates LLC v. Mattel, Inc.* the Court held that, even if parties agree in the arbitration agreement to allow for expanded judicial review of the arbitration award, the grounds for review specified in the FAA cannot be expanded upon.[174] The Court reiterated consistently in these cases that the language of the FAA promotes a public policy stance strongly in favor of arbitration, thus requiring a narrower reading of statutes that arguably suggest exceptions.

Conservatives in Congress increasingly sought to insert ADR techniques in a variety of policy areas as well. Perhaps the most heavily trafficked policy area for these proposals has continued to be health care reform and the treatment of medical malpractice claims. For example, as part of the effort to remedy the perceived onslaught of medical malpractice claims and to "weed out frivolous lawsuits"—a fixation for conservatives in the debate over how best to lower health care costs—Senator Lindsey Graham proposed the Fair Resolution of Medical Liability Disputes Act of 2009,[175] which stipulates that a covered health care malpractice action may not be brought in any state or federal court unless it is initially resolved in an ADR system. If the parties then contest the arbitrator's decision, they have a ninety-day window in which they may file an action in court for review. The bill also sets forth basic requirements for state ADR systems, including a requirement that they transmit to the state agency responsible for monitoring or disciplining health care providers any findings that a provider committed malpractice.[176] Even while Graham maintained "There is no better way to resolve a dispute than to have a jury do it," the bill's supporters argued that ADR mechanisms would be better suited to these particular cases, under these particular conditions, at least as a first step in the legal process.[177]

Conservatives have introduced legislation promoting the use of ADR in a variety of other areas as well. In 2000 Republican Representative Henry J. Hyde introduced legislation in which he proposed establishing a nonprofit organization, the "Asbestos Resolution Corporation," charged with the duty of adopting "rules, policies, and procedures for the fair and efficient conduct of medical review and alternative dispute resolution."[178] Because asbestos personal injury litigation is "unfair and inefficient, and imposes a crushing burden on litigants and taxpayers alike," he argued, redirecting such claims to the realm of ADR was arguably an obvious (though unrealized) potential remedy for the burden on the judicial system more broadly. Conservatives in Congress have also encouraged the use of ADR in areas like workplace disputes (proposing an ADR pilot program to assist the federal government in resolving "serious workplace disputes"),[179] in legislation "authorizing and encouraging" the president to establish and use ADR procedures regarding the award or denial of assistance to states, local governments, and private actors for damages suffered from hurricanes Katrina and Rita, as well as with regard to health care claims dealing with pregnancy trauma in particular.[180] While most of these bills die or remain in the committee stage, they reflect a concerted effort by Republicans to encourage "speedy resolution of claims" that notably takes place *outside* the traditional legal system.

Democrats have been active promoting their own proposals, particularly to end mandatory arbitration agreements in different industries. Legislators have frequently responded to Supreme Court decisions like *Circuit City* with statutory proposals designed to reinvigorate the rights of employees and consumers to a day in court. But these efforts have been piecemeal, frequently focusing on eliminating mandatory arbitration in areas ranging from automobile dealers to homebuilders to poultry and livestock producers to defense contractors to the credit card industry.[181] They have also consistently, with minor exceptions, failed to push these proposals beyond an initial hearing. Notably, however, the 2010 Dodd-Frank Wall Street Reform and Consumer Protection Act instructed the Consumer Financial Bureau to study the use of predispute arbitration provisions in consumer financial contracts. The bureau's report (cited in the introduction of this chapter) will at minimum keep the issue on Congress' radar as various bills looking to reform arbitration continue to spring up. For now, however, the debate continues to center on the reach of the FAA, with the Supreme Court largely at the helm.

In a series of cases since 2010, the Court has continued the trend of expansively interpreting the FAA so as to allow corporations to compel arbitration, even when arbitration clauses involve individuals contracting out of rights. For example, in *Rent-A-Center West, Inc. v. Jackson*,[182] the Court held that, under the FAA, where an agreement between employer and employee to arbitrate includes a provision that an arbitrator will determine the enforceability of the agreement, if a party challenges the enforceability of that specific provision, the district court considers the challenge. However, if a party challenges the enforceability of the agreement as a whole, final authority rests with the arbitrator.

The case arose from a Rent-A-Center employee who filed suit against the company alleging racial discrimination and retaliation. In response, Rent-A-Center moved to dismiss the proceedings and compel arbitration. Siding with the employer, the Court determined that Jackson (the employee) had, in fact, challenged the validity—and therefore enforceability—of the contract as a whole, thereby precluding judicial review and making the arbitrator in the dispute the last stop. The dissenters in the case, and Justice John Paul Stevens in particular, thought this reasoning was particularly suspicious, given that the majority adopted a position not proposed by either party when arguing the case. Nonetheless, the case clearly reflects the current Court's willingness to preclude judicial review of arbitration clauses specifically.

Since 2011 the Court has expanded its support for binding arbitration in a variety of ways. First, the Court addressed the issue of whether or not the FAA prevents states from conditioning the enforcement of an arbitration agreement on the availability of classwide arbitration procedures. The case, *AT&T Mobility LLC v. Concepcion*,[183] involved customers who brought a class action lawsuit against AT&T in California federal district court. The group of customers alleged that the contract they agreed to when signing up for AT&T mobile service contained a fraudulent provision (namely that the company's offer of a free phone to anyone who signed up for service was fraudulent to the extent the company charged the new subscriber sales tax on the retail value of each free phone). AT&T moved to compel arbitration based on the arbitration clause within its contract of service, and the district court denied its motion.

On appeal, the Ninth Circuit held that the arbitration clause—which required that consumers waive their class action rights—was unconscionable on the basis of a California common law rule that allowed consumers to avoid contracts in which they waived their class action rights. According to this rule, they reasoned, the arbitration clause was unenforceable under California state law, and the intent to preempt state laws regarding class action rights is neither explicitly stated nor implied in the congressional record regarding the FAA. The Supreme Court, however, found differently. In reversing the lower court decision, a 5-4 majority opinion (authored by Justice Antonin Scalia) held that the FAA *does*, in fact, preempt "state-law rules that stand as an obstacle to the accomplishment of the FAA's objectives." In response, the dissenters argued what has by now become a familiar line; that there is nothing in the legislative history of the FAA or in the act itself that indicates the intention to compel arbitration to such an extent.

The debate continues. Shortly after deciding the AT&T case, the Court agreed to hear a new arbitration dispute, this time seeking to reconcile the FAA with a federal law that is arguably incompatible by the Court's current standards. In 1996 Congress passed the Credit Repair Organizations Act (CROA),[184] which was put into place to protect consumers from unscrupulous practices by organizations that claim to repair credit. In addition to making consumers who use credit repair services aware of their rights and listing what these organizations cannot do, the act explicitly allows consumers to sue offending organizations for actual damages, punitive damages, and attorney's fees. The act also makes clear that credit repair organizations cannot ask consumers to sign any kind of form that waives their rights—including the right to sue—under the act.

Consumers accordingly sued CompuCredit Corporation in federal court, arguing that while they were promised $300 in available credit in their first year, the company also charged them $257 in fees. The corporation countered that the dispute must be handled through arbitration, as per an agreement that the customers signed in order to receive the card. As the CROA stipulates clearly and succinctly, "you have the right to sue a credit repair organization that violates the Credit Repair Organization Act," the Ninth Circuit ruled that the language was intended to bar arbitration of claims under the law, concluding "Congress meant what it said in using the term 'sue,' and that it did not mean 'arbitrate.' "[185] The Supreme Court reversed, citing its decision in FAA and *Concepcion*. Justice Scalia wrote the opinion for the 8-1 Court (with Justice Ginsburg dissenting), which held that any congressional exclusion of particular classes of contracts from arbitration must be clear. Statutory references to a "right to sue" and to "an action" in a statute are not sufficiently explicit.

In the aftermath of the Court's most recent decision in *American Express v. Italian Colors Restaurant* (in which the majority upheld an arbitration clause despite the fact that claimants would not be able to recover enough to afford the complex, expensive antitrust arbitration claim),[186] Andrew Pincus, the lawyer who defended both American Express and AT&T two years prior, argued that the Supreme Court "eliminated the last obstacle to adoption of fair, efficient arbitration systems that increase access to justice for consumers while reducing transaction costs for everyone."[187] Justice Elena Kagan's sharply worded dissent paints an even more dire picture for individual seeking redress against corporations: as she put it, the Court's decision means that "the monopolist gets to use its monopoly power to insist on a contract effectively depriving its victims of all legal recourse," and that the decision would encourage companies to "extract backdoor waivers of statutory rights" instead of adopting efficient arbitration procedures, as was intended by the FAA.[188] As such, the class action waiver has become "a favorite tool of corporate council" in seeking to insulate their clients from lawsuits.[189]

Conclusions

What is behind the support that conservatives have for these developments? Why is the Court so aggressively imposing the FAA's provisions onto such a wide array of statutes, arguably in ways that far exceed the intentions for the legislation? And why are conservatives in Congress increasingly promoting ADR procedures in legislation traversing a variety of policies? On the one hand, the Court seems to be normalizing ADR. Mediation and arbitration have become incorporated into courts at almost every level as a way to respond to increased case loads and budget cuts, and to promote less adversarial forms of conflict resolution.[190]

On the other hand, this series of decisions reaches well beyond merely an effort to bring arbitration onto even footing with litigation, raising skepticism regarding the Court's intentions, a skepticism that has certainly not escaped the attention of the Court's more liberal members. In *Circuit City*, Justice Stevens succinctly characterized the concerns of the Court's shrinking core of liberal justices, which have each voiced similar perspectives in their various dissents in this line of cases. He argued that the Court's recent decisions "have pushed the pendulum far beyond a neutral attitude and endorsed a policy that strongly favors private arbitration" over litigation. Such a strategy is functionally hostile to litigation, premised on the belief that there is nothing superior or special about litigation as a process for resolving disputes. While entirely consistent with the Rehnquist and Roberts Courts' antilitigation sentiment, the consequences for the quality of rights protections for certain groups make it a more complicated issue than the majority of the Court seems to let on.[191]

Regardless, the ways in which ADR procedures have been handled by largely conservative courts in recent years (often in stark contrast to the ways in which more liberal district and appeals courts handle the same claims) represents what is, on the one hand, a real turning of the tides for ADR. While the statutory and bureaucratic bases for the expansion of ADR were mostly achieved within the policy-specific arena of labor and industrial strife in the early twentieth century, the later monetary support, development of techniques, training, personnel supply were largely supported from private and frequently liberal sources. In the 1960s and 70s, the Ford Foundation funded and created the institutional infrastructure for most ADR activity (alongside other private donors), and the American Bar Association (along with law and graduate schools) appropriated many of these roles by the 1990s. To say that ADR was founded and driven by purely liberal and progressive goals is overly simplistic; groups and organizations such as the AAA supported ADR for economic and efficiency reasons while the Judicial Conference often promoted it out of a concern for better institutional maintenance of an increasingly overburdened judicial system. However, liberal actors coming specifically from the Democratic Party who were concerned for the rights protections of the poor, the stigmatized, and other disadvantaged groups played a pivotal and foundational role.

The success that conservatives, primarily on the Supreme Court (and as attempted in Congress) have had in co-opting these established ADR procedures track generally with efforts by conservatives to scale back access to the courts and judicial authority by tinkering with adjudicative procedures. The influence of conservatives in Congress and a conservative Supreme Court has meant that statutes originally intended to promote access to justice (e.g., the Rules Enabling Act, the Administrative Procedure Act, and certainly the FAA) have been redirected and reinterpreted for the pursuit of goals contrary to the original impetus for such legislation. This has allowed conservatives to support and convert institutional developments in areas of law like ADR as devices for defending corporate and wealthy interests by keeping disputes away from the costs and dangers of courtroom litigation.

Importantly, however, conservatives have been able to pursue this tactic for constricting access to the courts without needing to create *or* scale anything back; and because of this, the use of ADR is not often identified as a potent mechanism for retrenchment. In many ways, this is because conservative activists have simply built upon both an institutional and rhetorical apparatus constructed over time by liberals, merely extending the logic that ADR is suitable for minor disputes in a way that extends "minor" to just about anything that confronts corporate capital. It also largely escapes our analysis when seeking to identify the expanse of the antilitigation movement because the partisan component is complex. While conservatives have found ADR to be an especially amenable terrain to co-opt for the purpose of keeping certain litigants and cases out of court, a significant swath of Democrats continues to promote ADR as well. As such, even the recent conservative activity is hardly a simply partisan story.

Changing the Rules: The Battle to Control Civil Procedure

Introduction

In the days after the 9/11 attacks in New York and Washington, D.C., the federal government detained thousands of Muslim men in the United States. Javaid Iqbal, a Pakistani Muslim man living and working on Long Island, was arrested by the federal government on immigration charges and held in maximum security conditions, where he claimed that he was subject to daily body cavity searches, beatings, and horrible conditions because of his religion and national origin.[1] After being deported, he sued Attorney General John Ashcroft and F.B.I. Director Robert Meuller III, whom he believed authorized the abuse that he suffered while detained. In the 2009 term, however, the Supreme Court threw out his case.

For a case so clearly distressing in its details, the Court's decision in *Ashcroft v. Iqbal*[2] received relatively little media attention, and the coverage it did receive focused, unsurprisingly, on the allegations of alarming religious and racial discrimination at the hands of the U.S. government. As *New York Times* legal analyst Adam Liptak described, "On its face, the Iqbal decision concerned the aftermath of the Sept. 11 attacks," and most early media coverage of the case started and ended with that. Yet within two months, judges on the nation's lower courts had cited the case more than 500 times; and as Liptak also noted, it quickly became clear that the Court's findings were somehow relevant to a wide range of seemingly different cases, including, for example, both the case against former Bush administration lawyer John C. Yoo and that of the Duke lacrosse players accused of rape in 2006. Clearly, then, it seemed that something broader and more cross-cutting was at issue in the decision, and that "what attention it got was for the wrong reason."³

For the bulk of the past seventy-five years, initiating a lawsuit was easy. To start a case, a plaintiff needed only to state their grievance; "a short and plain statement of the claim" was all that was required to put a civil action into motion. And half a century before *Iqbal*, the Court weighed in on the importance of keeping it that simple. In the case, which involved an African American railroad employee who had received unequal protection from the union, a unanimous Court recognized that many injured plaintiffs might lack the resources necessary to prove their claim without pretrial discovery. Whether in discrimination or consumer protection cases (among others), an individual may well have been injured, yet lack enough evidence to effectively prove discrimination or negligence from the outset—at least until the initiation of a lawsuit would force a defendant to turn over any information relevant to the case. In terms of information necessary to start a legal proceeding, then, in 1957 the Court established that a plaintiff's allegations were to be considered true "unless it appears beyond doubt that the plaintiff can prove no set of facts in support of his claim which would entitle him to relief," giving rise to the familiar "notice pleading" system that characterized civil litigation in the second half of the twentieth century.⁴

Writing for the majority in 2009, however, Justice Anthony Kennedy took a different stance. While he agreed that pleading rules should be generous, he also argued that they do not "unlock the doors of discovery for a plaintiff armed with nothing more than conclusions." Unlike the earlier approach, where the facts as stated in a claim were to be construed as most favorable to the plaintiff, the Roberts Court raised the bar, requiring that judges determine at the outset "whether a complaint states a plausible claim for relief." This requires that a reviewing court "draw on its judicial experience and common sense" when making such a determination, unleashing a new degree of judicial discretion that was well on display in *Iqbal*, in which the Court determined that the plaintiff's claims were "bare assertions" that amounted to "nothing more than a 'formulaic recitation of the elements' of a constitutional discrimination claim" and thus should be considered "conclusory and not entitled to be assumed true."⁵ Where notice pleading could nearly be taken for granted, the new approach would be highly subjective.

This subjectivity was of deep concern to the liberals both on the Court and in Congress. In dissent, Justice David Souter stressed the need to accept accusations as true "no matter how skeptical the court may be," and Justice Stephen Breyer—who accepted the majority's premise that it is "important to prevent unwarranted litigation from interfering with the proper execution of the work of the government"—stressed that the law provides other mechanisms for preventing this unwarranted interference. Concerned Democrats on the House Judiciary Committee held hearings that fall on what they perceived as "Access to Justice Denied" and a proposed statute to overturn *Iqbal*. Jerrold Nadler, a representative from New York, argued that "often evidence of wrongdoing is in the hands of the defendants, of the wrongdoers, and the facts necessary to prove a valid claim can only be ascertained through discovery," an opportunity that became harder to come by under the Court's new standard. As such, he continued, "The *Iqbal* decision will effectively slam shut the courthouse door on legitimate plaintiffs based on the judge's take on the plausibility of a claim rather than on the actual evidence, which has not been put into court yet, or even discovered yet." While conservatives countered that litigation exacts "heavy costs" on the government that the Roberts Court rightly sought to reduce, to Nadler and other Democrats, the decision was part and parcel of "this conservative Court's apparent agenda to deny access to courts to people victimized by corporate or government misconduct."[6]

In this chapter, I examine the ways in which changing the rules that govern the process of adjudication can profoundly affect access to courts. The right to one's day in court is deeply embedded and celebrated in American legal culture, and a procedural system that enables this right is tied to our due process clause guarantees. As the near immediate and wide-ranging effects of the *Iqbal* decision made clear, rules that structure the legal process can be hugely effectual mechanisms for judicial retrenchment, and this case is far from the only example. At issue in *Iqbal*—the rule governing pleading that was up for consideration by the Court—was Rule 8(a)(2) of the Federal Rules of Civil Procedure, which govern the process of courtroom litigation. When an individual has suffered an injury as defined by substantive law, these rules then determine, procedurally, whether or not one has a valid legal claim. The rules also dictate the form that adjudication must take, who the relevant parties are to the claim, what information and evidence are applicable and available to the parties, as well as what opportunities exist for appeals, delays, and motions to end or move the claim from its initial courtroom. These rules, now codified under Title 11 of the United States Code, were first authorized by the Rules Enabling Act of 1934, which empowered the Supreme Court to promulgate rules of procedure for the federal courts that have the force and effect of law. The impetus for the initial rules was largely to make pleading—and therefore getting one's day in court—easier, and Rule 8(a)(2) was promulgated in 1938 with that goal in mind.

But as with the rules that govern any institution, such as the legislative process or the electoral arena, the rules that govern courtroom procedure have great consequence for substantive outcomes. Moving from the requirement that a plaintiff make "a short and plain statement of the claim" to requiring that a court assume a skeptical position when confronted with an alleged wrongdoing under the law clearly introduces a measure of discretion that might substantively affect, to any one judge's mind, what types of cases and claims warrant the full treatment of the legal process—and which do not. The effect of rule changes can be even more far-reaching; the rules that provide for mass litigation such as the class action, for example, make matters of civil procedure consequential not just for individual plaintiffs and defendants, but often for national public policy as well.[7] Changes to rules can lead to increases or decreases in litigation rates, as well as influence the role that litigation plays in enforcing public policy. Additionally, like any institution, the rules create a set of incentives for political behavior. As we will see, numerous actors, variously impacted by the rules, are keenly aware of the relevance of rulemaking and make concerted efforts to influence the process and outcomes of rule reform.[8] This is, in part, due to the complexity of the rulemaking process, which on the ground actually empowers not only the Supreme Court, but also Congress, as well as a variety of rulemaking committees housed in the judicial branch, to assert control over the civil rules.

Moreover, in making it easier for potential litigants to seek out legal remedies from the courts, these rules were also fundamental to the expansion and entrenchment of judicial authority and access to courts during the New Deal and rights revolution eras. As might be expected, then, would-be retrenchers have made reform of the rules a priority for decreasing judicial power and redress to courts, and multiple institutions and actors have fought to obtain more authority over the rulemaking process. Scholars have characterized the success of this strategy for scaling back access to courts as primarily the product of recent Supreme Court decision making[9]; but a historical institutional assessment of the campaign to retrench access through rule changes illuminates the complexity of the retrenchment process, which has gone through multiple stages involving very different interests, at different times including judicial administrators, legislators, judges, lawyers, and an assortment of interest groups. It began in the 1970s as a Democratic Party–led effort for legislators and litigators to gain control of the rulemaking process. As these actors continued to fight for further reforms in the 1980s, they were also joined by legal reformers internal to the rulemaking process who wanted—for less clearly partisan reasons—to find ways to address what they deemed a litigation crisis that was overwhelming court capacity. Rule reform only became a clearly partisan project after 1994, as Republican legislators and business lobbyists interested primarily in class action reform came to dominate the scene, and as an increasingly conservative, antilitigation Supreme Court significantly enabled their efforts.

Civil Procedure in the Early American State

The modern version of the federal civil rules was initially created during the New Deal era. The impetus for civil rules reform emerged in response to the "hyper-technicality" and lack of uniformity in the existing rule structure and materialized into a procedural reform movement in the states.[10] Scholars have attributed rule reform to various sources, including organizations of lawyers, such as the American Bar Association (ABA) and law professors who sought to increase the role of litigation in American society; conservatives who wanted to give more discretion to judges; and Progressive reformers who were intent on making the legal process more accessible and fair for the everyday citizen.[11] The procedural reform bills that evolved in the early twentieth century "prompted debate about matters as diverse as the convenience of lawyers, the efficiency of judicial administration, and the constitutional power of Congress to delegate rulemaking authority to the Supreme Court."[12]

Congress first granted rulemaking authority to the courts "to make and establish all necessary rules for the orderly conducting business in said courts" in the Judiciary Act of 1789.[13] In 1842 Congress specified that the Supreme Court was to promulgate rules for cases of common law, equity, and admiralty, and "generally to regulate the whole practice of said courts, so as to prevent delays, and to promote brevity ... and to abolish all unnecessary costs and expenses in any suit therein."[14] Although the Supreme Court adopted rules for equity and admiralty, it did not adopt general rules for cases at common law, which meant that federal district and circuit courts followed the procedural rules of the states in which they were located. Civil procedure in the early federal courts, then, was considered incoherent at its worst, and most charitably might have been described as following traditional common law procedure, but with much local variety. These local differences were further complicated by the development of rules for different types of civil cases, including "actions at law" versus courts of equity.

Various statutes passed by Congress, such as the Permanent Process Acts of 1789 and 1792, promoted the value of conformity in the "forms and modes of proceeding," meaning that judges should conform to the legal rules of the state from which the case at hand emanated. The Process Acts only confused matters further, however, in that they were written in such a way that it forced federal courts sitting in a given state to apply the common law rules of pleading and procedure that were in effect in the state not at present, but at the time that it joined the union—even if the state had modified its civil procedure rules since.[15] Further, both statutes left matters of procedure subject to "alteration by the respective courts or by rules which the Supreme Court of the United States might think proper to prescribe,"[16] and when states invoked conformity principles to defend their own procedural codes, federal courts consistently rejected them as being incompatible with broader features of justice. In 1825, for example, Chief Justice John Marshall rejected an appeal for conformity to a Kentucky law that gave relief to delinquent debtors because, he argued, Congress had empowered federal courts to regulate their own rules of practice, and such a system was designed "not for a consolidated people, but for distinct societies, already possessing distinct systems, and accustomed to laws, which, though originating in the same great principles, had been variously modified."[17]

By the mid-nineteenth century, matters only worsened as state civil procedures began to diverge from each other even more dramatically. By the 1840s, David Dudley Field—who would become a prominent legal reformist and author of the "Field Code"—launched a movement away from the practice of common law pleading. Common law pleading was a system inherited from English law, in the days where a plaintiff could only pursue a lawsuit by obtaining a writ from the king or king's chancellor. Over time these writs took on fixed forms, and a plaintiff could only pursue a legal claim if the language of his complaint fit one of the established forms of action. Forms of action became increasingly more rigid, and they took on the same overly technical quality under common law in the United States, leading many cases to be dismissed on procedural grounds. Despite its increasingly poor fit with the developing legal system, common law pleading continued to be used uncritically, more often than not simply because it was the way it had always been done. Those critical of common law pleading argued that it was flawed at its core, given that it did not take stock of whether or not those procedures still made sense in a changing legal climate. In an attempt to bring procedure into line with a changing judicial system, Field introduced the idea of "code pleading," in which a plaintiff would only need to provide a statement of fact that, if true, would justify legal relief. State legislatures could choose to adopt this uniform code of procedure, known as the Field Code (first adopted in 1948 by New York, his state), which functionally promoted a more standardized system of code pleading by merging courts of law and equity. The Field Code was adopted by dozens of states, though it too was ill-received by the Supreme Court, who deprecated its adoption by lower federal courts.[18]

Due to the continued complexity and confusion, Congress (influenced by lawyers who were very frustrated with having to follow obsolete procedures in their states every time they litigated in federal court) was more aggressive in promoting a unified set of court procedures. In 1872 they passed the Conformity Act, which required that "like cases" be treated by federal judges "as near as may be" with respect to the court practice and procedure of the state where the trial was being held. The goal was to make it easier for practicing lawyers by relieving them from having to learn differing systems of procedure, particularly when a case was removed from their state to a federal court. But here too, the act was criticized as "indiscriminate and unstable" in character and ultimately a "complete failure" because courts were given wide discretion that they used repeatedly to avoid conformity when it was thought to "defeat the ends of justice."[19] In the years that followed, Field led the ABA in pursuit of another uniform code of procedure that, importantly, would *not* place full power and control over the rules in the hands of state legislatures but rather transfer rulemaking power to the Supreme Court instead.[20]

Those ABA members who supported uniformity considered it to go hand-in-hand with judicial independence, or the idea that the courts can and should act separately from the political branches of government. One of the leading proponents, Thomas Shelton, repeatedly argued that judicial independence was under siege by "open mob violence and secret law enforcing societies," primarily in the form of arbitration boards that arguably allowed business to shape procedure in the states. As he put it, "No thoughtful man will deny that a weakening of the courts means a weakening of the government; and a loss of faith in the courts means the destruction of the government. When men desert the courts, nothing is left but force in the protection of property rights and civil liberty."[21] Shelton argued that "in its final analysis, the real trouble with judicial procedure is due to the fact that co-ordination has been absolutely destroyed by exclusive legislative control," and congressional reform that enabled procedural uniformity would "set the Supreme Court free" to govern its institution's own rules.[22] In his annual message in 1909, President William Howard Taft himself advised Congress of the need for rule reform for the federal and state courts, taking the position that "a change in judicial procedure, with a view to reducing its expense to private litigants in civil cases, and facilitate the dispatch of business and final decision in both civil and criminal cases, constitutes the greatest need in our American institutions."[23] Soon thereafter, President Woodrow Wilson took a similar position: "I do know that the United States in its judicial procedure is many decades behind every other civilized government in the world; and I say that it is an immediate and imperative call upon us to rectify that, because the speediness of justice, the inexpensiveness of justice, the ready access of justice, is the greater part of justice itself."[24] The existing Field Code itself, however, left the idea of procedural uniformity as something to be encouraged, but not required.

The ABA pressed the cause of civil procedure reform frequently in the first decades of the twentieth century, advocating for simple and uniform rules that would also give judges more discretion and lawyers more latitude in terms of how they framed their cases. In its pursuit, the ABA joined forces with Republicans in Congress who at the time sought to expand the authority of the federal judiciary, proposing in 1910 the first version of what would eventually become the Rules Enabling Act in 1934. The ABA claimed that the bill "represents and was drawn and approved by three professional elements—the bench, the practicing lawyer, and the university" and that it was designed to prevent appellate courts from rendering decisions on the basis of technical defects in procedure.[25] These early legislative proposals eventually took form in the Clayton Bill of 1912 and the Sutherland Bill of 1917, the latter of which would become the core substance of the subsequent Rules Enabling Act. As the debate over procedural reform progressed in the 1920s, the proposed bills began to include stipulations that, when promulgating rules, the Supreme Court would consult with a committee of judges and lawyers.[26] In addition, Taft recommended that the Court have the power to make rules at law as it had in equity, blending them into a code that would "make the procedure the same in all and as simple as possible."[27] These suggestions merged to shape the 1924 bill, cowritten by Taft and Senator Albert B. Cummins of Iowa, which carefully distinguished between matters of procedure and substantive law.[28] Although hearings on the act spanned two decades of debate, and the bill was hotly contested (meeting a series of defeats in the Senate Judiciary Committee), the universe of political actors involved was strikingly small, particularly—as we will see—when compared to the congressional debates over rules in the 1970s. The ABA was typically the only organization to testify in favor of the rules, with perhaps an occasional judge also speaking in favor of reform. Furthermore, these speakers addressed committees composed overwhelmingly, if not entirely, of lawyers and ABA members, including ABA notables such as Minnesota Senator

Frank Kellogg, a former president of the association. Even the chief opponent of the legislation, Democratic Senator Thomas Walsh, was a leading prosecutor and member of the Montana state bar.

The early opposition to rule reform frequently focused—as did Walsh's testimony—on the belief that most lawyers only worked in state courts, rarely engaged with federal law, and thus would find the uniformity of rules too stifling and unnecessary complicating to their practice. Although in some of his writings Shelton, then chair of the ABA's Committee on Uniform Judicial Procedure, would frequently defend rule reform as something that "people of this country in no uncertain manner demand,"[29] there is little indication from the popular press that anyone outside of the legal community was paying much attention to these issues, and brief mentions of the matter typically referred to it as of interest only to lawyers, judges, and law professors.[30] Shelton himself recognized the insular realm in which this debate was occurring, noting not only that the ABA was the sole organization testifying, but also referencing the fact that everyone in the room were lawyers and members of the bar.

Speaking on behalf of the ABA, in his proposal to Congress Shelton started by emphasizing that civil procedure reform would provide Congress with "absolute control over all fundamental matters, questions of jurisdiction and of permanent procedure and evidence and such other matters of a permanent nature as those with which you having been dealing to-day." But Shelton was also a strong believer in strengthening the judiciary and the ability of judges to have autonomy in developing procedural rules.[31] As he put it, "No government has ever stood that did not have its judiciary department absolutely separate and distinct from its legislative and its executive; and the very moment that this government seriously mingles its judiciary department with either of the other two, it is going to fall." He stressed that legislative bodies, both state and federal, held too much control over the rules process, binding "the hands of judges with bands of iron, and the court cannot decide upon the simplest thing of procedure except through and by these laws of Congress. It is the chiefest part of every trial and ought to be a mere incident."[32] Before a congressional committee in 1922, he stated more emphatically that the proposed bill would "vest in the Supreme Court the exclusive power to prepare for the trial courts all the necessary rules and regulations and gradually perfect them."[33] This, to Shelton and the ABA more broadly, would be an ideal state of affairs.

For a period of almost twenty years, however, Democrats on the Senate Judiciary Committee, led by Walsh, managed to derail the potential legislation.[34] The primary matter of contention was this question of who should be empowered to promulgate procedural rules. Both the ABA and most Republicans on the committee believed strongly that the Supreme Court, arguably immune from the pressures of electoral politics, was best suited for the task, where Democrats were wary of the rules stemming from so conservative and insulated a governing institution.[35] Walsh, a Democrat, was particularly worried that judges and lawyers controlling the rulemaking process would primarily serve ABA profiteers who aimed to nationalize their business. Further, he argued that most lawyers only practiced in their home state ("I am for the one hundred who stay at home as against the one who goes abroad") and in effect would only be confused and overwhelmed by federal conformity. As one of the leading Democratic Party progressives, and as FDR's initial pick for Attorney General,[36] he was also intensely skeptical that judicial control of rules might enable the courts to make substantive policy determinations. And while supporters vigorously denied and dismissed these fears, Walsh's concerns, in fact, foreshadowed a debate that would unfold over the relationship between procedure and substance decades later.[37]

Entrenching the Federal Rules, 1934–1973

By the 1930s, however, increased academic input (most prominently from Charles Clark, who became the dean of Yale Law School in 1929) and the appointment of Homer Cummings to Attorney General (who served to "fill the leadership vacuum in the reform movement" by helping to revive the ABA's campaign),[38] in combination with a growing concern for the efficiency of the judiciary, tipped the scale in the direction of the ABA/Republican proposal. In 1934 Congress finally succeeded in passing the Rules Enabling Act, which gave the Supreme Court centralized power to "prescribe general rules of practice and procedure" for the federal courts. Despite the controversy surrounding the proposed statutory directives of prior decades, Congress passed the law without giving it much attention; its passage was largely the result of the Roosevelt administration's support of the bill. On paper, the act gave the Supreme Court centralized control over a process that had formerly been diverse and decentralized, dominated by individual state and federal courts. In effect, the act also allowed the legal profession to dominate the initial promulgation and amendment of rules.[39] The resulting rules were crafted through a series of drafts by a Supreme Court Advisory Committee (composed of lawyers and law professors appointed by the Chief Justice), followed by extensive meetings and conversations with bar associations across the country.[40] The

Advisory Committee produced a preliminary draft of the proposed rules in 1936, which was followed by an intensive and unprecedented back and forth over the feedback that poured forth from judges and lawyers from every federal circuit and from state and local bar associations all over the country over the course of the following year.[41] After extensive revision, the rules were eventually adopted without congressional action in 1938.

The 1938 Federal Rules of Civil Procedure relaxed pleading rules, required information exchange, and ultimately made litigation easier. They engendered a rulemaking system of judicial committee development, Supreme Court approval, and transmission to Congress. The current rulemaking structure was put in place in 1957 and 1958, when the Supreme Court empowered the Judicial Conference of the United States—the primary policy-setting body for the courts—to oversee rulemaking. The Judicial Conference, composed of various federal judges and presided over by the Chief Justice of the Supreme Court, in turn created a two-tiered committee structure for rulemaking, including a Standing Committee on the Rules of Practice and Procedure and an Advisory Committee on Civil Rules. The latter, now largely responsible for regular review of the rules, is composed mostly of judges, as well as some practicing lawyers, law professors, and a representative from the Department of Justice. The dominance of judges on the rules committees marked a move away (largely facilitated by Chief Justice Earl Warren) from committees populated more evenly with members of the legal community. Proposed rule amendments were and are subject to review and revision by the Standing Committee, Judicial Conference, and Supreme Court before being sent to Congress for review.[42]

Although actors in the judicial branch dominate the rulemaking process, Congress has always retained the formal authority to play a meaningful role. However, the meaning and practical functioning of this shared responsibility have shifted greatly over time. The Rules Enabling Act provided that rules created by the Judicial Conference and approved by the Supreme Court would become law *unless* Congress acted to veto them within sixty days. In the 1950s, the Enabling Act was amended to change the procedure for reporting proposed rule changes to Congress, extending the time frame allotted for Congress' consideration to ninety days, and later (in the late 1980s) to seven months.[43] But until 1973, Congress never vetoed a rule change, much less even discussed the proposed rules that the Supreme Court gave them for review. In this sense, the initial insulation and power of judicial rulemaking resulted from the widespread sense among legislators that the rules committees—not Congress—had the proper expertise to make such decisions. As such, the rules of the 1930s were "founded upon judicial discretion."[44] Just a few years after the initial set of rules was promulgated, rulemakers were so accustomed to their control of the process that Justice Felix Frankfurter felt the need to remind his colleagues on the Court that the rules themselves were not the equivalent of laws and should not be equated with other acts of Congress. Writing in response to a Court-led proposal to radically alter Rule 35, he dissented on the grounds that such a proposal should require congressional action because having "due regard to the mechanics of legislation and the practical conditions surrounding the business of Congress when the Rules were submitted, to draw any inference from non-action by Congress is to appeal to unreality."[45] As legal scholars have argued of the early experience under the Rules Enabling Act, "Review of the work of the original Advisory Committee establishes that it proceeded without a coherent or consistent view of the limitations imposed by the act's procedure/substance dichotomy and that the Committee therefore resolved perceived problems of power on an *ad hoc* basis."[46]

The fact that legislators did not think the rules were political was integral to judicial dominance of the rulemaking process. The Rules Enabling Act itself granted the Supreme Court the power to promulgate rules of procedure for civil actions *only* so long as these procedural rules did not "abridge, enlarge, nor modify the substantive rights of any litigant." Rulemaking was considered "purely procedural," not substantive; that is, rules were considered "normatively distinct from and subordinate to substantive law." The distinction between procedure and substance was an important limiting component in Congress' delegation of rulemaking authority. "From these premises, it followed that a democratic process was not necessary to the legitimacy of procedure, for procedure involved no substantive value choices."[47] Involving legislators (potentially driven by electoral incentives) in the process was considered a threat to preserving procedural justice. Perhaps the strongest evidence that members of Congress at the time truly believed in this distinction was that they were willing to give this level of discretion and authority to the judiciary in the 1930s at all, when so much of the New Deal was based on distrust of the courts and attempts to limit their powers. But instead, for over three decades, the courts (and the lawyers and scholars who advised them) were viewed as "experts" who would best structure rules to protect the systemic integrity of the procedural system as a whole.

But rules are highly mutable, and actors often consider institutional rules a "tool kit" or vehicle for achieving alternative political goals or outcomes.[48] As preeminent legal scholars have noted, "Procedures inherently carry with them decisions about power distribution. In determining who has the obligation to do what in the litigation process, procedural rules and statutes in the United States distribute power among parties, lawyers, judges, experts, lay community, different branches of government, state and national governments, rich and poor, corporations and individuals."[49] Even more importantly, questions of civil procedure and litigation interact with social and political currents. During the Civil Rights era, the rules were increasingly used as a tool for opening the door to more litigants and to a wider range of cases.[50] Beginning in the mid-1960s, several major rulemaking reforms were directed to that end; the 1966 amendments to Rule 23, which governs class actions, helped enable diverse sets of litigants to present themselves as a group in court, made it easier for lawyers to represent them in a single case, and required extensive consideration when such litigation was permissible.[51] The related set of joinder rules was similarly revised at the same time.[52] Other examples include the rules addressing the scope of permissible discovery (primarily Rules 26 and 34) that were revised in 1970 to expand opportunities for litigants to obtain information about the opposing party.[53] Rule 53 was also amended to allow for the appointment of special masters—individuals, usually attorneys, appointed by a judge to carry out some action for the court, usually a court order. Special masters proved especially important, for example, in allowing judges to undertake massive prison reform beginning in the late 1960s.[54]

These rule changes, among others, played a major role in transforming the landscape of litigation in the years to follow, with a more concrete impact than those embracing the procedure/substance distinction would have anticipated. The sheer growth of litigation was immense. Due especially to the 1966 rule amendments to class actions and joinder, the nature of litigation also changed. Civil cases became multipartied and multiclaimed, and the rise of this complex litigation prompted a new set of concerns, from both judges and lawyers, as how best to handle the new volume and complexity. At the same time, the "supply side" continued to grow and diversify, with the birth of the Legal Services Program (later Legal Services Corporation) and the ABA's deepening commitment to legal aid.[55]

Congress also did its part in aiding these developments, especially by increasing the number of federal judges across the country and creating incentives for more litigation by providing provisions for the award of attorney's fees to winning plaintiffs.[56] But where judicial rulemaking was concerned, legislators left the process alone, despite the fact that many of the rules had clear political importance, and that the process of developing federal civil procedural rules has been called by the most influential scholars in the field the most remarkably successful "power grab by the judiciary" in history.[57]

But in 1973, when the Advisory Committee drafted the Federal Rules of Evidence, Congress not only vetoed the proposed rules, but also began a new era (with no end in sight) characterized by an institutional battle for control of rulemaking. As I will argue, a variety of retrenchment advocates played a role in this battle. But these retrenchers were of many different mindsets, interests, and ideological backgrounds. Indeed, some of these actors were not so much classic "retrenchers" as much as they were motivated by making the judiciary run more efficiently, with better capacity to handle a plethora of new problems stemming from the dramatic increase in volume and complexity of litigation. Initial efforts at introducing a more prominent role for Congress were motivated primarily by a variety of pro-judiciary actors and legislators who saw this fight as part of a bigger set of political battles that had less to do with courts than with congressional authority. However, once Congress became more active in rulemaking reform, it opened the door to new actors with more concerted desires to scale back access to the judiciary and judicial authority—some out of self-interest, and others for ideological reasons.

The 1973 Rules of Evidence and the Beginnings of an Institutional Battle over Rules

With the luxury of hindsight, it seems striking and surprising that anyone would have argued that the Federal Rules of Civil Procedure were in any way, and at any time, "apolitical." Given the impetus for the Civil Rights movement, it is hardly surprising that the rules were used as tools for social reform. The 1966 amendments to Rule 23, for instance, involved changes to the ability of a single plaintiff to represent a "class" of people—subsequently allowing the class action to become one of the biggest and most powerful devices of the Civil Rights movement. When this rule change was discussed in the mid-1960s, the rules committee explicitly mentioned a substantive issue in its notes, referencing the famous civil rights desegregation case, *Brown v. Board of Education*,[58] as a positive example of why class actions matter. John Frank, a member of the Advisory Committee at that time, said later of his experience regarding the class action reforms: "Rule 23 was in work in direct parallel to the Civil Rights Act of 1964, and the race relations echo of that decade was always in the committee room. If there was single, undoubted goal of the committee, the energizing force which motivated the whole rule, it was the firm determination to create a class action system which could deal with civil rights and, explicitly, segregation."[59]

But the question of whether or not the rules were political would not grab Congress' attention until the rules episode of 1973, which clearly marked the end of unquestioned judicial dominance in rulemaking. Senator Sam Ervin of North Carolina began the process of exposing the substantive component of rulemaking (most likely unwittingly) at the end of January, promoting a bill that would have given Congress additional time beyond the ordinary ninety days to consider what had become highly controversial amendments to the proposed Federal Rules of Evidence. Ervin's proposal aimed "to promote the separation of constitutional powers by securing to the Congress additional time in which to consider the rules of evidence," and he argued that while lawyers and legal scholars had become familiar with the newly revised rules, neither members of Congress nor the ABA had an opportunity to "subject the rules and their recent changes to the careful scrutiny which one would consider appropriate in such a major undertaking."[60] Hearings before a judiciary subcommittee in the House began the following week.[61] On March 6, 1973, following debate in the Senate, the House Judiciary Committee voted to postpone indefinitely the effective date for the proposed Federal Rules of Evidence. The evidence rules were contentious on several fronts. Rule 505, governing husband–wife confidentiality, would have required a spouse to reveal the other's confidential admissions in a courtroom. The proposed Rule 504 similarly threatened patient–doctor confidentiality. Rule 509, the so-called "State Secrets Privilege," provided protection for secret information regarding national defense, but was written by the Judicial Conference such that it could be asserted by virtually any attorney representing the government at any level.

The rules committees had seemingly overreached on several points. As former Supreme Court Justice Arthur Goldberg said in his testimony before the House committee, "Some of the proposed rules extend beyond mere matters of procedure and represent real changes in the substantive rights and duties of persons throughout the country."[62] Robert Clare of the New York Trial Lawyers Committee stated in his testimony that, while he endorsed the continuing role of courts in making rules, mistakes had been made in recent years, starting with the Rule 23 revisions of the mid-1960s for making substantive changes in the law, and that "the bar was asleep."[63] The *New York Times* approached the rules controversy with a question: "Can the Supreme Court make fundamental changes in the rights of accused criminals by administrative fiat?"[64] The proposed Federal Rules of Evidence, then—similar to the

class action changes of 1966—compromised the "purely procedural" var-
nish that the rulemakers applied to their activities and made their substantive motivations more overt. In other words, rulemakers exposed that their
actions were both politically motivated and consequential, something that
caught not only the attention of Congress, but also some of the justices on
the Supreme Court.[65] In fact, the 1973 rules provide a rare example where a
Supreme Court Justice (William O. Douglas) dissented on their merits.

But if the rules committees had, in fact, used the rules as vehicles for
substantive rights reform at least since the Civil Rights era, what caused
Congress to pay attention in 1973? There are arguably two explanations for
Congress' sudden interest in rulemaking. First, in response to the proposed
evidence rules, Congress was barraged by concern from interest groups
that either disagreed with the content of the rules or believed that they
were given short shrift in the rulemaking process. The ABA, for example,
expressed frustration that rulemakers did not formally include input from
the bar. With the 1973 rules specifically, they were angered that changes were
made to the rules at the very last second, leaving them with no chance to
provide comment at all. Lawyers from the Washington Council of Lawyers
argued that "Congress should take a fresh look at the rulemaking process"
to ensure both greater congressional scrutiny as well as more "meaningful
participation of the entire legal profession" that includes "all elements of
the bar."[66] Self interest took other forms as well. For example, when rulemakers considered revising the rule involving patient–doctor privilege, the
American Medical Association (AMA) made its intense displeasure known
to Congress. Related, the Association of Trial Lawyers of America (ATLA)
was alarmed that the same proposed changes would threaten its own enterprise. Testifying before the House Judiciary Committee, James Schaeffer,
head of ATLA, echoed the AMA's concern that, for example, "a rule empowering the court to appoint an expert would virtually abolish any opportunity
of success in medical negligence cases."[67]

Second, in an era defined by the intensive Watergate investigations and
battles with President Richard Nixon over a range of constitutional powers, Democrats in Congress were particularly sensitive to real and imagined
encroachments on their power. The *New York Times* picked up on this theme
immediately, presenting the debate over the rules as a move by Congress "to
curb justices."[68] Representative Elizabeth Holtzman provided the opening
remarks at the hearings in February, arguing that it was imperative to pay careful attention to the rule changes both because of their "tremendous impact"
and because of "nationwide discussions of the newspaperman's privilege and

Government secrets."⁶⁹ New York Representative Bertram Podell followed her, worrying that "we constantly hear that our prerogatives are being threatened by the expansion of Executive power. The encroachment of the judiciary upon the Congress is equally dangerous." If the rule changes were allowed to go through, he argued, "the Supreme Court will have established the right to make whatever changes in our court system it sees fit."⁷⁰ Moments later, he declared the Rules Enabling Act "perhaps the most open and most concerted attack on the powers of Congress in history."⁷¹ In general, separation of powers concerns pervaded Congress' discussion of the proposed evidence rules, especially with regard to the proposed rules of privilege, which were thought to be legislative and therefore necessarily enacted by Congress. Members of Congress were further alarmed when they learned from Judge Albert Maris, the chairman of the Judicial Conference's Standing Committee on Practice and Procedure, that his committee had been influenced by a member of the Justice Department when drafting the rule involving the "state's secret privilege." Such an admission, at a time when Nixon administration officials were continually invoking executive privilege to avoid testifying in the Watergate hearings, caught their attention and furthered their suspicion that something political was afoot in rulemaking.

As a result, 1973 was a transitional moment where Congress came to value more control over the judicial rulemaking process and more authority vis-à-vis the Supreme Court. When legislators first began discussions of the rules in February, many were aghast and outraged that they had not been more actively involved all along. Rulemaking, as Justice Goldberg pointed out, was something that was entirely "confined to the bar," and House members, particularly Republicans, feared that they lacked the expertise to participate in such matters.⁷² Many seemingly learned about the rulemaking process for the first time on the floor as other members spoke, with frequent questions about the basics of rulemaking. For instance, House members quickly objected to the fact that the Rules Enabling Act gave them only a limited period of time in which to review and potentially veto such technical and complicated material—a feature that had been in effect as long as the rules existed. The fact that the rules were written and developed by the Judicial Conference, not the Supreme Court, was also lost on both Congress and the national media. The *New York Times* continually found it surprising when Supreme Court justices claimed that they had not played an active role in the rulemaking process, pointing out, correctly, that the rules were written by a committee only vaguely overseen by the Court. To the *Times*, however, this was clearly a battle between the Supreme Court and Congress.⁷³

At the time, members of Congress were by no means opposed to the policy ends that the rules were furthering. The backlash to the proposed evidence rules did *not* stem from dissatisfaction with the broader project of the rights revolution and social reform; that is, anti-civil rights legislators did not motivate congressional action in 1973, nor were they yet motivated by a desire to begin the process of scaling back the role of litigation in promoting and enforcing social policy. Indeed, just three years later, Congress passed the Civil Rights Attorney's Fees Award Act, which fostered further litigation on behalf of civil rights plaintiffs. Similar types of pro-litigation legislation were enacted frequently at least through the Civil Rights Act of 1991,[74] and Democratic majorities in Congress were consistently at battle with an increasingly conservative Supreme Court over the interpretation of numerous pieces of Civil Rights era legislation. At this historic juncture, then, what largely (though, we will see, not solely) prompted congressional involvement was the fact that legislators themselves wanted to play a larger role in the *process* of rulemaking. In so desiring, however, they unwittingly catalyzed what would become decades of constrictions on judicial power and access to the courts.

The 1973 debates led to legislation that garnered strong support from both parties in Congress the following year. The legislation produced the nation's first uniform rules of evidence, though with significant changes to the controversial provisions proposed by the rulemaking committees. Perhaps most notably, Congress stripped the Supreme Court of its power to make rules and determinations of evidentiary privilege.[75] At the same time, while there was no significant institutional change to the rulemaking process (although Congress did extend its review period from 90 to 180 days), legislative involvement would completely change the landscape of federal rulemaking in the years to follow.[76] Legislators began to conduct hearings on how they could get more involved in the rulemaking process, and they quite regularly both delayed accepting rule changes (as they would with the evidence rules, which did not go into effect until 1975) and passed statutes of their own that effectively altered the wording and meaning of rule changes that they did not like.[77] Interest groups, from plaintiff attorneys to businesses, realized that they could lobby Congress to gain a greater voice in a process that previously left them on the sidelines; equally, legislators found a new avenue through which they could cater to interests (like ATLA) that tended to give a lot of money in political campaigns. It would be another two decades before the interests that we tend to associate with retrenchment—namely conservatives in the Republican Party mounting an assault on the power of plaintiff attorneys and liberal-activist judges—would come to the foreground. The first irony of retrenchment in rulemaking, then, is that all of the actors initially involved came from the Democratic side of the aisle, often prompted and buttressed by liberal lobbyists. Republicans, to the degree they were involved, tended to be on the other side of the debate, as conservative judges and other judicial actors were most often in a position of defending the authority of the Nixon administration during ongoing impeachment hearings.

The 1980s—Judges Versus Plaintiff Lawyers and Their Democratic Party Allies

As retrenchment through rulemaking reform proceeded into the 1980s, the defining characteristics of the 1970s persisted; Republicans in Congress, for the most part, were still quiet on this front. Although Ronald Reagan was beginning to tout "tort reform" as part of the policy agenda of the Republican Party, and although conservative legal organizations like the Federalist Society were in their beginnings, the debate over rules remained largely waged by Democratic legislators. In this vein, they managed several major legislative rulemaking achievements: most notably, they successfully restructured the rulemaking process and further empowered their own role with the Judicial Improvements and Access to Justice Act of 1988, as well as passed sweeping legislation under the Civil Justice Reform Act (CJRA) in 1990, which decentralized rulemaking to the district court level, removing a significant degree of power from the federal rulemaking committees. The Democratic legislators who passed these reforms did so under the intense lobby of the ABA, ATLA, and other groups of public interest lawyers, all of whom wanted the rules to open up access to litigation.

Most importantly, however, the 1980s was also a period when new interests joined to reform civil rules. The significant shifts in rulemaking authority that defined the decade ultimately stemmed from a territorial battle internal to the judiciary. By the 1980s, the concept of a "litigation crisis" was in widespread circulation. The strain that the dramatic growth in litigation, as well as the development of "complex litigation," created for the courts made greater case management by judges imperative. Case management was another hot topic at the Pound Conference of 1976, and its momentum continued into the early 1980s.[78] In order to overcome growing problems of expense, abuse, and delay, judges increasingly believed that they needed to take more control of judicial proceedings. And given that federal judges dominate the membership of the civil rules committees, they were perfectly positioned to institute procedural changes that would help to keep the justice system functioning and intact in the face of this increased demand. But taking control in this way, which included imposing firm dates and deadlines for discovery and creating sanctions for abusive lawyer tactics, conflicted with the concentrated interests of lawyers, for whom doing exactly these things is precisely the way to win cases and procure attorney's fees. In other words, judges "favored procedural mechanisms that empowered judges at the expense of others, including lawyers, litigants, and juries."[79] For judges, these changes were not at all partisan in nature, but self-avowedly aimed at "fixing" the problems caused by an explosion in litigation that was taxing their resources.

Nonetheless, judicial committee members began to implement changes that, for the first time since the Civil Rights–era expansions, began to constrict access to the courts. This streamlining of the judicial process caused a rift to develop between lawyers and judges, leading major legal organizations such as the ABA and ATLA to join with Democrats in Congress in their pursuit of rulemaking reform, instead of joining with judges and rulemakers. Because Democrats were generally supportive of expansive litigation and access to courts, it made sense for lawyer groups to approach Democrats rather than Republicans on this issue, if leading to ironic consequences in the long term.[80] As prominent civil rules scholar Stephen Burbank aptly summarizes, "It is no coincidence that at the very time when the federal judiciary was wresting power from lawyers (and their clients) by putting in place general rules that not only enabled but encouraged trial judges to take control of all civil litigation, and required them to root out abuse, the judiciary began to lose what had been essentially a monopoly of power to fashion the rules of the game."[81]

Formal Rule Changes

In the early 1980s, the rules committees under the Judicial Conference implemented their first major rule changes aimed at constricting litigation. This included amendments to Rule 26 in 1980, which promoted case management by judges in requiring an early discovery conference of counsel in most cases (aimed at disposing of the case without trial); changes to Rule 11 in 1983, which imposed disciplinary sanctions for attorneys in order to curb abusive tactics; Rule 16 (also in 1983), which strongly empowered active trial management and authorized judicial involvement with settlement promotion for the first time; and Rule 26(b), which authorized district judges to restrict discovery for several reasons, including on a cost–benefit basis. In addition, Rule 11–type sanctions were written into the other rule amendments as an additional measure for constraining abuses. Prominent scholars of the rules use these developments (as well as changes to the rules governing pleading and summary judgment) to bookend the start of a "new era" in the history of American civil procedure, built of rule reforms that are "correlated and enduring because, since the 1970s, they have pointed largely in one direction: constricting access to courts, limiting discovery, and denying trials."[82]

While these amendments were major retrenchment successes for rulemakers, not all of their proposals fared so well. The struggle between rulemakers, Congress, and interest groups over proposed changes to Rules 4 and 68 typified the tensions that had come to divide the groups. To take one example, Congress managed to table consideration of the proposed amendments to "put teeth into" Rule 68. The Advisory Committee sought to make the original rule—which was designed to provide an incentive to settle by requiring that a prevailing claimant who has declined a more favorable offer of judgment pay post-offer "costs"—a two-way street, allowing both plaintiffs and defendants to make offers and counteroffers. Specifically, the proposal provided that a party who rejected an offer under Rule 68 and failed to obtain a more favorable judgment at trial would have to pay the costs and expenses, including reasonable attorney's fees, incurred by the offering party after the offer was made (at the judge's discretion).

Although sanctions were fairly uncontroversial cornerstones of the amendments to Rules 11, 16, and 26, many major legal groups came out strongly against incorporating them into Rule 68. The National Bar Association, ACLU, Alliance for Justice, and the NAACP Legal Defense and Educational Fund all testified against the 1983 proposal. These groups feared that the proposed changes would keep civil rights plaintiffs out of court because, if they were to lose, they would have to be able to pay the defendant's attorney's fees as well as their own—a financial burden too large for many civil rights plaintiffs to bear. Also, because judges would have the discretion to coerce settlements by threatening sanctions, these groups worried that civil rights plaintiffs would be forced to accept plainly inadequate settlement offers out of fear that if they went to trial and lost, they would not be able to pay.[83] Critics also argued that the rule changes were in conflict with various statutes that authorized attorney's fees for prevailing parties, as well as with the "supersession provision" of the Rules Enabling Act,[84] which had been interpreted by courts to allow procedural rules to trump statutory mechanisms designed to provide "remedial rights fashioned by Congress as essential to the enforcement of substantive law."[85] These lobbying efforts effectively quashed the proposal, and Rule 68 has not since undergone reform.

Some of these rules—most prominently Rules 11 and 26—caused controversy again in the early 1990s. The now compulsory nature of Rule 11, coupled with defense attorneys' rampant use of it, led to thousands of additional sanctions and opinions—precisely the opposite effect of what was intended by the 1983 reforms. More importantly, significant concern developed that, as initially feared, these sanctions were being used disproportionately against civil rights plaintiffs in order to impede public interest litigation.[86] Given that the sanctions embedded in Rule 26 were used similarly, rulemakers proposed amendments to both in hopes of softening their impact by making sanctions discretionary. These proposed amendments were met with unprecedented resistance, the strength of which was undoubtedly fueled once again by a stark divide between lawyers, judges, and other interested parties. District Judge Robert E. Keeton, chairman of the Standing Committee on Rules of Practice and Procedure, commented at the start of the House subcommittee hearings: "It is not accidental that you are hearing from more constituencies, because as the processes of administration of justice come under greater stress and more complex litigation is presented, there are increasing concerns by participants in that process that they would like to get an edge in the procedural aspects of the matter."[87] As a Federal Judicial Center survey at the time indicated, civil rights lawyers despised Rule 11, while 80 percent of judges supported it.[88] This division also manifested itself in a change in the alignment of rules committee supporters: lawyer groups found themselves largely on board with rulemakers, businesses (notably insurance companies like Aetna) vehemently opposed the amendments, and rulemakers themselves still maintained an outwardly nonpartisan concern for the practical functioning of the judiciary. Judge Keeton reminded the rules committees that they must "resist all pressures" to give into interest lobbying, as their statutory mandate requires that "the rules are to be substantively neutral."[89]

The new alliances were not perfect; the ABA, for instance, wanted to remedy the increased problems of delay by relying on more case management from judges, while the rules committees leaned toward increasing lawyer responsibility.[90] In the end, both rule reforms passed, but only after the discovery amendments—which would have required litigants to provide "core" materials at the outset of trial without waiting for a formal discovery request—included a provision permitting individual courts to opt out of the requirement, thereby bringing lawyers on board. The final rule changes did, however, draw dissent from Supreme Court Justices Antonin Scalia and Clarence Thomas, who claimed that the amendments would make Rule 11 "toothless" and that the disclosure rule conflicted with the duties of

American lawyers never to turn over any information harmful to their client without a proper request from the opposing party.[91]

Reforming the Rulemaking Process

Congress provided the conduit for rulemaking involvement that legal organizations and other interest groups could not find with the rules committees. And given that groups like ATLA tend to be major campaign donors, Congress had ample reason to join forces with them. These alliances fueled Congress' growing effort throughout the 1980s to increase its own (and subsequently its patrons') role in the rulemaking process. To this end, Congress debated overhauling the entire structure of rulemaking; specifically, from 1980 to 1985 it conducted multiple hearings regarding the question of whether or not to abolish the role of the Supreme Court (and/or the Judicial Conference) entirely in the rulemaking process.[92] In response to complaints from different state bar associations, in 1982 Congress rejected the rule changes put forth that year by the Court, substituting its own amendments to Rule 4 regarding delivery of summons.[93] By the mid-1980s, a significant congressional reform coalition mobilized, leading to a series of hearings before the House Judiciary Committee in which its chairman, Robert Kastenmeier, described the efforts as the first "comprehensive congressional review of the rulemaking process" since its initial passage fifty years prior.[94] Kastenmeier followed the lead of the ABA, which called for drastic reforms that would remove the Supreme Court from the rulemaking process and promoted greater ABA and congressional involvement in the early stages of drafting rule changes.[95]

More often than not, however, the hearings focused less on diminishing the role of judges and more on the possibility of involving other groups—especially Congress—in the early stages of drafting rule changes. During hearings before the House Subcommittee on Courts, Civil Liberties, and the Administration of Justice in April of 1983, Judge Edward Thaxter Gignoux, the chairman of the Standing Committee, sidestepped the issue in a manner characteristic of the rules committee members of the time. He argued, for example, that the problem with incorporating groups like the ABA into the rulemaking process was that it would take prohibitively long to allow them time for comment, and that "as far as the members of Congress themselves are concerned, their participation might be helpful, but I wonder if you do not have enough to do without sitting through two days of discussion of the details of the rules."[96]

Congress disagreed. Despite Judge Gignoux's position that there is "nothing the Standing Committee does which would be of any public interest,"[97] Congress felt isolated from a process that it considered democratically relevant, as well as relevant to the interests that supported them. Democratic Representative Howard Berman, who admitted he was "totally unaware of this process and that Congress had a role in the Federal Rules of Civil Procedure," nonetheless reported that he was receiving copious mail from concerned law professors who believed that ongoing rule reforms were controversial and worthy of congressional attention.[98] By contrast, judicial rulemakers believed that the input of outside parties would be purely reflective of "rank self-interest" and would only get in the way of systematic, nonpartisan deliberation over purely procedural concerns; but members of Congress and their supporters from the bar argued that rulemaking was a "quasi-legislative process" that necessitated outside supervision and representation. This disjuncture was a recipe for major change. Kastenmeier's Judiciary Committee issued a report in 1985 promoting "openness in the rulemaking process" by requiring more representative Judicial Conference committees, more reasonable notice for public comment on the proposed rules, more time for Congress to review the promulgated rules, and the elimination of the supersession clause.[99] By the end of the decade, the desire for public accountability through enhanced participation and political oversight overwhelmed claims by rulemakers of the importance of technical expertise; as Robert Bone argues, "Concerns about efficacy and legitimacy pushed the process toward an interest group model that assimilates rulemaking to legislation."[100] Indeed, Congress emerged victorious in the institutional battle by passing two major reforms at the end of the decade: The Judicial Improvements and Access to Justice Act (1988) and the Civil Justice Reform Act (1990).

The Judicial Improvements and Access to Justice Act codified long-sought efforts to open up the rulemaking process to broad public participation by requiring public hearings, open meetings, publicly available minutes, and longer periods for public commentary.[101] This formally obligated the rulemaking committees to hear from the plethora of interests knocking down Congress' door.[102] As a result, the Advisory Committee began to receive hundreds of comments whenever it circulated a draft of a proposed rule change and regularly heard testimony from a much broader array of groups than before.[103] In effect, this has led to explicit political lobbying of the judiciary, the one branch of government we struggle to conceive of as immune from political influence. Despite this, the committees seemed to maintain their focus on what "made sense" for the courts in terms of practical functioning and fairness and did not appear to be "swayed by groups merely advocating revisions to the rules that will be better for their particular interests."[104] While the committees were now officially "open" to outside interests, the interests that lost in this forum simply repeated their efforts in Congress.

Accordingly, the continued politicization of the rules made Congress even more willing to initiate its own rule changes, albeit outside of the formal process for creating and amending rules. With the Civil Justice Reform Act (CJRA), Congress significantly disrupted the judiciary's rulemaking monopoly by decentralizing it. In an attempt to curtail the cost and delay of civil litigation, the act directed each of the ninety-four U.S. district courts to convene advisory groups in order to design district-level procedures to achieve these objectives, thus embracing a "bottom-up" approach to procedural reform. It directed these local groups to consider certain principles of reform, chief among them a familiar mandate: increased judicial management of litigation. Finally, it required federal judicial districts to develop civil justice expense and delay reduction plans.

The legislation was perceived as bipartisan, with the real conflict manifesting itself in the institutional-level battle between legislators and the judiciary. In Senate hearings, the chairman of the Judiciary Committee and the bill's main sponsor, Joseph Biden, commented repeatedly how amazing it was that corporate law, ATLA, insurance groups, and consumers were all on the same side of the issue. Biden portrayed the legislation as an apt response to a litigation "crisis of major dimensions,"[105] and interest group lobbyists clearly agreed. An insurance lawyer for Aetna, for example, complained that the corporation had spent $370 million that year alone on litigation.[106] Bill Wagner, the head of ATLA, was less concerned about expenses, and more concerned about having firm trial dates, which would promote settlements: "The most important thing is, I think, that this has an idea that the plans to make these tracks work are developed and monitored by the people who use the system. And I don't mean to be overly critical of federal judges, but let's face it, they see their problems, and they are federal judges and they can order us to do what they want to."[107] Understandably, judges viewed the legislation as an attack on both their authority and the idea of procedural fairness through uniformity. Members of the Judicial Conference, while validating the problems voiced by Congress, argued that the rules committees should remain the venue for reform, and that the bill was "extraordinarily intrusive into the internal workings of the judicial branch."[108]

In the end, the CJRA was an experiment that came and went, as the legislation was never renewed. In its aftermath, judges considered themselves "right" insofar as the act led to a messy morass of district-level rules that were not consistent with the federal rules (as the legislation required), and later studies indicated that it did not, in fact, serve to reduce expense or delay. Simply, the CJRA did not achieve its goals. And because the act required implementation by judges, what the judiciary perceived as a refusal to heed its advice came with a major cost. At the same time, Congress had made its mark; its willingness to initiate rules would grow substantially in the 1990s.

Retrenchment Through the Courts

Even though a coalition of Democrats was largely responsible for the retrenchment of the 1980s, the decade was by no means devoid of politically motivated retrenchment. The Reagan administration was active in attempting to cut the supply side of litigation by "defunding the Left" and even trying to abolish entities such as the Legal Services Corporation.[109] But its biggest successes were arguably put into motion through court appointments; President Reagan made two key conservative appointments to the Supreme Court in the 1980s (Antonin Scalia in 1982 and Anthony Kennedy in 1988), elevated William Rehnquist to Chief Justice, and appointed eighty-three judges to the U.S. Courts of Appeals and 290 to the U.S. district courts. Through these appointments, the final years of the Burger Court—and more notably the Rehnquist Court years—became fiercely antilitigation in nature.[110] And in addition to the other components of the deepening antilitigation agenda (including constricting the availability of attorney's fees, limiting remedies and causes of action, enhancing governmental immunities, enforcing mandatory arbitration agreements, and limiting punitive damages awards), in the mid-1980s, the Supreme Court began its own discussion of legal concepts that overlap with the federal rules.

Specifically, the Court began to reconsider its role in summary judgment, a legal practice governed by Rule 56. Summary judgment is considered the last potential gatekeeping function before a case goes to trial, addressing whether or not the claim at hand should go before and judge and jury. A motion for summary judgment is filed with supporting evidence, and if the judge agrees to it, he or she has essentially found either that (1) there are no issues of material fact that require a trial for their resolution, or (2) in applying the law to the undisputed facts, one party is clearly entitled to judgment. As such, this gives judges the discretion to provide a judgment without a trial and without a jury.

In the so-called Trilogy Cases of 1986—*Celotex Corp. v. Catrett, Anderson v. Liberty Lobby*, and *Matsushita Elec. Indus. Co. v. Zenith Radio Corp.*[111]—the

Supreme Court made summary judgment markedly easier to obtain.[112] Increased summary judgment activity was well under way in the lower federal courts prior to the trilogy.[113] *Celotex*, the most famous of the cases, involved a wrongful death suit regarding a man who died from exposure to the defendant's asbestos products while on the job. The Court responded to the dispute with a new summary judgment standard, whereby if the party moving for summary judgment does not have the underlying burden of proof at trial, it need not provide evidence negating the other party's claim; instead, it may simply show that the opposing party has failed to provide evidence behind a critical part of his or her claim.[114] The vast majority of the time, this has had the effect of requiring that plaintiffs "who normally have the burden of proof at trial, must come up with evidence earlier on, simply to defeat defendant's motion for summary judgment."[115] This forces a plaintiff to show his or her hand before the trial even begins. In aggregate, these cases have favored defendants by enabling them, far more so than plaintiffs, to ask the judge to end a trial prior to giving the plaintiff the opportunity to engage in discovery. Subsequently, by moderate estimates, rates of summary judgment in federal civil cases rose from 1.8 percent of cases in 1960 to 7.7 percent of cases in 2000, with a recent Federal Judicial Center study indicating that approximately 60 percent of summary judgment motions are granted, in whole or in part. Importantly, increased summary judgment activity appears to affect certain types of cases and groups of plaintiffs more than others. The rate of motions granted in civil rights cases is higher than the national average, where over 70 percent of summary judgment motions in employment discrimination cases in particular are granted.[116] These doctrinal changes, in combination with procedural reform, have served to constrict access to the courts for minority groups and the poor pursuing civil rights claims—a major shift from the doctrinal and procedural innovations and goals of the rights revolution era.

From the 1990s Onward: Partisan Rule Reform

"Tort reform" first became a subject of media attention in the 1980s, gathering steam and success initially at the state level.[117] At the federal level, President Reagan created a Tort Policy Working Group and told national audiences "tort tales"—outrageous stories of lawyers profiting from a legal system out of control.[118] In 1992 Dan Quayle made tort reform a primary issue in the attempt to reelect George H. W. Bush, while Bush himself declared in his acceptance speech to the Republican National Convention that opponent

Bill Clinton was backed "by every trial lawyer who ever wore a tasseled loafer."[119] A Bush pollster at the time noted the potential for electoral gains inherent in attacking trial lawyers: "Trial lawyers today have the same favorability rating as Richard Nixon in 1974."[120] In 1994 Republicans, led by Newt Gingrich, made tort reform a tenet of the "Contract with America," demanding with it what they deemed to be "common sense legal reform." And with a Republican majority in the House for the first time in four decades, retrenchment through the rules (or rule-related matters) became more the story we would have expected it to be all along; a Republican-dominated Congress using its political unity to sidestep the formal rulemaking process. Legal and interest group alliances fell into familiar patterns, with plaintiff groups and lawyers supporting Democrats, and business and the corporate defense legal community lining up with Republicans. In addition, with the Rehnquist Court now in full operation, the Supreme Court itself continued to further its own antilitigation agenda.

By this time, rulemaking authority had thoroughly shifted from the traditional judicial model stressing the importance of "experts" to legislative dominance of the rulemaking process. Given that members of Congress were now lobbied regularly regarding rule-related matters (often in response to the amendments proposed by rulemakers themselves), Congress and other elected officials seemed legitimated in exercising an increased freedom to propose their own rule reforms through legislation. An important component, for instance, of Dan Quayle's promotion of tort reform included detailed changes to discovery rules aimed at lowering both legal expenses and the number of lawsuits.[121] At the same time, the rules committees managed to retain some measure of authority—if not directly for themselves, for judges— even amidst clear legislative dominance. They did so primarily by loosening mandatory sanctions and discovery procedures and increasing judicial discretion over the processes. When the Rule 26 disclosure obligation and the scope of discovery were revisited in 2000, the proposed reforms—which narrowed the obligation of initial disclosure and both narrowed the scope of discovery and made it nationally binding—went into effect without congressional intervention, in sharp contrast to the explosive political opposition that similar reforms prompted in decades prior. This was consistent with what was by then the House and Senate's propensity to go along with anything that even remotely promised less civil litigation.[122] This tactic also clearly relied on the political tone of the time; with Republicans and conservative judges in the majority, reforms aimed at increasing the discretion of judges were by nature compatible with efforts to lower litigation rates and judicial overburden.

Congress Tackles Procedural Reform

Evidencing this shift in governing authority, Congress pursued a variety of litigation reform platforms in the 1990s, with some notable success. The 104th Republican Congress moved quickly to seek "common sense legal reform," and—as a central tenet of their Contract with America—the proposed reforms were decidedly antilitigation in nature. The extent of their legislative success, however, was thwarted unsurprisingly by a series of vetoes from President Bill Clinton. In 1996 Clinton vetoed the Product Liability Fairness Act, which would have limited the amounts that plaintiffs could receive in punitive damages in product liability cases. In doing so, Clinton defended consumer groups (and, more quietly, trial lawyers) against Republican presidential candidate Robert Dole's active support of the legislation.[123] The same year he vetoed the antilitigation-driven Attorney Accountability Act, which would have codified a "loser pays" attorney's fees system and placed limits on punitive damages.[124]

Clinton also vetoed the Private Securities Litigation Reform Act (PSLRA), which amended Rules 9 and 11, only to see Congress' first successful override of his administration. The legislation amended Rule 11 so as to reverse much of its 1993 reform, once again making the threat of lawyer sanctions more imposing for cases arising under the law. Importantly, in so doing, Congress effectively superseded Rule 9, which deals with the amount of particularity and specificity that an investor needs to provide in order to bring litigation on the grounds of security fraud, and in heightening pleading requirements statutorily. As noted, the civil rules were originally written such that pleading—the act of bringing litigation in courts—was fairly easy; a potential plaintiff needed relatively little information about the defendant beyond a stated legal grievance when first filing a claim in court. The rules were further designed so that, once actually in court, the plaintiff could then acquire relevant materials about an opponent through the process of discovery. But in the 1990s, high-tech firms in Silicon Valley in particular pushed hard for reform that would make pleading more difficult. Intel and other Silicon Valley start-ups, as well as the defense bar, sought reform that would make it more difficult for investors presuming fraud to sue without preexisting factual knowledge; they claimed that the volatility of the stock market was leading investors to sue to recoup their losses regardless of whether they believed fraud had occurred, and that the companies found themselves settling out of court to avoid litigation costs.[125] On the other side, investors wanted the opportunity, when their investments plummeted, to use discovery to get access to materials potentially indicative of fraud that might have caused their dramatic financial losses.

Twenty Democrats joined the vast majority of Republicans in the Senate (except four members, including Arlen Specter and John McCain), while ninety-one Democrats joined a unanimous Republican party in the House in overriding the Clinton veto. Key Democrats seemed torn between conflicting ties to the numerous big interests involved: trial lawyers, public interest groups, and the American Association of Retired People (AARP) on one side, and technology firms, big business, and insurance (which helped sway the head of the Democratic National Committee, Chris Dodd, because of the importance of insurance to Connecticut politics) on the other. This was not terribly surprising, since many of these Democrats had been pushing for the reforms prior to the Republican takeover. During Senate hearings in 1993, Senator Pete Domenici proudly introduced Tom Dunlap, the general counsel for Intel, a company with "a presence in my State of New Mexico," and one that had been involved in seven lawsuits that, "as I understand it, each triggered when the stock dropped in price." Domenici celebrated Intel's defeat of the "incredulous" lawsuits, but "the bad news is that it took more than 6 months and the expenditures of substantial resources and legal fees to convince the plaintiffs they had no case."[126] Democrats were also angered that Clinton had vetoed the bill for what, as Senator Harry Reid suggested, "seemed to be pandering to the trial lawyers, who have been generous in their support of him."[127]

The interests of the president and Congress coalesced with ease, however, on one antilitigation piece of legislation: the Prison Litigation Reform Act. Passed as part of a larger appropriations bill, the law constricts the remedies available to prisoners bringing conditions of confinement lawsuits and makes it more difficult for prisoners to find remedy in federal courts. With regard to civil rules specifically, Section 1997e(a) of the law requires that prisoners exhaust all administrative remedies before they can file a valid suit alleging violations in their prison conditions.[128] The law itself, however, is not explicit as to which party the burden to plead remedial exhaustion falls upon; and because of this, courts are split as to whether or not this duty lies with plaintiffs. Where it is determined that it does, this may well be considered yet another increase in pleading standards, in that they must ensure that their grievance has progressed through the prison's multistep series of grievance procedures before a lawsuit is commenced. While the Supreme Court has held that failure to exhaust is an affirmative defense that must be raised by the prison (and not a pleading requirement per se), if the court finds that a prisoner has not, in fact, navigated the administrative process completely, the case is dismissed.[129] Even in the absence of a new pleading standard, this arguably creates a substantial burden on prisoners, already likely lacking significant support to help them navigate the legal process.

Moving onward from "common sense legal reform," Republicans in both houses began pursuing a more ambitious goal: class action reform. Starting in 1997 and over the course of the next eight years, Republicans held a series of committee hearings on the topic, brought votes to the floor, and often found themselves close—but without the bipartisan numbers—to obtain a Senate cloture vote. With Republicans setting the agenda, the committee hearing participants changed dramatically from the Democrat-led hearings of the 1980s; notably, appearances by rules committee members from the Judicial Conference became increasingly infrequent. The debate within Congress over whether the two houses had authority to reform the rules had ceased, and the judicial committees became fairly marginal in their efforts to fight congressional rulemaking. Even so, it was the rules committees that first managed some measure of class action reform, enacting several uncontroversial, though effectual, amendments in 2003 with the goal of providing district courts the tools, authority, and discretion to closely supervise class actions. Meanwhile, some of the most prominent Democrats to participate in the reforms of the 1970s through the 90s were now some of the most fervent opponents of reform. For example, as then Senator Joseph Biden pronounced of his support for trial lawyers, "I'll pay the bottom feeders their high fees to stop the wrongdoers from doing bad things."[130]

Continuing to further the cause, George W. Bush put tort reform high on his agenda from the beginning of his run for president in 2000. An early version of what would become the Class Action Fairness Act first passed the House in 2001, and came within a vote of cloture in the Senate in 2003 and 2004. When the bill was once again considered in 2005, the successes of interest groups like the Chamber of Commerce in defeating high-ranking Senate Democrats opposed to tort reform (such as Tom Daschle in 2004), and a significant number of Democrats willing to cross the aisle (fifty members in the House and nineteen in the Senate, including notables such as Christopher Dodd, Dianne Feinstein, and Barack Obama), pushed the numbers in the Senate high enough to comfortably override a filibuster attempt.[131] On February 18, 2005, President Bush and other Republican leaders trumpeted the passage of the Class Action Fairness Act (CAFA). On the eve of its passage, President Bush declared that "a capitalist society depends on the capacity for people willing to take risks and say there's a better future. ... [L]egal reform is part of a larger agenda to make sure this economy of ours continues to grow."[132] Unlike in 1995, when the major news media paid scant attention to the passage of the PSLRA (despite its ongoing significance),[133] the class action legislation made front-page news in the *Washington Post* and *New York Times*.

CAFA expanded upon the 2003 rule amendments, which had provided greater judicial control over when a class may be certified, who may be appointed attorney and when, and the amount of attorney's fees available for successful plaintiffs. While the earlier amendments relied on judicial discretion as a means for constraining litigation, CAFA codified this goal by superseding Rule 23 in several respects. Specifically, it (1) altered federal diversity jurisdiction so that only "minimal" instead of "complete" diversity is required for large interstate cases[134]; (2) it changed the rules for removing cases from state to federal court; and (3) it imposed limits on the amounts that can be recovered by class members and their attorneys. Changes to federal diversity jurisdiction—based in Article III of the Constitution, which provides that jurisdiction for controversies "between Citizens of different States" is within the judicial power of the United States—have a long history of involvement in discussions about whether and how to encourage or discourage litigation. Through laws like the Judiciary Act, the Local Prejudice Act, and the Jurisdiction and Removal Act, and in landmark Supreme Court decisions like *Swift v. Tyson* and *Erie Railroad Company v. Tompkins*,[135] Congress and courts have at times altered the minimum amount in controversy and removal requirements in order to make it more or less difficult for certain types of cases to be heard in federal court. In general, these changes have largely been directed toward promoting or constricting opportunities for interstate business corporations to "forum shop" when they feared a less favorable reception in state courts. CAFA directly factors into this debate by expanding federal jurisdiction over class actions in which minimum diversity exists and where the aggregate of all claims is in excess of $5 million.[136]

The act is somewhat counterintuitive in terms of its potential for retrenchment; it works by shifting many class action lawsuits involving diverse parties from the state to the federal level, with the goal of bringing as many class actions to federal court as possible. This at first does not sound like retrenchment at all. However, the legislation was premised on the belief that fewer class actions would be certified in federal court than in state courts. As such, this change in venue serves to alleviate the rampant forum shopping for state jurisdictions that are historically most receptive to class action suits, which (some argue) only serve to enrich trial lawyers. The goal of the act, then, was to lessen the incentive to bring frivolous suits and to lower monetary awards.

Retrenchers interested in scaling back litigation against corporations were ecstatic. Insurance stock prices surged dramatically immediately after the passage of the law.[137] Business interests credited their own "massive effort:" "These are the level of resources it takes to beat the trial lawyers in the U.S. Senate."[138] It is as of yet entirely clear, of course, what effect the law has had. At the same time the act was passed, several of the states considered to be especially pro-plaintiff (namely Alabama, Louisiana, and Mississippi) were already themselves starting to crack down on class actions.[139] Initial reports from the Federal Judicial Center indicate that there has been a dramatic increase in the number of diversity class actions filed as original proceedings in the federal courts since the act was passed, increasing from 11.9 filings per month pre-CAFA to 34.5 per month in 2007, and a 72 percent overall increase in class action activity has occurred in the eighty-eight district courts studied more generally. The growth has largely been due to increases in the number of contract, consumer protection/fraud, and torts-property damage class actions being filed in or removed to federal courts in the post-CAFA period. However, it is not self-evident that the federal courts will decide most cases any differently,[140] as this would rely on federal judges acting far more favorably to defense interests than do state court judges. However, data as of yet lend little support to the claim, and the monetary amount of damage awards has thus far evened out in the wash. Nonetheless, at least politically, CAFA has been touted as a major retrenchment success for Republicans.

Rule Retrenchment in the Courts

The antilitigation work of the Rehnquist Court continued fairly seamlessly into the 1990s and 2000s, and has at times served to retrench rules in places where elected officials have failed. In finding ways to keep plaintiffs out of courts, the Supreme Court continued to reduce its willingness to find private rights to action in statutes, narrowed standing, developed "qualified immunity" for government officials accused of violating the civil rights of private citizens, and construed the Eleventh Amendment such as to make it nearly impossible to receive damages from states. In matters more closely related to the federal rules, the Court has maneuvered to keep would-be litigants out of court in two important ways: by further raising the requirements for pleading (increasing the amount of facts that must be stated in a complaint for a lawsuit to move forward) and by making it more difficult for litigants suffering a similar injury to certify as a class for purposes of pursuing a class action. Together, these changes are clear examples of "how a seemingly technical decision about court procedures can have a profound effect in keeping plaintiffs from being able to sue and in systematically favoring defendants who have allegedly violated the Constitutional and federal laws."[141]

As we have seen, it has long been at issue how much detail you need to have in order to file an actual complaint in civil court. If the threshold is too low, we run the risk of enabling frivolous, potentially costly suits that clog up an increasingly overburdened judicial system, which undermines the rationale for having pleading requirements in the first place. But if the threshold for necessary detail is too high, then many plaintiffs with potentially successful claims will be unable to proceed if they do not have the resources to obtain such detail prior to the process of discovery. However, a plaintiff cannot reach the stage of taking depositions, conducting interrogatories, and requesting documents in the service of making its claims more detailed and specific unless it meets the initial pleading requirements. As such, discovery and pleading rules are importantly interrelated.

Originally, American courts adopted the English rules for pleading, which were strict; but in the mid-nineteenth century, courts began to devise their own rules for pleading,[142] and eventually the federal rules introduced the practice of "notice pleading" that strongly favored plaintiffs getting into court. As described, under a notice pleading system, all that is required of plaintiffs is a short, plain statement of the facts of their claim—just enough to "give notice" to the potential defendants and the court as to the nature of the claim, and just enough to show that it would not be impossible for the plaintiffs to win. The Supreme Court first addressed the notice pleading system in *Conley v. Gibson* in 1957, determining that under Rule 8 of the federal rules, a complaint cannot be dismissed by a judge unless there are *no* set of facts upon which relief could potentially be granted. Specifically, the Court ruled that general allegations of discrimination were sufficient to fulfill the Rule 8 requirement of a "short plain statement" because liberal discovery guidelines allow the complaint to become far more specific in advance of the trial. Importantly, the Court established a set of "assumptions" for judges considering whether a plaintiff meets the pleading threshold: (1) the plaintiff's allegations are to be considered true; (2) in this early stage, the facts are to be construed in a way that is most favorable to the plaintiff; and (3) a judge cannot dismiss a case unless proven beyond a doubt that the plaintiff can prove no set of facts meriting a legal claim.[143] Unsurprisingly, then, liberalized pleading meant liberalized access to courts in the decades that followed.

But in 2007, the Court dramatically reversed course. While just in 1993 the Court had determined that courts could *not* impose a higher standard of specificity for claims than those detailed by Rule 9(b),[144] it substantially raised its pleading requirements in *Bell Atlantic v. Twombly*. The case, in which plaintiffs brought a class action against Bell Atlantic for alleged anti-competitive behavior under the Sherman Antitrust Act, was dismissed at the district court level for failure to allege sufficient facts to state a claim for violation of the act. The Second Circuit reversed, and the Supreme Court subsequently reversed them, dismissing the complaint for failure to state a claim under Rule 12(b)(6) of the federal rules, which sets the judicial standards for dismissing a case. The Court's opinion also changed the existing interpretation of Rule 8(a)(2) from the *Conley* standard—whereby a complainant need only put forth a "conceivable" set of facts to support the claim—to a new "plausibility" standard, requiring that there be "enough facts to raise a reasonable expectation that discovery will reveal evidence of illegal agreement."[145]

While the new "plausibility" standard established in *Twombly* only applied to antitrust cases, the Court established the general applicability of these heightened pleading requirements two years later in *Ashcroft v. Iqbal* (as discussed in this chapter's introduction). Justice Kennedy's opinion in the case established two important changes to the pleading standards. First, he argued that "the tenet that a court must accept as true all of the allegations contained in a complaint is inapplicable to legal conclusions," and second, that "only a complaint that states a plausible claim for relief survives a motion to dismiss." What would determine whether a claim was plausible? The Court's new two-pronged approach considers establishing plausibility "a context-specific task that requires the reviewing court to draw on its judicial experience and common sense. In keeping with these principles a court considering a motion to dismiss can choose to begin by identifying pleadings that, because they are no more than conclusions, are not entitled to the assumption of truth. While legal conclusions can provide the framework of a complaint, they must be supported by factual allegations. When there are well-pleaded factual allegations, a court should assume their veracity and then determine whether they plausibly give rise to an entitlement of relief."[146]

Both cases have already had a profound effect on both litigation behavior and results, though studies vary in their conclusions as to just how much.[147] But as recent expert testimony before Congress on the effects of these cases made clear, a sample of lower court cases already indicates that more complaints have been dismissed than would have prior to these newly heightened standards.[148] Others have noted that by April 2010—a mere eight months after the decision—more than 8,000 lower federal court cases cited *Iqbal*, and hundreds of those had been dismissed.[149] While motions to dismiss for failure to state a claim have increased, these motions [filed under Rule 12(b)(6) of the civil rules] can contain an option to amend the complaint, and this appears to be helping to stem the tide by reducing the overall rate at which those seeking to throw out a claim prevail from 75 percent to 63 percent.[150] Still, the most troublesome concern is that, in aggregate, *Twombly* and *Iqbal* have had a disproportionately adverse impact on the usual victims of "procedural" reform: civil rights plaintiffs.[151]

Congress responded swiftly with calls for legislative action to reverse the Court's new standard, but to date such efforts stalled at the committee level. In 2009, moderate Republican Senator Arlen Specter introduced the Notice Pleading Restoration Act with the goal of changing the pleading rules back to the standard that had previously been in place for seventy years. The goal of the bill was very clear: keep judicial discretion away from the issue of pleading. As the "purpose" of the bill read, "Except as otherwise expressly provided by an Act of Congress or by an amendment to the Federal Rules of Civil Procedure which takes effect after the date of enactment of this Act, a Federal court shall not dismiss a complaint ... except under the standards set forth by the Supreme Court of the United States in *Conley v. Gibson*."[152] Senator Patrick Leahy started the hearings in December 2009 by arguing that the two cases would deny litigants "access to the facts necessary to prove wrongdoing" and demanded that judges not ignore "the reality that a defendant often holds the keys to critical information which a litigant needs to prove unlawful conduct."[153] Professor Stephen Burbank of the University of Pennsylvania Law School expressed concern that the decisions would "contribute to the phenomenon of vanishing trials, the degradation of the Seventh Amendment right to jury trial, and the emasculation of private civil litigation as a means of enforcing public law."[154] A similar bill was introduced in the House shortly thereafter (the Open Access to Courts Act of 2009), which mirrored the Senate bill, but without referring to *Conley* by name. The bill sought to prohibit U.S. district courts from dismissing a complaint unless it appeared "beyond doubt" that the plaintiff could prove a set of facts to support the claim.[155] But with Republicans taking control of the House in 2010, the bill stalled in committee.

In terms of further retrenchment in rule-related matters, the Supreme Court's recent activity with regard to the use of class actions in civil rights cases is so far-reaching in its effects as to serve as the opening example in this book. In its 2011 *Wal-Mart* decision, the Court refused to certify what was the nation's largest class action lawsuit in history. In declining to do so, the Court set a precedent that will no doubt also constrain the ability of similar litigants to join together in a class action.[156] This was a dramatic departure from the driving motivations for creating the class action in the first place: to make it easier for like litigants to get to court, and to ease the judiciary from the overburden stemming from a multitude of similar cases that could efficiently be dealt with together. While these changes shifted public and political attention toward the importance of procedural rules (prompting the Senate Judiciary Committee to hold hearings on the availability of class actions in 2011),[157] the *Wal-Mart* decision in many ways came and went as the latest example of the important gatekeeping mechanism that those in control of procedure can play. Shortly thereafter, the spotlight quickly shifted to whether and how another procedural concern—the doctrine of standing—would factor into the fate of gay marriage rights in the United States. No sooner did the Supreme Court grant cert to *U.S. v. Windsor* and *Hollingsworth v. Perry* than did a national conversation about another previously marginal justiciability consideration begin,[158] continuing to highlight the degree to which control of the "rules of the game" can come with the power to meaningfully constrict who has their day in court. And as the *Perry* and *Windsor* cases show, procedural rules not only stand to affect individual rights, but national policy as well.

Conclusions

The historical trajectory of rule reform in the United States elucidates the profound effect that targeting the "rules of the game" can have on access to justice. The "right to be heard"—so deeply embedded in our constitutional structure and legal culture—can be easily affected by a variety of procedural changes. As scholars of the civil rules have recently described, "Dismissals at the pleading stage diminish that right. Reduced or eliminated discovery deprives parties of facts they need in order to have a fair hearing. And summary judgments limit access to trials."[159] Yet it is all too easy to overlook this retrenchment strategy.

But analyzing this strategy also unearths the multiplicity of ideological motivations—far beyond mere partisan backlash—that can drive judicial retrenchment. In the battle for authority over the Federal Rules of Civil Procedure, institutional actors either endogenous to the judiciary, or who derived significant benefits from it, drove the initial retrenchment efforts.

Specifically, liberal lawyers and Democrats led judicial retrenchment in the 1970s in an institutional venue largely independent of the Supreme Court. In the 1980s, this coalition was joined by yet more nonideologically motivated actors—namely legal reformers internal to the rulemaking process who sought to adjust the structure of the judiciary so as to better handle the growing burdens upon it. These actors were not motivated by a partisan interest in scaling back the power and scope of judicial authority. Some simply wanted a greater say in the rulemaking process. Others were primarily concerned with protecting the systemic integrity and practical functioning of the judicial system, and still others unwittingly instigated retrenchment by acting to protect their own institutional position. Once these actors reformed the rules process, they opened the door for alignments of actors with intentions that fit a more conventional understanding of political retrenchment. By the mid-1990s, retrenchment efforts were dominated by Republican legislators and lobbyists who wanted to cut down on public interest litigation.

It is important to note that the entrenchment of the civil rules emerged in an unusual environment in American politics. There were very low barriers to authoritative change; the rules committees operated with a high level of deference from others on the grounds that these rules were merely "technical." In addition, the rules proved highly malleable, or easy to convert. As a result, entrepreneurial trial lawyers and judges could easily stretch them to find new ways to bring cases to the federal courts. Ironically, this combination not only set the stage for the development of new judicial powers but also planted the seeds of retrenchment, because this environment made it easy for the courts and lawyers to overreach. This overreaching, in turn, set the stage for the split between trial lawyers, who favored ever-wider access to the courts, and judges, who found themselves swamped by a large influx of claims and were concerned about the functioning of the courts.

Meanwhile, the political environment shifted, as Watergate encouraged Congress to become more concerned about protecting its prerogatives and opening up the rulemaking process. The result was that the barriers for authoritative change rose as fights over the rules shifted to the normal legislative process. This had two effects in terms of institutional change. On the one hand, efforts to make authoritative changes became much less effective, as indicated by the checkered record of tort reform at the federal level, even during periods of unified Republican government.[160] On the other hand, conversion in the Supreme Court emerged as a key mode of retrenchment, as conservative justices developed ways to make dockets more manageable and by constricting access to the courts.

A major reason why there were such low barriers to authoritative change in this case was because the federal rules themselves were long considered to be "purely procedural," technical, and therefore the province of experts. It was these characteristics that gave rulemakers such a high level of discretion that went uninterrupted for so long. Rulemakers eventually overreached—a common hazard of such a situation—and subsequently lost their insularity. But even once control over rulemaking exploded into an institutional battle, and even after Congress began to engage in rulemaking itself, rulemakers retained a fair amount of discretion. When Congress has subsequently diverted its attention to its own rule reform pursuits (as was the case with class action reform), rulemakers have still been able to promulgate rule changes without much attention or interference. The very presence of these malleable, institutional rules that afford those who control them a high degree of discretion and insularity makes the difference in this case, helping to enable reformers in their quest to scale back access to courts. Institutional rules, then, are ideal levers for reform, and controlling them in conditions of relative insularity increases the likelihood of successful institutional change.

In sum, retrenchment of and through the federal civil rules in the years following the New Deal illuminates retrenchment as the product of what might be called an "institutional maintenance" imperative.[161] Foundational efforts to constrict access to courts were born of a concern for the increasingly overburdened legal system in the rights revolution era. The initial groups and government actors involved in retrenchment were on the one hand largely supportive of the expanded rights protections that were the product of the era; on the other hand, however, they also recognized the practical perils that these changes wrought for the judiciary. In seeking to protect the systemic integrity of the justice system by easing the growing burdens of expense, delay, and complex litigation, these groups found themselves sometimes fighting alongside—and sometimes against—lawyers operating with their professional (as opposed to political) interests in mind. As the scope of conflict expanded beyond judges and lawyers, and as institutional maintenance efforts were increasingly intertwined with political battles, more and more groups were drawn into the fray—often unwittingly, or at least without retrenchment as their primary motive.[162] With the continued expansion of the scope of conflict, retrenchment efforts in recent years have fallen into the political alignments and patterns that resonate with the familiar narrative of partisan backlash to the rights revolution; but this is only a very recent phase of what is a much longer and more complicated institutional story.

5

Changing the Venue: The Quasi-Judicial Realm of the Administrative State

Introduction

Just three years after "the switch in time that saved nine," Franklin Roosevelt's newly established administrative state was once again under fierce attack from both New Deal opponents and a legal community accusing him of "totalitarianism and administrative absolutism."[1] The American Bar Association (ABA) put its weight into the passage of the Walter-Logan Bill in December 1940, which would have provided extensive judicial review of administrative agency actions that previously could not be challenged in court. The President, however, vetoed the bill. In part, he justified his actions on the grounds that his own committee had yet to issue its recommendations as to how best to reform the administrative process. But at the same time, his veto was also a sharply worded defense of the regulatory state as one "of the most significant and useful trends of the twentieth century in legal administration" and constituted a pointed attack on the legal establishment, which he claimed "desire to have all processes of government conducted through lawsuits."[2] Were the bill to become law, he argued, the power of agencies to resolve disputes internally would be greatly constrained. This was problematic, to FDR's mind, given that the administrative state "has its origin in the recognition even by the courts themselves that the conventional processes of the courts are not adapted to handling controversies in the mass. Court procedure is adapted to the intensive investigation of individual controversies. But it is impossible to subject the daily routine of fact-finding in many of our agencies to court procedure.

Litigation has become costly beyond the ability of the average person to bear." By contrast, administrative tribunals were designed to simplify and expedite the judicial process with "simple and non-technical hearings [that] take the place of court trials." For FDR and other proponents of the administrative state, this was a crucial innovation.

Roosevelt singled out the legal establishment in particular for carrying on a fight against the hallmark of the New Deal regulatory state, having "never reconciled itself to the existence of the administrative tribunal." Lawyers, he argued, "prefer the stately ritual of the courts, in which lawyers play all the speaking parts, to the simple procedure of administrative hearings which a client can understand and even participate in. Many of the lawyers prefer that decisions be influenced by a shrewd play upon technical rules of evidence in which the lawyers are the only experts."[3] Despite a passionate response from the bill's advocates in the House, who claimed that the president was denying Americans the basic and fundamental right of a day in court, they failed to garner the necessary two-thirds vote to override the veto. For at least another day, Roosevelt's administrative state was saved.[4]

These debates over the powers of the administrative state are part of a broader conversation involving competing understandings about the jurisdiction of the judicial branch, and where, how, and by whom it may properly be altered.[5] The New Deal attack on courts was hardly the first or the last of its kind and is importantly situated in an even broader, historical conversation about whether and when a branch of government may properly delegate its constitutional powers to another—a conversation that predates the birth of FDR's administrative state. For example, as George Lovell has shown, the ambiguity of early 1900s labor statutes like the Clayton Act meant that "legislators deliberately created conditions that empowered judges to make important substantive decisions on labor policy;" and even in creating and empowering administrative bodies like the National Labor Relations Board (with robust power to adjudicate claims in its purview), Congress' decision to provide for some measure of judicial review is indicative of an early, enduring concern with keeping the courts *in* as a check on agency discretion.[6] And, of course, judges themselves were certainly concerned with policing the boundaries of delegation, as evidenced in the famous *Schechter Poultry* decision, wherein the Supreme Court unanimously found Congress' National Industrial Recovery Act to be an impermissible delegation of legislative power to the executive branch.[7]

At the same time, however, legislators have an even longer history of trying to keep the courts *out* of the legislative process. Congress has frequently

included explicit statutory provisions in its legislation that deny judicial
review to parties alleging harm at the hands of an administrative body. For
example, although the Wagner Act has provisions enabling judicial review,
it also gives the National Labor Relations Board (NLRB) "exclusive jurisdiction to prevent and redress unfair labor practices."[8] A 1933 law concerning
the powers of the newly created Veterans Administration explicitly cut the
courts out with virtually no discussion whatsoever, specifying that "no other
official or court of the United States shall have jurisdiction to review" any of
the agency's decisions. And perhaps most prominently, both before and after
the New Deal, legislators have regularly attempted to pass laws and initiate constitutional amendments that aim to strip courts of their jurisdiction
over certain kinds of cases. These efforts began nearly as early as the nation's
founding, prompting particularly dramatic debates in the early 1800s, 30s,
and 70s. As many as seven amendments to the Constitution can be construed as having served to strip courts of jurisdiction, ranging over time from
the Eleventh Amendment in 1795 to the Twenty-Sixth Amendment in 1971.[9]
Unsurprisingly, "court curbing" bills became a hallmark of the modern era
and were introduced frequently during the Civil Rights era and at present,
largely in response to partisan disagreement with controversial Supreme
Court rulings involving school prayer, busing, abortion,[10] and later gay
marriage.

Yet despite the fact that it is widely noted that these measures rarely make
it out of committee,[11] current research on these grand acts of legislative court
curbing dominates the academic literature when it comes to studying judicial retrenchment.[12] While these proposals have at times succeeded in severely
limiting access to courts to groups of litigants (the recent Antiterrorism and
Effective Death Penalty Act is a prominent example), these accounts of court
curbing have failed to capture what has become one of the most extensive
shifts in institutional authority away from the judicial branch: Congress'
increasing willingness to pass laws that restrict judicial review of agency decision making. As part of the development of our now vast regulatory apparatus, Congress created hundreds of administrative agencies, with over thirty
housing their own administrative law judges (prominently among them the
NLRB, the Social Security Administration, the Departments of Agriculture,
Interior, Labor, Transportation, Justice, Health and Human Services, and the
Environmental Protection Agency) and many others that statutorily insulate
their decision making from judicial review. In these quasi-adjudicative processes, most additional review takes place within the given agency—not the
courts—by its own internal appellate body.[13]

In this chapter, I examine the jurisdiction stripping effects inherent in the creation of the administrative state as it began in the postbellum era and matured in the New Deal and Cold War years. Although this is a widely studied, transformative moment in American politics, it has surprisingly been largely ignored as a powerful form of jurisdiction stripping.[14] But it warrants a closer look. The growth and development of a more traditional administrative state brought with it a fundamental shift in the venue where many disputes were adjudicated, namely from traditional legal proceedings in a courtroom to adjudication by regulatory agencies themselves, under the authority of the executive branch. In general, the more that disputes are resolved by agencies themselves, the less access individuals have to courts for the adjudication of claims—and this may come at the cost of losing fundamental rights to due process, a right to a fair trial by a jury of one's peers, and a constitutional "check" on the activities of the elected branches.

Perhaps the clearest evidence stressing the importance of viewing the development of the administrative state through the lens of judicial retrenchment is the deep concern and downright hostility that motivated the legal community to fight to constrain these developments. No sooner had the dust settled from the New Deal era power struggles between FDR's administration and the Supreme Court than did another wave of legal reformers organize, deeply concerned that the executive branch was appropriating for itself powers that, constitutionally, rightly rest with the judiciary. As a prominent member of the ABA described in 1935, "The trouble is not with administrative tribunals; the trouble lies in the breadth of power given to such tribunals," for if an agency decision regarding a statute is *not* subject to judicial review, "the jurisdiction of the Courts is gone."[15]

The ABA's first fight for legislation to constrain the degree to which agencies engaged in judicial functions failed in 1940. It would have greater success later with the passage of the Administrative Procedure Act (APA) of 1946, but that too did not go far in assuaging the ABA's concern that the right to trial be protected from perceived encroachments by the executive branch. And despite decades more of efforts to "proceduralize" agency adjudication, the legal community—joined by a varied and sometimes counterintuitive coalition of liberal rights revolution activists and the business community—has largely failed to amend the APA in any significant way. During the Civil Rights era, lawyers and activists were comforted by the fact that, if nothing else, the nation's courts kept a watchful eye as agencies themselves resolved a notable swath of what once were traditional legal claims; but in the modern era of conservative courts concerned with keeping "political" matters in the hands of the elected branches, judicial review of agency activity has become far more discretionary. In short, both courts and the organized bar saw the rise of the administrative state as a direct threat to their authority, and many today continue to view it as problematic for access to justice in the United States.

But although increasingly routine, and often sold—as many retrenchment efforts are—as a more expedient way to handle legal disputes, this shift in venue is not unproblematic, and has led to "an unprecedented debate over the constitutional allocation of federal, executive, and legislative powers."[16] In addition to the problems of political accountability that came with the development of independent agencies, then, the very existence of agencies threatened long-cherished constitutional concepts like separation of powers and due process, which were considered to be put at risk where agencies combined executive and judicial functions by engaging in adjudication that is informal compared to that of the judiciary.[17] Honoring these concepts in their historic form, however, directly conflicted with the very impetus for the New Deal, as responding to these concerns would mean dampening the government's ability to act in response to a quickly changing society with serious economic problems. As the initial crisis of the New Deal resolved, however, the critique of regulatory politics shifted from concerns about the appropriate realm of administrative activity to the discretion that agencies had gained in both their rulemaking and adjudicative processes. To address these concerns, Congress passed the APA in 1946 with the overall purpose of governing the ways in which administrative agencies could propose and establish regulations. The APA is considered the foundation of "administrative law" in the United States, "a complex mixture of constitutional, statutory, regulatory, and 'common law' principles that govern the structure, decision processes, and behavior of administrative agencies,"[18] as well as the "bill of rights for the new regulatory state."[19] In practice, it gives procedural protection to interests affected by agency decisions by providing a new statutory cause of action to obtain judicial review against administrative agencies. Because modern agencies are considered to perform legislative, executive, and judicial roles, quests to legitimate and detract from their authority have motivated consistent reform efforts since the APA's adoption.

The APA itself has been characterized as "unusually impervious to change,"[20] subject to only a handful of successful legislative amendments. But where legislators have failed or refrained from amending the overarching law itself, they have instead (1) used enabling statutes to declare agency decision making "conclusive" and therefore exempt from the APA's provisions for judicial review, and (2) have found it politically expedient to allow the other branches to develop reforms within its purview—a delegation of authority that, when combined with a lack of overt legislative reform of the APA, has left the judiciary in a position to innovate. While the APA codifies a general presumption that final administrative action is judicially reviewable, lawmakers have often skirted this requirement by taking advantage of an exception also created by the law, allowing Congress to "preclude judicial review" explicitly in statutes governing the powers of new administrative bodies (the creation of the Veterans Administration is a notable example). In an attempt to contain this, the ABA and other advocates for reform largely directed their efforts toward creating uniform "rules for administrative procedure" that—much as with the Federal Rules of Civil Procedure—would give the legal community a hand in protecting core judicial functions.

But when the ABA and its allies in Congress failed in the 1960s and 70s to codify a set of administrative procedural rules, agencies themselves maintained a high degree of discretion. At the time, however, the Supreme Court carefully oversaw and often constrained that discretion with active judicial review; it read the provisions of the APA governing "statutory preclusion" and "matters committed to agency discretion" narrowly, making it relatively more difficult for agencies to be insulated from judicial review; and the Court broadly supported making the rulemaking process more transparent to the public. But in the 1980s, the Supreme Court adopted a more restrained approach to the review of administrative decisions, restricting or eliminating almost all of the activist techniques previously employed to police agency discretion. In so doing, the courts now often act as arbitrators of linguistic disputes, leaving larger questions of both law and policy to the quasi-judicial adjudication of agencies themselves. Further, in creating doctrines like "Chevron deference," the Court in effect created a legal tool that has arguably served to camouflage the ideological component to an individual judge's choice as to whether or not to defer to agency decisions. These shifts have—to varying degrees at different historic moments—led to a persistent pattern of reduced access to courts for those alleging that their rights have not been protected as a result of agency action or inaction.

Agency Jurisdiction in the New Administrative State

In 1946 Congress passed the APA to govern the ways in which administrative agencies propose and establish regulations. The APA also establishes a process for judicial review of agency activity and, in so doing, provides procedural

protection to those affected by agency decisions. As the "founding document" for administrative law, the basic purposes of the APA are (1) to require
agencies to keep the public informed of their organization, procedures, and
rules; (2) to provide for public participation in the rulemaking process; (3) to
establish uniform standards for the conduct of formal rulemaking and adjudication; and (4) to define the scope of judicial review.[21] When enacted, the
act was praised as "the most important statute affecting the administration of
justice in the Federal field since the passage of the Judiciary Act of 1789" and
as "a comprehensive charter of private liberty."

Under the act, federal administrative activity is broken into two parts: adjudication and rulemaking. Adjudication, or the "agency process for the formu-
lation of an order," is considered either "formal" or "informal," with formal
adjudication giving rise to trial-like hearings with witness testimony, a written
record, and a final decision that is subject to judicial review (with exceptions).
Formal agency rulemaking consists of procedures similar to those for formal
adjudication, but with the goal of producing a rule for prescribing, interpreting, and/or implementing a law or policy. Rules that are a product of formal
rulemaking under the APA are often called "substantive" or "legislative" rules,
in that they are considered to create new law and are binding on the public and the agency. Importantly, these rules are made on the record after an
agency hearing, which makes the process relatively transparent. The general
review provisions of Section 10 of the APA also create a legal cause of action,
establishing that "a person suffering legal wrong because of agency action, or
adversely affected or aggrieved by agency action within the meaning of a relevant statute, is entitled to judicial review thereof," particularly when "there is
no other adequate remedy in a court ... subject to judicial review."[22] In order
for the courts to overturn a formal agency decision, however, they must find
it to be "arbitrary and capricious, an abuse of discretion, or otherwise not in
accordance with the law."[23]

With informal adjudication, which characterizes most agency activity,
decisions are made using negotiations, conferences, and inspections, and
these procedures are not outlined in the APA. Informal agency rulemaking
consists of procedures similar to those for formal rulemaking, often following
a "notice and comment" model, but do not require a courtroom-style hearing. These so-called interpretive rules are typically statements that advise the
public of the agency's construction of its statute, and these rules and take various forms, including handbooks designed to guide in the process of applying
agency regulations, opinion letters, policy statements, and published guidance documents. Informal rulemaking may follow a quasi-legislative process

similar to that of formal rulemaking, but it is not required to. And generally speaking, where the role of courts is concerned, interpretative rules are not subject to judicial review under the APA.

More often than not, the courts permit individual agencies to choose which type of decision making process to use in a given situation. An entire area of court doctrine, beginning with *Vermont Yankee Nuclear Power Corp. v. Natural Resources Defense Council, Inc.* in 1978, has developed around the question of whether or not the courts owe discretion to agencies overall or in any particular type of case, as well as whether or not federal courts can impose additional procedural requirements on administrative agencies beyond those set out in the APA.[24] Through what is widely known as "Chevron deference" (named for the case that doctrinalized the test),[25] the Court has sought to balance the procedural requirements of the APA with the issue of what any particular instance of agency action or inaction means for the constitutional guarantee of procedural due process and the protection of rights. These factors constrain the ways in which agencies can act to limit liberties, rights, or property interests, and in general, judicial review tends to be more stringent for formal proceedings and questions of law as opposed to questions of fact or exercises of discretion.[26]

The highly durable and entrenched nature of the APA, however, is in many ways misleading, as the legislation was very much a bitter compromise and the product of an intensely political debate years in the making, described as "a pitched political battle for the life of the New Deal."[27] The political processes leading to the passage of the act mirrored the growth of the administrative state, which itself grew in a series of fits and starts. Questions of administrative power raised important issues of constitutional legitimacy, judicial control, and effective governance long before the first proliferation of federal regulatory agencies in the latter half of the 1800s. *Marbury v. Madison*, in addition to establishing judicial review, also involved a suit against an agency official, namely the secretary of state.[28] As Jerry Mashaw has argued, national administrative discretion percolated throughout the antebellum era in policy domains including embargos, commerce, and property, and courts at all levels participated by allowing the early administrative state to take root.[29] But efforts to establish the regulatory state's intrusion into the budding railroad industry, banks, and insurance companies remained largely at the state level during that time period, and were rarely successful.[30] The small size and minimal capacity of the federal government, in turn, led it to rely frequently on a decentralized system of "courts and parties" that importantly promoted the development of a national economy without the presence of a large bureaucratic system.[31]

In this institutional arrangement, courts were "the American surrogate for a more fully developed administrative apparatus."[32] But with the onset of industrialization and the demands it created for centralized governance to intervene and remedy the inequities caused by unregulated capitalism, "the less appropriate the structure of courts and parties became.[33]

By the end of the nineteenth century, the pressures of industrialism, escalating strife between employers and laborers, and growing Progressive movement opposition to entrenched party leaders and judges shifted the conversation toward the inevitability of a new American administrative state. The establishment of the Interstate Commerce Commission (ICC) in 1887 was followed by a series of laws that gradually enabled its construction. Importantly, these same laws also began to strip federal courts of jurisdiction.[34] In 1914 Congress passed the Clayton Antitrust Act, which restricted the authority of courts to enjoin labor strikes, and on the eve of the New Deal it passed the Norris-La Guardia Act in another attempt to restrict the jurisdiction of federal courts to enjoin strikes in labor disputes.[35] Notably, however, these efforts to constrict jurisdiction unfolded alongside an enduring concern that courts had a role to play in the developing American state. For example, the Supreme Court struck down key provisions of the ICC and Clayton Antitrust Act, and Congress enabled continued court involvement by providing important ambiguity and exceptions in their laws that allowed for—and perhaps even invited—judicial intervention.[36]

With the impending New Deal, then, "it was no longer a question of whether or not America was going to build a state that could support administrative power but of who was going to control administrative power in the new state that was to be built."[37] It was also a time of great transformation for the courts: as the famous lawyer and statesman Elihu Root said in his presidential address to the ABA in 1916, "We are entering upon the creation of a body of administrative law quite different in its machinery, its remedies, and its necessary safeguards from the old methods of specific statutes enforced by the courts."[38] While the major regulatory initiatives of the Progressive era began to make inroads for government intervention in specific areas of the economy, the election of Franklin Roosevelt in 1932 fundamentally transformed the American regulatory state through the New Deal agenda. Legislation like the National Industrial Recovery Act and the Agricultural Adjustment Act "were regulations of a new magnitude," aimed to control the market in a far more comprehensive way; and the passage of the National Labor Relations Act, followed by the subsequent decision of the Supreme Court to defer to the authority of Congress to make determinations of what constituted proper regulation of interstate commerce, firmly entrenched the new bureaucratic order.[39]

But no sooner did the administrative state rise than did opposition mobilize in response to curb its reach. A 1929 proposal by Senator Norris, chairman of the Judiciary Committee, to create a "Court of Administrative Justice" was fundamentally designed to encourage judicial review of the conduct of these newly empowered administrative agencies. Although the bill (which would have merged the Court of Claims, the Board of Tax Appeals, the Customs Court, and the Court of Patent Appeals into one court) stemmed from opposition to agency policies, it received bipartisan support. But given the relative lack of New Deal opponents willing to vote for a law that would encourage active oversight of agency proceedings, Congress took no action on the bill. Nonetheless, the Norris Bill would become the basis for a spate of further legislative attempts to exercise *some* control over agencies in the early and mid-1930s. It was reintroduced in 1933 as the Logan Bill, largely fueled by what was considered a nonpartisan interest in the improvement of administrative procedures. But this bill—which notably sought once again to give courts clear-cut, centralized power to review agency decisions—also failed due to the New Deal's popularity.[40]

Concerned members of Congress were soon joined by another powerful group, itself deeply suspicious of the adjudicative power of administrative agencies. Since early in the 1930s, the ABA had expressed concern with the degree to which agency administrators were engaging in judicial activities. As Morton Horwitz points out, "The rise of administrative regulation represented a renewed threat to common law conceptions of legality, which had already resisted the earlier challenge of codification."[41] This fear, combined with a wave of political opposition from the legal community to the implementation of the New Deal, prompted the ABA to form a Special Committee on Administrative Law in 1933. The ABA was particularly concerned with whether the executive branch was eroding judicial independence and speculated that combining judicial, legislative, and executive functions within one government body would leave courts without the jurisdiction to intervene in agency decision making. Committee chairman Louis Caldwell worried that agency adjudication amounted to "something that looks like a court and acts like a court but somehow escapes being classified as a court whenever you attempt to impose any limitations on its power." Given that agency adjudication transferred power from lawyers to bureaucrats, thereby standing to decrease the importance of courts and lawyers, the committee also expressed some fear for the fate of its profession, prematurely lamenting "dark days which are said to be facing the legal profession."[42] To the committee's mind, there were three possible solutions for these problems: stricter procedural rules for agency adjudication, enhanced judicial review, or the creation of separate administrative court.[43] The committee settled on the third option in 1934, joining with members of Congress and issuing a report that recommended the creation of a federal administrative court. Preferable to administrative tribunals, they argued, an administrative court would exist truly independently from the legislative and executive branches in a way that agency tribunals by nature could not.[44]

The ABA continued to recommend a separate court throughout the mid-1930s, at times lending its support to similar proposals from members of Congress. In 1936 the committee (although not the ABA as a whole) opted to back the Logan-Celler Administrative Court Bill. Now with the support of Emanuel Celler, a New Deal Democrat with a legal background and an interest in legal reform, this more extreme proposal pushed to extract further jurisdiction from agencies and proposed the creation of two additional courts to remove specific complaints from the realm of agency adjudication.[45] Although the bill died in committee, the ABA-backed legislative coalition did succeed in passing the Federal Register Act in 1935, requiring the publication of all agency rules and regulations in order to ensure transparency.[46]

With Justice Roberts' "switch in time that saved nine"[47] and the aftermath of a court-packing plan that politically weakened FDR, this reform movement changed in the late 1930s in important ways. Given that a Supreme Court–led approach to reform would now be unlikely to succeed, the ABA abandoned its support for an administrative court in favor of a stricter bill that would require that the decisions of every department of the federal government that housed its own review board be subject to judicial review. In the proposal, any citizen "aggrieved" by an agency could demand a hearing with a three-person board, the outcome of which would be subject to review in court. Where agency rulemaking was concerned, the ABA committee also recommended public hearings in order to ensure further transparency.

In 1938, however, the Supreme Court decision *Morgan v. United States* set off a new controversy between the Roosevelt administration and the courts. The Court, warning of a "vast expansion" in the field of administrative regulation, substantially widened the scope of judicial inquiry into the workings of administrative bodies in its decision, setting aside an order that established the maximum rates that commission agents could charge farmers at a Kansas City stockyard. Chief Justice Hughes argued that the agency had not provided a full hearing to the aggrieved parties, something he argued was an "inexorable safeguard" that was "essential alike to the legal validity of the administrative regulation and to the maintenance of public confidence in the value and soundness of this important government process."[48] Agencies, Hughes argued, *must* use procedures that followed "the ordinary legal manner" of common law courts; for "whatever the shortcomings of the courts, and whatever the need of administrative bodies, it is still the courts which stand out as exemplars of the tradition of independence and impartiality."[49] Secretary of Agriculture Henry A. Wallace protested, prophesying "yet another battle" between the Roosevelt administration and the Supreme Court.[50] This decision prompted several agencies to make revisions to their internal procedures (with the NLRB notably withdrawing several cases that it had before appeals courts), and it prompted President Roosevelt to create a commission to study the "extent to which decisions of administrative agencies are reviewable in the courts."[51]

With Roscoe Pound taking control of the ABA Committee in 1938, the ABA as a whole continued to criticize agencies publicly and to highlight the importance of independent judicial review, now demanding far more expansive judicial oversight over all agency orders under a proposed "clearly erroneous" scope of review.[52] Pound's 1938 report was highly incendiary, explicitly attacking the legitimacy of judicial activity within administrative agencies and likening administrative "absolutism" to the type of law and politics supported by Marxists and judges in the Soviet Union. He further asserted that unless "the bar takes upon itself to act, there is nothing to check the tendency of administrative bureaus to extend the scope of their operations indefinitely even to the extent of supplanting our traditional judicial regime by an administrative regime."[53] The report listed and lamented various problematic "tendencies" of administrative officials (such as their tendency to decide cases without conducting hearings), many of which, if true, reflected a gross lack of protection for procedural rights and due process by agency officials. Ironically, some of the "tendencies" were features shared by the judiciary, and other tendencies were more likely the result of abuses by particular individuals in places of power.[54] But nonetheless, and although other prominent law professors like Louis Jaffe and James Landis took issue with Pound's characterizations, his view became the official position of the ABA and the basis for the organization's own legislative proposal.[55] As Morton Horwitz describes, the APA later became a triumph of the Pound Report by reestablishing a legalist mindset that attacked administrative law as part of a larger attack on the regulatory state.[56]

By the end of the decade, New Deal opponents in Congress were stepping up their attacks against numerous agencies, most notably the NLRB, which was continually a lightening rod for conservatives who believed that the Roosevelt administration was imposing socialist forms of economic policy.[57] Committee hearings by Virginia Democrat Howard W. Smith attempted to expose the NLRB for being politically and unethically tied to the AFL-CIO and for failing to create a proper separation between judicial and administrative functions.[58] The committee went so far as to recommend stripping the board of its prosecuting function. Senator Robert Wagner—who five years prior had led the fight to create the NLRB—responded to the proposed amendments critically, calling them an attack on the rights of workers and "a feast for a few lawyers, an insuperable problem for the courts, an insurmountable obstacle to any efficient administration of the law, a blessing to those anxious to disobey the law and a merry-go-round for the employers and workers affected by the law."[59] He proposed increasing the size of the board and providing more bodies to better oversee any potential errors in agency discretion instead.

Meanwhile, lawyers were also dividing along the lines of New Deal supporters and opponents. On the one hand, the Committee on Administrative Law of the Federal Bar Association surprised the legal community by opposing the ABA's administrative law bill, describing it as "impracticable and not in the public interest; and that should such legislation be enacted by any chance the work of a majority of the Federal agencies would be substantially handicapped." On the other hand, a committee minority report countered that "it is the right of every American, rich or poor, weak or powerful, to contest in the courts the legality and fairness of any administrative action." The minority report complained further that government attorneys were currently shut out of a process where "administrative officials raise the technical issue, wherever possible, that the courts do not have jurisdiction to review the particular Federal administrative decisions or, if this cannot be raised, they seek to limit the extent to which the courts may examine the administrative record and findings of facts to see whether such findings are supported by substantial evidence, are not clearly erroneous, and that a full and fair hearing has been accorded."[60] It argued that the administrative law bill was problematic in that it would "place all government administrators on the 'spot' ... through the requirement that their handiwork in the exercise of quasi-legislative or quasi-judicial functions may be subjected, if the aggrieved individual so desires, to the acid test on the merits of the controversy (not the technical points of jurisdiction) before the judicial branch of the Government which is wholly free and uninfluenced."[61]

The legislation that ultimately came before Congress, the Walter-Logan Bill, was considered "the high water mark of judicialization," a reflection of the ABA's desire to seek "remedies in the form of procedures that would grant individuals and firms greater rights within the regulatory process, greater access to the courts for judicial review, and stronger tools for the judiciary to review and intervene in agency procedures."[62] Accordingly, the bill focused mostly on providing opportunities for judicial review, both at the level of procedure (requiring, for example, standards for hearing evidence), and more broadly in giving jurisdiction to the Court of Appeals to review all agency rules and regulations. Agency officials charged that the bill would effectively incapacitate agencies by causing extreme delay and requested that consideration of the bill be postponed until the Attorney General's committee report was issued. But the ABA continued to link administrative governance with "absolutism;" in his comments on the bill, chairman of the ABA's Special Committee on Administrative Law, O. R. McGuire, referenced Sir Thomas Moore, who began a long line of "utopian" propaganda joined by Communists, Fascists, and dictators who are all "united in their dislike of both law and lawyers."[63] He claimed that "administrative absolutism" now results in "the suppression of religious worship, the confiscation of property, the persecution of races, the concentration camps, the exiles to the snows of Siberia or to the burning sands of the Sahara, the deaths in foreign legions for causes not of their concern, and the firing squads."[64] The U.S. administrative state, he argued, had replaced "our tripartite governmental system, under the traditions of the common law," with "an Executive-controlled Government on the model of imperial Rome." As such, the ABA would serve as a final line of defense against what he called sequel to the court-packing debate of 1937: "the constitutional struggle, 1938."[65]

The ABA was opposed both by liberal lawyers from the Federal Bar Association and National Lawyers Guild and federal agency heads, who believed the legislation was designed to take away their ability to implement policy swiftly and efficiently and would allow far more leeway for courts to use judicial review to reject agency decisions. Chester Lane, general counsel of the Securities and Exchange Commission (SEC), complained that the law would allow courts to intervene even when the agency came to a conclusion based on "substantial evidence" if that court "just don't think it was right." As he saw it, this would mean that "the court of appeals, which has not had the expert equipment to handle the case in the first place, which has not seen the witness, not known just what was going on, may remake the findings to its own desire even though they are supported by substantial evidence."[66]

Nonetheless, the House Judiciary Committee (including northern Democrats, many of whom had ties to the ABA) approved the bill.[67] On

the House floor, opponents made clear that they understood that the bill
was meant to constrain the New Deal and were acutely fearful that the bill
could have the effect of hampering labor's power in the interest of big business, who expected to get better results from courts than agencies.[68] Given
that the ABA and anti-labor groups were closely allied at the time, opponents
accused supporters of promoting the bill because it benefited lawyers, and
ultimately feared that the bill would introduce judicial totalitarianism by
allowing the judiciary to paralyze executive agencies. Supporters advocated
slowing down agency decision making to help ensure that rules and regulations adhered to the legislation passed by Congress and would therefore
be faithful in protecting individual rights. The House passed the bill, with
Republicans and Southern Democrats in favor, and about three-fourths of
northern Democrats against it. The Senate version of the bill also passed in
1939, but by a narrow margin of two votes.[69]

As discussed above, President Roosevelt vetoed the bill—fiercely attacking
the legal community and defending the regulatory state in the process—and
he also proposed that his own committee take responsibility for reviewing and
improving agency decision making. Unsurprisingly, the recommendations
from the President's Committee on Administrative Procedure were far less
extreme than the proposals that had inspired the Walter-Logan Bill. Notably,
the committee proposed leaving significantly more discretion to agencies. The
committee report did not recommend expanding judicial review of administrative action, arguing that "further extension of court review would result
in needless litigation and would place an undue and improper burden upon
the courts."[70] Instead, the committee suggested requiring the publication of
agency rules and interpretations, using hearing commissioners for adjudicative proceedings, and creating an office with the power to appoint said hearing commissioners.[71] A minority report written by Carl McFarland, former
Assistant Attorney General; E. Blythe Stasson, the dean of the University of
Michigan Law School; and Arthur T. Vanderbilt, a former ABA president,
criticized other members of the committee for falling short in terms of proposing meaningful reform, arguing that the report recommendations "cannot achieve the complete independence that is essential for the exercise of the
adjudicatory function." They contended instead that agency hearings must be
"judicial in nature," with their conduct governed by "the accepted canons of
judicial ethics"; and until such time as Congress was willing to make effective
reforms, they recommended greater "availability and scope of judicial review
in order to reduce uncertainty and variability."[72] But as Paul Verkuil has noted,
the real significance of the administration's report was that it formulated an

argument resisting the judicial model of administration as put forth in the Walter-Logan Bill, asserting a new "independent" model of administrative procedure that emphasized procedure over adversarial hearings. This was, in fact, the model later adopted with the passage of the APA.[73]

Interestingly, this model—which would largely insulate agency decision making from judicial review—had both historical weight and, later, support from the Supreme Court as well. The "common law of judicial review" that predated provisions for judicial review under the APA required courts to determine, prior to hearing the merits of a case, whether Congress had intended to authorize judicial review of the particular administrative action in question. As such, Congress was considered free to insulate agency decision making, whether explicitly or implicitly (in the congressional record) when passing laws enabling new agencies. The Court supported this approach in 1943 in *Switchmen's Union of North America v. National Mediation Board*, holding that the Board's decision to certify a union to represent railway men under the Railway Labor Act was not judicially reviewable.[74] From the perspective of the broader legal community, however, an explicit provision for judicial review could (and should) supersede the Court's position.

By 1944 the ABA nonetheless supported the passage of the proposed APA as a way to eliminate the existence of "kangaroo courts," complaining in particular about the Office of Price Administration, which had recently charged a group of wholesale meat dealers in Chicago and was accused of denying counsel and court reporters at their hearing. The proposed legislation was aimed, according to ABA President Joseph W. Henderson, "at the uncontrolled bureaucrats who are disregarding the rights of citizens and regimenting their lives."[75] Months later, he declared before the ABA's annual meeting that the rights of individuals to liberty had been "seriously affected" by "the rise and growth of administrative agencies which cannot be curbed by the courts or sufficiently controlled by Congress," and that "lawyers above all other citizens should be vigilant and bold ... and should never be cynical, indifferent or timid in the presence of any piecemeal breaking-down of our cherished liberty or the constitutional system which made our freedom real."[76]

But what ultimately passed Congress in 1946 had important strands of both the Roosevelt proposal *and* that of the ABA.[77] On the one hand, the Administrative Procedure Act pleased New Deal opponents by specifying that formal agency processes were to be governed by trial-like procedures that would be subject to judicial review. The APA granted the judiciary the presumptive reviewability of all final agency actions and provided broad standing for affected parties seeking judicial oversight. In total, the APA's grant of power to the judiciary stipulates that reviewing courts shall decide "all relevant questions of law, including the interpretation of constitutional or statutory provisions and the determination of the meaning or applicability of any agency action." The general review provisions of Section 10 effectively codify a presumption that final administrative action is judicially reviewable and create a cause of action for those "suffering legal wrong because of an agency action," as well as for review of "final agency action for which there is no other adequate remedy in court."[78] As Cass Sunstein has described, these general review provisions were especially important "in light of the awkward constitutional position of the administrative agency" and no doubt appealed to those concerned because of the "perceived need to constrain the exercise of discretionary power by administrative agencies" that the provisions sought to address.[79]

The APA *did* recognize, however, that Congress may, within constitutional limits, preclude or restrict judicial review; and if the statute at hand does "preclude judicial review" within the meaning of Section 10, the law affords no access to the courts. Importantly, the terms of these exceptions— which include statutes that preclude judicial review, as well as those where agency action is "committed to agency discretion by law"—would become the focus of much Supreme Court attention and contention in years to come. But in general, the explicit inclusion of a role for courts led many groups to celebrate the APA, even labeling it an industry "bill of rights" because they believed it forced agencies to be more accountable.[80] The business community, for example, had criticized agencies as biased by the discretion of the administrators, arguing that testimony from government staff members was "naturally prejudiced in that they had to consider their source of employment," a consideration that led the prosecutor, plaintiff, and judge to all side against the industry.[81]

Nonetheless, there were also important liberal victories. On adjudication, the Pound/ABA coalition lost in its demand for a separate tribunal.[82] The act also reinforced the liberal demand that rulemaking by agencies be considered an explicit and legitimate delegation of Congress' lawmaking power.[83] Moreover, the Walter-Logan coalition lost out on another point; all agency activity that was considered to fall in "the vast realm of informal adjudication" was not to be considered as governed by the APA.[84] This, too, was ultimately a liberal victory, as it favored agency discretion.

In passing the APA, Congress clearly believed that it was both providing a new statutory cause of action for judicial review against administrative agencies and also limiting the ability of courts to make the law that would govern what occurred in such cases. That is, the APA sought to define the scope of its powers of judicial review. As one member of Congress summarized, "In the all-important field of judicial review, section 10 is a complete statement of the subject. It prescribes briefly when there may be judicial review and how far the courts may go in examining into a given case."[85]

Why did the 1946 act pass—with no formal vote—after nearly two decades of legislative battle and with little congressional debate, especially in the Senate? As we have seen, the most ardent New Deal Democrats opposed procedural limits on agencies until 1946 because these limits were perceived as a direct assault on the implementation of New Deal policy. Because they were secure in their political control of government in the early New Deal years, they did not see it necessary to sacrifice or compromise. By 1941 a barrage of public criticism left New Deal supporters reliant on the president's veto. By 1946, however, their numbers in both houses and their political security had eroded, and faced with the probability of a Republican president, many New Dealers supported the APA, favoring administrative constraints on a soon-to-be president whose policy goals would likely be at odds with the New Deal. This also explains why they supported a compromise that at least somewhat favored review by courts, for a Republican-controlled agency could sabotage New Deal programs by "interpreting" statutes narrowly. In addition, as FDR had appointed eight of the nine Supreme Court justices and 184 federal and appeals court judges, New Deal Democrats felt that their causes stood a better chance with the courts, heavily populated by judges sympathetic to the New Deal. As McNollgast has argued, "By 1946, the New Dealers in Congress had an interest in consolidating their policy gains against the possible antipathy of a Republican presidency, and they could finally count on the courts to favor New Deal programs in adjudicating procedural provisions."[86]

The APA, then, was a hard-fought compromise that ended an era and began a new one. In terms of judicial retrenchment, it is clear that, from the very origins of the modern administrative state, the legal community viewed the creation of agencies empowered to adjudicate disputes internally as a development that shifted the work of the courts away from the judiciary, with the consequence of constricting access to courts for aggrieved individuals. While the APA was very much the product of compromise and therefore mixed in its results, it did codify a role for the courts in the administrative state. However, early efforts to effectively narrow or proceduralize agency adjudication failed. With that in mind, the bar association launched a second series of attempts to "judicialize" administrative procedure and therefore exert additional control over agency decision making in the decades that followed.

The Judicialization of Administrative Procedure

Given that it was the product of significant compromise, the APA has proven remarkably durable. Congress has only substantively altered it on three occasions, none of which provided significant changes to the substance of the law. But the living consequences of the APA have transformed dramatically since the 1940s. Despite little change from Congress, the act has in many ways become "judicialized." As prominent administrative law scholars have commented, the reality is that "perhaps about nine-tenths of American administrative law is judge-made law, the other tenth statutory."[87] What accounts, then, for the development of greater judicial control over administrative decision making in the years following the passage of the APA?

Importantly, neither the ABA nor other opponents of the administrative state were content with the terms of the law. Shortly after its passage, Senator Pat McCarran of Nevada, the Senate sponsor of the law, continued to attack the regulatory state, indicating to the bar association that further revision of the act was most certainly necessary and arguing that both legislators and courts were left out of the administrative process with little vital work to do. Assuming the position that where law ends, arbitrary power begins, he proposed a return to "the ordinary courts of the land" as well as the creation of new courts that would serve to take back the judicial function from agencies.[88] Roscoe Pound saw what was accomplished in the APA a necessary step toward making administrative law "law in the lawyer's sense," but cautioned that courts and lawyers should remain vigilant "to prevent the setting up of an administrative regime free of constitutional and statutory checks."[89] Judge William L. Ransom, editor of the *American Bar Association Journal*, urged Congress to assure the ABA of "the substance and reality of plenary review by law-governed Courts," since "judicial abdication and agency manipulation are defeating and denying the intended actuality of review."[90] A few years later, the ABA once more increased its pressure on the administrative state, conducting a test of examiners in fourteen federal agencies, and making national news with its findings that only 70 percent of the examiners were qualified to adjudicate (within the NLRB, the test found only half of the examiners to be qualified).[91] Defenders of the courts derided administrators for falsely claiming the mantle of "expert" as a way to mask their partisan biases. "They sit as judges in their own cause," Welburn Maycock, the general counsel to the Democratic National Committee, told a conference of judges in the summer of 1949, whereas "it is the judicial process that strives to protect the liberties of the people."[92]

Despite position-taking on behalf of individual members, Congress as a whole largely stayed out of these debates, allowing the other branches of government to deal with crises that emerged under the APA. Most importantly, Congress was willing to allow both the executive and judicial branches to make extra-legislative changes to the law, a process that began almost immediately after the APA's passage. In response to the compromise that constituted the act, the *Attorney General's Manual on the Administrative Procedure Act*, published in 1947, attempted to appease an uneasy bar and courts. To this end, when writing the manual, Attorney General Clark "shrewdly characterized the APA provisions governing judicial review as merely a 'restatement' and thereby invited courts and the bar to treat the Act as something less than a statute, as subservient to judge-made doctrine."[93] At the time, of course, there was no evidence that the APA was simply a restatement; but the characterization nonetheless went a long way in suggesting to the courts that the APA was to be considered less binding than your average statute.

Characterizing the law in this way worked. The Supreme Court in particular wasted no time before handing down several decisions that sought to control the exercise of administrative discretion by "judicializing" agency adjudication.[94] This judicialization took three forms. First, as early as 1950, the Supreme Court began to insist upon a broader range of procedural safeguards than those required by the APA. For example, in *Wong Yang Sung v. McGrath*, the Court required that the INS provide a deportation hearing even though the Immigration Act did not require it. As the Supreme Court saw it, the APA was intended to reconcile two "evils": (1) a lack of uniformity of procedure, and (2) a lack of standardization of administrative practice across agencies. Given this, and given that the Immigration Act did not specify a particular form of adjudication for deportations, the Supreme Court reasoned that the APA must do so, as the due process clause requires a hearing of some kind in all cases.[95]

Second, the Supreme Court was quick to question the standards of evidence that agencies used in their hearings. In *Universal Camera Corp. v. NLRB*, the Court reiterated its duty to defer to agencies' findings of fact (as per the APA), but it also indicated that it would only do so where such findings were supported by "substantial evidence on the record considered as a whole."[96] Third and finally, the Court also began to demand a clear statement of legislative purpose as a means of restraining agency discretion in cases where fundamental liberties were at stake. This trend toward balancing the provisions of the APA with the protection of basic rights was apparent by the end of the 1950s. In two notable First Amendment cases—*Kent v. Dulles*

(1958) and *Greene v. McElroy* (1959)—the Supreme Court struck down decisions of the Secretary of State on the grounds that Congress had not explicitly authorized constricting individual liberty as far as the State Department
had.[97] In all, these cases represent the first judicial efforts to answer the question of how best to hold administrators legally accountable under the APA.
These efforts continued to proliferate due to the general political momentum
that fueled a growth in judicial activism in the years to follow. Still, the initial
process of "judicializing" the APA was not seamless; in 1948, for example, the
Court operationalized the "statutory preclusion" clause of the APA when it
held that the Alien Enemy Act precluded judicial review of a wartime alien
deportation order.[98]

Efforts to involve the judiciary in the administrative process came from
more than just the Supreme Court, however. With the Republican take-over
of government in 1952, conservatives had high hopes that newly elected
President Dwight Eisenhower would promptly take on bureaucracy, which
was already gaining its corrupt, inefficient, "red tape-bound" reputation for
the greater public.[99] While Eisenhower's efforts to refine the administrative
state were far more incremental than his party had hoped, his Task Force
on Legal Services and Procedures (commissioned less than 10 years after
the APA's passage) made much more sweeping recommendations for com-
prehensively revising agency procedures and judicial review. The report was
strikingly skeptical and even hostile to administrators and recommended
shifting as much work as possible to the federal courts.[100] Sensing another
window into revising the processes and procedures of the APA, the bar association appointed a Special Committee on Legal Services and Procedures and
charged it with assessing the current state of affairs and issuing recommendations. While the ABA had been in favor of some provisions of the APA, it still
sought to codify clearer constraints on the "judicial" functions of administrative agencies, as was its intent a decade prior. The President's appointment of
a task force gave them the perfect opportunity to once again pursue this goal.

In 1956 the ABA proposed a permanent congressional committee on
administrative procedure, fearing that Congress had "surrendered" its control
of policy making to the realm of agency rulemaking, a problem only "heightened by the fact that the courts are showing more and more reluctance" to
review administrative decisions.[101] Members of the ABA argued that the
Judiciary Committee, which oversaw the creation of the APA, was swamped
at the time with issues of crime and civil liberties, leading it to ignore the
administrative process as special interest groups better captured its attention. Their litany of fears were similar to those of a decade prior: fear that

administrative agents "drew up the laws as he [they] went along"; frustration with the lack of uniformity of rules and procedures ("the average trial lawyer who thinks he is pretty good in his own field, before an administrative agency feels lost and throws up his hands"); and angry charges that administrators were simply reckless disobeyers of law ("Some of us would like to get some of the men who practice before administrative agencies before a court and jury.")[102] David Maxwell, president-elect of the ABA, added, "If I get a case before an administrative tribunal, I haven't the foggiest notion of how to approach it. It is all a mystery to me." For these among other reasons, the rules needed to be uniform. Meanwhile, David Peck, justice of the New York Supreme Court, lamented publically that agencies had usurped core judicial functions: "Administrative agencies have outstripped the courts in the volume and importance of the matters within their jurisdiction."[103]

What the ABA ultimately proposed was a "Code of Federal Administrative Procedure" in the mold of other procedural rules, like the Federal Rules of Civil Procedure, to replace the APA. As proposed, this code would have made judicial review of agency action more stringent, required more evidentiary hearings, and made those hearings more formal.[104] The ABA committee submitted a draft of its proposal to Congress in 1959, where opposition was less based in partisan affiliation and more from federal agencies contending that the bill would unduly interfere with the efficient operation of government.[105] Elmer B. Staats, Deputy Director of the Bureau of the Budget, complained vociferously: "We have reached a point, largely because of cumbersome procedure, where serious questions have been raised about the capacity of the regulatory agencies to achieve the objectives laid out for them by the Congress." He argued that because of what he perceived as excessive concern with due process, true justice was now being denied because of procedural delay. To achieve due process, agencies need not copy the court model, according to Staats, since many regulatory functions were primarily quasi-legislative in nature, not quasi-judicial. Quoting Justice Felix Frankfurter from a 1945 dissenting opinion, he pointed out that "agencies deal largely with the vindication of the public interest and not the enforcement of private rights, this Court ought not to imply hampering restrictions, not imposed by Congress, upon the effectiveness of the administrative process. One reason for the expansion of the administrative agencies has been the recognition that procedures appropriate for the adjudication of private rights in the courts may be inappropriate for the kind of determinations which administrative agencies are called upon to make." Staats continued by arguing that "the process of judicialization" had led agency activity to "be carried out with an eye on the

...ate possibility of court review, where the decision may turn on procedural detail rather than broad public interest, equity, or statutory authority. Formal procedure may be used in some instances where informal procedure is permitted by law and would be more effective and more expeditious."[106]

Staats' statement was followed by one from Donald C. Beelar, chairman of the new ABA committee on the Federal Administrative Practice Act, who (unsurprisingly) painted a very different picture of administrative justice. "The trend toward government by administrative agency," he argued, "has significantly impaired the rights and freedoms of the individual. The agency machinery which we have combined the total powers of Government is no well-tuned cymbal of democracy. The much evangelized administrative process is no substitute for the democratic process."[107] He continued,

> The main source of anxiety we believe has to do with justice and fair play in agency litigation. If we are going to have government by administrative agency, public confidence will not be satisfied until we provide some kind of governmental machinery which is competent to handle litigation of disputes between citizens and between the citizen and the Government, which will give the citizen unquestioned assurance of justice and fair play. Three decades of experience with government by administrative agency has failed to achieve that order of public confidence.[108]

To his mind, agencies act as both judge and prosecutor and therefore have a tendency to prejudge the merits without providing an impartial hearing. Since the agency has already been associated with the case, and is often a litigant in the case, it puts the citizen at a significant disadvantage.

He also promoted further opportunities for judicial review. "Our main objective ... is that we must have litigation conducted which will be impartial and comply with the principles of fair play. This, if it can be achieved in the agency environment, is fine. If not, we will have to have some other organization."[109] However, he was skeptical at best as to whether agencies could, in fact, ensure such a thing. In addition, "from the citizen's point of view, the purposes of litigation are essentially the same without regard to the difference in cause of action or the type of tribunal having jurisdiction. Litigation provides an orderly means for the settlement of disputes. A citizen is not to be criticized if he expects from agency proceedings that quality of justice which he feels is rightfully his before the courts."[110]

But as it became clear that a complete overhaul of the APA was not politically feasible, the bar association changed its approach. The following year Senator Everett Dirksen, who was a minority member on the Senate Judiciary subcommittee, proposed the ABA reforms in a new format: a set of rules governing federal administrative agency proceedings, much like the federal civil and criminal rules of procedure, to exist *alongside* the APA. However, this also prompted a barrage of criticism, this time on the basis that uniform rules were not feasible across agencies that dealt with different types of policy issues. Nonetheless—and perhaps influenced by its experience with the civil rules—the ABA persisted on this point. As it would state in defense of a later version of the bill, the ABA believed that a uniform procedure for agency proceedings was crucial, as agencies "exercise legislative, executive, and judicial functions. They establish policies which have the force of law; they administer those policies; and they act as a tribunal to decide cases involving those policies."[111]

After several more years of no success (including a failed bill that would have simplified the admission of qualified lawyers to practice before federal agencies),[112] ABA representatives met with the Senate subcommittee to discuss the issue at length.[113] Following the meeting, Dirksen once again proposed his bill to Congress in March 1965, with a notable twist in its language; this time, the goal of the proposed legislation was to create "a set of procedures which would meet the needs of the public as well as the needs of the agencies. It is important that both needs be met because there is scarcely a facet of our life which is not affected by the decisions of these administrative agencies."[114] In seconding Dirksen's recommendation, Senator Edward Long of Missouri argued that whereas agencies were created because they were thought to deal with issues more expeditiously than by legislative or judicial procedures, there was now "doubt on this basic premise. Administrative procedures have become tremendously complicated, often very lengthy, and usually terribly expensive. Indeed, it has been said that the courts have made more progress in modernizing and streamlining their procedures than agencies have made. There are even suggestions made today that the administrative process be abandoned because it is so much slower than the judicial process."[115] Many agencies voiced concern over what they still believed were the "objectionable aspects" of such legislation, including "the unneeded infusion of delay-producing judicialized hearings and appellate procedures into the Commission's present, comparatively simply, case-processing techniques," and "the shifting of decisional responsibility from the duly appointed agency members to hearing examiners."[116] While Dirksen and the ABA were finally able to overcome these concerns in the Senate in 1966, their opposition in the House was unrelenting.

Meanwhile, during this same time period, the bar, the courts, and both the executive and legislative branches came together to create an advisory body whose recommendations would help to regulate the regulators by streamlining the administrative process, ensuring due process, and reducing cost and delay. The contours of such a committee were initially drawn by the Judicial Conference of the United States, which was seen as a parallel entity to this new body. A temporary conference was put in place under President Eisenhower and was populated by a mix of officials from regulatory agencies, judges, and a dozen practicing lawyers.[117] The ABA was closely consulted in the drafting of the legislation and given the opportunity to pick delegates to the conference.[118] It had the endorsement of Chief Justice Earl Warren, who had argued in 1959 that "such a conference—composed basically of agency representatives, but with practicing lawyers and other participants as well, is sorely needed to conduct continuing and practical studies of ways to eliminate undue delay, expense, and volume of hearing record; to develop uniform rules of practice and procedure, and generally to promote greater efficiency and economy in the administrative process."[119]

Given the level of tension and disagreement developing around revisions to the APA, in 1961 President John F. Kennedy issued an executive order that officially created the Administrative Conference of the United States (ACUS). Kennedy argued that the ACUS would "bring a sense of unity to out administrative agencies and a desirable degree of uniformity in their procedures." Kennedy did not go as far as some in the legal community wanted; while "judicialization—the method of determining the content of a controversy by processes akin to those followed by the judiciary—may well be the answer in many cases," he wanted to maintain the power of administrative agencies to use "informal methods and mobilizing the techniques of other disciplines" as well.[120] Recommendations from the new ACUS led the Securities and Exchange Commission to adopt rules in 1964 that provided a right to counsel for witnesses before the commission, as well as provided an opportunity for those accused to appear, cross examine other witnesses, and produce rebuttal evidence.[121]

Congress initially allowed the statutory basis for the ACUS to expire before President Lyndon Johnson signed a permanent commission into law in August 1964. As he described it, "The Administrative Conference is no superagency, but will stand in a similar relationship to the Federal agencies as the permanent and successful Judicial Conference stands in relationship to the Federal judiciary."[122] The ACUS was considered a necessary response to "the steady expansion of the Federal administrative process during the past several years [that] has been attended by increasing concern over the efficiency and adequacy of department and agency procedures."[123] Therefore, it became a federal advisory agency charged with making recommendations for the improvement of administrative agencies and their procedures. Although it was considered an independent agency much like the Judicial Conference, the ACUS was only given the power to make recommendations, not to promulgate actual binding rules.

The conference, at various times numbering 75 to 101 individuals, drew its members from agencies, academia, and the private sector. The ACUS is governed by a chair, appointed by the president for a five-year term, and a council of ten members, five of whom are always senior federal officials. The council members, also appointed by the president, serve three-year terms. The remaining members, chosen by the council, form the assembly—a majority of whom come from within the government. In terms of recommending improvements to Congress and the agencies, the ACUS most often acts by commissioning studies by law professors that are then reviewed by one of their six more specialized standing committees.[124] Its subsequent recommendation is then considered for adoption by the assembly, which meets usually twice a year.

When the ABA proposals for an administrative code were repeatedly rejected, advocates abandoned the code and crafted yet another series of individual amendments of the APA in hopes of achieving the same end. In 1970 the ABA's House of Delegates approved twelve resolutions calling for amendments, many of which reflected the bar association's ongoing concern regarding the need for uniform rules to govern informal adjudicative proceedings, authorizing appeal boards, and deleting exemptions from the requirement of notice and public participation in rulemaking proceedings.[125] In promoting the new set of resolutions, they joined forces with the ACUS, who endorsed four of the ABA's proposed amendments: those that redefined "rule" and "order" to better distinguish between rulemaking and adjudication activities, expanded the coverage of the notice and rulemaking requirements, established boards of appeal for administrative decisions, and granted agencies broader subpoena power in their formal proceedings.[126] During the broader period in which the ACUS served, it made approximately 200 recommendations, most of which were implemented to some degree.[127] Ironically, however, the only ABA proposal enacted by Congress was *not* one of the amendments endorsed by the ACUS, but rather something that it expressed reservations about: prohibiting ex parte communications in evidentiary hearings. Congress codified this procedural change in the Sunshine Act of 1976, the main thrust of which required agencies to hold their meetings regularly in public session.[128] The ABA shared the same goal, but supported achieving it through new rules instead. But given that the bill was drafted in the wake of the Watergate scandals, the section on evidentiary hearings hardly slowed its passage, or drew much attention.

Ultimately, the ABA managed only one reform through Congress in the first twenty years of the act. Its success—the Freedom of Information Act (FOIA), which passed in 1966—differed from the ABA's other efforts in politically notable ways. FOIA rewrote Section 3 of the original APA, defining agency records subject to disclosure and the procedures for procuring them. It also made agencies subject to penalty for hindering the process of a petition for information, granting recourse to federal court if there was suspicion that an agency had illegally tampered with records or delayed in sending them. Importantly, however, it did not alter the basic structure of the legislation, nor did it address the contentious issue of judicial review. It therefore did not produce the same kind of politically intense disputes that had interrupted the ABA's attempts to enact a new code of procedure.[129]

Some scholars have argued that procedural reform simply does garner enough attention to succeed. But when we juxtapose the quest for rules of administrative procedure with the experience under the early years of the Federal Rules of Civil Procedure (where the ABA and other actors were successful), it is clear that there must be an alternate explanation. The legal community had very different experiences when seeking uniform, procedural rules in each area of law. William Warfield Ross, chairman of the ABA Special Committee on Administrative Law, seemed to get at the heart of this difference. As he put it, "No consequential proposals to change administrative procedures are truly non-controversial"; instead, they are "perceived as politically important, and hence controversial, because they are perceived as strengthening or weakening one or more government or private factions against others in the incessant struggle for advantage that marks the political process."[130] While the judicial administrators who wielded substantial control over the civil rules were able to use the rules to affect matters of politics and policy, they benefited from decades of insularity from the broader political process—insularity that came from the widespread sense that the rules were not, in fact, "politically important." In other words, they were able to avoid precisely what advocates for administrative rules could not: exposure that procedural rules mattered for political outcomes. In its quest for procedural uniformity in administrative procedure, the legal community was not able to wrest control of the rules from agencies precisely because it was widely understood, from the start, that to do so would mean weakening the powers of the executive branch.

Administrative Law in the Rights Revolution Era

By the 1960s, the legal community increasingly believed that government could not be trusted blindly to protect the rights of all its citizens. And they weren't the only ones. The 1960s and 70s was a period when "those enthusiastic about regulation were especially dissatisfied with administrative autonomy." During this time, agencies appeared equally unenthusiastic about their mandates. The phenomenon of "capture" received widespread attention, and in an era defined by judicial innovation in the area of fundamental rights, judicial review of agency activity was widely believed to be an essential part of ensuring that rights and regulatory statutes were implemented in practice. As Cass Sunstein describes, "In a surprising reversal of New Deal alliances, those who were critical of the effects of regulation by the 1980s frequently insisted on administrative autonomy and the perverse effects of legalism—whereas critics seeking to bring about greater regulatory protections saw administrative independence and autonomy as the problem rather than the solution."[131] Social activists sought to remedy this through major legislation encompassing broader and broader policy areas, but they also became keenly aware of the fact that what they had won in Congress could easily be lost in the exercise of rulemaking by administrators unsympathetic—or worse, antagonistic—to their causes.

Even as Congress increasingly opted to take advantage of the statutory preclusion clause of the APA, thereby insulating individual agencies from judicial review as a matter of statute, many activists continued to devote their efforts to reforming the overall law itself. The focus on the APA is unsurprising, given that success in amending the monumental law as a whole would constitute "one stop shopping" for obtaining reforms would affect *all* agencies. This new wave of proposals sought to differentiate more cleanly between activities that constituted agency "rulemaking" versus "adjudication." Recognizing what was at stake, the executive branch also began to keep a closer eye on agency rulemaking activities, establishing a federal advisory agency to comment on the potential "improvement" of administrative agencies and their procedures. Consistent with the lesson of the 1940s and 50s, however, reform of rulemaking was most successful in the courts—so much so that it became hardly expedient for activists to even try their hand in Congress. But as much as the courts were active at first in enhancing judicial oversight of agency rule-making, by the early 1970s, the first signs of retreat (or at least complication) began to appear.

In the 1970s, Congress continued what had become the fairly regular practice of passing legislation that skirted the APA where convenient. For example, both the Economic Stabilization Act and the Emergency Petroleum Allocation Act expressly stated that APA would not apply to its provisions.[132] At the same time, however, the Ford administration also began what is the now common process of issuing executive orders to constrain agency rulemaking. Specifically, President Gerald Ford required that an "inflationary impact statement" accompany all "major legislative proposals, regulations, and rules" promulgated by executive agencies, including an explicit cost–benefit analysis for the potential effects of proposed rules and regulations.[133] The Carter administration continued this practice in 1978 with Executive Order 12,044, which required a "regulatory analysis" both when rules were proposed and when they were finalized.[134] While limited in their direct effects, these orders set a structural precedent for what would be a much more hands-on approach to overseeing the activities of administrative agencies by presidents Ronald Reagan and Bill Clinton.

In 1976 the Senate held hearings on fourteen bills that had been proposed to expand and improve the APA in order to help government agencies "proceed more fairly, openly, and responsively in their duties."[135] Senator Edward Kennedy began the hearings by stating, "Rules and regulations promulgated through the rulemaking provisions of the APA affect our lives and incomes as workers, consumers, businessmen and women, farmers, pensioners, doctors and patients, families, teachers, and Government employees. From the unborn child to the elderly, from the field to the dinner table, from the oceans to the skies, hardly any person, place, thing, or activity escapes some form of Federal programing or regulation."[136] The most critical amendment up for consideration, which was recommended by the joint ABA/ACUS alliance, was designed to eliminate the ability of the federal government and its officials to avoid suits arising from agency decision making.[137] Specifically, Congress amended the judicial review provision of the APA so as to eliminate sovereign immunity as a defense in suits against the government for money damages. As a member of the ACUS described it, the bill constituted "a major step in rationalizing the law of judicial review of agency action. It might not change many outcomes, but it would force the courts to ask and to answer the right questions. It would force them to decide whether the challenged action is in fact in the range of discretionary authority granted to the officer under law."[138] Although the bill was considered unnecessary by some (among them then Assistant Attorney General Antonin Scalia),[139] in testifying in support of the bill on behalf of Public Citizen, Ralph Nader put the need for it most strenuously:

> This bill is particularly necessary not only because of this legacy of governmental shutout of citizen involvement, but because recent Supreme Court decisions by the Burger majority have transformed this technical issue into a virtual monster that is allowing Government actions to go entirely uncorrected, and that is leaving citizens completely helpless when they try to ensure that Government officials will be held accountable for their actions. In addition, those decisions have created a vast confusion in this area of the law which has in turn led to excessive use by Government attorneys of standing as a defense and has caused the courts to issue decisions which are inconsistent with each other, and many of which are inconsistent with the fundamental tenets of our legal system.[140]

When Senator Kennedy asked whether it would be better for the public to hold the federal government accountable through the legislature as opposed to looking to the judicial branch to do so, Nader responded that Congress could never "match the enormous ability of the citizenry to challenge a large variety of actions ... [the public] can go to court and not feel that its only alternative is to mount a congressional campaign." The ABA, meanwhile, continued to levy its ongoing criticisms: that the APA as codified was fundamentally flawed in allowing the same person to be a prosecutor and judge, and that there continued to be a problematic lack of uniformity among agency procedures.[141]

With regard to the continued "judicialization" of administrative law, the Supreme Court was arguably the most active participant in the developments of the 1960s and 70s, undoubtedly part of the broader trajectory of a rise in court activism. What activists achieved in the courts has been the subject of innumerable law review articles on the development of the field of administrative law, though there are several developments specifically relevant to its subsequent "delegalization." Where judicial review of administrative action is concerned, despite some early fits and starts in the years following the passage of the APA, the Supreme Court quickly established a presumption in *favor* of reviewability, unless the statute at hand precluded such review "on its face." This presumption was at its clearest in a decision in a 1967 case, *Abbott Labs v. Gardner*, in which drug manufacturers sought judicial review of regulations on drug labeling issued under the Federal Food, Drug, and Cosmetic Act (the law that created the FDA). The government tried to block such review, arguing that the law precluded judicial review by implication. In rejecting the government's claim, the Court declared that the APA "embodies the basic presumption of judicial review" to one "suitably aggrieved by agency action so long as no statute precludes such relief or the action is not one committed to law by agency discretion."[142] In so doing, the Court made explicit that the starting premise for the reviewing agency actions should be to consider them available for judicial review.

Soon thereafter, the Court also pinned down a standard of review for the messier realm of informal rulemaking and adjudication. In *Citizens of Overton Park v. Volpe*, the Court found that a decision of the secretary of transportation to construct a highway through Overton Park was not a matter "committed to agency discretion." A concerned group of citizens alleged that the secretary's decision ran afoul of a section of the Department of Transportation Act that prohibited the secretary from authorizing the use of federal funds to finance the construction of highways through public parks if there was a "feasible and prudent" alternative route. The secretary was not able to produce formal documents indicating why he did not believe there to be a feasible alternative, and argued that he need not, as his decision making process was a matter of agency discretion under the APA. While the Court decided that formal findings were not required under Section 706 of the law, it asserted that a court *must* become involved in overseeing agency actions if the court "becomes aware, especially from a combination of danger signals, that the agency has not really taken a 'hard look' at the salient problems" involved in its decision making. In creating the so-called "hard look" doctrine and the "arbitrary and capricious" standard of review, the Court carved out a clear role for courts in reviewing even informal agency decisions.[143]

Expansion in the broader doctrine of standing was complementary to this clear standard of judicial review under the APA and therefore bears note. Briefly, standing is one of several criteria that legal issues must meet in order to be heard in court; as the Supreme Court has described it, "In essence the question of standing is whether the litigant is entitled to have the court decide on the merits of the dispute or of particular issues." While the APA itself established a new cause of action for bringing a case to court, the question of whether an individual or group has standing to seek review in the first place is distinct from reviewability under a law. As such, changes in the standing doctrine have both positively and negatively affected standing to challenge agency action. At first, standing under the APA was expanded along with the broader doctrine, from the "legal wrong" test in place at the time the APA was passed to the later "injury in fact" test that emerged from *Association of Data Processing Service Organizations v. Camp* in 1970.[144] As with other standing inquiries at the time, then, the plaintiff needed only to show that an alleged injury was within the "zone of interests" that a statute was intended to protect.

On the one hand, the decision was a victory for those favoring the "presumption of reviewability," following the *Abbott Labs* framework in finding that a decision of the Comptroller of the Currency was not precluded from review by any "relevant" statute. But on the other, the case created the basis for later restrictions on litigant standing. Section 702 of the APA addresses standing under the act, extending a right of judicial review to any person "suffering legal wrong because of agency action, or adversely affected or aggrieved by agency action within the meaning of a relevant statute." While the judiciary might have treated the APA as a codification of the test for establishing standing, at least for cases arising under the act, it opted to separate its standing analysis from the substantive legal issues in the case, claiming that "standing is different" from a hearing on the merits because it concerns the question of "whether the interest sought to be protected by the complainant is arguably within the zone of interests to be protected or regulated by the statute or constitutional guarantee in question."[145] This meant that questions of standing under the APA would be subject to the Court's increasingly restrictive standing doctrine over time, instead of dealing with the standing provision of the APA on its own terms.[146]

What is more, despite the presumptive clarity of the *Abbott Labs* framework for assessing when courts do or do not owe deference to agency decision making, the Court began to constrict its standards of review in the early 1970s, primarily through what has been characterized as the "delegalization" of administrative law and procedure. In its earliest manifestation, this shift took form in the Court's growing reluctance to interpret enabling acts to require formal rulemaking. As early as 1972 in *United States v. Allegheny-Ludlum Steel Corporation*, the Court established that even statutes that required hearings in connection with rulemaking should *not* be read to trigger formal proceedings unless Congress explicitly stated that it desired trial-type procedures.[147] This did not turn out to be an aberration in the Court's position; the following year, in *United States v. East Coast Railway Co.*, the Court held that agency "hearings" required by statutes would not trigger the APA's provisions for formal rulemaking, and would instead be satisfied by informal rulemaking procedures.[148] Together, the cases instructed reviewing courts to largely ignore congressional provisions for hearings in conjunction with agency rulemaking.

The fundamental turning point for the Court, however—where it made its clearest statement of the trends that had begun to develop in the 1970s (and to which Nader referred)—came with *Vermont Yankee Nuclear Power Company v. Natural Resources Defense Council.*[149] In this 1978 case, the Court forbade judicial imposition of procedures that were not expressly mandated by the APA, specifying that a reviewing court could not "impose upon the agency its own notion of which procedures are 'best' or are most likely to further some vague, undefined public good," as this would exceed the statutory limits of judicial review of agency action.[150] The Court's new position also had the effect of undermining the position that courts have the ultimate power to interpret statutes, now locating that power with agencies themselves. Antonin Scalia, in a law review article that he wrote before becoming a federal judge, called *Vermont Yankee* "a remarkably self-denying opinion" in "an era of judicial activism."[151] Scalia claimed that "one of the functions of procedure is to limit power—not just the power to be unfair, but the power to act in a political mode, or the power to act at all." Citing *Roe v. Wade* as an example of a recent court decision motivated by "publicly appointed counsel and public-interest law firms, and of opinions regularly drawn with legislative breadth," he argued that procedure is one area that "continues to serve as a restriction upon the areas of law on which the Court may pronounce." It is "a restriction upon the power of the courts, impairing (however crudely) their ability and thus their inclination to make social policy."[152] In essence, Scalia recognized the ways in which deference, or lack thereof, could serve partisan and ideological ends, and he supported a reigning-in of Supreme Court discretion in an era of liberal policy making. He also recognized that liberal groups, particularly environmental organizations, were using the power of delay through judicial review to prevent businesses from operating and expanding.[153]

An increasingly conservative Supreme Court began to reflect Scalia's concerns in two ways. First, the Court began to dismantle its tradition of reasoning that statutes that named certain parties or actions were not necessarily meant to preclude others. It made this new predilection even clearer in 1984 when it held in *Block v. Community Nutrition Institute*[154] that consumers of milk could not bring suit under the marketing orders issued by the secretary of agriculture. Even though the Court noted that the enabling act in question included a congressional concern for consumer interests, it also interpreted the fact that the act explicitly gave review rights to producers and handlers of dairy products as proof that Congress did not intend such rights for consumers. The Court's new approach, therefore, centered on the question of whether or not Congress' intent to preclude judicial review was "fairly discernable in the statutory scheme,"¹⁵⁵ whereas the standard in *Abbott Labs* was notably more strict, requiring "clear and convincing evidence."¹⁵⁶

Related, the Supreme Court also began to expand the APA exceptions to judicial review, moving decidedly away from its *Overton Park* approach. This trend began in *Heckler v. Chaney*,¹⁵⁷ a case involving a suit by inmates on death row scheduled to be executed by lethal injection. These inmates argued that the drugs to be used in their execution had not been tested and labeled for use in human executions, and that—in the hands of untrained professionals— they could cause "tortuous pain rather the quick and painless death." As such, they argued that this use violated the "misbranding" and "new drug" provision of the Food, Drug, and Cosmetic Act, and they asked the FDA to take enforcement action to prevent their use.

The FDA declined to act, claiming that it did not have jurisdiction over the use of drugs for human execution and that, even if it did, it also had the "inherent discretion" *not* to act unless (as per the FDA's enabling statute) there was "a serious danger to the public health."¹⁵⁸ In an opinion by Justice Rehnquist, the Court held that an agency's decision not to pursue enforcement is presumptively *unreviewable*, as such actions are "committed to agency discretion by law" under section 701(a)(2) of the APA. This stood in complete opposition to the Court's *Abbott* approach from the prior decade. Instead, the Court now reasoned that "an agency decision not to enforce often involves a complicated balancing of a number of factors which are peculiarly within its expertise," and because of this, "the agency is far better equipped than the courts to deal with the many variables involved in the proper ordering of its priorities," thereby making it the type of decision "committed to agency discretion" under the APA.¹⁵⁹ Notably, while liberal members of the Court like Justice Thurgood Marshall wrote separate concurrences to stress that the conclusion in the case ought not imply a general refusal to review agency inaction, it is important to note that the members of the Court were unanimous on these points. The Court has since built upon *Chaney* by invoking the exception to justify not only agency inaction, but also an agency's decision to *take* certain actions as well.¹⁶⁰

In a second development, the Court doctrinalized a new standard of deference to administrative agency interpretations of congressional statutes in *Chevron U.S.A., Inc. v. Natural Resources Defense Council*, a decision that has subsequently become the most cited case in administrative law, and a decision that Cass Sunstein has labeled "one of the very few defining cases in the last twenty years of American public law," altering "the distribution of national powers among courts, Congress, and administrative agencies."[161] Prior to the decision, there was inconsistency, especially in the lower courts, as to whether it fell to agencies or courts to resolve ambiguities in statutes. The significance of *Chevron* is that it resolved this uncertainty in favor of agencies. Justice John Paul Stevens, writing for a unanimous 6-0 majority, rejected the NRDC's challenge of what it perceived to be an overly lenient interpretation by the Environmental Protection Agency (EPA) as to what constituted a "stationary source" at an industrial plant that emits pollutants into the air. According to the decision, the EPA was entitled to deference because the agencies, not courts, are delegated the responsibility from Congress to make policy decisions in matters where the original statutory history was ambiguous. As Justice Stevens wrote, "While agencies are not directly accountable to the people, the Chief Executive is, and it is entirely appropriate for this political branch of the Government to make such policy choices—resolving the competing interests which Congress itself either inadvertently did not resolve, or intentionally left to be resolved by the agency charged with the administration of the statute in light of everyday realities."[162] The Court, in turn, established the doctrine of "Chevron deference," a two-part analysis for deciding whether or not a reviewing court should defer to an agency's own reading of a statute. Under the *Chevron* doctrine, the Court established that a reviewing court must first determine (1) whether a statute is ambiguous or whether there is a gap that Congress intended the agency to fill, and if so, (2) whether the agency's interpretation of the statute is permissible. To be "permissible," the Court decided, the agency's interpretation needs only to be "reasonable." This major shift required courts to make two changes to their practices; it moved from considering the interpretation of ambiguous statutes as "questions of law" to a "policy choice," and it redirected the focus of reviewing courts from statutory purpose to statutory text.[163]

The Court's decision in *Chevron* was widely expected to have the effect of eliminating the role of policy judgments on the behalf of individual judges in judicial review of agency interpretations of law. In practice, judges and justices vary in how much they defer to agency interpretations. A recent study found that, for example, Justice Scalia—the most vocal supporter of *Chevron*—was also the least deferential to administrative interpretations overall, whereas Justice Stephen Breyer (the most vocal critic) was the most deferential. There are also important partisan patterns that have developed over time; for example, while conservative justices vote to validate agency decisions less often than liberal justices, they were increasingly willing to do so when President Bush succeeded President Clinton.[164] But in the direct aftermath of the decision, the outcome did not seem to be particularly ideologically driven; the decision was unanimous (despite that we might have expected the facts of the case to prompt the Court's liberal justices *not* to defer), was written by a liberal justice, and has been described as an "accidental landmark" amidst evidence that Justice Stevens intended *Chevron* to be merely a "restatement" of existing law.[165] Given that the case seemed to reflect Scalia's preference for textualism and was decided at a moment where increased deference would have meant more deference to Reagan-appointed administrators, it is tempting to assume that this was a "purely procedural" decision in disguise. But while the turn to textualism has over time provided a vehicle for infusing ideology into a judge's decision whether or not to defer to an agency, the case was ultimately "little noticed when it was decided, and came to be regarded as a landmark case only some years later."[166]

Other scholars have viewed the case as a mechanism for retrenchment. As per the two-step analysis, it is rare that Congress' intent is uncontroversially clear; more often than not, then, reviewing courts determine that Congress intended an agency to fill in the gaps through the process of rulemaking. In practice, this means that reviewing courts proceed directly to the second step of the *Chevron* analysis—determining whether or not an agency determination is "permissible"—and the standards of permissibility make it difficult for the courts not to defer. This is not a novel approach to interpreting the effects of *Chevron*; as Keith Werhan describes, "The *Chevron* revision of the traditional approach to judicial review of administrative action, although startling, is entirely consistent with a delegalization of the administrative process," and "reviewing courts have applied *Chevron* in the spirit of delegalization."[167] When you add this presumption against judicial review to the legal community's failure to appropriate any control in terms of "proceduralizing" the administrative process, where access to courts in this area of law is concerned, the "rules of the game" are strongly against individuals seeking redress from administrative agencies.

Administrative Reform from Reagan to Obama

It is worth noting that these constrictions in judicial review, at the hands of the Court itself, occurred alongside a spate of jurisdiction stripping proposals. In the 1970s and 80s, Congress found itself responding to another series of controversial Supreme Court decisions. In response to the Court's decisions regarding school prayer,[168] busing,[169] and abortion,[170] opponents argued that the justices on the Supreme Court were regularly making what should have been legislative determinations, thereby interfering with the core functions assigned to Congress in the Constitution. As a member of Congress described during the 1980s:

> The courts today are perceived as exceeding their traditional authority in numerous instances. The public is skeptical of federal judges who appear to be assuming the administration of some state functions. They are angered by what they view as sweeping judicial orders that effectively prevent individuals from exercising control over significant aspects of their daily lives. They are also disturbed by decisions that they regard as preventing state and local governments from exercising traditional powers.[171]

These proposals ultimately failed, and the role of the courts in agency oversight actually grew to enjoy a new set of supporters. As Sidney Shapiro characterizes, administrative law in the 1980s was defined by "presidential oversight"; in addition to continued efforts from Congress, President Reagan in particular made a concerted effort to constrain the scope and extent of regulation. Regulatory reform was, of course, a much larger movement; but in terms of judicial retrenchment, the most relevant issues involve the ways in which the movement put pressure on reviewing courts to be *less* deferential to agencies.[172] This marked a shift in the development of administrative law, away from fixating on rules governing specific proceedings (e.g., formal evidentiary hearings) to making rules of general applicability.[173] Because general rules affect a much broader swath of interests—not just specific industries, but all three branches of government as well—they proved even harder to reform. As such, the APA itself continued relatively unscathed, although not without significant related developments occurring in the courts.

President Reagan, like the two presidents before him, used his ability to issue executive orders to impose extra-statutory requirements on the agency rulemaking process. Unsurprisingly, given his antiregulation point of view, Reagan's requirements were more extensive than those of the presidents that preceded him. He not only required agencies to perform an explicit cost–benefit analysis and to issue a regulatory impact report for major rules, but he also required that these analyses specifically address the impact of the proposed and final rule on issues of family, federalism, property, and trade. Even more importantly, Reagan's executive order empowered the Office of Management and Budget (OMB) to review all major rules before they could be issued.[174] Finally, the order flat out prohibited agencies from issuing major rules "unless the potential benefits to society ... outweigh the potential costs."[175] An advisory committee established by Reagan to study the housing industry, meanwhile, promoted even more sweeping changes to the APA, recommending that agencies "should carry the burden of proving compliance with the statutory tests and not be aided by presumptions favoring the validity of agency actions."[176]

While Reagan's orders did not impact judicial review specifically, they are clearly reflective of the degree to which the administration was skeptical of and antagonistic to "big government" in the form of expansive bureaucratic power. The oversight exercised by the OMB, for example, was not considered to be reviewable in court, as OMB action was labeled "managerial."[177] But one of the more ironic consequences of this skepticism is that it led to increasing calls for the courts to again become *more* active in reviewing agency activities and less deferential to agency determinations. In this iteration, proponents of judicial review were conservative.

Although the larger regulatory reform movement ultimately failed to amend the APA, one prominent near-success illustrates the politics of Republican's new support of judicial review. There was bipartisan support for the "Bumpers Amendment" to the proposed Regulatory Reform Act, named for its sponsor, Democrat Dale Bumpers, which explicitly directed that the courts be less deferential to agencies, instructing reviewing courts to (1) set aside any agency rule found to lack substantial support in the rulemaking file; (2) determine the authority or jurisdiction of the agency on the basis of the language of the authorizing statute or other evidence of legislative intent; and (3) accord no presumption in favor of or against agency action.[178] For Bumpers and the amendment's other supporters (which included a broad swath of Republicans as well as the ABA), the need for such a change was obvious: "A fundamental premise of our system of government is that the courts interpret and apply the law; they are the ultimate authority on all legal questions. It simply makes sense for courts to decide independently whether an agency has exceeded its authority, without deference to the agency's interpretation regarding the extent of its authority."[179] The Senate Judiciary Committee's report argued that "the judicially created doctrine of deference to agency interpretations of law, which some courts have elevated to a virtual presumption of correctness, places the bureaucratic thumb on the scales of justice, weighting them against the citizen. We intend to re-establish an equal balance."[180]

The amendment passed the Senate easily in March 1982 but met significant opposition in the House. In particular, House members seemed to have
no patience for altering the scope of judicial review, despite Bumpers' assertion that the provision was "hardly a Draconian burden on agencies." Clearly,
however, that was not how members of the House perceived it; as one legislator put it, "This judicial review section would eliminate the presumption
of validity currently afforded agency determinations of law. Furthermore,
agencies would have to justify decisions made during an informal rulemaking
proceeding through substantial support in the new rulemaking file."[181]

Congress once again attempted to amend the APA in the mid-1990s
with the "Comprehensive Regulatory Reform Act," popularly known as the
Dole Bill. The bill sought to codify and extend the executive extra-statutory
changes that had already been imposed on the APA, such as requiring agencies to perform a cost–benefit analysis when proposing new rules and regulations. For example, the bill specified at length exactly what the procedures
for an adequate cost–benefit analysis should be, required that the analysis be
produced for less expensive rules as well as more costly ones, and even mandated that agencies provide an analysis of reasonable alternatives to the proposed rule. It also proposed allowing interested parties to petition agencies
to review existing rules in terms of these new requirements and would have
subjected unreviewed rules to sunset provisions.[182]

As the product of a Republican Congress concerned with the perils of
"overregulation," the proposal, which ultimately failed, was unsurprising in
terms of its goals. A bipartisan coalition of Republicans and conservative
Democrats argued that adding these risk assessment and cost–benefit provisions was crucial for assessing agency decisions on the basis of the APA's own
standards. As both the Democratic Lousiana Senator Bennett Johnston and
Republicans argued, "only by making them part of the record and considering that can you understand whether the final agency action is arbitrary
and capricious. In effect, it would be a rule of common sense."[183] Many of the
reforms were endorsed by both the bar association and the ACUS; one, for
example, proposed amending Section 625 of the APA so that "judicial review
of agency action taken pursuant to the requirements of this section shall be
limited to review of compliance or noncompliance with the requirements of
this section." As Orrin Hatch argued in support of the ABA/ACUS reforms,
"Judicial review of cost-benefit analysis is effectively impossible" without
them.[184]

Those who opposed the bill, however, both denied that overregulation
was a problem and argued that imposing such strict procedures would cause

considerable delays in administrative decision making. They agreed that courts had a role to play in the process, often arguing that "the courts should be used to ensure that final agency rules are based on adequate analysis"; but they also believed that "regulatory reform should not be a lawyer's dream with unending ways for special interests to bog down agencies in litigation."[185] They referred to the part of the bill allowing "any person" to petition for cost–benefit analysis of any existing regulation as problematic, fearing that instead of creating reform, it would lead to "regulatory and judicial gridlock. It opens up to those who would thwart a particular piece of legislation that might be in the public good. They can thwart it and stop it dead in its tracks by keeping it in court. So this is a way to keep agencies from doing their jobs and keeping lawyers happy and prosperous."[186]

The bill was ultimately referred to the Senate Judiciary Committee, where both the liberal ABA and the conservative American Enterprise Institute (AEI) expressed their support for reform. Christopher DeMuth, president of AEI, argued that "regulatory officials have too much discretion" and urged that the reforms "should not be particularly controversial; its policies and procedures should be considered rudimentary good practice by those on all sides of particular regulatory debates."[187] The ABA agreed, arguing that the reforms were necessary to eliminate further uncertainty over the proper standard of judicial review and, in fact, to cut down on litigation over that standard.[188] But the real enemies of the reform—agencies themselves, supported by a handful of academics—won out in the end, stalling the bill indefinitely in committee.[189]

The Clinton administration followed the Reagan precedent in its active management of agency rulemaking. Although he technically revoked Reagan's executive orders and replaced them with his own, President Clinton left the administration's planning and review process basically intact.[190] He maintained the regulatory plan requirement, requiring that both the OMB and, additionally, the vice president, review the report. The vice president was then required to circulate the document to various White House officials and agencies potentially affected by the proposed rule change. In vesting this additional power in the vice president, Clinton's procedures undoubtedly slowed down the development and implementation of rules, much as was criticized of the Republican plan in Congress. Given the composition of the courts at the time, however, Clinton had reason to be skeptical at best as to whether or not the courts would protect the administrative state.

The courts gave Clinton plenty of reason to worry, although the reasons were complex. Following *Chevron*, the Supreme Court entrenched an increasingly textualist practice of statutory interpretation. In 1992 the Court was its most explicit to date in redirecting reviewing courts from the purpose of the statute to its text, using phrases like the "plain language" of the statute, and concluding that "in ascertaining whether the agency's interpretation is a permissible construction of the language, a court must look to the structure and language of the statute as a whole. If the text is ambiguous and so open to interpretation in some respects, a degree of deference is granted to the agency, though a reviewing court need not accept an interpretation which is unreasonable."[191] The move from purpose to language in many ways represents a victory of Justice Scalia's perspective on matters of interpretation.

On the one hand, less judicial review during a period when agencies were populated by Clinton appointees might have been seen as a good thing (to the administration and Democrats in Congress), as it left more discretion in the hands of his government. But from a retrenchment point of view, diminished judicial review was cause for concern in freeing agency policy from legal accountability and for allowing the choice of whether or not to defer to agencies to become more ideological in nature. Consistent with other retrenchment strategies, the "rules" of deference have been used increasingly in recent years for partisan ends, as evidenced by the finding that, in lower court decisions from 1990 to 2004 involving the EPA and NLRB, Republican appointees on the courts were more willing to invalidate agency decisions than those judges appointed by a Democrat. Retrenchment seemed to occur, not only because the textualist approach helped further "delegalization" by providing a mechanism for keeping the courts out, but also because this textualism gives judges *additional* discretion to interpret such "rules" of deference, at times in order to promote or detract from agency actions based on their ideological and policy preferences as individuals.[192]

Although Scalia's approach to administrative law reigned supreme for most of the 1990s, the tides have begun to turn. In the early 2000s, the Court issued a trilogy of decisions affecting what has come to be known as *Chevron* "Step Zero," or a reviewing court's decision as to whether the *Chevron* framework should be applied in a case at all. These decisions represent the assertion of Justice Breyer's position on agency discretion; namely that the courts should take a case-by-case approach rather than viewing the *Chevron* decision as a total grant of law-interpreting powers to agencies. In effect, the three cases—*Christensen v. Harris County, United States v. Mead Corporation*, and *Barnhart v. Walton*—somewhat limit the scope of agency actions that receive *Chevron* deference.

At issue in the first case, *Christensen v. Harris County*, was a decision by the Harris County Sheriff's Department to force employees to use their accumulated compensatory time before it reached the limit that would require overtime payments.[193] In response, the Department of Labor had issued an opinion letter stating that the forced use of compensatory time violated provisions of the Fair Labor Standards Act. In assessing the degree of deference that the letters should receive from the courts, the Supreme Court pointed out that *Chevron* was not the only doctrine governing administrative deference in existence. The majority opinion spoke to an issue that long required clarification: whether the doctrine of deference predating *Chevron* survived it, and if so, in what capacity. In *Skidmore v. Swift Co.*, a 1944 case, the Court had established a different type of deference meant to apply to *informal* agency decisions, whereby an administrative agency's interpretive rules were given deference according to their persuasiveness. "Persuasiveness," as described in the opinion, was to be judged on the basis of a four-factor test that examined "the thoroughness evident in its [the agency's] consideration, the validity of its reasoning, its consistency with earlier and later pronouncements, and all those factors which give it power to persuade, if lacking power to control."[194] While it had been unclear to date whether this doctrine survived *Chevron*, the Court quickly dismissed the government's contention that it was owed *Chevron* deference, arguing that *Chevron* only applied to agency interpretations having "the force of law." The decision made clear that interpretations "such as those in opinion letters—like interpretations contained in policy statements, agency manuals, and enforcement guidelines, all of which lack the force of law—do not warrant *Chevron*-style deference."[195] Instead, they would merit the less deferential *Skidmore* standard.

The decision was highly important in validating *Chevron* "Step Zero" as an independent inquiry. But it was unclear on other matters, such as whether interpretations that lack the force of law or that are not the product of formal procedures are *always* to be assessed under *Skidmore*. The Court promptly addressed this issue in a second case, *United States v. Mead Corporation*, in 2001.[196] Finding that classification decisions made by the regional office of the U.S. Customs Services did not merit *Chevron* deference, the Court again applied the *Skidmore* standard, this time clarifying that "administrative implementation of a particular statutory provision qualifies for *Chevron* deference when it appears that Congress delegated authority to the agency generally to make rules carrying the force of law, and that the agency interpretation claiming deference was promulgated in the exercise of authority."[197] The Court's final clarification came a year later in *Barnhart v. Walton*, which made clear that the use of informal procedures in establishing a rule did not insulate the subsequent agency decision from *Chevron* deference; while the interpretive method was important, so too was "the nature of the question at issue."[198] In aggregate, these decisions help to guide lower courts where it had previously been highly unclear as to whether or not *Chevron* applied to interpretations adopted from informal adjudications and informal documents like advisory letters, interpretive rules, and policy statements. And given the increased propensity of agency administrators to prefer this type of rulemaking, such a clarification was essential.

Importantly, the "delegalization" of administrative law that progressed in the 1990s occurred alongside another outpouring of prominent legislative court curbing proposals. Some of these were successful; in 1996, for example, Congress limited judicial review of rights claims brought by prisoners and noncitizens when it passed the Antiterrorism and Effective Death Penalty Act (AEDPA) and the Illegal Immigration Reform and Responsibility Act, both with bipartisan support. But the 1990s and 2000s were far from a heyday for proponents of jurisdiction stripping, illustrating the persistent political difficulties inherent in grand acts of politics as strategies for judicial retrenchment. The Oklahoma City bombing no doubt drove Republicans and Democrats to coalesce in their interests and to pass the AEDPA (which limits the number of habeas corpus petitions available to prison inmates, as well as the judiciary's ability to grant habeas), but this proved to be an exceptional moment.[199] In the past two decades members of Congress have continued to promote court curbing proposals for controversial issues involving the Pledge of Allegiance, abortion, pornography, school prayer, and gay marriage.[200] The small group of representatives and senators who regularly propose them are clearly devoted to these efforts. As Spencer Bachus explained in hearings for the Marriage Protection Act, "The circumstances that we find ourselves in are occasioned by an increasingly intrusive and tyrannical judiciary."[201] Representative Todd Akin remarked similarly two years later, "Essentially, what our bill does, if you want to put it in a simple word picture, we are creating a fence. The fence goes around the Federal judiciary. We do that because we don't trust them."[202]

Nonetheless, proposals to expand judicial oversight of administrative activity also persist. At the hearings on the 60th anniversary of the APA held before the House Judiciary Committee, the ABA once again promoted expanding judicial review, particularly to include those areas of rulemaking that currently escape formal adjudication procedures under the law: disputes involving immigration and asylum issues, veteran's benefits, Medicare cases, NLRB decisions on bargaining units, and IRS collection disputes, among others.[203] Yet even in the face of what has become far more court deference to agency adjudication and rulemaking than existed prior to the 1970s (the Court's *Chevron* doctrine led circuit courts to affirm agency decisions at a rate of 81 percent just one year after the decision, up from 76 percent the year prior),[204] the ABA lauded the judiciary's role in one regard. Where agency rulemaking—as opposed to adjudication—is concerned, "since 1970, however, the Supreme Court and the federal courts of appeals have virtually singlehandedly reshaped the structure of informal rulemaking in a series of decisions expanding both the obligations of agencies and the role of the reviewing courts. The result has been a transformation, without the benefit of legislative amendment, of informal rulemaking into an on-the-record proceeding that has fostered widespread public participation in the process."[205] In other words, creative judicial interpretation of the APA has made rulemaking dramatically more accessible to the public and procedurally formal, and the "hard look" doctrine means in practice that reviewing courts are no longer content to assume that policy as announced adequately conforms with statutes as written.[206] Where agency adjudication is concerned, however, the role and degree of judicial oversight are still questionable in their effects.

Conclusions

The growth of the administrative state—and especially the practice of agency adjudication—has had profound and unmistakable effects for moving and insulating disputes from the courts. The growth and development of administrative agencies with their own internal apparatus for dispute resolution have, in effect, led to a change in venue for individuals and groups pursuing various would-be legal claims. As groups like the ABA began to fear that agencies were in essence performing core judicial functions without providing basic due process guarantees, and as opponents of the New Deal in Congress feared losing the executive branch expansions that they had long struggled to gain, reformers sought to codify rules of "administrative procedure" to protect the best interest of aggrieved individuals. While Congress did pass the Administrative Procedure Act in 1946 with the goal of establishing guidelines for agency rulemaking and adjudication, agencies retained significant discretion. And although courts served in an important watchdog role over agency adjudication for much of the 1950s and 60s, increased deference to quasi-judicial administrative rulings and diminished opportunity for judicial review have left many wary about the quality of rights protection that agencies provide.

The initial compromise that resulted in the APA was a partisan one, but the Republican side of that compromise was notably buttressed by both legal academics and the ABA. Over time, these groups, joined by judicial administrators, played a major role in proposing most changes to the APA. But once the nation moved onward from the ideologically polarized New Deal era, the real enemies to further change were not Republicans or Democrats, but federal agencies concerned about losing their discretion. This proved to be true regardless of which party was in power, making the APA very difficult for legislators to use for strategic political purposes. Similarly, presidents have exercised a heavier hand in overseeing agency discretion over time, regardless of the party in power. With regard to courts in particular, the initial moves toward lessening active judicial oversight were put into motion by a liberal justice. Since then, debates over administrative deference on the Supreme Court have become more ideological, though still not strictly partisan; Justices Scalia and Breyer, while advocating positions that stem from their broad judicial ideologies, have *not* changed those positions based on the party that is in power.

In terms of the politics and processes of institutional change, barriers to authoritative changes in administrative law and procedure have always been high. Both Republicans and Democrats are subject to it, making the APA difficult to manipulate for overtly political strategic reform efforts. While a majority party might favor increased discretion, it surely does not feel the same when its opponents are in power. Further, the more deeply that agencies are entrenched, the more difficult a political project taking away their discretion becomes. For these very reasons, scholars have argued that, over time, Congress chose to delegate control of the administrative process in order to enhance its legitimacy: "When Congress amends the APA, it adopts procedures that apply across the board. When Congress permits the other two branches to develop procedures within the general ambit of the APA, it opens the door to adjusting the mix of values in different institutional settings or even in specific cases. Such adjustments can fine-tune the administrative process while retaining the general uniformity achieved by the APA."[207]

Because of these high barriers to change, retrenchment in administrative law and procedure has largely been a story of drift and conversion. Because the amount of veto players available on the Supreme Court is always small, we are most likely to see conversion. As such, in the hands of administrators, the APA constantly "drifted" toward more insularity and discretion, while the courts converted their own doctrines toward the exercise of less discretion over agency decision making.

Given the overlap in the historical time frame and given their similarities as objects for reform, the question arises of why the cases of the federal civil rules and the APA worked out so differently as targets for retrenchment. While the ACUS was influential in matters involving administrative procedure, it was a less effective party than the Judicial Conference was for civil rules. While the Judicial Conference could promulgate rule changes, the ACUS was only empowered to make recommendations, not to implement them. But even so, both cases were the product of interbranch relationships where the distribution of authority was far from clear. Congress could have acted to stop the president and the courts from appropriating authority over agency activity and informally "amending" procedure, much as occurred with the federal rules. And yet they seemed content to allow the courts in particular to innovate.

Why? The difference comes down to rules themselves. The ABA failed to procure a "Code of Administrative Procedure" that would have been parallel to the federal civil and criminal rules. While it was politically expedient for Congress to delegate (if informally) some degree of authority over agencies to the other branches, without a set of rules for parties to manipulate behind closed doors, they also had less to fear in terms of incremental erosion. A set of federal rules for administrative procedure might therefore have altered the trajectory of institutional change entirely, especially by enhancing the power of the ACUS to implement more effectual changes with ease and regularity over time.

6

Changing the Incentives: Leaving Rights and Removing Remedies

Introduction

In 2009 the details of a prominent Supreme Court decision instigated controversy over the issue of exactly how much discretion school officials should have when enforcing antidrug and violence policies. On the one hand, it is arguably considered to be in the best interest of students for school officials to have space to craft and exercise policies to keep their student body safe; but on the other, it was widely concerning to some that this discretion had the potential to compromise the constitutional rights of young students. This was certainly the position taken by Savana Redding, as well as both her angry mother and concerned lawyer.

Accused by a fellow student of harboring two prescription-strength Advils, and therefore potentially violating the school's zero-tolerance drug policy, the 13-year-old middle school student was strip-searched by the school secretary and nurse when a search of her backpack and outer clothing failed to reveal the pills. The search, in which she was asked to strip down to her bra and underwear and to move each garment aside for inspection, did not reveal anything either. For Savana, the ordeal hardly ended there. She did not return to school for months, for fear of having to face the nurse and secretary again; she developed stomach ulcers and eventually transferred schools. Lawyers defending the school district in the subsequent case later argued that school officials have every reason to be vigilant about the abuse of over-the-counter medications by preteen students—a trend on the rise—and their position was bolstered by a 1985 legal precedent allowing school officials to search a student's purse for drugs without a warrant, so long as their suspicions were considered "reasonable."[1] But the Arizona school's policy—which her law-yer described as "strip-search first and ask questions later"—seemed not to take into account whether these accusations were, in fact, reasonable, and the Ninth Circuit Court of Appeals was concerned as well. As Judge Kim McLane Wardlaw put it, "It does not require a constitutional scholar to conclude that the nude search of a 13-year-old child is an invasion of constitutional rights."[2]

The Supreme Court agreed. Writing for a 7-2 majority, Justice David Souter determined that the strip search violated the Fourth Amendment ban on unreasonable searches, given that the school lacked reason to suspect that the drugs presented a danger, or that they were, in fact, concealed in her underwear.[3] But while the decision was pivotal for clarifying the constitutional rights of students, the Court also held that, because its position was not clearly established law prior to the case, the school officials themselves were shielded from liability. While not approving the particulars of the search, which Justice Souter characterized as "embarrassing, frightening and humiliating," the Court seemed sympathetic to a concern raised by legal scholars in the months preceding the decision. "Do we really want to encourage cases," Professor Richard Arum inquired, "where students and parents are seeking monetary damages against educators in such school-specific matters where reasonable people can disagree about what is appropriate under the circumstances?"[4] In fact, school officials asserted that they could not be held accountable for the search, under the doctrine of qualified immunity, from the start of Redding's case. Qualified immunity shields government officials from liability for the violation of an individual's federal constitutional rights where their actions, even if later found to be unlawful, did not violate "clearly established law." In effect, then, despite a violation of her constitutional rights, the school officials violating those rights could not be held legally accountable for their actions.

This distance between rights and remedies—which refer to the means by which rights are enforced, or the means by which the violation of rights is prevented, redressed, or compensated—also creates a space in which would-be retrenchers can make significant changes to rights without challenging them directly. Although *Marbury v. Madison* long ago established that "it is a general and indisputable rule, that where there is a legal right, there is also a legal remedy by suit, or action at law, whenever that right is invaded … every right, when withheld, must have a remedy, and every injury its proper redress,"[5] the relationship between a successful rights claim and recovering remedies is not always so simple. As Peter Schuck argues, "In an ideal world, the distinction between right and remedy would have no significance. Rights, once recognized and defined, would be secure; citizens would enjoy them without the state having to intervene. Remedies would be superfluous, or at least unproblematic."[6] Perhaps for this reason, much of the focus of public law scholarship in political science is on the question of rights: specifically when we have them, where we should have them, and how the Supreme Court defines them. However, focusing only on these albeit important questions ignores the reality that rights can exist even when an appropriate remedy is removed, a practice that has been described as one of the most "insidious" ways for courts or other actors to erode access to justice.[7] And without a remedy, the meaning of a right—and access to obtaining or enforcing it—is often severely limited.

This chapter deals with the retrenchment of judicial remedies, which ultimately incentivize and/or enable would-be litigants to bring their grievances to court. Considering the availability of remedies through the lens of access to courts illuminates a complex calculus involving who you can sue, for what, and who has the power to make such determinations. While there are many aspects to the process of redressing legal claims, I focus on two specific strategies employed by those seeking to constrict access to courts: (1) creating doctrines of immunity and narrowing causes of action in order to limit who can be sued and what types of claims are considered legally valid; and (2) efforts aimed at constricting the monetary remedies awarded to successful claimants. While it is clear how reducing the amount of money that you can recover in a successful lawsuit could de-incentivize the choice to initiate a legal claim, it is also important to recognize that *access* to those remedies is dependent on one's ability to get into court in the first place. As such, questions of remedy are more complicated than they at first seem. Because any constriction levied upon court jurisdiction, who you can sue, and what constitutes a valid claim also limits the power of the court to provide remedies, retrenchment in this arena is fundamentally about redress to the courts as much as it is about actual monetary damages or injunctions.

In order to successfully initiate a case, after all, one must have both a cause of action and legal standing.[8] While both are relatively clear in the realm of criminal violations, they have been subject to significant discretion, contestation, and change over time where civil cases are concerned. This has been especially true in the area of civil suits against government actors, for as statutory rights expanded over the course of the twentieth century, so too did the potential for violative behavior on the part of government officials. At times this has created significant controversy over whether private individuals can sue government officials, with courts exercising significant discretion in settling the question. But from early in the nation's history, politicians and judges have struggled to determine which branch of government ultimately has the constitutional power to determine remedies. Congress has at times weighed in on questions of governmental immunities, and presidents have sought to promote their own idea of who should properly find themselves before a court, and for what types of disputes. Add in the Supreme Court's discretion to determine *who* has the primary power to establish who has access to court, and it is clear that questions of remedy are subject to just as much political and institutional strife as in the other areas of judicial retrenchment that we have thus far seen.[9]

This issue has become more complicated because the nature of available remedies has changed over time as well. Often by act of Congress, the courts have amassed other tools and methods for remunerating successful plaintiffs beyond classic compensatory damages. Attorney's fees, which have a long history of use in the United States, may be made available to winning plaintiffs as part of the "costs" of a lawsuit.[10] Aimed to defray the costs of filing a suit, and therefore to incentivize litigation, the courts' ability to award such fees has constituted a crucial remedy in politically divisive moments—particularly during the Civil Rights era—as the promise of recovering such fees made it more lucrative for lawyers to represent poor and disadvantaged clients who would otherwise be unlikely to have their day in court. In recent decades, courts have also increased the practice of awarding punitive damages, which vary from traditional damages in an important way; while damages are usually intended to compensate plaintiffs for their losses, punitive damages are awarded in order to punish defendants for egregious conduct and to deter defendants and others from future offenses. While they are the subject of significant controversy, usually due to their perceived "excessive" nature, these awards provide an additional fund, on top of traditional remedies, from which plaintiffs can recover attorney's fees and cover other costs of litigation. In effect, these so-called "damages enhancements" also aim to incentivize litigation.[11]

The process of awarding remedies, then, is clearly political. In addition to concerns regarding the costliness of modern remedies, this is in large part because of the array of actors empowered to weigh in on a process that, at first blush, appears to be the sole province of the courts. In Part I of the chapter, I examine these interbranch negotiations in the context of the development of doctrines of immunity, causes of action, and legal remedies in the early American state. Despite the complicated political arrangement regarding questions of redress to courts that manifested by the rights revolution era, under the private law model that defined the early part of the twentieth century, questions of standing, injury, and remedy were relatively uncomplicated. The right to suit was linked to a group of well-defined common law injuries arising from tort, violation of property rights, and breach of contract. Congress did not need to specify remedies; because the vast majority of cases involved common law violations, the courts could simply imply the remedies of common law. With the growth and entrenchment of the national administrative state, however, the relationship between justiciability, adjudication, and remedies became increasingly complicated. As we have seen in previous chapters, the earliest effects of these changes on the judicial system, such as the advent of multi-party, multi-claim cases and a vastly increased caseload, seriously impacted procedures governing access to the courts. While government institutions responded fairly quickly to these developments (by establishing new justiciability doctrines to facilitate more wide-ranging litigation, for example), they did not establish a parallel "doctrine" of remedies until the Civil Rights era.

As we know, however, concerns about and frustrations with the rapidly expanding national government manifested much earlier, in two seemingly contradictory ways. In response to the social welfare goals that served as the impetus for the growth of a national administrative state, government quickly became "a breathtakingly complex system of social welfare programs," and those programs raised concern in that they "delegate[d] enormous powers to frontline inspectors and other field operatives, creating numerous risks for error and abuse."[12] And as the government increasingly intervened in the national economy, expanding its propensity not only to benefit, but also to harm private citizens, government immunity came under attack. Citizens and Congress quickly began to see the need for a system of public tort law that would allow citizens to redress harm that public officials may have caused to their person or property. But at the same time, however, the Supreme Court created and refined a set of justiciability doctrines to maintain proper separation of powers between branches by constricting the use of citizen suits that aimed to enlist the judiciary to oversee the executive branch's compliance with congressional action.[13]

While Congress and the Supreme Court have fought for control over the power to provide remedies since early in the nation's history, over the past three decades in particular, the availability of civil rights remedies has been significantly constricted. I examine these constrictions in Part II. After failing to pass legislation restricting remedies from the 1940s to 90s, Congress has had some success in recent decades, particularly since the Republican takeover of the House in 2004. At the behest of the Supreme Court, late in the Civil Rights era, Congress also created a statutory basis for the provision of attorney's fees and has at times attempted to legislate the upper limits for punitive damages. The Supreme Court has also exercised its authority over remedies, first expanding opportunities for litigants to claim damages—through the rights revolution era, and largely in the form of Section 1983 actions—and later restricting them through a narrow interpretation of the same statutory provisions. Notably, this constriction has reached to punitive damages as well. In total, the power struggle between the branches has meaningfully separated questions of right from remedy (as manifested in developments regarding the form and availability of remedies, causes of action, and immunities), at times with a chilling effect on the incentives that individual citizens have for asking that their rights violations be heard in court.

Unlike the other retrenchment strategies discussed, Congress has had much less success scaling back remedies. While legislators have tried at times to limit attorney's fees and occasionally succeeded, mostly at the state level, in capping punitive damages, judicial innovation in the area of causes of action and immunities is the dominant story. But given what we know about the conditions for retrenchment, this is largely unsurprising. Monetary incentives like attorney's fees, for example, are a concentrated benefit, and a highly visible one at that. They both benefit the highly entrenched legal profession *and* have a cross-party appeal; that is, whether liberal or conservative, individuals filing a lawsuit benefit from enhanced monetary incentives. This notable confluence of interests in and of itself makes attempts at overt legislative reform more difficult than with regard to many other retrenchment strategies. Add to this the reality that legislative changes to attorney's fees are open to political contestation, and we clearly have a slate of conditions that make retrenchment most difficult. These conditions stand in stark contrast to judicial treatment of doctrines like qualified immunity, where insulated judges have the largely uncontested power to control the rules of the game. In practice, then, this becomes a highly court-dominated area of reform.

Part I: The Historical Development of Remedies and Legal Redress

Rights and Remedies in the Early American State
Immunities and Causes of Action

In the nineteenth century, officer suits were the primary mechanism for involving the judiciary in disputes between the government and private individuals, and hence for obtaining judicial review. If a government officer harmed a private person and claimed official privilege as a defense, the plaintiff could be successful only if the officer was found to have engaged in a private wrongdoing outside of his official privilege. Even then, however, many injuries that arose from the government were not due to wrongdoings on the part of officers personally. Because the legal system was centered on private rights, even in cases involving the government or its officials, relief could also only be granted if the legislature waived its sovereign immunity—the presumption that the federal government may not be sued without its consent.[14]

It is this dynamic that generates the elements involved in the provision of remedies. In order to bring a claim before a court, individuals must have a cause of action, or a set of facts sufficient to justify the right to sue. The idea of a "cause of action," such as breach of contract or torts stemming from injury, encompasses both a theory of the legal wrong the plaintiff claims to have suffered and a corresponding remedy that a court can provide in order to compensate them for that wrong.[15] In addition, a litigant must establish that they have legal standing—that is, that they are the proper party to bring a particular dispute to court. As with other areas of the law, causes of action and questions of standing were simpler concepts prior to the development of the national administrative state, when they primarily corresponded with a well-defined group of traditional common law injuries. As the administrative state developed, however, so did the potential for legal conflict between private individuals and government actors.

Over time, this created two problems for the courts. First, because Congress increasingly included provisions for legal redress within its statutes, judges were faced with the question of whether individuals should be allowed to enforce a right or benefit in court where Congress did not explicitly include such a provision. This dilemma led to the birth of what is known as a "private right of action" (also known as "implied causes of action"). Private rights of action refer to instances where a court finds that a law that creates rights also allows private parties to bring a lawsuit, even if no such remedy is explicitly provided for in the law. Beginning in the 1960s and continuing well into the 1970s, the Supreme Court adopted a stance that federal courts had the power to infer remedies—including private rights of action for either injunctive or monetary relief—from both the Constitution itself and from statutes otherwise silent about private enforcement.

Second, because the expansion of statutory rights increased the likelihood of suits arising from the allegedly violative behavior of administrative officials, the courts have had to revisit their doctrines of official immunity. In addition to the nineteenth-century doctrines protecting the federal government from suit, two other major types of government immunity predated the administrative state: *sovereign immunity*, which refers to the Eleventh Amendment protection for states and state agencies against suit without their consent; and *absolute immunity*, which protects presidents while in office, and judges, lawyers, legislators performing legislative tasks, and police officers who testify as witnesses from lawsuits brought against them for their official conduct.[16] The Constitution is not altogether clear about the extent of governmental immunities. At the time it was written, states were largely considered immune from lawsuits unless they consented to them, making the idea that they intended states to be open to lawsuits by their own citizens even more improbable.[17] However, charters in several colonies (including Connecticut, Massachusetts, and Rhode Island) expressly indicated that their state governments *could*, in fact, be subject to lawsuit. Evidence from the state ratifying conventions is unclear, with several Founders (including Madison and Hamilton) arguing that states could not be sued by citizens in federal court, while other evidence indicates that the Framers may have even intended to preclude governmental immunity.[18] Perhaps because of this lack of clarity, the issue quickly garnered national attention, culminating in the Supreme Court's 1793 decision in *Chisholm v. Georgia*. While the state of Georgia had successfully asserted its immunity against a breach of contract suit and refused to appear in the case in lower court, the Court proceeded without the state and held on behalf of the plaintiff, arguing that Article III in fact abrogated the state's claim of sovereign immunity and that, in ratifying the Constitution, the states had consented to be legally accountable to the people. As such, the Court affirmatively granted federal courts the power to hear disputes between private citizens and states.[19]

This was not well received by the states, which feared that they would be confronted with a series of similar lawsuits. Accordingly, the Court's decision in *Chisholm* was almost immediately superseded by the passage of the Eleventh Amendment. The amendment, which drew widespread support and was quickly ratified in 1794, established that "the Judicial power of the United States shall not be construed to extend to any suit in law or equity, commenced or prosecuted, against one of the United States by Citizens of another State, or by Citizens or Subjects of any Foreign State" and thereby nullified the effect of *Chisholm* by reasserting common law immunity for the states.[20] Over the course of the next century, however, the Supreme Court weakened the amendment by allowing litigants to use the federal courts to challenge state officials in their individual capacities, even when acting under the authority of state law. In this model, so long as a state itself was not named as a defendant in the case, and so long as relief would not come from the state treasury, the amendment was not construed to preclude citizens from suing. The Court continued to promote limits on the reach of the amendment throughout the 1800s (with some mixed signals, most notably in its 1890 decision in *Hans v. Louisiana*),[21] establishing that it did not grant immunities to local governments within the states and later clarifying that, when a state official is accused of misconduct, "he is in that case stripped of his official or representative character and is subjected in his person to the consequences of his individual conduct."[22] As such, the state could not grant him immunity.

In terms of absolute immunity, the Supreme Court granted it to prosecutors in 1927[23] and to the "quasi-judicial and regulatory organs of the welfare state" in 1938.[24] Beginning in the nineteenth century, a tradition also arose of providing immunity, in some circumstances, to executive officials sued in tort. While official immunity originated as a common law doctrine, its rationale was based in the realm of policy; failure to provide immunity, it was thought, would "dampen the ardor of all but the most resolute, or the most irresponsible [public officials], in the unflinching discharge of their duties.... [I]n this instance, it has been thought in the end better to leave unredressed the wrongs done by dishonest officers than to subject those who try to do their duty to the constant dread of retaliation."[25] When immunity was granted, a plaintiff injured by an official's tortious conduct was denied a damages remedy, even if damages were the only effective form of redress.[26]

With the onset of the New Deal era, as government increasingly intervened in the economy, in turn expanding its potential to harm private citizens, Congress began to take issue with immunity as a vehicle for shutting down the adjudication of claims against the government. Subsequently, while the courts continued to expand immunity, Congress began to attack it. Their early-twentieth-century efforts came to fruition in 1946 with the passage of the Federal Tort Claims Act (FTCA),[27] designed primarily in order to make filing tort claims in federal court easier. The law was in many ways the culmination of years of efforts in which Congress introduced more than 1000 private claims bills a year for property damage and personal injury caused by the government.[28] At the same time, the FTCA established a limited waiver of sovereign immunity for the federal government, providing for damages for personal injury, death, or property damage caused by "negligent or wrongful act or omission" of any federal employee acting within the scope of his or her employment.[29] In addition, however, it effectively strengthened immunity for government officials by stipulating that if the United States was found at fault in a particular case, plaintiffs were precluded from seeking indemnification from the official whose misconduct caused the judgment. The act also contained several explicit "exceptions," perhaps most importantly specifying that the FTCA's provisions would not apply to "any claim ... based upon the exercise or performance or the failure to exercise a discretionary function or duty ... whether or not the discretion involved be abused."[30] In discussing the bill, members of Congress made explicit that "the bill is not intended to authorize a suit for damages to test the validity of or provide a remedy on account of such discretionary acts, even though negligently performed and involving an abuse of discretion."[31] Congress' position was so clear, in fact, that the Supreme Court denied jurisdiction to several cases under the act in the 1950s, going as far as to hold—with regard to constitutional torts committed by the United States and federal officials—that Congress, not the Court, had the power to define remedies.[32]

Attorney's Fees in the Early American State

In the early part of the twentieth century, the legislative and judicial branches began what would also become a century long back-and-forth to establish and control one specific remedy available to successful litigants. Attorney's fees, which refer to money awarded to successful plaintiffs in order to defray the costs of filing a lawsuit, are awarded as "costs" of a case. Historically, the Supreme Court has considered attorney's fees a type of remedy, at least in public interest cases, where they provide the plaintiff with another tool for asserting rights. Generally, however, attorney's fees are not recoverable in most types of cases, as they are not traditionally awarded to the prevailing party absent statute, contract, or satisfying certain equitable remedies. Where such fees are made available, they are determined on the basis of the "American Rule," whereby each party bears its own costs of litigation. This is in contrast to the historic English approach, where the winning party recovers litigation expenses from the losing party. The United States chose its system on the grounds that refraining from awarding attorney's fees to the winning party would avoid penalizing a party for its reasonable claim or defense that was ultimately unsuccessful. Given that the losing party has not done anything wrong in participating in a legal action, the logic goes, imposing fees may discourage legitimate use of the judicial system. The historical justification for the American Rule, then, is founded upon a commitment to providing citizens with access to justice; for "if a wronged party is deterred from filing and prosecuting a suit by the risk that he will have to pay the opposing party's attorney's fees if the suit is unsuccessful, there is a concern that many wrongs could go unremedied in our society. That rationale is effectively pro-litigation, even pro-plaintiff, in the sense that it reflects a view that access to courts by claimants should not be discouraged by the threat of substantial, potential penalties for losing."[33]

Attorney's fees have a long history in the United States. During the first years of the federal court system, Congress established that the federal courts were to follow the practices of the states with respect to awarding attorney's fees. Five days after passing the Federal Judiciary Act of 1789, Congress enacted further legislation regulating court processes. Among them, Congress determined "that until further provision shall be made, and except where by this act or other statutes of the United States is otherwise provided ... rates of fees, except fees to judges, in the circuit and district courts, in suits at common law, shall be the same in each state respectively as are now used or allowed in the supreme courts of the same.[34] For a brief period of about five years, Congress stipulated that it would allow the award of attorney's fees to the prevailing party in the Supreme, circuit, and district courts.[35] By 1800, however, all statutes governing fees had either expired or been repealed.

Around the same time, the Supreme Court also established its early position on attorney's fees. In 1796 the Court ruled that the judiciary itself should not create a general rule, independent of a statute, allowing awards of attorney's fees in federal courts. In *Arcambel v. Wiseman*, the inclusion of attorney's fees as damages was overturned on the grounds that "[t]he general practice of the *United States* is in opposition [*sic*] to it; and even if that practice were not strictly correct in principle, it is entitled to the respect of the court till it is changed, or modified, by statute."[36] Importantly, the Supreme Court has adhered to this position to the present, often finding itself in conflict with congressional fee-shifting statutes as a result.[37]

Following this brief period of congressional regulation, in the mid-nineteenth century, New York's highly influential Field Code of Civil Procedure explicitly rejected any regulations "establishing or regulating the costs or fees of attorneys" and declared that "hereafter the measure of such compensation shall be left to the agreement, express or implied, of the parties." The Field Code also suggested that, in stark contrast to both our historical and contemporary views, a "loser pays" system might actually be justified by the costs that attorneys could otherwise impose on innocent victims simply by virtue of filing a lawsuit.[38] In the years that followed, however, fee-shifting provisions benefiting plaintiffs became the norm. As a consequence, and in line with the American "access to justice" predisposition, "the result has been an abdication of any significant limits on the power of attorneys to file lawsuits, the encouragement of filing lawsuits through fee-shifting rules that benefit plaintiffs alone, and—with the rise of the numbers and influence of attorneys in America—the triumph of rules that only create additional demand for attorneys."[39]

Although Congress declined in its early years to codify a general rule governing the provision of fees, they passed three early federal statutes—the Civil Rights Act of 1870 (also known as the Force Act, or the Enforcement Act), the Interstate Commerce Act of 1887, and the Sherman Act of 1890—that allowed successful plaintiffs, but not successful defendants, to recover their legal expenses. Throughout the Progressive era, many states followed suit, largely in hopes of encouraging attorneys to represent poor plaintiffs suing larger corporations. These state laws allowed for the award of attorney's fees and costs to prevailing plaintiffs, but generally only when the losing party responsible for paying such fees was a large corporation.[40] Unsurprisingly, the Supreme Court struck down statutes of this nature for violating the equal protection clause.[41]

But beginning as early as the New Deal era, Congress began to include attorney's fees provisions in its various statutes in order to allow the recovery of attorney's fees by a prevailing party. Major New Deal statutes like the Securities Act of 1933, the Securities Exchange Act of 1934, and the Fair Labor Standards Act of 1938 all provided for attorney's fees as a potential remedy for litigants bringing suit under the law. The justification for fee-shifting was based on (1) providing an incentive for plaintiffs to vindicate their rights under a particular statute, and (2) in classic remedial terms, to "make them whole" again by not diminishing their award by forcing them to pay their own attorney's fees. While in a seeming departure from the American Rule, these fee-shifting statutes were inspired by its same "access to justice" spirit, "serving as an exception that actually reinforces the pro-plaintiff rationale of the American Rule."[42]

As discussed in the context of the development of the federal civil rules, attorney's fees provisions became critical for incentivizing rights claims during the Civil Rights era, as the potential for recovering fees made it more lucrative for attorneys to represent poor and disadvantaged parties. As Congress continued to provide for attorney's fees by individual statutes—later even enacting provisions that swept whole areas of litigation into the fee award system—the legality of these provisions quickly became a topic of concern for the courts.[43] Courts have always maintained some power to grant exceptions to the traditional American Rule,[44] awarding "reasonable" attorney's fees to a prevailing party when the losing party has acted in "bad faith" in the conduct of litigation, for example. In the 1960s and 70s, the Supreme Court read these fee-shifting statutes broadly, drawing from them an underlying rationale and assumption that civil rights statutes should encourage enforcement by "private attorneys general."[45] But over time, these fees became the object of an interbranch struggle, casting doubt on their ability to incentivize litigation on behalf of poor and disadvantaged litigants.

Remedies and the Rights Revolution
The Foundations of Private Enforcement

The availability of attorney's fees for successful plaintiffs proliferated, however, in the 1960s. This was in no small part due to the successful fight to include fee-shifting provisions in major civil rights legislation, as well as the reality that such provisions are "not the unique province of any particular ideological or partisan program, nor have they been exclusively deployed to serve a specific type of constituency."[46] While Democrat-controlled congresses have more often enacted private enforcement regimes to regulate business, more conservative congresses have also embraced the appeal of attorney's fees for successful plaintiffs; the Taft-Hartley Act of 1947, for example, gave companies a cause to pursue economic damages against unions engaged in labor actions proscribed by the act.[47] Given the bipartisan appeal of this tool for incentivizing litigation, Congress increasingly chose to use fee-shifting provisions to implement "private enforcement regimes" whereby private individuals, and subsequently courts, were deputized to enforce major rights litigation.

The attorney's fee provision included in the Civil Rights Act of 1964—which Sean Farhang describes as "clearly intended to facilitate, rather than merely permit, private enforcement litigation"—in many ways provided the foundation for the use of private enforcement regimes.[48] The version of the act that passed the House did not contain such a provision; but in the compromise amendments offered in the Senate, courts were granted the authority to waive filing fees and to appoint an attorney for plaintiffs, as well as to award winning plaintiffs attorney's fees and other costs of the suit (to be paid by defendants). While some Republicans in the Senate (predominantly Strom Thurmond) tried to strike the fee-shifting provision from the amendment, civil rights activists ultimately prevailed by expressing their fear that the right to sue would be hollow without a fee-shifting provision. Scholars have observed a similar story for other Civil Rights–era legislation as well; as Farhang describes of the Fair Housing Act of 1968, for example, "Pivotal conservative Republicans, empowered by a divided Democratic Party and super majoritarian legislative institutions, imposed private litigation, with mobilizing incentives such as fee-shifting and appointment of counsel, in order to defeat bureaucratic state-building by liberal civil rights advocates."[49] And even amidst a campaign to amend Title VII to give the EEOC more traditional, bureaucratic "cease and desist" powers, civil rights advocates refused to let go of private lawsuits with fee-shifting, evidence of the degree to which such provisions were viewed as providing a powerful incentive for individual litigants to seek enforcement of civil rights statutes in court. As the American Bar Association (ABA) informed a judiciary subcommittee at the time, "The right or privilege of being represented by counsel ... becomes hollow if the private party is prohibited from paying his attorney other than a subnormal fee. Retaining one's own counsel is a private right which deserves safeguarding in fact as well as in theory."[50]

As the political and practical value of private enforcement regimes became clear, and as fee-shifting provisions proliferated,[51] the courts found themselves facing a complementary question: In the era of burgeoning rights legislation (inspired in many ways by deepened appreciation for equality under the law and hinging on equal access to justice), should individuals have the right to seek redress in court for the enforcement of statutes where Congress failed to explicitly provide that right? While private individuals long played a key role in enforcing federal rights, the explosion of citizen suit provisions eventually prompted the question of what to do in their absence. This dilemma led to the birth of what is known as a private right of action, which refers to instances where a court finds that a law creating rights also allows private parties to bring a lawsuit, even if no such remedy was explicitly provided for in the relevant law itself. During the Civil Rights era the Supreme Court took the position that the federal courts had the discretion to infer remedies, including private rights of action, even if a statute is otherwise silent about private enforcement.

The idea that statutory causes of action might be implied, however, was not solely a rights revolution–era construction. As early as *Marbury v. Madison*, the Court espoused the view that, since rights are premised on the availability of remedies, when Congress fails to provide for one, the court must do so. And they typically did. Because of this, there is little to no reference to legislative intent in early cases addressing whether individuals had the right to sue under specific laws, as "the right of courts to imply a cause of action from an act of Congress simply was not thought to depend on the will of Congress."[52] Rather, the focus of the early courts was on remedial adequacy and the need to provide relief to injured plaintiffs.

The idea that congressional intent was an integral component for determining whether to recognize a private right of action arose in the late nineteenth and early twentieth centuries. When considering a railroad safety
dispute in 1904, for example, the Supreme Court relied upon a determination
that the purpose of the statute at hand (the Railroad Safety Appliance Act of
1893) was to protect travelers from injury.[53] The case often cited as the first
to recognize an implied cause of action, however, involved another railroad
dispute in 1916. In *Texas & Pacific Railway Company v. Rigsby*,[54] the Court
applied a simple test (again with regard to the Safety Appliance Act)[55] in order
to determine the availability of an implied private remedy: if a statute was
enacted for the benefit of a special class, the courts would recognize a remedy
for members of that class. While the federal courts henceforth regarded the
possibility of denying a remedy the exception rather than the rule, even with
the proliferation of New Deal federal legislation, the Court gave mixed signals on whether and when to recognize the right of a private individual to go
to court absent express statutory authorization. On the one hand, in 1934 the
Court reversed its 1916 *Rigsby* decision, holding that the adjudicatory consequences of the Safety Appliance Act were limited to those expressly provided
by Congress,[56] and in the years following the Court's landmark *Erie* decision
(which denied the federal court's ability to create common law in diversity
cases), the Court frequently denied private rights of action, focusing instead
on the availability of other means to enforce statutory duties (a mediation
board, for example).[57] On the other hand, however, where there appeared
to be *no* other source of potential remedy for injured claimants, the Court
consistently erred on the side of allowing a case to move forward.[58]

In a pair of cases during the rights revolution, the Court explicitly recognized private rights of action as such and made clear its willingness to allow
for private enforcement of statutes. In *J.I. Case Company v. Borak* in 1964, the
Court held that, given the purpose and legislative history of the Securities
Exchange Act, a private right of action should be implied under the act. More
importantly, the Court announced a "duty of the courts to be alert to provide such remedies as are necessary to make effective congressional purpose,"
in many ways making explicit the historic presumption that congressional
silence was insufficient reason to deny a remedy to the members of a class
that a statute seeks to protect. In addition, in *Bivens v. Six Unknown Named
Agents*,[59] the Court dealt with private rights of action for constitutional rights,
holding that an individual whose Fourth Amendment freedom from unreasonable search and seizure had been violated by federal agents could sue for
violation of the amendment itself, despite the fact that there was no federal

statute authorizing the suit. With regard to remedies, the Court did argue, however, that it only found the implied cause of action because Congress had not provided for an adequate alternative remedy. Nonetheless, together the cases made clear to politicians and citizens alike that the courts would be available for the private enforcement of both rights revolution era–statutes and constitutional rights, with great effects for the activists of that era.

In the context of a Court willing to recognize both private rights of action and fee-shifting provisions, the civil rights bar also sought to extend the Civil Rights Act of 1964's fee-shifting provision to cover all the civil rights laws that allowed for private enforcement but did not stipulate attorney's fee recovery specifically. In so doing, the Court hoped to expand further its funding to support enforcement, to enlarge the civil rights bar by attracting more lawyers to practice, and to add a more significant economic penalty in order to better deter potential civil rights violators.[60] As a result, civil rights groups, especially the NAACP, also began to lobby Democrats in Congress to extend the fee-shifting provisions of the CRA to other civil rights laws lacking them. This led the Senate Judiciary Committee to take up the matter in 1973; but Congress ultimately failed to act.[61] Still, including fee-shifting provisions in individual statutes became a near-automatic practice in various areas of policy, among them school desegregation (the Emergency School Aid Act of 1972); voting rights (Section 402 of the Voting Rights Amendments of 1975); consumer litigation (e.g., the Truth-in-Lending Act, Motor Vehicle Information and Cost Savings Act, and the Consumer Product Safety Act, all of 1975); and environmental legislation (Federal Water Pollution Control Amendments of 1972 and the Ocean Dumping Act of 1975). In addition to a legislative strategy, both non-profit and for-profit civil rights lawyers pressed the courts to infer the availability of attorney's fees under those historic civil rights statutes lacking fee-shifting provisions, including the Civil Rights Acts of 1866 and 1871.[62]

Lawsuits "Under Color of State Law"

Amidst all of these congressional developments, however, by the 1960s the Supreme Court had also laid the foundations for its own framework for assessing constitutional injuries for which federal judicial remedies could and could not be withheld. This framework arose from a landmark 1961 case, *Monroe v. Pape*.[63] The case effectively resurrected a section of the post–Civil War federal civil rights act, the Civil Rights Act of 1871, now codified as Section 1983 of the United States Code.[64] The law—popularly known as the Ku Klux Klan Act, designed "to enforce the Provisions of the Fourteenth Amendment to the Constitution of the United States"[65]—was enacted to protect southern blacks from KKK violence by providing a civil remedy for the abuses being committed in the South. The act therefore made state officials liable in federal court for depriving anyone of their civil rights or equal protection of the laws; it also made a number of the KKK's intimidation tactics into federal offenses, authorized the president to call out the militia to suppress conspiracies against the operation of the federal government, and prohibited those suspected of complicity in these conspiracies to serve on juries related to the Klan's activities. In effect, Section 1983 of the act made monetary damages available to those whose constitutional rights had been violated by a person acting under state authority. Accordingly, when thirteen Chicago police officers broke into Mr. Monroe's residence, forcing him and his wife to stand naked in the living room while they ransacked his house and subsequently interrogated him—without a search or arrest warrant—the plaintiffs filed a complaint against the police officers of Chicago under Section 1983, which reads: "Every person who, under color of any statute ... subjects, or causes to be subjected, any citizen of the United States or other person within the jurisdiction thereof to the deprivation of any rights, privileges, or immunities secured by the Constitution and laws, shall be liable to the party injured in an action at law, suit in equity, or other proper proceeding for redress."

While Section 1983 appears to be a sweeping remedy—in fact, it was used extensively by the Department of Justice under President Ulysses Grant[66]—in the years following its passage, its reach was limited by a narrow definition of what actually constituted the "rights, privileges, or immunities" provided by the Constitution; if the courts did not recognize the infringement of a right, there would be no duty to provide a remedy under 1983. This was in no small part due to the Supreme Court's narrow interpretation of the Reconstruction Amendments; in the *Slaughterhouse Cases*, for example, the Court argued that the Fourteenth Amendment protection of "privileges and immunities" safeguarded only a small number of rights associated with a citizen's relationship to the federal government. And under such a narrow definition, there were few opportunities for plaintiffs to rely on Section 1983 to sue state and local officials for alleged wrongdoings.[67] The potential scope of 1983 was complicated even further by cases like *United States v. Cruikshank* and *United States v. Harris*, in which the Court found that the First Amendment right to assembly "was not intended to limit the powers of the State governments in respect to their own citizens" and that the federal government could not punish private conspiracies without proof that the state had failed in its efforts to protect rights (respectively).[68] As such, it was invoked only in a very limited sense prior to 1939 and used successfully only in cases that challenged unconstitutional restrictions on voting for African Americans.[69] Despite this period of dormancy, Section 1983 was essential for bringing the white primary to an end; because the Supreme Court had argued in *United States v. Classic* (1941) that the primary was an integral part of state electoral machinery, therefore concluding that an official who had committed fraud was, in fact, acting "under the color of law,"[70] the Court was able to overturn the Democratic Party's use of an all-white primary in Texas with a similar rationale.[71] Importantly, however, *Monroe v. Pape* laid the foundation for the expansion of 1983 into other areas as well.[72]

In *Monroe,* the Court rejected the police officer's argument that the "under color of state law" provision of Section 1983 limited liability to cases in which state law authorized acts that violated the Constitution. The Court argued that, in enacting the Civil Rights Act of 1871, Congress had intended to give a remedy to parties deprived of constitutional rights, privileges, and immunities by an officer's abuse of his or her discretion. Further, the statutory words "under the color of any statute, ordinance, regulation, custom, or usage, or any State or Territory" did not exclude the actions of a police official who can show no authority under state law. In so deciding, the Court established Section 1983 as an independent basis for remedies for acts, whether authorized by state law or not, that were violative of the Constitution or federal law.

As many have argued, it is difficult to overstate the importance of this case; without it, constitutional litigation against state officials in the absence of an express statutory remedy would have been extremely difficult. Just two years after the case, Section 1983 litigation grew by over 60 percent, making it "the legal bulwark of the ripening civil rights movement."[73] Three years later, the Court handed down another landmark decision with the effect of opening up access to courts—this time for suits against federal officers for alleged constitutional violations. In *Bivens* (as discussed above), the Court argued that it would recognize an implied cause of action because Congress had not provided for an alternative remedy that the Court believed to be adequate.[74] When Federal Bureau of Narcotics officers searched the house of Webster Bivens and arrested him without a warrant, the government argued that the Fourth Amendment itself provided no cause of action for Bivens; but based on the principle that for every wrong, there must be a remedy, Justice William Brennan established that the Court would infer a private right of action for monetary damages when there is no other federal remedy available for the vindication of a constitutional right. In total, then, *Monroe* and *Bivens* enabled citizens to seek compensation for injuries suffered at the hands of state and federal officials committing both constitutional and statutory violations, at times even in the absence of an explicit statutory cause of action.

The cases, however, did not create an unblemished precedent for allowing injured citizens to sue government officials in court. In a 1951 case, the Supreme Court held that Section 1983 created a civil damages remedy against any government official causing "the deprivation of any rights, privileges, or immunities secured by the Constitution and laws"[75]; but by incorporating Section 1983 into the common law of immunity, the Court also extended its "official immunity" protections. Because of this, a plaintiff who demonstrates the deprivation of a constitutional or statutory right may not be entitled to recovery if the government official proves an entitlement to qualified immunity. The recognition that, in some circumstances, immunity for government officials should not be absolute, but *qualified*, both opened a window for plaintiffs seeking remedy against the actions of government officials and gave the Court another doctrinal device by which to keep litigants out of court. Even *Monroe v. Pape* excluded some government entities, such as municipalities, from coverage as a "person" under Section 1983. And while a set standard for qualified immunity did not arise until well after the Civil Rights era, the phrase itself was first used in *Scheuer v. Rhodes* in 1974, in the statement "the immunity of officers of the executive branch of a state government for their acts is not absolute, but qualified, and of varying degree, depending upon the scope of discretion and responsibilities of the particular office and the circumstances existing at the time the challenged action was taken."[76] The concept was applied to *Bivens* and Section 1983 actions alike, granting federal officials immunity from damages liability unless he "knew or reasonably should have known that the action he took within his sphere of official responsibility would violate the constitutional rights of the [plaintiff], or if he took the action with the malicious intention to cause [injury].[77]

The Court's decision two years later in *Imbler v. Pachtman*[78] was among a series of cases surrounding Section 1983; but this one in particular caught the attention of liberal Democrats in Congress. In *Imbler*, while the plaintiff had been convicted after a trial in which the prosecutor had knowingly introduced false testimony, the Court nonetheless maintained that prosecutors enjoy immunity. In response, Democrats sought to revise Section 1983 to expand its definition of government actors. One of the legislation's sponsors, Senator Charles Mathias of Maryland, said in hearings that the legislation was aimed to ensure that Section 1983—the "primary vehicle" that kept the federal courthouse door open in the Civil Rights era—would continue to be interpreted in the broad fashion established by the Warren

Court: "Courthouse doors, which had been open so wide, have begun to close little by little. Access to the Federal court system is being constricted."[79] Mathias added that "we must not forget that rights that cannot be enforced through the legal process are worthless. Such a situation breeds cynicism about the basic fairness of our judicial system. We in Congress must do what we can to insure that our Federal courts remain open to those in greatest need."[80] But Judge Edward Gignoux, who was representing the Judicial Conference, disagreed with Mathias, pointing out that litigation statistics told a different story than claims that courthouse doors were closing to civil rights plaintiffs. He therefore opposed the bill on grounds that it would increase tensions between federal and state courts and "precipitate a substantial amount of new litigation in the Federal district courts."[81] Congress failed to reach a vote; and by the early 1980s, Republican control of the Senate meant that Section 1983 was still criticized, but from a very different angle. For example, John Ashcroft, then Attorney General for the state of Missouri, criticized courts for using Section 1983 to intimidate local law enforcers and for clogging courts.[82]

Private Rights of Action and Government Officials in Court

In practice, there are several stages to providing a remedy. A court must distinguish what type of remedy fits the injury suffered and determine how best to implement the chosen remedy. Finally, a judge may choose to take into account what effect a remedy will have on the state, locality, or institution charged with providing such. Compensatory damages can be costly, and injunctions directed to future government conduct are even more so.[83]

As the Supreme Court continued to develop a doctrine determining remedies in cases with alleged constitutional violations, it increasingly took these factors into account. In the 1970s, and as the product of several major desegregation decisions, the Court developed an explicit test.[84] As finalized in 1977 in *Milliken v. Bradley*, the test had three parts: a remedy (1) must be determined by the nature and scope of the constitutional violation, (2) must be "remedial" in nature, and (3) in devising a remedy, the court must "take into account the interest of state and local authorities in managing their own affairs."[85] Due especially to the third prong, however, the test provided courts with substantial discretion. As a result, the Supreme Court has largely left the lower courts alone in terms of the remedies they decide upon in a given case.[86] However, where the issue of private rights of action was concerned, the Court developed a distinct test, which allowed the Court to recognize the right to sue for damages under the equal protection component of the Fifth

Amendment's due process clause and the Eighth Amendment's prohibition on cruel and unusual punishment in the late 1970s.[87]

While questions of private rights of action typically arose (and were widely granted) in civil cases, in *Cort v. Ash* in 1975 the Court dealt with the question of whether a court may imply a cause of action from criminal statutes. While the Court declined to find a private right of action in the case, it did create a new method for analyzing implication questions—one that would apply to both criminal and civil laws—and in contrast to its earlier position, one that relied more heavily on congressional intent. Specifically, the Court's new four-part test stipulated that courts must consider (1) whether the plaintiff is part of the class of persons "for whose especial benefit" the statute was enacted; (2) whether the legislative history suggests that Congress *intended* to create a cause of action; (3) whether granting an implied cause of action would support the underlying remedial scheme established by the statute at hand; and (4) whether the issue would traditionally be left to state law.[88]

While the Court applied the test flexibly in the years to follow,[89] it was not long before the Court increasingly fixated on legislative intent. This was perhaps clearest in *Cannon v. University of Chicago*, where a plaintiff sued the University of Chicago under Title IX of the Education Amendments of 1972, alleging that the university denied her admission on the basis of her sex.[90] The Court explicitly employed its *Cort* test, finding that all four factors pointed to an implied right of action; it determined that the female plaintiff was within the class protected by the statute, and that a private right of action was consistent with the remedial purpose that Congress had in mind. The Court came to this conclusion without differentiating between the statute and its implementation provisions that, while providing for attorney's fees, did not specify a cause of action. In the absence of a clear statutory mandate, the dissenters in the case (primarily Justice Lewis Powell) claimed that the Court's approach to private rights of action was incompatible with separation of powers, as it was only defensible for the Court to enforce an action where Congress explicitly demonstrated that it intended to create that remedy.

While Powell's argument would become the majority position under the Rehnquist Court, at the time the Supreme Court continued to find private rights of action expansively, further legitimating their use in constitutional cases as well. The following year in *Carlson v. Green*, for example, the Court provided for a *Bivens* remedy under the cruel and unusual clause of the Eighth Amendment for a prisoner who suffered from injuries, and later died when prison officials failed to give him proper medical attention.[91] However, in its *Cannon* decision, the Court overtly characterized the test as primarily a mechanism for discerning congressional intent, providing a basis for moving away from the four-factor test and toward an exclusive reliance on the congressional record. As Justice John Paul Stevens put it, "Before concluding that Congress intended to make a remedy available to a special class of plaintiffs, a court must carefully analyze the following four factors that *Cort v. Ash* identifies as indicative of such intent."[92] While the Court did not reverse its position until the 1990s, this shift, along with the growing traction of Justice Powell's separation of powers concerns, combined in later years to create a movement away from the idea that a right must come with a remedy, and therefore also away from the idea that it is the duty of the courts to recognize a cause of action when Congress fails to provide for it.

Shortly after the *Cannon* decision, the Court continued to indicate that legislative intent would be its primary determining factor in implication cases. In declining to find an implied cause of action under a section of the Securities Exchange Act of 1934 in the same year, the justices made clear that the relevant question was "whether Congress intended to create, either expressly or by implication, a private cause of action" and specified that the first three factors of the *Cort* test were, in fact, only meant to be used for determining legislative intent.[93] In practice, this meant that reviewing courts were not to assess independently whether or not a statute could support legal redress outside of explicit legislative history. The Court made the new centrality of intent even clearer in *Transamerica Mortgage Advisors, Inc. v. Lewis*, where the Court declined to find a right of action because there was no evidence in the legislative history suggesting any such intent[94] and began to find similarly in constitutional cases as well.[95] In aggregate, these decisions evidenced a major shift away from the *Marbury* position that the Court once embraced, whereby a right *must* come with a remedy in order to be legitimate.

Nonetheless, in the 1970s and early 80s, Section 1983 litigation also continued to grow; where 280 suits were filed under all civil rights statutes in 1960, in 1972, 8,000 Section 1983 claims specifically were filed.[96] The proliferation of 1983 actions was largely due to a series of favorable Supreme Court decisions, some of which appeared to be a double-edged sword for how available the doctrine would be to individuals. As discussed, in 1974 the Supreme Court determined that the immunity of officials (in this case, university officials and members of the National Guard) is not absolute, but "qualified," depending on the scope of discretion, responsibilities of the individual, and circumstances existing at the time that the challenged action was taken. The degree of immunity for a specific government official would therefore be determined after a trial on the issue of "good faith."[97] But shortly thereafter, the Court ruled that the "good faith" standard required not only that a jury inquire into the offending official's subjective attitude, but also that it objectively evaluate what the official reasonably *should* have known about the state of applicable law—a far more stringent requirement for holding offending officials responsible for their harmful behaviors.[98] While these decisions opened the door for suits against executive officials, the Court left ambiguous when immunity would be qualified and "where ... absolute immunity is essential for the conduct of public business."[99]

As Congress debated statutory changes to Section 1983, in 1978 the Court chose to extend its application to cases against local governments.[100] In *Monell v. Department of Social Services of the City of New York*, the Court decided that municipalities ought to be considered "persons" subject to liability under Section 1 of the Civil Rights Act of 1871. The case began in 1971 as a challenge to the New York City Board of Education's forced maternity leave policy, and in 1978 the Supreme Court ruled that cities could also be held liable for damages under the Civil Rights Act. This resolution created a precedent that for the first time established local government accountability for unconstitutional acts and created the right to obtain damages from municipalities in such cases. A 1980 case gave government officials the burden of actually pleading immunity and, more importantly, implied that they would bear the burden of proof as well.[101] Another case suggested that even a state supreme court might be denied absolute immunity and therefore be subject to declaratory and injunctive relief, potentially paying the plaintiff attorney's fees as well.[102] And still another prominent case—*Maine v. Thiboutot*—expanded Section 1983 to cases involving the deprivation of rights under any U.S. law, therefore allowing for suit against both state and local officials. The case, which arguably led to an explosion of Section 1983 cases (rising 129 percent from 1976 to 1986) prompted Republicans in congress to propose a "Municipal Liability Law" to shield local official from suit.[103]

Part II: Remedies Drift from Rights
From the Rights Revolution to Republican Party Resurgence
Seeds of Constriction: Suing the Government

Despite the developments increasing and incentivizing access to the courts during the 1960s and 70s, the many successes were ultimately short-lived. For example, *Monroe v. Pape* really marked the high point of 1983 litigation, and by the start of the 1980s, it was clear that the Court was "having some second thoughts about its recent handiwork."[104] As a result, the Burger Court began once again to limit Section 1983 actions in order to control the rapid multiplication of their use, and it did so in a variety of ways. First, in 1981 the Court held that Congress, in establishing a comprehensive scheme to regulate water pollution, had intended to preclude private enforcement under Section 1983.[105] This change of heart dovetailed with the Court's decreased willingness to find private rights of action in statutes by the late 1980s and early 1990s.[106] Second, the Court began to narrow its interpretation of Fourteenth Amendment due process rights in Section 1983 claims. In *DeShaney v. Winnebago County*, for example, the Court found that the due process clause did not impose a "special duty" on the federal government to protect the public from the harms of private actors unless it could be proven that the government itself created that harm. In the case, four-year-old Joshua DeShaney had been beaten into a coma by his father, the culmination of a long series of physical abuses thoroughly documented by the Winnebago County Department of Social Services. Despite this history, the Department declined to remove Joshua from his father; and when Joshua became comatose, his mother sued the Department of Social Service, alleging that its inaction had deprived her son of his "liberty interest in bodily integrity, in violation of his rights under the substantive component of the Fourteenth Amendment Due Process Clause, by failing to intervene to protect him against his father's violence."[107] But because the state itself did not *create* the harm Joshua suffered, the Court declined to allow for a successful Section 1983 claim; instead, it held that the due process clause would not be interpreted to allow torts committed by state actors to be considered constitutional violations.[108] While just one example, the case characterizes the Court's constricted understanding of the availability of 1983 claims for due process rights.

Third, the Burger Court also sought to extend immunity doctrines in order to cut back on access to courts for 1983 claims, largely by granting individual officer defendants immunity in Section 1983 cases. Although judges and lawyers have had absolute immunity in civil cases for centuries,[109] historically it has been permissible to prosecute them for criminally willful deprivations of constitutional rights under 18 U.S.C. 242, which is the criminal analog of Section 1983. Despite this, qualified immunity quickly became a means for denying damages to individuals—even those having suffered a constitutional violation of their rights—and qualified immunity in civil cases has followed a similar trajectory. Together, changes to retroactivity, along with the expansive application of the harmless error doctrine and limits on federal habeas relief, have together insulated many convictions against reversal, even in the case of intentional violations. Also, because more than 90 percent of sentences at the federal level stem from plea bargains, prosecutorial conduct is subject to very little judicial oversight in the vast majority of cases to begin with.[110]

The same has proven to be true in civil cases. In reshaping the standards for qualified immunity, in *Harlow v. Fitzgerald*,[111] Justice Powell elucidated the plethora of perceived deficiencies in the existing immunity law. According to his majority opinion, the previous standard allowed for too many torts, many of them deemed frivolous, with far too much time and energy lost by government officials having to defend themselves. Powell also lamented that the threat of suit, even an insubstantial one, both "chilled" officials in the performance of their duties and deterred able individuals from entering public service. To remedy these deficiencies, the Court provided a screening device; under *Harlow*, "government officials performing discretionary functions generally are shielded from liability for civil damages insofar as their conduct does not violate clearly established statutory or constitutional rights of which a reasonable person would have known."[112] In practice, the standard operates as a threshold; until a judge can determine that rights were "clearly established" at the time of an alleged violation, "discovery should not be allowed."[113]

On one level, the doctrine is not at all controversial; where a right is novel and its legal status unforeseen, it could be unfair to hold an individual officer liable. Prior to *Harlow*, early immunity decisions made precisely this point.[114] At the same time, however, the standards for discerning what "a reasonable person should have known" and "clearly established law" are not at all self-evident, and *Harlow* provided no further guidance. This lack of guidance has created a major problem for the courts over time; since "qualified immunity jurisprudence is prone to judicial manipulation ... the hundreds of appellate opinions, and even within judicial circuits ... are often inconsistent."[115] The Court ran into this difficulty shortly after *Harlow*; for example, in *Malley v. Briggs*, the Court claimed that the doctrine of qualified immunity protects all but the "plainly incompetent" or those who intentionally violate rights, suggesting that the objective standard of what a reasonably trained officer should have known provides expansive protection.[116] In *Andersen v. Creighton*, the Court also extended the doctrine to immunize conduct that violates plainly foreseeable violations, leaving substantial room to grant immunity to reasonable officers who might be "confused"; in addressing whether a federal law enforcement officer who participates in a search that violates the Fourth Amendment may be personally held liable for money damages if a reasonable officer could have believed that a search comported with the amendment (even in error), the Court granted immunity to the officer. These decisions foreshadowed further extension of protections under the doctrine authored under Chief Justice William Rehnquist.

Running parallel to the development of qualified immunity, the Court also began to assert a doctrine of state sovereign immunity. In the wake of *Monell* it was unclear how municipalities and states would be treated under Section 1983, and the Court ultimately resolved this dilemma in its subsequent state sovereign immunity jurisprudence. After the Court's 1793 decision in *Chisholm v. Georgia* (allowing a private citizen to sue the state), states were concerned that they would be confronted with a series of similar lawsuits, and critics of the decision pushed for a constitutional amendment to nullify its effects, restoring the states' common law immunity.[117] The subsequent Eleventh Amendment, however, only altered federal diversity jurisdiction, and so it was assumed that only lawsuits brought under state law were covered. Its protections were invoked roughly a century later when states grew concerned that bondholders might bring suits to recover unpaid interest on their state bonds. In *Hans v. Louisiana*, a bondholder brought exactly such a suit; and while the case did not involve diversity jurisdiction, the Court *did* invoke the Eleventh Amendment to protect the state from suit. Many years later, the Court argued more broadly that states could claim sovereign immunity in any case for damages where the state itself was the named defendant[118]—but this decision was not without its detractors. In 1972, when Congress amended Title VII of the Civil Rights Act of 1964 to authorize private suits for monetary damages, it did so by citing its authority under Section 5 of the Fourteenth Amendment, which gives Congress the power to enforce, by appropriate legislation, the provisions of the act. The plaintiffs, who were male retirees suing the state of Connecticut for sex discrimination in their retirement policies, had lost in lower federal court, with the courts allowing only monetary and not injunctive relief, based on the state's claim of Eleventh Amendment sovereign immunity. In this decision—written by Justice Rehnquist, perhaps an unlikely supporter—the Court held that statutes brought pursuant to congressional authority under Section 5 should, in fact, be understood to abrogate state sovereign immunity. Rehnquist reasoned that, since the Fourteenth Amendment was written to limit the powers of the states (with the purpose of enforcing civil rights guarantees against them), Congress had the power under the amendment to abrogate state sovereign immunity.[119]

Under the Court's state sovereign immunity doctrine, however, Section 1983 actions met a different fate. In *Quern v. Jordan* in 1979,[120] the Court found that Congress did not intend to abrogate state sovereign immunity when it drafted the Civil Rights Act of 1871, leading the Rehnquist majority to conclude that Congress did not intend to revoke state immunity from lawsuit in federal courts under Section 1983. In the debates, Rehnquist wrote, there was no mention of the Eleventh Amendment, leaving him "unwilling to believe, on the basis of such slender 'evidence,' that Congress intended by the general language of Section 1983 to override the traditional sovereign immunity of the states." The ruling did not preclude constitutional tort claims against state governments in state courts, but the Court later eliminated this option in 1989 when it declared that a state is not a "person" under 1983.[121] Because of this, the state itself cannot be sued for damages under the law in either state *or* federal court. As such, this interpretation has gone far in dramatically limiting the availability of Section 1983 claims, and subsequently the ability of litigants to go to court for claims against the government.

Attorney's Fees and Institutional Authority

While attorney's fees provisions were regularly included in congressional statutes throughout the 1970s and 80s, the Supreme Court began to develop a different perspective on the matter. Perhaps having been pushed too far, the Court responded to Congress' rampant use of fee-shifting provisions in *Alyeska Pipeline Service Co. v. Wilderness Society* in 1975, holding that federal courts should not impose fee awards without independent statutory authority to do so.[122] In other words, in the absence of a sweeping statutory directive giving courts the power to recognize and enforce fee-shifting provisions as part of a remedy, the justices argued that the Court should not enforce them. The decision fundamentally relied on the Fee Bill of 1853, in which Congress restricted the Court's equitable powers to award attorney's fees. While civil rights groups had already been lobbying Congress for further civil rights fee-shifting legislation, the *Alyeska* decision fueled groups (organized and represented by NAACP lobbyist Clarence Mitchell) to lean on Democrats in Congress.[123]

Accordingly, the Senate Judiciary Committee recommenced its consideration of broad attorney's fee legislation.[124] As the discussion moved to the House and Senate floor and the initial versions of what would become the Civil Rights Attorney's Fees Award Act (CRAFAA) were proposed, partisan disagreement was far more muted than it had been with regard to the civil rights laws of the decade prior,[125] as Senator Robert Byrd led a bipartisan coalition that worked together in both houses. The bill's major detractors in the Senate, James Allen and Jesse Helms, expressed concern that the bill would simply be a "bonanza for the legal profession," promoting yet more legislation. Helms also lamented that civil rights litigation, in his opinion, had come to constitute far too large a percentage of the annual federal caseload, and that the Senate ought not pass legislation that would promote further growth.[126]

For the most part, however, members of Congress agreed that the experience of the Civil Rights era suggested that the "fee-shifting mechanism has proved a particularly equitable and efficient means of enforcing the [civil rights] laws by enlisting private citizens as law enforcement officials."[127] Since attorney's fees also rely upon adequate funding, fee-shifting was an attractive way of subsidizing "the Justice Department, which obviously does not have the resources to bring suit for every civil rights violation."[128] In the end, a majority—including both Democrats and Republicans—agreed with Senator Kennedy's characterization: "Fee shifting provides a mechanism which can give full effect to our civil rights laws … at no added cost to government."[129]

Congress swiftly responded to the Court just a year after *Alyeska*, authorizing recovery of attorney's fees to prevailing parties under a wide variety of civil rights, environmental, and other statutes involving the public interest. It did so with a single sentence: "The court, in its discretion, may allow the prevailing party, other than the United States, a reasonable attorney's fee as part of the costs." Congress considered these provisions essential for enabling potential plaintiffs who might not otherwise be able to afford it to get into court to vindicate their rights claims. "By compelling losing parties to subsidize the attorneys of those whose civil rights they violate, Congress endorsed civil rights litigation as an essential mechanism of individual dispute resolution and as a legitimate weapon."[130] And while a group of mostly Southern senators filibustered the bill for seven days, the Senate voted for cloture for a margin of 63-26 and passed the bill with a vote of 57-15. Passage was easier in the House, where the vote was 306–68, and President Gerald Ford signed the bill into law on October 19, 1976.

The CRAFAA not only restored fee-shifting to its previous state, but it also strengthened it in two important ways. The act included the Reconstruction civil rights acts (including Section 1983) within the coverage of the law, making attorney's fees applicable to a broader range of cases. The act also clarified several ambiguities that existed until the Supreme Court's *Alyeska* decision. Prior to the case, the decision to award attorney's fees rested with the judge who, at his or her discretion, could easily deny fees. As such, "this made public interest litigation twice the gamble" of traditional litigation. "Receipt of a fee depended not only upon winning the case, but also upon a judge's discretion whether or not to award a fee once the case was won."[131] Additionally, the discussion in the legislative history of the CRAFAA as to what constituted a "reasonable" award directed courts to look to more expensive cases, like antitrust, thereby removing a tendency on the part of individual judges to give small awards—often amounting to less than what lawyers were charging per hour at the time for litigation. Finally, whereas the courts frequently declined to award attorney's fees in cases where a state claimed Eleventh Amendment immunity, the act made clear that fees are authorized against state and local officials, as well as governments, whether or not they are named parties.

Interestingly, Republicans introduced a bill shortly thereafter—the Equal Access to Justice Act, which was passed in 1980—that also aimed to reduce the disadvantage in economic resources faced by parties who challenge governmental actions. The legislation, which has evolved through amendment over time, did so in two ways. First, it gave the courts discretion to impose fees on the federal government to the same extent as private parties, and second, the act authorized attorney's fees to a prevailing party unless "the position of the United States was substantially justified or that special circumstances make an award unjust."[132] The assessment of fees under this provision is mandatory, except for stipulated special circumstances. As such, the act created a presumption in favor of a prevailing party and shifted the burden to the government to demonstrate that its acts were reasonable.

While civil rights plaintiffs—who are typically at the center of the ongoing conversation about attorney's fees—have had more than ample reason to bring claims against the federal government over time, it is easy to forget that they are not the only plaintiffs interested in suing the government. The changes provided through the EAJA were not only intended to serve liberal causes; in fact, the proponents of the original 1980 act were primarily conservatives who wanted to encourage businesses and corporations to litigate against the federal government. Republicans introduced the original legislation, and the Senate debates that followed were so clearly nonpartisan as to be accurately characterized as "nondebates."[133] As we will see, then, the Supreme Court's continued constriction of attorney's fees stands to hamper not only liberal causes, but conservative ones as well.

The Drift Continues: Remedies and
the Antilitigation Movement
Diminishing Incentives

One way in which the antilitigation sentiment of the Burger and Rehnquist Courts manifested itself was in the Court's treatment of attorney's fees provisions, as the Court began to chip away at the CRAFAA. In 1980 the Court clarified the condition of attorney's fees awards in a way that would be used to curtail fees further in later years. In *Hanrahan v. Hampton* (1980), when reviewing CRAFAA, the Court claimed, "Congress intended to permit the interim award of counsel fees only when a party has prevailed on the merits of at least some of his claims."[134] Because fee-shifting statutes typically provide for the recovery of these fees for "prevailing plaintiffs," a considerable amount of litigation has been directed toward defining what counts as a prevailing party, giving the Supreme Court another method for constricting awards. The Court outlined a basic approach for fee eligibility a few years later in *Hensley v. Eckerhart*, ruling that a plaintiff is considered a prevailing party if it succeeds on "any significant issue in litigation which achieves some of the benefit the parties sought in bringing suit."[135]

Shortly thereafter, however, the Court began defining many groups *out* of its "prevailing party" definition. In *Hewitt v. Helms* in 1987, the Court determined that even when a violation of a plaintiff's rights are found (here, a prisoner), without an entry of a formal declaratory judgment or injunction, the prisoner is not to be considered a "prevailing party" able to recoup fees.[136] And a year later in *Rhodes v. Stewart*, the Court held similarly that a declaratory judgment is itself insufficient if it is entered at a point in time where it does not provide any substantive benefit to the litigant.[137] The *Hensley* standard was further refined in *Texas State Teachers Association v. Garland Independent School District* in 1989, where the Court held that, in order to recover fees, the party must succeed on a "significant issue in the litigation which achieves some of the benefit they sought in bringing the suit." The Court stipulated further that the degree of overall success should relate to the measurement of the fee, and no awards should be made for minimal or technical successes.[138]

The Court also took CRAFAA on directly. In *Marek v. Chesny*, the Court considered how to reconcile Rule 68 of the Federal Rules of Civil Procedure (which deals with the costs of litigation) with Section 1988 of the CRAFAA, which entitles the prevailing party in a civil rights action to reasonable attorney's fees "as part of the costs." Because Section 1988 defines attorney's fees as costs, and because Rule 68 mandates that a plaintiff whose judgment fails to exceed a Rule 68 offer at trial "must pay the costs incurred after the making of the offer," the Court found that the rule therefore barred the plaintiff from recovering post-offer attorney's fees. And in his majority opinion, Justice Warren Burger explicitly rejected the argument that this would discourage civil rights litigation.[139]

From the perspective of the civil rights bar, however, the decision was viewed as a backdoor way to deny certain groups of plaintiffs access to the courts. It also created the potential for creative use of Rule 68 offers by defendants by allowing them to make a lump sum offer to the opposing party, specifically intended to include costs. This created a dilemma for lawyers, as the client would have the ability to accept or reject any settlement offer, thereby potentially bargaining away attorney fee awards in the process. The Court intensified this dilemma in *Evans v. Jeff D.*, which involved a Section 1983 class action suit in which the plaintiffs agreed to a settlement in which they received their desired relief (a consent decree) in exchange for waiving their right to recover attorney's fees. Much to the dismay of trial lawyers, the Court ruled that plaintiffs can, in fact, bargain away their statutory attorney's fees in a settlement, just as they can any other form of relief.[140] This structure creates a tension between lawyers and classes, particularly in cases where the class is seeking non-monetary relief and might not be able to pay for its legal representation if it is not awarded attorney's fees by the court.

In response to the Supreme Court's decisions in the late 1980s, Congress entered the 1990s aiming once again to expand the availability of attorney's fees. It passed an updated Equal Access to Justice Act early in the decade with the effect of granting the courts discretion to award attorney's fees to prevailing parties unless "special circumstances" would make the award unjust, and it expanded the amount of monetary remedies that successful plaintiffs could recover in cases brought under the Civil Rights Act of 1991.[141] But underlying the legislative enthusiasm for attorney's fees was a rising tide of antilitigation activists rallying around the idea of tort reform.[142] Although the movement would not achieve much by way of success until Republican majorities took hold in the House with the midterm elections of 1994, as early as the mid-1970s there was a growing push for reforms that would reduce lawyer fees and cap damages. These reform proposals began at the state level (most prominently in California) in debates concerning rising insurance premiums for product liability and medical malpractice, and they came from Democrats as much as Republicans. In September 1976 the House Committee on Small Business held hearings on what it deemed a burgeoning crisis in public liability insurance. Much of the focus during these hearings was on issues of rising insurance premiums and other costs, as well as failed regulatory policies and insurance schemes to protect against economic disaster; but questions of lawyers and the implications of attorney's fees permeated throughout.[143] Robert Begam, president of ATLA, responded to such claims by blaming the insurance industry for rising costs: "Under the guise of the high-sounding phrase, 'tort reform,' the insurance industry would erode the rights of the American consumer killed and maimed by a defective product, by regressive statutes of limitations that would deprive people of their rights before they are injured; with arbitrary limits on recovery; with measures that would effectively deprive not just the poor, but the average income consumer of his right to counsel; in short with a new system much more convenient and expedient to the insurer."[144] Committee members were friendly in response as they used their follow-up questions seemingly to learn from his expertise and not to challenge his interpretation of the facts. This tone characterized hearings the following year as well, when a subgroup of five committee members (three Republicans and two Democrats) convened to conduct a survey about product liability litigation. Again, the focus was more on insurance economics than law; in fact, many of those surveyed complained about premiums going up despite never having been faced with a lawsuit. But the issue of attorney's fees was again raised repeatedly in the hearings: "A number of correspondents blamed 'litigation happy lawyers' and contingency fee arrangements for the rise in product liability claims." They simply concluded at the time that further research was necessary.[145] Andrew Ireland, a Republican congressman from Florida, reinvigorated the issue in committee, claiming, "I get a lot of complaints that it is practically a conspiracy by the bar" that their premiums were rising so sharply; but his Republican counterpart, Charles Whalen of Ohio, retorted that they did not know whether the fault was "the lawyers that are seeking out people who are injured, or whether it is the other way around," and added "while perhaps some might wish to blame the lawyers, I think perhaps it is also possible that it is part of this entire consumer advocacy thrust."[146]

Although ATLA and ABA members continued to downplay the role that lawyers arguably played in increasing costs for businesses, those calling for tort reform and limitations on attorney's fees grew more strident in the early 1990s as conservatives running for elected office prominently attacked liberal candidates for defending rich trial lawyers, arguably at the expense of the working and middle class. Vice President Dan Quayle played a prominent role in this campaign, overseeing an extensive plan to reform civil litigation that included both limiting punitive damages and "extending" the loser pays rule through a proposed "fairness rule," the purpose of which was create additional fear and uncertainty for potential litigants contemplating initiating a lawsuit.[147] Medical malpractice suits in particular became a lightening rod for these reform proposals. In 1992 and again in 1993, Democratic Senator Dennis DeConcini introduced the Attorney Accountability Act with the goal of addressing "the inequity that arises when an individual is forced to defend a lawsuit where he has done nothing wrong. As we all know, the costs of litigation can be enormous."[148] As he saw it, "America's love affair with litigation, and the pursuit of a deep pocket has inappropriately made the courts the forum for redistributing wealth in this country. Accountability, especially on the part of attorneys bringing nonmeritorious cases, needs to be established."[149] The legislation sought to reimburse prevailing *defendants* for legal fees incurred in the costly process of defending themselves. The bill was designed to impose accountability on lawyers who take cases on a contingency fee basis by requiring that they share both rewards and risks. DeConcini was clear: "I recognize that this bill will discourage people from filing suit. That is one of its purposes. … [W]hat this bill will do is discourage claims initiated with the goal of settlement, claims without merit and defendant shopping."[150]

Although the bill enjoyed some support from high-profile Democrats—President Bill Clinton proposed caps on damage awards as part of his health care plan in 1993—the bill was given new life when the Gingrich Republicans came to power in the midterm elections of 1994. Perhaps the most thorough attack on the American "access to justice"-inspired system to date arose as part of the new Congress' proposed "Contract with America." In a multifaceted piece of legislation originally titled the Common Sense Legal Reform Act of 1995,[151] Republicans in the House sought to preempt state laws with a uniform, federal standard for adjudicating claims against companies whose products maim or otherwise harm people; to reduce the liability of retailers who unwittingly sell defective products; and to cap damages that courts impose with the goal of punishing malicious business practices (specifically limiting them to three times the compensatory damages awarded to a victim). The legislation also aimed to restrict expert witnesses' statements, disallow comments from those whose pay depends on a client winning the case, and limit lawsuits brought by shareholders whose stocks have plummeted possibly due to fraud.[152]

Republicans also sought to instate Quayle's "loser pays" proposal in actions arising under state law that were brought in the federal courts under diversity jurisdiction.[153] According to the House report on the proposed bill, its impetus stemmed from the concern that "our nation is overly litigious, the civil justice system is overcrowded, sluggish, and excessively costly and the costs of lawsuits, both direct and indirect, are inflicting serious and unnecessary injury on the national economy."[154] Initially, this aspect of the bill—which later became a proposal of its own—was crafted such that attorney's fees recovered by the winning party could not exceed those of the losing party, and it gave judges the discretion to limit awards under special circumstances. As opposition to the "loser pays" approach arose, a second bill was introduced with a provision that allowed any party to make an offer of judgment to the opposing party; if such an offer were refused, and the court's judgment was not ultimately more favorable, the offeree would be required to pay the offeror's costs, including attorney's fees (up to the amount of the offeree's attorney's fees). The House passed this bill, the Attorney Accountability Act, on March 7, 1995, with all but sixteen Democrats voting against it.[155] In the same week the House also passed the Private Securities Litigation Reform Act, which sought to discourage investors from bringing lawsuits charging companies abroad, and the Common Sense Product Liability and Legal Reform Act, which limited punitive damages in cases involving defective products and personal injuries, including medical malpractice claims.

Unsurprisingly, as the Senate considered the bill, an alarmed ABA rushed to put together a task force in order to produce a counterproposal that would provide an alternative framework. The ABA task force's drafting committee was especially concerned that the new rule, whatever it may be, must not impede access to the courts or the rights of citizens to a jury trial. The final proposal, which only narrowly passed the ABA's House of Delegates in the spring of 1995, expanded the offer of judgment through Rule 68 so that plaintiffs and not only defendants could invoke it, also allowing for the shifting of attorney's fees.[156] The proposal "requires that an offer must be to settle all of the monetary claims the offeror has against the adverse party in the suit," which is intended "to prevent parties from making offers to settle as to less than all the monetary claims and thus to discourage piece-meal settlement ... that may not expedite the ultimate resolution of the suit." In an attempt to protect access to the courts, the proposal also contained several safeguards, such as authorizing the court to "reduce or eliminate" an award of costs and attorney's fees for any of three reasons: "to avoid undue hardship"; "in the interest of justice"; or for "any other compelling reason that justifies the offeree party having sought judicial resolution."[157] In all, the terms of the proposal were crafted to incentivize offers to settle early in the suit while not unduly pressuring a party toward settlement.

The version of the Attorney Accountability Act that had passed the House, however, eventually stalled in the Senate, with no action taken on the bill. A similar bill was reintroduced in 1997, and the ABA again strongly opposed it.[158] While both legislative efforts were instigated by a coalition within the Republican Party, both episodes also ultimately reflected the substantial degree of bipartisan support for attorney's fees. In the debates over the 1997 proposal to limit them, for example, even Orrin Hatch reflected, "If we allow ourselves to start dictating what fees have to be paid to certain professions in our society, however tempting, then I think we are starting down a dangerous road. How can conservatives support setting fees in a free market system?"[159] As has historically been the case with retrenchment in other areas, both parties have maintained significant constituencies that, when push comes to shove, support access to the judicial branch for a variety of political, theoretical, or practical reasons.

On this issue, however, the Supreme Court continued to deal crippling blows into the new millennium. The Court significantly limited attorney's fees again in 2001 with its decision in *Buckhannon Board and Care Home, Inc. v. West Virginia Department of Health and Human Resources*, in which it determined that voluntary changes in behavior, without securing a court order, did not suffice for a fee award unless the change is made binding by judicial decree. In other words, attorneys are not eligible to collect fees on behalf of a plaintiff whose lawsuit prompts a defendant to change his or her behavior voluntarily, without a court order. As the majority concluded, "a defendant's voluntary change in conduct, although perhaps accomplishing what the plaintiff sought to achieve by the lawsuit, lacks the necessary judicial *imprimatur* on the change. Our precedents thus counsel against holding that the term 'prevailing party' authorizes an award of attorney's fees *without* a corresponding alteration in the legal relationship of the parties." The Court rendered this decision despite the fact that the vast majority of lower courts (nine out of the ten circuits) had adopted the so-called "catalyst theory" that the Court rejected.

In effect, the Court's ruling permits defendants to litigate equitable claims to the point of judgment, and then to avoid fees by consenting to the relief requested. The Court's hostility to legislation that was intended to broaden access to the courts in civil rights cases is reflected in Justice Antonin Scalia's comments regarding the comparative interests at stake:

> It could be argued, perhaps, that insofar as abstract justice is concerned, there is little to choose between the dissent's outcome and the Court's: If the former sometimes rewards the plaintiff with a phony claim (there is no way of knowing), the latter sometimes denies fees to the plaintiff with a solid case whose adversary slinks away on the eve of judgment. But it seems to me the evil of the former far outweighs the evil of the latter. There is all the difference in the world between a rule that denies the extraordinary boon of attorney's fees to some plaintiffs who are no less "deserving" of them than others who receive them, and a rule that causes the law to be the very instrument of wrong—exacting the payment of attorney's fees to the extortionist.[160]

In effect, *Buckhannon* adds an additional complicating factor that makes it substantially more difficult and costly for attorneys to undertake civil rights litigation.[161] Due to the decision, now an attorney who is considering taking on a case must also consider whether or not relief will likely come through a judicially enforceable judgment or decree.

The Supreme Court has also attacked congressional efforts to incentivize private litigation in another prominent way in recent years. While damages are usually intended to compensate plaintiffs for their losses, over the course of the twentieth century, Congress increasingly provided for punitive damages, which are awarded in order to punish defendants for egregious conduct and to deter them and others from future offenses. These "damages enhancing" provisions serve as a potent mechanism for incentivizing litigation.[162] However, jurisdictions vary in how they define the standard for awarding them, typically including calculations like whether a defendant's conduct reflects a subjectively malicious intent or objectively demonstrates gross recklessness or a willful disregard for the rights of others. Factors guiding the measurement of damages also vary, typically including the defendant's financial condition (including whether it profited from the illegal actions), the nature of the defendant's conduct and the seriousness and duration of the harm (as well as whether it tried to conceal the misconduct), whether or not the defendant was aware of the potential for harm, the extent to which the conduct offends the public sense of justice, and the total deterrent effect of other damages already imposed upon the defendant. While punitive damage awards are given on top of traditional remedies, they also provide a fund from which plaintiffs can recover the costs of litigation.

Although the practice of awarding punitive damages dates back to the late 1700s, it has recently become highly controversial. Proponents argue that punitive damage awards are necessary to assess the true societal costs of gross misconduct. Opponents, however, levy several potentially damning critiques. While punitive damages are quasi-criminal in nature, they are imposed without the benefit of traditional constitutional safeguards that apply in criminal trials. Juries are given a high degree of discretion in deciding on the amount of punitive damages awards, which often results in the award of large sums. Related, opponents argue that the potential for procuring punitive damags may also encourage unnecessary litigation. Many state legislatures have imposed limits on punitive damages; Nebraska, for example, does not allow for them at all, and others, like Ohio, have imposed caps stipulating that punitive damages cannot be more than double the amount of compensatory damages awarded.[163] But while some states remain notorious for providing large awards, the Supreme Court never reversed a punitive damage award as excessive until 1996.

As another venue for reducing litigation and remedies, punitive damages have always been closely connected to the tort reform debate. On the one hand, they represent a substantial portion of the costs of our current legal regime; additionally, however, critics have "increasingly questioned whether the perpetuation of such damages continues to reflect a majoritarian political choice or instead reflects only the entrenched interests of lawyers and judges, who profit respectively from the substantial fees produced by large damage awards and the power implicit in formulating the rules that govern American business practices."[164] Given these concerns, the Supreme Court has considered various constitutional and statutory questions related to punitive damages over the past three decades, issuing at least eight significant challenges to state court awards in a sixteen-year period. Together, these decisions have the effect of creating a more intrusive federal doctrine that limits their availability. And in effect, these constrictions potentially scale back incentives for individuals looking to bring suit against large and powerful corporations. That conservative justices have largely authored these innovations has led critics to conclude "the Supreme Court's creation of constitutional limits on punitive damages also is inconsistent with the traditional conservative claim of deference to the political process."[165]

The Court has succeeded in limiting punitive damages in three ways: by providing procedural protections for defendants, by affirming the general principle that the Constitution imposes substantive limitations on the amounts of damages, and by defining and applying specific constitutional standards to strike down "excessive" awards. The Court's modern treatment of punitive damages began in the late 1980s with cases like *Banker's Life and Casualty Co. v. Crenshaw*, where the justices discussed but declined to answer questions about the constitutionality of punitive damage awards.[166] The Court similarly avoided addressing all of the available constitutional issues in *Browning-Ferris Industries v. Kelco Disposal, Inc.* in 1989, where the Court held that the "excessive fines" clause of the Eighth Amendment did not apply to a civil jury award of punitive damages in civil cases between private parties. Although the goals of punishment and deterrence underlie both punitive awards and criminal law, it found that the extent of any overlap was not sufficient to impose the same constitutional limitations. It therefore declined to set aside a $6 million punitive damage award as excessive in the case.

In *Pacific Mutual Life Insurance Co. v. Haslip*, however, although the majority refused to strike down an award that was 200 times the amount of the compensatory damages awarded, for the first time, the Court gestured toward a doctrine for reviewing punitive damages. In his opinion, Justice Harry Blackmun raised concern that punitive damages had "run wild" due to unlimited jury and judicial discretion, but he declined to establish a "mathematical bright line" for constitutionally acceptable awards.[167] Nonetheless, he did suggest that perhaps, as a general rule, punitive damage awards of "more than four times the amount of compensatory damages" might be "close to the line of constitutional impropriety." At any rate, by the early 1990s, the Court had made their role clear, arguing that the due process clause requires meaningful judicial review to prevent the arbitrary deprivation of property through an excessive award.[168]

Two years later the Court specified that the due process clause prohibits a state from imposing a "grossly excessive punishment on a tortfeasor," but it still refrained from imposing a clear measurement standard for what should be considered "excessive.[169] However, when Congress passed—and President Clinton vetoed—legislation for punitive damage reform, the Court finally provided its own clear guidelines.[170] Interestingly, the Court has pursued this strategy by constructing a constitutional law of punitive damages, resting primarily on the due process clause of the Fourteenth Amendment. In several cases, most prominently *BMW of North American, Inc. v. Gore,*[171] the Court established a set of "guideposts" for determining when a punitive damages award could be considered so excessive as to be unconstitutional. In *Gore*, the Alabama Supreme Court had found that an award of $4 million was excessive, and cut it in half. The Supreme Court agreed, for the first time striking down an award on substantive grounds under the due process clause. While the Court still declined to set a total that awards could not exceed (though it did note that a ratio of 500:1 would almost certainly be excessive), it nonetheless directed courts to consider (1) the degree of reprehensibility of the person's conduct, (2) the reasonableness of the ratio between the harm or potential harm suffered by the victim and the size of his or her award, and (3) the comparison of the punitive damage award and the civil or criminal penalties authorized or imposed in comparable cases.[172]

Unlike in other areas of the tort reform movement, here, "the Justices are not simply interpreting statutes or crafting common law doctrines that might be overturned by congressional enactment. Instead, they are taking the bold step of determining that certain aspects of our existing litigation culture so transcend the Constitution's basic fairness norms that they are per se verboten."[173] Because the province of determining the constitutionality of an area of law is theirs alone, the justices benefit from significant insularity in these retrenchment efforts. By constitutionalizing a means of tort reform, they also appropriate legitimacy for the project that is hard to match or attack. While the Court has attempted to retrench remedies in other areas by restricting access to judgment, on this topic the Court has gone to great lengths to make sure that the topic remains in its hands.

This certainly has not stopped conservatives in Congress from trying to weigh in on the punitive damages debate. In recent years they have proposed laws that would accomplish this in one of two ways: either by carefully defining the circumstances under which individuals may be awarded punitive damages, or by capping the numeric amount. These efforts, which are more successful the more cautiously they are crafted, sprung up quickly alongside the Court's late-1990s efforts. In the area of medical malpractice in particular, throughout the 1990s and 2000s conservatives in Congress proposed legislation to cap damages on numerous occasions. The Common Sense Medical Malpractice Reform Act of 2001, for example, proposed the standard "in no event shall the amount of punitive damages awarded exceed two times the amount of compensatory damages awarded or $250,000, whichever is greater."[174] The same language was used in the proposed Help Efficient, Accessible, Low Cost, Timely Health Care Act and the Medicare Solvency and Enhanced Benefits Acts of 2002 as well.[175] But while a small handful of bills protecting a constituency also supported by liberals have passed (the Volunteer Protection Act of 2007, for example, limits the degree to which volunteers can be held responsible for punitive damages and was passed by a margin of 99-1 in the Senate),[176] the Supreme Court remains the major source of constriction for punitive damages and other damages enhancements.

And constrict it has; the Court has struck down punitive damage awards as excessive in several high-profile cases in the last decade. In 2003 in *State Farm v. Campbell*, the Court struck down a $145 million punitive damage award as so excessive that it violated the due process clause of the Fourteenth Amendment; in a case against the tobacco industry giant Philip Morris, it declined to rule on whether a $79.5 million award was excessive but stated that "the Constitution's Due Process Clause forbids a State to use a punitive damages award to punish a defendant for injury that it inflicts upon non-parties;" and it agreed that $500 billion in punitive damages against Exxon Valdez was constitutionally impermissible as well. With each case, the Court has become more precise; in *State Farm*, for example, the majority elaborated on its previous three-pronged test by stipulating that punitive damages can only be up to nine times greater than the amount of compensatory damages awarded in a case.[177] But by the time of *Exxon Shipping v. Baker*, the Court determined that a 1:1 ratio between compensatory and punitive damages was "a fair upper limit" in maritime cases involving recklessness. "The real problem," Justice David Souter wrote for the majority, "is the stark unpredictability of punitive awards."

Who Can Be Sued Today? For What?

In the last two decades, the Supreme Court has handed down at least a dozen major opinions involving outright debate over remedial questions. Early in the 1990s, the Court continued to employ a more conservative approach when choosing whether to recognize private rights of action in particular. For example, notwithstanding its Section 1983 jurisprudence, in 1992 in *Suter v. Artist M.* the Court determined that the Adoption Assistance and Child Welfare Act did not confer a private right enforceable in a Section 1983 action.[178] The Court reasoned that because Congress was silent on the issue, adopted children and their representatives do not have a right to bring private suit against state adoption programs and their administrators. In this case, Democrats in Congress did succeed, however, in passing legislation related to the *Suter* decision through an appropriations bill in order to counter the Court's holding.

With regard to qualified immunity and private rights of action, the Court's analysis today seems to be built on the assumption that litigants should not have access to remedy in suits involving federal officials.[179] This has been evidenced in both statutory and constitutional cases. In the statutory context, in *Gonzaga University v. Doe*—a case involving the privacy of student academic records—the majority concluded that, absent specific directive from Congress, no private rights of action would be inferred. In a striking departure from its earlier cases, the Court also announced that no private rights of action could be enabled by Section 1983 either. Rather, it took the position that "if Congress wishes to create new rights enforceable under Section 1983, it must do so in clear and unambiguous terms."[180]

Similarly, in *Alexander v. Sandoval* the majority concluded that the disparate impact regulations promulgated under Title VI of the Civil Rights Act of 1964 would not be enforceable by private litigants. While Title VI does not explicitly provide a cause of action to those individuals denied the rights that it protects, the Court had previously construed it to create a private remedy.[181] Nonetheless, in a 5-4 decision the Court held that no such remedy existed; as Scalia wrote, "Title VI directly reaches only instances of intentional discrimination," and "neither as originally enacted nor as later amended does Title VI display intent to create a freestanding private right of action." As he argued, because Section 602 of the statute authorizes agencies to enforce their regulations by terminating funding to programs that violate them, and because statutory construction generally counsels that the express provision of one method of enforcement should be taken to preclude others, Congress therefore did not intend to have private lawsuits enforce Title VI—and that should be the end of the story, from his perspective.[182]

While the case leaves open the possibility of congressional or administrative enforcement, it effectively eliminates the function of private attorneys general in this area. By focusing on whether or not the statute created individuals rights, it ignores the "social benefit" impetus for the citizen suit provision, precluding the possibility that the authority to sue can come from the broader public interest in enforcing a policy. There have been similar developments in the Court's standing doctrine, where the "injury in fact" requirement came to preclude this as well.[183] And while the Court had been generally more sympathetic in recognizing causes of action for constitutional violations, the death knell came that same year when the Court refused to find a private right of action even with respect to the constitutional rights of a prisoner.[184]

Sandoval also arguably left unclear whether, and to what extent, federal agencies can shape private rights of action. It implied that agencies can only play a limited role in creating them, but it still left substantial room for agencies to shape the contours of that role.[185] This lack of clarity has created confusion in the lower courts in terms of how to square the primacy of legislative intent with the Court's *Chevron* decision (whereby agencies retain substantial discretion when it comes to rulemaking). In practice, it seems that if an agency wishes to create a private right of action, it must explicitly promulgate its regulation as an interpretation of the statutory language for which the agency claims a private right of action exists. But while an agency is limited in this respect, it can still "functionally create private rights to action by expanding and defining those private rights of action that Congress (or the Court) has created. Even if agencies can only play the 'sorcerer's apprentice,' that role is of considerable power."[186] Where this understanding of agency discretion leaves individuals who seek to access to courts through a private right of action, however, is unclear at best.

Where immunities are concerned, in recent years the most significant constrictions on access to courts to sue for governmental wrongdoing have come through the continued development of the state sovereign immunity doctrine, derived from the Eleventh Amendment. Where the Eleventh Amendment serves to insulate the federal government from suit against its will, in the 1990s and 2000s the Supreme Court constructed a parallel "state" sovereign immunity, insulating states and state agencies from suit for damages or equitable relief as well. In 1996 the Supreme Court declared unconstitutional a provision of the federal Indian Gaming Law that required state governments to negotiate in good faith with Native American tribes. In so doing, the Court determined that states are sovereign entities under the Eleventh Amendment, and that such sovereignty implies that they may not be sued by private individuals without consent.[187] In quick succession, the Court used its new doctrine to strike down federal laws authorizing suits against states for patent infringement,[188] age discrimination in employment,[189] gender-motivated violence,[190] and discrimination against disabled persons.[191]

The state sovereign immunity doctrine has been heavily criticized for allowing state governments to violate the Constitution or the law and not be held accountable, making it fundamentally "inconsistent with a central maxim of American government: no one, not even the government, is above the law."[192] Justice Kennedy addressed this criticism directly in *Alden v. Maine*, arguing that "we are unwilling to assume the States will refuse to honor the Constitution or obey the binding laws of the United States. The good faith of the States thus provides an important assurance that [the Constitution and laws will be supreme]."[193] Putting the issue of "good faith" aside, in practice the doctrine creates a means by which rights can remain in place while the availability of remedies becomes questionable. In all of the recent landmark cases, the claimants—the probation officers in *Alden*, the company in *Florida Prepaid*, and the employees in *Kimel*—had a right under federal law, but no available remedy. In this way, not only does the doctrine "frustrate compensation and deterrence," but the reality is also that "individuals injured by government wrong-doing are left without a remedy."[194]

While the Court's decisions with regard to private rights of action and government immunity have made it seem as though the justices simply prefer Congress to be the central source for both rights and remedies, even when litigants find themselves "properly" before the courts (via explicit statutory provision), the Court increasingly turns them away—by presuming constraints on its *own* remedial powers. Three recent cases reflect this trend. In the first (while no statutory provision was on the table), *Correctional Service v. Malesko*, the Supreme Court held in a 5-4 decision that a *Bivens* action was not available given the facts of the case, in which a federal prisoner held in a private correctional facility sought damages against the corporation administering the prison for violation of the Eighth Amendment's cruel and unusual punishment guarantees.[195] In *Great-West Life Annuity & Insurance Company v. Knudson*, the Court denied having the ability to offer a remedy to the plaintiff, despite the fact that the statute at hand, the Employee Retirement Income Security Act of 1974, expressly authorized "appropriate equitable relief." Instead, the Scalia majority skirted its statutory responsibility by concluding that what the plaintiff sought was a "remedy at law," not available under ERISA.[196]

Similarly, in *Grupo Mexicano de DeSarrollo, S.A., v. Alliance Bond Fund, Inc.*, a creditor sought an injunction to prevent the dissipation of its assets while it pursued its contractual rights for money damages against Grupo, who—unable to meet his financial obligations—restructured his debts by assigning priority to the Mexican government and other creditors. The lower court had granted the injunction on the basis of two federal civil rules: Rule 64, which authorizes the use of remedies available under state law "for the purpose of securing satisfaction" of judgments, and Rule 65, which provides for preliminary injunctive relief. But the Supreme Court overturned the lower court's holding, claiming that because the remedy would not historically have been available in a court of equity, the lower court did not have the power to prevent the dissipation of assets prior to adjudication.[197]

In the case, in addition to basing its conclusion on a controversial reading of history,[198] the Court engaged in the unprecedented practice of using the federal rules as a source for judicial restraint. While neither party had raised the issue, Scalia noted that because Rule 18 (which deals with joinder of claims) did not authorize preliminary relief when monetary damages were sought, it therefore implied a bar on the provision of such remedies.[199] Because, as per the Rules Enabling Act, the Judicial Conference cannot promulgate rules that "abridge, modify, or enlarge" substantive rights, remedial creativity has to be exercised by a different party, otherwise the rules would be in violation of their mandate. As such, the rules ought not be read to remove the power of a court to create remedies. Yet that is exactly what Scalia did.[200]

For its part, Congress has continued its efforts to limit both the jurisdiction and remedial power of the federal courts from the 1990s to the present. While the overwhelming majority of its attempts have continued to fail, jurisdiction and remedy-stripping proposals had unprecedented success in the mid-1990s. While Congress continued to pursue removing remedies in policy areas like abortion and school prayer, it expanded its proposals to issues involving prisoners and illegal aliens as well. In targeting groups without much political power or support, Congress has successfully imposed wide-ranging limitations on access to the courts for prisoners seeking to litigate conditions of confinement cases, inmates seeking to challenge convictions by means of federal habeas corpus, and immigrants seeking to challenge government efforts at deportation and incarceration. Congress has also continued to limit the types of cases litigated and the judicial relief requested by Legal Services Corporation lawyers, which have disfavored these same groups.

Most directly affecting remedies in particular, the Prison Litigation Reform Act (PLRA), passed in 1996, restricts the "remedies that a judge can provide in civil litigation relating to prison conditions." Designed to "address the alarming explosion in the number of frivolous lawsuits filed by State and Federal prisoners," the act limits the injunctive powers of federal courts in prisoner rights cases by requiring that prisoners exhaust administrative remedies, reducing attorney's fees to prevailing plaintiffs, creating a "three strike" provision disallowing filings where courts have earlier dismissed actions by that inmate, and precluding compensatory damage awards for "mental or emotional injury" from proven constitutional violations where the inmate has not suffered "physical injury."[201] Additionally, judges are instructed to give "substantial weight to any adverse impact on public safety or the operation of a criminal justice system caused by the relief."[202] In aggregate, this legislation arguably discourages private lawyers from taking prisoner civil rights cases to trial by eliminating the potential for recovering a reasonable fee. Additionally, before the PLRA was passed, many suits brought by prisoners alleging unconstitutional conditions were settled through pretrial consent decrees where—without admitting liability—officials could agree to change the conditions at issue.[203] Under the act, however, prison officials are now required to admit that they violated the constitutional rights of prisoners, and those admissions make the officials vulnerable to personal liability lawsuits. As a result, then, more cases go to trial, which is an ironic consequence given the jurisdiction stripping aspirations of the law.[204]

Conclusions

Perhaps more tangibly than with other retrenchment strategies, it is clear how restricting incentives to bring a lawsuit restricts access to courts. But this fairly simple project has taken on a variety of forms, which have varied in their levels of success. In terms of immunities, courts have at once created doctrines, like state sovereign immunity, and gutted others, like Section 1983 actions. Where the rewards for successful litigation are concerned, both judges and elected officials have alternatively expanded and attempted to constrict the monetary incentives for bringing a case to court. Courts and Congress have also continually negotiated who has the proper authority to address questions of remedy, and this institutional battle has at times masked the extent to which remedies can be divorced from rights. But the roles of insularity, ideology, and temporality are on clear display in this arena.

Both ideologically liberal and conservative Courts sought to shield the federal government from providing remedies to successful plaintiffs early in the twentieth century. For the most part, members of Congress from both sides of the aisle have also worked to ensure the widespread provision of remedies over time. While these overall trends do not square with what a regime politics approach might predict, the patterns of groups lobbying for the availability or constriction of remedies do; during the Civil Rights era, for example, classically liberal groups such as the American Bar Association and the NAACP pushed to open the courts to a wider variety of suits. An increasingly conservative Court also acted as we might expect over time, creating a constitutional law of punitive damages late in the century in order to cut down on frivolous lawsuits and exorbitant awards. However, some of Congress' most successful efforts to limit remedies were bipartisan; the Prison Litigation Reform Act, for example, was passed with bipartisan majorities and signed into law by a Democratic president.

The power to provide remedies has been the subject of much contention and significant push and pull between the judicial and legislative branches. While we might expect remedies to fall solely under the discretion of the judiciary, conversion by the Supreme Court is only part of the story. As the Court converted its standards for providing remedies for rights claims, notably through its immunities doctrines, Congress not only attempted to undermine this authority, but also layered its own statutory apparatus on top of it, through legislation like the FTCA and the PLRA.

Still, it is clear that courts enjoy a high degree of discretion in creating the "rules" by which they provide remedies. They have in their arsenal a wide array of remedial tools, and as such, as long as the courts have power to adjudicate cases, they retain significant flexibility and authority, with low barriers to both authoritative change and to internal adaptation except in cases where there is a strongly established and prominent precedent, making barriers to authoritative change higher. With qualified immunity, the precedent was in favor of enabling retrenchment of access to the courts. Since the Supreme Court had historically granted absolute immunity to several groups and government bodies, converting the doctrine to one of qualified immunity was hardly difficult. With private rights of action, there was very little precedent at all, making outright revision of their policy easy. In the language of "rules," both doctrines were highly mutable for the Court, for the same reasons.

This is partially also a structural benefit; because the political spotlight focuses on the Court's treatment of rights, this enables it to limit remedies without calling much attention to its activities. Congress can and has attempted to create its own rules governing remedies, with some degree of success. But their success more often than not has taken the form of creating new remedies rather than scaling them back. Given what we know about the political and practical dilemmas at the heart of retrenchment—the difficulty in taking away concentrated benefits for diffuse gains—this is not surprising. The difficulty is perhaps even more pronounced in the area of remedies, given that both the legal community and any individual hoping to maximize their chance for success in court has an entrenched interest in preserving benefits like attorney's fees. Congress' attempts to constrict remedies suffer another unfortunate flaw, in that the legislative process is wide open to political scrutiny and all the hazards that go with it. While the effects of this lack of insularity are clear, it seems not to dissuade legislators in their attempts; various forms of the Attorney Accountability Act have appeared before Congress repeatedly since the Gingrich Congress, including in 2013. But it remains unclear what mechanism could be available to legislators seeking to ensure meaningful access to remedies, given all of these complicated developments.

7

Conclusion

Before the law sits a gatekeeper.
FRANZ KAFKA, *The Trial*

THE LEGACY OF the rights revolution era is, in many ways, still unfolding. There continues to be an ongoing struggle over both the meaning and the practical effects of this pivotal period in American political and legal development, in which increased access to courts was considered both a goal in and of itself and a critical vehicle for enforcing new rights guarantees.[1] Private litigation now plays a vital role for enforcing policy in areas ranging from job discrimination and affirmative action policy to welfare policy, special education, playground safety, tobacco and asbestos litigation, the safety of vaccines, antitrust enforcement, police brutality, and prison reform, among others. The enhanced role that courts have played in this process is necessarily presaged by the availability of legal redress for a much wider variety of litigants. That is, courts and judges can have no role to play in the enforcement of rights and the implementation of policy unless the relevant plaintiffs can make it through the courthouse door to begin with. Thus, the rights revolution was not just about the passage of landmark legislation like the Civil Rights Act, but was also necessarily fueled by a dramatic expansion of procedural mechanisms, causes of action, and a deep support structure to enable disadvantaged groups to get their day in court.

These expansions in access to courts and judicial power have since run headlong into the conservative legal movement, built of a coalition with a very different view on the role that courts and judges should play in American politics. Most scholars have described the subsequent clash between the old rights regime and legal retrenchers as simply a matter of electoral and partisan politics; voters who desire a rollback of rights elect legislators who appoint and authorize judges to carry out their mandate. As Mark Tushnet describes, "The Rehnquist Court resembles the Warren Court in implementing a constitutional vision associated with the nation's dominant political party."[2] For many scholars and pundits alike, then, the conservative legal era is understood as just electoral politics in another branch.

In this book, I have recounted a different component of the story. Foundational efforts to constrict access to courts were largely born of a concern for an increasingly overburdened legal system, beginning early in the twentieth century and escalating during the rights revolution era. Many of the initial groups and government actors involved in retrenchment were on the one hand largely supportive of the improved and expanded rights protections that were the product of the Civil Rights era; at the same time, however, they also recognized the practical perils that these changes brought for the efficient functioning of the judiciary. In seeking to protect the systemic integrity of the justice system by easing the growing burdens of expense, delay, and complex litigation, these groups found themselves sometimes fighting alongside— and sometimes against—lawyers who were operating with their professional interests in mind. As the scope of conflict expanded beyond judges and lawyers and as institutional maintenance efforts were increasingly entwined in political battles, more and more groups were drawn into the fray—often unwittingly, or at least without retrenchment as their primary motive. And with the continued expansion in the scope of conflict, retrenchment efforts in recent years have fallen more into the political alignments and patterns that we might have expected all along. While more traditional approaches to studying the conservative legal era capture retrenchment efforts as we see them today, this is only a very recent phase of a much longer and more complicated institutional story.

In turn, by broadening our conception of the range of actors who seek to weigh in on questions of judicial power, I have sought to bring the more hidden world of procedural reform to the surface. Whereas conservative activists have to date largely failed to overturn the critical statutes and landmark legal precedents of the rights revolution, actual procedural changes *have*, in fact, had a demonstrable effect on access to the courts. In contrast to those who focus on overt legislative proposals aimed at altering judicial power— which are almost always unsuccessful—it is clear that, as E.E. Schattschneider has famously written, "the rules of the game determine the requirements for success" when it comes to judicial retrenchment.[3]

However, in stressing the institutional component of backlash, I do not mean to suggest that the partisan story should be ignored, particularly as party competition may align with ideological divisions over the meaning of "access to justice." We must be careful not to undervalue the role that political power and material resources play in these reform efforts. Ultimately, changes in the technical rules governing access to courts are best navigated by "repeat players;" often corporations with the resources necessary to stay on top of these developments, and even to use them to their advantage.[4] And perhaps most importantly, regardless of whether constrictions in access to courts are driven by conservatives, liberals, or both, the political salience of these retrenchment efforts is acute for the groups that they affect, no matter who drives them. In the remainder of the chapter, therefore, I summarize my key theoretical findings regarding what the politics and processes of judicial retrenchment help us to understand about the importance of rules and insularity as means for retrenchment, the ideologies that drive reform, and the processes of institutional change more broadly. I then conclude by reflecting on the relationship between reform efforts of this nature and foundational questions of political power.

Insularity

There are really two aspects of the role that insularity plays in the story of judicial retrenchment. First and foremost, actors must enjoy a significant level of discretion over the institutional rules and procedures that they hope to wield in the service of their reform goals. Second, success varies within and across the case studies that I have provided with the degree to which reformers can avoid having their efforts subject to political contestation. As is clear in all four cases, because institutional and procedural rules govern such a wide variety of activity within the judiciary, changes to them can have dramatic consequences for incentivizing lawyers and litigants to seek justice through the courts, as opposed to focusing their efforts toward other institutional venues. When would-be retrenchers can target these rules and successfully avoid the multitude of veto points inherent in the political process, the potential for successfully constricting access to courts is at its highest.

Importantly, the availability of malleable rules amenable to change behind closed doors shifts meaningfully over time. In the first half of the twentieth century in particular, many of the rules relevant to the judicial process were widely accepted as "purely procedural" and therefore irrelevant to the concerns of elected officials. In characterizing these rules as the province of "experts," early reforms (both in the direction of expanding and constricting access to courts) did not draw much in the way of political attention. Accordingly, during this time various groups and individuals interested in reforming access to courts found themselves pleasantly isolated from the political process and therefore able to have a great effect on the accessibility of litigation. As the reality that changes to legal rules could profoundly affect substantive outcomes became more visible, and as we entered the more recent period of partisan conflict over the role of the courts, a wider variety of actors clearly came to appreciate the power inherent in controlling these "rules of the game." Given that "whoever decides what the game is about decides who can get into the game," for this very reason, groups and institutions continue to struggle mightily over that power.[5]

But this is not a monolithic story. Despite a general trend from relative insularity to overt partisan contention, the multitude of institutions and actors involved greatly complicates the trajectory. In the case of those interested in developing ADR, for example, insularity from the political process has always been relatively low. This is no doubt because the benefits of ADR itself can and have been cast at times as near-universal, appealing to both political parties and many groups of actors, and are therefore perceived to be highly portable. This is especially reflected in the sheer amount of interest that professional associations and even private individuals have had in supporting ADR. Because of this, the major benefits of insularity have, over time, really come to rest with the Supreme Court, which is structurally well positioned to interpret ADR's foundational legislation. Where the Federal Rules of Civil Procedure are concerned, however, the trajectory is different. The struggle for the authority to control these rules, in fact, is in many ways the most striking case for the value of insularity. The civil rules were promulgated in a very unusual environment in American politics, where barriers to authoritative change were quite low. Accordingly, it is in this case where the argument that institutional rules are "purely procedural" gained the most traction. It is also an especially striking example of how much power is lost when that insularity is compromised. Once it became clear that the rules could, in many ways, be considered "political" in nature, the amount of groups and interests drawn into the fray was immense.

With administrative rules, the power to control them was in many ways insular all along. Early reformers were clearly concerned about the discretion of administrative agencies, and the Administrative Procedure Act was passed at a notable political moment wherein concerned parties sought to utilize institutional rules to contain that discretion. The American Bar Association's continued efforts to promote a "Federal Rules of Administrative Procedure" reflect a recognition of the power of insularity as well. Here, the juxtaposition between the civil rules and the failure to create a set of parallel, insulated administrative procedural rules is especially illuminative. With the story of civil rules in mind, it is clear that federal rules for administrative procedure might well have altered the trajectory of institutional change entirely, especially by enhancing the power of the Administrative Conference of the United States to implement more effectual changes with ease and regularity over time.

Finally, while Congress and the courts have fought for discretion over the rules governing legal remedies, the courts have, in many ways, largely won the battle. Congress has been relatively more successful in creating remedies than in constricting them; but the courts have gone further, both in constricting monetary remedies and in creating doctrines of immunity that greatly constrain who can be held legally accountable, and for what. Characterizing this as a "win," however, is somewhat misleading, as the success that judges have had is in many ways the product of a structural benefit. Because the political spotlight focuses so directly on the Court's treatment of rights, judges can be quite effectual in limiting remedies without calling much attention to themselves. In this vein, Congress' attempts to constrict remedies tend to suffer a fatal flaw, in that the legislative process is wide open to political scrutiny and all the hazards that go with it. While the effects of this lack of insularity are clear, it seems not to dissuade legislators in their attempts, as legislative proposals for constricting remedies have persisted to the present.

Ideology

Some retrenchment efforts are clearly partisan in nature. Jurisdiction stripping proposals by members of Congress in the 1960s, 70s, and 80s were openly ideological, fueled by substantive disagreement with the Supreme Court's position on issues such as busing, abortion, and school prayer. Similarly, the Rehnquist Court's treatment of legal devices like private rights of action and qualified immunity undoubtedly reflects a conservative position on the proper scope of litigation. But as these cases also show, retrenchment is often pursued by a multitude of actors primarily concerned with protecting or improving the practical functioning of our system of justice as well. Thus, I argue that these cases suggest two interrelated conclusions about the nature of judicial retrenchment and the groups that pursue it: (1) Retrenchment is far from always a conservative backlash to the promises of the entrenched, liberal-legal state; and (2) the project of retrenchment, while still ideological in nature and politically salient in its effects, may also have a nonpartisan impetus, driven instead by a desire to protect institutional turf.

Here too, the story has changed over time, as there is meaningful variation in the ideologies of those seeking retrenchment, as well in the ways that these groups and institutions confront each other at a given historical moment. While the political resurgence of the Republican Party beginning in the 1970s and the growth of a conservative legal movement led in subsequent years to the more overtly partisan battle over the power of courts that we see today, the politics of previous periods looked quite different. This is reflected not only in the prevalence of the "institutional maintenance" ideology, but also in the ways that different antilitigation reforms engendered different forms of politics. While reforms aimed to limit the attractiveness of litigation (such as changes to the rules governing discovery or class actions, for example) spawned partisan battles between trial lawyers and their Democratic allies and business groups and their Republican allies, the project of "changing the decision makers" (as in the case of ADR) enjoyed bipartisan appeal, and reforms characterized as essential for alleviating the burdens of an overworked judicial branch at times often skirted a partisan conversation of any kind. In this way, retrenchment seems neither solely driven nor entirely explained by partisan politics.

Over its long history, ADR has been promoted at times—and even in overlapping fashion—by both liberals and conservatives. As we have seen, this is largely because both Democrats and Republicans see it as an ideal "solution," but for different problems. In the years following the passage of the Federal Arbitration Act, liberals promoted ADR as a great way to ensure access to justice to those struggling for it in traditional courts. Republicans were always part of the debate, as business supported it in these early years as well. Over time, however, an even broader swath of conservatives came to see its appeal for keeping "lesser" cases out of court, and increasingly conservative Supreme Courts have facilitated the use of ADR for this end. But as I have argued, because the partisan component is complex, political scientists have thus far largely overlooked ADR when assessing the expanse of antilitigation strategies.

Through this lens, using the reform of the civil rules as a retrenchment strategy is also complicated, as it is both a clear example of the development and persistence of the "institutional maintenance" ideology and of the ways in which actors within the *same* political party can have divergent interests. Early efforts to constrict access to courts were born of a concern for the increasingly overburdened legal system in the New Deal and rights revolution eras. The initial groups and government actors involved in retrenchment were, on the one hand, largely supportive of the expanded rights protections that were the product of the era; but on the other hand, they also recognized that these developments would contribute to an overburdened judiciary. The changes they pursued, however, led to a split between judges and lawyers, which expanded outward into the political arena as the legal community joined with Democrats to constrict judicial authority over the rules. The story of the growth of the administrative state and its effects on "changing the venue" is similar. While support and opposition initially broke down along partisan lines, once the nation moved onward from the polarized era of New Deal politics, it became clear that the real enemies for those seeking to maintain a role for the courts were not Republicans or Democrats, but rather federal agencies concerned about losing their discretion. This made it difficult for legislators to use the APA for strategic political purposes, ironically leaving significant discretion in the hands of the judges. Today, this also means that the choice of whether or not to review agency action is potentially subject to the political or policy preferences of individual judges.

In terms of remedies, both ideologically liberal and conservative courts sought to keep the federal government out of the business of determining remedies early in the twentieth century. Similarly, members of Congress from both sides of the aisle have sought to ensure the widespread provision of remedies over time. While this bipartisan confluence of interests may be surprising, the patterns of groups lobbying for the availability or constriction of remedies is more as we might expect. Especially during the Civil Rights era, for example, liberal groups like the ABA generally pushed to open the court-house door to a wider range of disputes; and later in the century, an increasingly large cohort of conservative judges and justices worked to cut down on what they considered frivolous litigation and exorbitant awards, notably by creating a constitutional law of limitations on punitive damages. Even so, however, some of Congress' most successful efforts to limit remedies to date, like the Prison Litigation Reform Act, were passed by bipartisan majorities in Congress and signed into law by a Democratic president. That this cohesion of interests primarily seems to occur on the topic of access to courts for stigmatized groups is both problematic and telling.

Temporality

While much of the literature on jurisdiction stripping has focused on authoritative legislative change, in this book I have sought to uncover less visible retrenchment strategies and to situate them in a narrative of institutional change over time. As Jacob Hacker has prominently shown, the ground-level operation of policies can change in a variety of ways—whether through drift, conversion, or layering—and studies that focus on "grand acts of politics" often miss these changes. Because retrenchment is a difficult political project, especially in cases where policies are embedded in ways that insulate them from authoritative reform, actors seeking change often find it best not to attack institutions directly. Further, retrenchment efforts are often subsumed within a pervasive narrative of state growth and development, or otherwise lumped into the politics of a single historical period dominated by the conservative legal movement. What is lost in these approaches—and what I argue that these case studies show—is that institutional change can take different forms over time, as reformers respond to the particular constellation of political and institutional barriers that they face. Just as the ideological affiliations of those promoting retrenchment have changed over time, so too have the methods for retrenchment.

In order to capture the nature of these strategies, I have tried here to operationalize Hacker's typology of forms of retrenchment and apply it to reform efforts aimed at constricting access to courts. What the details of these cases make clear is that, in order for this typology to have any explanatory value, it must be examined over time. The effects of path dependence make it important to examine the process of entrenching these legal procedures and rules prior to examining their use in the project of retrenchment, as the politics of entrenchment importantly shape the politics and institutional constraints governing later efforts at reform. In this regard, it also becomes clear that recognizing the sequence and timing of retrenchment efforts is critical, as some succeed because of their ability to co-opt existing institutional mechanisms— some of which were put in place for entirely different political and functional reasons—for the purpose of restricting access to courts.

Many ADR procedures were entrenched decades prior to the beginnings of the conservative legal movement, and the fact that these procedures were well established made co-opting them for purposes of retrenchment even easier, as reformers did not need to dismantle the "litigation state" or develop ADR themselves in order to pursue their goals. The influence of Republicans in Congress and a conservative Supreme Court has meant that statutes originally intended to promote access to justice—the Federal Arbitration Act in this case, and certainly the Rules Enabling Act and the Administrative Procedure Act in others—have been redirected and reinterpreted for the pursuit of goals contrary to the original impetus for such legislation. This has allowed conservatives to support and convert institutional mechanisms like ADR as devices for defending corporate and wealthy interests by diverting disputes away from the costly realm of litigation. But because conservatives have been able to accomplish this without creating new legal procedures *or* constricting others, the use of ADR is not often identified through the lens of retrenchment. This strategy of "changing the decision makers," then, is a clear case of "conversion," and one that we would miss if only looking for overt "revision" or formal policy change.

Where the case of ADR usefully illuminates a subterranean mechanism for retrenchment, the case of the civil rules show how multiple mechanisms can be employed over time in a single case.[6] Initially, the barriers to authoritative change in the rulemaking process were very low, as rulemakers enjoyed a high degree of discretion. But as the political power of rule changes became apparent, and as barriers to authoritative change began to rise, judges and lawyers still maintained some ability to stretch the rules for their purposes, largely through "drift." When the Watergate scandal prompted Congress to become more concerned with protecting its prerogatives and opening up the rulemaking process, on the one hand, efforts to make authoritative changes became much less effective, even during periods of unified Republican government. But on the other, conversion in the Supreme Court became a primary mode of retrenchment, as conservative justices increasingly constricted access to courts.

Retrenchment aimed at the administrative state has also been a story of drift and conversion. Barriers to authoritative changes in administrative law and procedure have always been high, since everyone—Republican or Democrat—is subject to the law, making the APA difficult to manipulate for politically strategic reform efforts. While a majority party might temporarily favor increased discretion, it does not necessarily promote it when its opponents are in positions of power. Further, the more thoroughly administrative agencies are entrenched, the more difficult eroding their discretion becomes. This is evidenced by how little the APA has changed over the last sixty years. But as we have seen, the ways in which its provisions are used and interpreted has actually changed dramatically. Congress has often found it politically expedient to allow the other branches to develop reforms of the administrative state, and this has given the judiciary substantial room in which to innovate. As such, in the hands of administrators the APA constantly drifted toward more insularity and discretion, while the courts converted their own doctrines toward the exercise of less discretion over agency decision making.

Finally, given what we know about the political and practical dilemmas at the heart of retrenchment, the fact that the elected branches struggle to restrict remedies is not surprising. The difficulties of formal retrenchment more generally are most pronounced here, given that it is not only the legal community with an entrenched interest in preserving benefits like attorney's fees, but also *any* individual or group hoping to maximize their chance for success and profitability from a lawsuit. Nonetheless, the power to provide remedies has been subject to a significant amount of push and pull between the judicial and legislative branches. While we might expect remedies to fall solely under the discretion of the judiciary, conversion by the Supreme Court is only part of the story. As the Court converted its standards for providing remedies for rights claims (and also largely through its immunities doctrines), Congress not only tugged at this authority, but also "layered" its own statutory apparatus on top of it, most notably through legislation like the Federal Tort Claims Act and the Prison Litigation Reform Act.

Retrenchment and Political Power

The subtitle of this book, "Access to Justice and the Politics of Judicial Retrenchment," makes two implicit assumptions: first, that courts can provide an adequate forum for justice, and second, that the politics of judicial retrenchment are at least in part an attack on this forum. But both of these assumptions are complicated. The idea that courts can provide "access to justice" arose in the rights revolution when groups that were excluded from other avenues of justice—notably the political process—looked to courts as a site of last resort. Courts became an attractive option partially because, during the Civil Rights era, they seemed uniquely open to such groups, and partially because elected officials found it in their own interest to push them to that venue.[7] The term "access to justice" itself was popularized in the 1970s as legal activists pushed the courtroom doors open further for the poor and disadvantaged, and everyone from the ABA to NGOs to the federal government (which established the Legal Services Corporation for purposes of providing legal counsel to the nation's poor) seemingly embraced it.[8] There were and are certainly reasons to believe that courts are the ideal site for access to justice. As Judith Resnik writes, "the particular and peculiar practices of adjudication produce, redistribute, and curb power among disputants who disagree in public about the import of legal rights." We advocate courts because they "oblige disputants to treat each other as equals and to provide one another with information ... and upon evaluating the interactions of fact and norm, juries render verdicts or judges provide justifications for their decisions. The mandate of courts to operate in public endows their audience with the capacity to and the authority of critique."[9]

Whether courts live up to this ideal is much debated. After all, as Linda Greenhouse describes, "Our egalitarian ambitions for courts have grown over the years, perhaps outstripping our will to provide the means to fulfill our promises."[10] But the power of the ideal—in which individuals and groups can succeed in having courts legitimate their rights claims—makes the erosion of rights through erosions in access to justice particularly troubling. By and large, the legislative developments of the Civil Rights era remain in place, as do the core of many of the movement's landmark legal precedents.[11] Conservatives, despite their escalating efforts, have few signature statutory victories to show for their decades of attacks on the legal establishment. And even as attacks on the legacies of the rights revolution have been increasingly direct—the Supreme Court's 2012 decision striking down the heart of the Voting Rights Act is a prime example—the direct repeal by Congress of a landmark law like the Civil Rights Act of 1964 still seems relatively unlikely. However, conservative reform efforts have been channeled elsewhere, and with great effect; and given the high political and structural barriers to overt reform, as well as what we know about the politics of retrenchment, it is unsurprising that those seeking to diminish the rights revolution's effects have targeted the subterranean realm of procedural rules. While less visible, these reforms are highly consequential.

Even in the context of the birth and persistence of what I have characterized as a nonpartisan, "institutional maintenance" motivation for constricting access to the courts, then, it is no doubt true that targeting procedural mechanisms can be an attractive way to disguise reform efforts laced with political motivations. There is certainly evidence, for example, that judges are far more likely to decide "against" rights in procedural cases than in cases on the merits.[12] In addition, even bipartisan support for a retrenchment policy does not necessarily mean that a politically salient outcome is not at stake, but only that the interests of Democrats and Republicans coalesced on a particular issue. As we have seen, the politics (or lack thereof) surrounding the passage of the Prison Litigation Reform Act is a striking example, as are the cases of the Antiterrorism and Effective Death Penalty Act and the Illegal Immigration Reform and Immigrant Responsibility Acts of 1996, which constricted access to courts for prisoners and immigrants with bipartisan support. Further, where political power and electoral politics are concerned, both parties have acted at times to protect powerful corporations from lawsuits.

The Farmer Assurance Provision of a 2013 appropriations bill—called the "Monsanto Protection Act" by its critics—effectively barred federal courts from halting the sale or planting of controversial genetically modified or engineered seeds, regardless of any health issues that might arise from their use. As I have argued, the use of statutory provisions like these is not rare; but it is clear that the language of the law serves not only to insulate the review powers of the USDA, but also the interests of the powerful Monsanto Company as well.

In presenting an institutional narrative, I have sought to complement the partisan dimension of retrenchment, not to deny it. In fact, the "institutional maintenance" imperative arguably adds another ideological component to the story, if not one that is neatly conservative or liberal. After all, the values attached to the project of distinguishing when the judiciary is the proper venue for resolving a dispute are certainly ideological, as are those concerned with the long-term ability of the courts to be open and available for individuals. While it might be tempting to write off these concerns as convenient disguises for politics, I hope that the evidence I have presented here counsels against it. There is no doubt that political posturing occurs, and the institutional maintenance motivation may sometimes be co-opted; in fact, it is clear that procedural changes have been used for both retrenchment (whether in the *Wal-Mart* case, for example, or in the selective use of "Chevron deference" by judges), as well as in the service of the rights revolution (as with expansions to the rules governing class actions). But the development of legal and professional movements aimed at maintaining an available, effective, enduring legal system in the face of the proliferation of new rights claims and plaintiffs must also be taken seriously. Without it, from an academic point of view, we risk under-theorizing the processes of retrenchment and could subsequently miss the sites where retrenchment occurs most.

The practical consequences, however, are far more important.[13] Complicating the universe of ideologies involved in judicial retrenchment is also essential for monitoring the effects of the rights revolution on the ground. On the one hand, the legalistic rules and procedures born in the 1950s and 60s have continued to be adopted in the last quarter-century, even by local-level bureaucrats convinced that complying with federal rights policy is in their best interest. As Charles Epp describes, "Contrary to the widespread perception that this era was a time of retreat from the pursuit of egalitarian reform through law, activists and bureaucratic reformers pushed through law-modeled reforms that radically reframed the core assumptions and tools of government administration."[14] But while the spread of legalistic rules and procedures is not widely questioned, it remains unclear how effective they are in enforcing and protecting rights policies. On the other hand, then, it can be tempting to take comfort in the proliferation of rules and procedures as evidence that we are actively seeking the enforcement of rights.

But that may not be the case. Ultimately, the form and function of procedures are shaped by those in a position to control them. At any given moment in time, they might be controlled by those concerned with maintaining the integrity of the legal system, but not necessarily or primarily with better protecting rights, or—more problematically—by those seeking to use the institutional mechanisms of the "litigation state" for the opposite goal entirely. Because of this, the institutional mechanisms developed to promote access to courts can also be used to scale it back. Manipulating institutional rules and procedures to constrain state power and constrict access to courts may only chip at the edges of the litigation state; but this has a disproportionate effect on civil rights plaintiffs in particular.

Thus, institutional rules and procedures are essential components of ongoing debates about policy and power. As levers for reform, rules play an indispensable role in political change, which is fundamentally "accompanied by the accumulation and persistence of competing controls within the institutions of government."[15] The development of judicial capacity and access to courts has not been a linear expansion over time, but is—at any given moment—the product of multiple agendas in contest with each other, maneuvering within our complex institutional universe. This suggests that we must keep promoting revised accounts of the rights revolution and its backlash, as "arbitrarily one chooses that moment of experience from which to look back or from which to look ahead."[16]

Notes

CHAPTER 1

1. See *Arizona Christian School Tuition Organization v. Winn* (131 S.Ct. 1436 [2011]), *Connick v. Thompson* (131 S.Ct. 1350 [2011]), *American Electric Power Company v. Connecticut* (131 S.Ct. 2527 [2011]), and *AT&T Mobility LLC v. Vincent Concepcion* (563 U.S. 321 [2011]), respectively.

2. Richard Thompson Ford, "Everyday Discrimination: Why the Wal-Mart Sex-Bias Lawsuit Is the Most Important Case the Supreme Court Will Hear This Year," *Slate Magazine*, March 28, 2011. http://www.slate.com/articles/news_and_politics/jurisprudence/2011/03/everyday_discrimination.html.

3. Ibid.

4. *Wal-Mart Stores, Inc. v. Betty Dukes, et al.*, 131 S.Ct. 2541 (2011).

5. The Court unanimously determined that the plaintiffs' claims for back pay were improperly certified in the lower courts under Rule 23(b)(2), arguing that claims for monetary relief cannot be certified under that provision when the monetary relief is not incidental to the requested injunctive or declaratory relief.

6. The Court's liberal wing—Justices Ruth Bader Ginsburg, Stephen Breyer, Elena Kagan, and Sonia Sotomayor—concurred in part and dissented in part. While they agreed that the class should not have been certified under Rule 23(b)(2), Justice Ginsburg suggested that the case should be remanded for consideration as to whether the class met the requirements of Rule 23(b)(3), which was not before the Court. The majority effectively precluded consideration by holding that the class did not meet the "commonality" threshold set by Rule 23(a)(2), however, which effectively (as Ginsburg put it) "disqualifies the class at the starting gate."

7. Comments presented at Princeton University, "Full Court Press: The Supreme Court, the Media, and Public Understanding," sponsored by the Program in Law and Public Affairs, November 11, 2009.

8. "Access to justice" was a phrase commonly used by public advocates during the rights revolution when promoting the rights of groups typically disadvantaged by both the political and legal systems. The phrase continues to be used by groups advocating on behalf of remedying inequalities in the legal process today.

9. *Shelby County v. Holder*, 133 S.Ct. 2612 (2013).

10. See, for example, Steven M. Teles, *The Rise of the Conservative Legal Movement: The Battle for Control of the Law* (Princeton, NJ: Princeton University Press, 2008); Ann Southworth, *Lawyers of the Right: Professionalizing the Conservative Coalition* (Chicago: University of Chicago Press, 2008).

11. For example, see Judith Resnik, "Fairness in Numbers: A Comment on *AT&T v. Concepcion, Wal-Mart v. Dukes*, and *Turner v. Rogers*," *Harvard Law Review* 125 (2011), 78–170.

12. See *American Express v. Italian Colors Restaurant*, 133 S. Ct. 2304 (2013); *AT&T Mobility v. Concepcion*, 131 S. Ct. 1740 (2011); *Comcast Corp. v. Behrend*, 133 S. Ct. 1426 (2013); *Compucredit Corp. v. Greenwood*, 132 S. Ct. 665 (2012).

13. See, for example, Malcolm M. Feeley and Edward L. Rubin, *Judicial Policy Making and the Modern State: How the Courts Reformed America's Prisons* (New York: Cambridge University Press, 2000); R. Shep Melnick, *Between the Lines: Interpreting Welfare Rights* (Washington, DC: Brookings Institution Press, 1994).

14. See, for example, Howard Gillman, "Party Politics and Constitutional Change: The Political Origins of Liberal Judicial Activism," in Ronald Kahn and Ken I. Kersch, eds., *The Supreme Court and American Political Development* (Lawrence: University of Kansas Press, 2006), 138; Richard A. Posner, *The Federal Courts: Challenge and Reform* (Cambridge, MA: Harvard University Press, 1985), chapter five.

15. For more on the "support structure" that made the developments of the rights revolution possible, see Charles R. Epp, *The Rights Revolution: Lawyers, Activists, and Supreme Courts in Comparative Perspective* (Chicago: University of Chicago Press, 1998). For the role of the judiciary in the American state, see Charles R. Epp, *Making Rights Real: Activists, Bureaucrats, and the Creation of the Legalistic State* (Chicago: University of Chicago Press, 2010); Sean Farhang, *The Litigation State: Public Regulation and Private Lawsuits in the U.S.* (Princeton, NJ: Princeton University Press, 2010); Feeley and Rubin, *Judicial Policy Making and the Modern State*; Paul Frymer, *Black and Blue: African Americans, the Labor Movement, and the Decline of the Democratic Party* (Princeton, NJ: Princeton University Press, 2008); Melnick, *Between the Lines*; Gordon Silverstein, *Law's Allure: How Law Shapes, Constrains, Saves, and Kills Politics* (New York: Cambridge University Press, 2009); John D. Skrentny, "Law and the American State," *Annual Review of Sociology* 32 (2006), 213–44; Cass Sunstein, *After the Rights Revolution* (Cambridge, MA: Harvard University Press, 1990).

16. See, for example, Thomas F. Burke, *Lawyers, Lawsuits, and Legal Rights: The Struggle Over Litigation in American Society* (Berkeley: University of California

Press, 2002); William Haltom and Michael McCann, *Distorting the Law: Politics, Media, and the Litigation Crisis* (Chicago: University of Chicago Press, 2004).

17. *Chevron U.S.A., Inc., v. National Resources Defense Council,* 467 U.S. 837 (1984).

18. Marc Galanter, "Why the 'Haves' Come Out Ahead: Speculations on the Limits of Legal Change," *Law and Society Review* 9 (1974), 95–160.

19. The total number of federal civil cases reaching a judgment by a court per year, for example, has dropped from 10,155 in 1997 to 5,478 in 2012. See Federal Judicial Caseload Statistics, Judicial Business, www.uscourts.gov/statistics.aspx.

20. Marc Galanter, "The Vanishing Trial: An Examination of Trials and Related Matters in Federal and State Courts," *Journal of Empirical Legal Studies* 1 (2004), 459–570; Marc Galanter and Mia Cahill, "Most Cases Settle: Judicial Promotion and Regulation of Settlements," *Stanford Law Review* 46 (1994), 1339.

21. Whether individuals and groups can benefit settling out of court is a question that deserves further attention. For example, Catherine Albiston examines the question of whether plaintiffs can "win" through pre-trial settlements. See Catherine Albiston, "The Rule of Law and the Litigation Process: The Paradox of Winning by Losing," *Law & Society Review* 33 (1999), 869. Indeed, it was argued prior to the *Wal-Mart* decision that the company's female employees had seen improvement in their working conditions because of changes that the company made while under the threat of litigation. See Liza Featherstone, "Suit Has Spurred Wal-Mart," *Newsday*, March 31, 2011. However, it has also been argued that changes to procedure such as these may lead disadvantaged groups in particular to fail to attain a lawyer and subsequently to reach an advantageous settlement. See Catherine R. Albiston and Laura Beth Nielsen, "The Procedural Attack on Civil Rights: The Empirical Reality of *Buckhannon* for the Private Attorney General," *UCLA Law Review* 54 (2007), 1087.

22. Jacob Hacker uses this term in "Privatizing Risk without Privatizing the Welfare State: The Hidden Politics of Social Policy Retrenchment in the United States," *American Political Science Review* 98 (2004), 243–60.

23. See, for example, Tom S. Clark, *The Limits of Judicial Independence* (New York: Cambridge University Press, 2010); Stephen M. Engel, *American Politicians Confront the Court: Opposition Politics and Changing Responses to Judicial Power* (New York: Cambridge University Press, 2011).

24. Although certain trends in criminal law do parallel those in civil law—for example, there is a similar decline in the number of criminal cases that go to trial— backlash to the rights revolution has also dramatically increased incarceration rates, a phenomenon that scholars have referred to as the growth of the "carceral state." See, for example, Marie Gottschalk, *The Prison and the Gallows: The Politics of Mass Incareration in America* (New York: Cambridge University Press, 2006); Naomi Murakawa, *The First Civil Right: How Liberals Built Prison America* (New York: Oxford University Press, 2014); Vesla Weaver, "Frontlash: Race and the Development of Punitive Crime Policy," *Studies in American Political Development* 21 (2007), 230–65.

25. The issue of access to courts is a topic well-traversed by law professors interested in trends in litigation. For an example of these discussions, see the collection of essays in *Journal of Empirical Legal Studies* 1 (2004), 459–984.

26. See, for example, Hacker, "Privatizing Risk without Privatizing the Welfare State"; Paul Pierson, *Dismantling the Welfare State? Reagan, Thatcher, and the Politics of Retrenchment* (New York: Cambridge University Press, 1995).

27. For a thorough discussion of how actors importantly construct their own institutional insularity, see Daniel P. Carpenter, *The Forging of Bureaucratic Autonomy: Reputations, Networks, and Policy Innovation in Executive Agencies, 1862–1928* (Princeton, NJ: Princeton University Press, 2001). For a discussion more specific to legal actors, see Justin E. Crowe, "The Forging of Judicial Autonomy: Political Entrepreneurship and the Reforms of William Howard Taft," *Journal of Politics* 69 (2007), 73–87.

28. In his work on asbestos litigation, Jeb Barnes has elucidated the importance of this approach. See Jeb Barnes, "Courts and the Puzzle of Institutional Stability and Change: Administrative Drift and Judicial Innovation in the Case of Asbestos," *Political Research Quarterly* 61 (2008), 636–48.

29. Pamela S. Karlan, "Dismantling the Private Attorney General," *University of Illinois Law Review* (2003), 185.

CHAPTER 2

1. The success of the litigation strategy is itself, however, a topic of much debate. See, for example, Paul Frymer, "Acting When Elected Officials Won't: Federal Courts and Civil Rights Enforcement in U.S. Labor Unions," *American Political Science Review* 97 (2003), 483–99; Michael W. McCann, *Rights at Work: Pay Equity Reform and the Politics of Legal Mobilization* (Chicago: University of Chicago Press, 1994); Gerald Rosenberg, *The Hollow Hope: Can Courts Bring about Social Change* (Chicago: University of Chicago Press, 1991).

2. Charles Fishman, *The Wal-Mart Effect: How The World's Most Powerful Company Really Works—And How It's Transforming the American Economy* (New York: Penguin, 2006).

3. See Liza Featherstone, *Selling Women Short: The Landmark Battle for Workers' Rights at Wal-Mart* (New York: Basic Books, 2005), 2–4.

4. Ralph Richard Banks, "A Cruel Paradox," *New York Times* online, updated June 21, 2011.

5. For a discussion of "subterranean" forms of retrenchment, see Jacob Hacker, "Privatizing Risk without Privatizing the Welfare State: The Hidden Politics of Social Policy Retrenchment in the United States," *American Political Science Review* 98 (2004), 243–60.

6. John Donahue and Peter Siegelman, "The Changing Nature of Employment Discrimination Litigation," *Stanford Law Review* 46 (1991), 983–1033. For a

more recent discussion of litigation trends in employment discrimination, see Laura Beth Nielsen, Robert L. Nelson, and Ryon Lancaster, "Individual Justice or Collective Legal Mobilization? Employment Discrimination Litigation in the Post-Civil Rights United States," *Journal of Empirical Legal Studies* 7 (2010), 175.

7. Administrative Office of the United States Courts, Table X-5, "U.S. District Courts—Class Action Civil Cases Commenced, by Basis of Jurisdiction and Nature of Suit" (1976–2004).

8. Administrative Office of the United States Courts, Table C-4, "U.S. District Courts—Civil Cases Terminated, By Nature of Suit and Action Taken" (1976–2013). For a comprehensive account of these legislative changes to the Civil Rights Act of 1964 (and "damages enhancements" more generally), see Sean Farhang, *The Litigation State: Public Regulation and Private Lawsuits in the U.S.* (Princeton, NJ: Princeton University Press, 2010).

9. Marc Galanter, "The Vanishing Trial: An Examination of Trials and Related Matters in Federal and State Courts," *Journal of Empirical Legal Studies* 1 (2004), 461.

10. U.S. Courts, Table C-4 (1976–2013).

11. Ibid.

12. Marc Galanter, "Why the 'Haves' Come Out Ahead: Speculations on the Limits of Legal Change," *Law and Society Review* 9 (1974), 95–160.

13. For an overview of these trends within political science, see Keith E. Whittington, "Once More Unto the Breach: Post-Behavioralist Approaches to Judicial Politics," *Law and Social Inquiry* 25 (2000), 601–34.

14. William Sewell, "Three Temporalities: Toward an Eventful Sociology," in Terrence J. McDonald, ed., *The Historic Turn in the Human Sciences* (Ann Arbor: University of Michigan Press, 1996), 262–64.

15. Paul Pierson, "Increasing Returns, Path Dependence, and the Study of Politics," *American Political Science Review* 94 (2000), 251. See also Ruth Berins Collier and David Collier, *Shaping the Political Arena: Critical Junctures, the Labor Movement, and Regime Dynamics in Latin America* (Princeton, NJ: Princeton University Press, 1991); S. J. Liebowitz and Stephen E. Margolis, "Path Dependence, Lock-In, and History," *Journal of Law, Economics, and Organization* 11 (1995), 205–26; Margaret Levi, "A Model, a Method, and a Map: Rational Choice in Comparative and Historical Analysis," in Mark I. Lichbach and Alan S. Zuckerman, eds., *Comparative Politics: Rationality, Culture, and Structure,* (New York: Cambridge University Press, 1997), 19; Kathleen Thelen, "Historical Institutionalism and Comparative Politics," *Annual Review of Political Science* 2 (1999), 369–404.

16. See James Mahoney and Kathleen Thelen, "A Theory of Gradual Institutional Change," in James Mahoney and Kathleen Thelen, eds., *Explaining Institutional Change: Ambiguity, Agency, and Power* (New York: Cambridge University Press, 2010), 1–37; Wolfgang Streeck and Kathleen Thelen, eds., *Beyond Continuity: Institutional Change in Advanced Political Economies* (New York:

Oxford University Press, 2005); Kathleen Thelen, *How Institutions Evolve: The Political Economy of Skills in Germany, Britain, the United States, and Japan* (New York: Cambridge University Press, 2004).

17. Karen Orren and Stephen Skowronek, *The Search for American Political Development* (New York: Cambridge University Press, 2004), 114.

18. See, for example, Howard Gillman, "How Political Parties Can Use the Courts to Advance Their Agendas: Federal Courts in the United States, 1875–1891," *American Political Science Review* 96 (2002), 511–24; Mark A. Graber, "The Non-Majoritarian Difficulty: Legislative Deference to the Judiciary," *Studies in American Political Development* 7 (1993), 35–72; Mark A. Graber, "The Countermajoritarian Difficulty: From Courts to Congress to Constitutional Order," *Annual Review of Law and Social Sciences* 4 (2008), 361–84; Mark Tushnet, "The Supreme Court and the National Political Order: Collaboration and Confrontation," in Ronald Kahn and Ken I. Kersch, eds., *The Supreme Court and American Political Development* (Lawrence: University of Kansas Press, 2006), 117; Keith E. Whittington, *Political Foundations of Judicial Supremacy: The Presidency, the Supreme Court, and Constitutional Leadership in U.S. History* (Princeton, NJ: Princeton University Press, 2007).

19. This mirrors (indeed paraphrases) Eric Schickler's characterization of national legislatures in *Disjointed Pluralism: Institutional Innovation and the Development of the United States Congress* (Princeton, NJ: Princeton University Press, 2001), 3: "Whatever else a national legislature may be, it is a complex of rules, procedures, and specialized internal institutions, such as committees and leadership instruments. Particular configurations of these rules, procedures, committees, and leadership instruments may serve the interests of individual members, parties, pressure groups, sectors of society, or the legislature as a whole. As a result, as any legislature evolves through time, little is more fundamental to its politics than recurrent, often intense, efforts to *change* its institutions."

20. Charles Epp, *The Rights Revolution: Lawyers, Activists, and Supreme Courts in Comparative Perspective* (Chicago: University of Chicago Press, 1998).

21. Robert A. Kagan, *Adversarial Legalism: The American Way of Law* (Cambridge, MA: Harvard University Press, 2003).

22. Gordon Silverstein, *Law's Allure: How Law Shapes, Constrains, Saves, and Kills Politics* (New York: Cambridge University Press, 2009), 2.

23. Gillman, "How Political Parties Can Use the Courts."

24. Graber, "The Non-Majoritarian Difficulty."

25. Tushnet, "The Supreme Court and the National Political Order."

26. Whittington, *Political Foundations of Judicial Supremacy*.

27. See, for example, Anthony S. Chen, *The Fifth Freedom: Jobs, Politics, and Civil Rights in the United States* (Princeton, NJ: Princeton University Press, 2009); Ken I. Kersch, *Constructing Civil Liberties: Discontinuities in the Development of American Constitutional Law* (New York: Cambridge University Press, 2004);

George I. Lovell, *Legislative Deferrals: Statutory Ambiguity, Judicial Power, and American Democracy* (New York: Cambridge University Press, 2003); Kevin J. McMahon, *Reconsidering Roosevelt on Race: How the Presidency Paved the Road to Brown* (Chicago: University of Chicago Press, 2004); Julie Novkov, *Racial Union: Law, Intimacy, and the White State in Alabama, 1865–1954* (Ann Arbor: University of Michigan Press, 2008); Silverstein, *Law's Allure*; John David Skrentny, *The Ironies of Affirmative Action: Politics, Culture, and Justice in America* (Chicago: University of Chicago Press, 1996); Mariah Zeisberg, *War Powers: The Politics of Constitutional Authority* (Princeton, NJ: Princeton University Press, 2013).

28. See, for example, Thomas F. Burke, *Lawyers, Lawsuits, and Legal Rights: The Battle Over Litigation in American Society* (Berkeley: University of California Press, 2002); Dawn M. Chutkow, "Litigation, Ideology, and Congressional Control of the Courts," *The Journal of Politics* 70 (2008); Tom S. Clark, *The Limits of Judicial Independence* (New York: Cambridge University Press, 2010); Stephen M. Engel, *American Politicians Confront the Court: Opposition Politics and Changing Responses to Judicial Power* (New York: Cambridge University Press, 2011); Edward Keynes with Randall K. Miller, *The Court v. Congress: Prayer, Busing, and Abortion* (Durham, NC: Duke University Press, 1989); Stuart S. Nagel, "Court-Curbing Periods in American History," *Vanderbilt Law Review* 18 (1965), 925–44.

29. Kagan, *Adversarial Legalism.*

30. Burke, *Lawyers, Lawsuits, and Legal Rights.*

31. Farhang, *The Litigation State*; R. Shep Melnick, "Courts and Agencies," in Mark C. Miller and Jeb Barnes, eds., *Making Policy, Making Law: An Interbranch Perspective* (Washington, DC: Georgetown University Press, 2004), 89, respectively.

32. In the area of asbestos policy reform, for example, Jeb Barnes shows that judges themselves were at the forefront of "court-based tort reform" precisely because they sought to create more efficient ways to handle the onslaught of asbestos cases in the federal courts. See Jeb Barnes, *Dust Up: Asbestos Litigation and the Failure of Commonsense Policy Reform* (Washington, DC: Georgetown University Press, 2011).

33. Epp, *The Rights Revolution*; William Haltom and Michael McCann, *Distorting the Law: Politics, Media, and the Litigation Crisis* (Chicago: University of Chicago Press, 2004).

34. Though see Justin Crowe, *Building the Judiciary: Law, Courts, and the Politics of Institutional Development* (Princeton, NJ: Princeton University Press, 2012); Sarah Staszak, "Institutions, Rulemaking, and the Politics of Judicial Retrenchment," *Studies in American Political Development* 24 (2010), 168–89.

35. See, for example, Joanna L. Grisinger, *The Unwieldy American State* (New York: Cambridge University Press, 2012).

36. For an overall discussion of the APD approach to studying institutional change, see Karen Orren and Stephen Skowronek, *The Search for American Political Development* (New York: Cambridge University Press, 2004).

37. See Paul Pierson, "Path Dependence, Increasing Returns, and the Study of Politics," and *Politics in Time: History, Institutions, and Social Analysis* (Princeton, NJ: Princeton University Press, 2004), 251–67.

38. See Stephen Skowronek, *The Politics Presidents Make: Leadership from John Adams to Bill Clinton* (Cambridge, MA: Belknap Press of Harvard University Press, 1997).

39. See Daniel P. Carpenter, *The Forging of Bureaucratic Autonomy: Reputations, Networks, and Policy Innovation in Executive Agencies, 1862–1928* (Princeton, NJ: Princeton University Press, 2001); Gillman, "How Political Parties Can Use the Courts."

40. Orren and Skowronek, *The Search for American Political Development*; Schickler, *Disjointed Pluralism*; Stephen Skowronek, *Building a New American State: The Expansion of National Administrative Capacities, 1877-1920* (New York: Cambridge University Press 1982).

41. For example, see Justin Crowe, "The Forging of Judicial Autonomy: Political Entrepreneurship and the Reforms of William Howard Taft," *Journal of Politics* 69 (2007), 73–87; Gillman, "How Political Parties Can Use the Courts;" Whittington, *Political Foundations of Judicial Supremacy*.

42. Karen Orren, *Belated Feudalism: Labor, the Law, and Liberal Development in the United States* (New York: Cambridge University Press, 1992); Theda Skocpol, *Protecting Soldiers and Mothers: The Political Origins of Social Policy in the United States* (Cambridge, MA: Belknap Press, 1995).

43. See Stephen B. Burbank, "Hearing on Whether the Supreme Court Has Limited Americans' Access to Courts," prepared statement, Hearings Before the Senate Judiciary Committee, December 2, 2009; Burke, *Lawyers, Lawsuits, and Legal Rights*; Lynda Dodd, "*DeShaney v. Winnebago County*: Governmental Neglect and the 'Blessings of Liberty,'" in Myriam Gilles and Risa Golubuff, eds., *Civil Rights Stories* (New York: Foundation Press, 2007), 185; Galanter, "The Vanishing Trial."

44. See generally Pierson, *Politics in Time*.

45. Eric M. Patashnik, *Reforms at Risk: What Happens After Major Policy Changes Are Enacted* (Princeton, NJ: Princeton University Press, 2008).

46. *Marbury v. Madison*, 5 U.S. 137 (1803).

47. See, for example, Burke, *Lawyers, Lawsuits, and Legal Rights*; Richard H. Fallon, "The 'Conservative' Paths of the Rehnquist Court's Federalism Decisions," *University of Chicago Law Review* 69 (2002), 429–94; Engel, *American Politicians Confront the Court*; Andrew M. Siegel, "The Court Against Courts: Hostility to Litigation as an Organizing Theme in the Rehnquist Court's Jurisprudence," *Texas Law Review* 64 (2006), 1097.

48. See, for example, Thomas M. Keck, *The Most Activist Supreme Court in History: The Road to Modern Judicial Conservatism* (Chicago: University of Chicago Press,

2010); Mark Tushnet, *A Court Divided: The Rehnquist Court and the Future of Constitutional Law* (New York: W.W. Norton, 2005).

49. See, for example, Lawrence M. Friedman, *Total Justice* (New York: Russell Sage Foundation 1994); Kagan, *Adversarial Legalism*.

50. Steven M. Teles, *The Rise of the Conservative Legal Movement: The Battle for Control of the Law* (Princeton, NJ: Princeton University Press, 2008).

51. Haltom and McCann, *Distorting the Law.*.

52. See E. E. Schattschneider, *The Semisovereign People: A Realist's View of Democracy in America* (Boston: Wadsworth Cengage Learning, 1975).

53. As I proceed temporally through each chapter, I employ the research method of a "structured, focused comparison." As Alexander George and Andrew Bennett describe, this method involves asking general questions that reflect one's research objective and asking them of each case. In each case study chapter, I evaluate the cases I have examined in terms of the insularity, ideology, and temporality hypotheses. See Alexander L. George and Andrew Bennett, *Case Studies and Theory Development in the Social Sciences* (Cambridge, MA, and London: MIT Press, 2005), 67–72.

54. Elisabeth S. Clemens and James M. Cook, "Politics and Institutionalism: Explaining Durability and Change," *Annual Review of Sociology*, 25 (1999), 448.

55. See Carpenter, *The Forging of Bureaucratic Autonomy*; Crowe, "The Forging of Judicial Autonomy"; Adam Sheingate, "Political Entrepreneurship, Institutional Change, and American Political Development," *Studies in American Political Development* 17 (2002), 185–203.

56. Burke, *Lawyers, Lawsuits, and Legal Rights*.

57. Carpenter, *The Forging of Bureaucratic Autonomy*, 5.

58. Hacker, "Privatizing Risk without Privatizing the Welfare State." 245. See also Mahoney and Thelen, *Explaining Institutional Change*; Patashnik, *Reforms at Risk*; Pierson, *Dismantling the Welfare State*.

59. Hacker, "Privatizing Risk without Privatizing the Welfare State," 244–46. In addition to identifying these forms of retrenchment, Hacker does a great service in associating these mechanisms with the conditions under which they are likely to occur. For example, he argues that outright "revision" is generally unlikely because it necessitates that both barriers to internal adaptation (where those in power have high levels of discretion and a policy has weak support) and barriers to authoritative change are low. When both are high—most often the case in American politics—"drift" is the most likely method of change. When barriers to authoritative change are high and the barriers to internal adaptation are low, "conversion" is most likely. Finally, when the barriers to authoritative change are low and those to internal adaptation are high, layering is likely to emerge. Eric Patashnik has developed a similar predicative typology with regard to the question of whether and when policy reforms are likely to become entrenched; see *Reforms at Risk*.

60. Jeb Barnes, "Courts and the Puzzle of Institutional Stability and Change: Administrative Drift and Judicial Innovation in the Case of Asbestos," *Political Research Quarterly* 61 (2008), 646. In his study of asbestos litigation, Barnes has found that administrative drift led to periods of judicial conversion and layering, indicating that drift (and presumably other forms of institutional change) can best be understood as transitional.

CHAPTER 3

1. See Stuart T. Rossman, Director of Litigation, National Consumer Law Center, "Recent Developments in the Forced Arbitration Market and the Continued Need for Protective Legislation," Subcommittee on Commercial and Administrative Law, House Committee on the Judiciary, September 15, 2009; "Firm Agrees to End Role in Arbitrating Card Debt," *New York Times*, July 19, 2009.

2. Public Citizen, "The Arbitration Trap: How Credit Card Companies Ensnare Consumers," September 2007; City Attorneys' complaint, *People of the State of California v. National Arbitration Forum, Inc. et al,* San Francisco Superior Court No. 473–569 (March 24, 2008).

3. Public Citizen, "Forced Arbitration: Unfair and Everywhere," September 14, 2009.

4. See Consumer Financial Protection Bureau, "Arbitration Study Preliminary Results: Section 1,028(a) Study Results to Date," December 12, 2013, 12, http://files.consumerfinance.gov/f/201312_cfpb_arbitration-study-preliminary-results.pdf.

5. Regarding the partisan nature of the current antilitigation movement, see, for example, Thomas F. Burke, *Lawyers, Lawsuits, and Legal Rights: The Battle over Litigation in American Society* (Berkeley: University of California Press, 2002); William Haltom and Michael McCann, *Distorting the Law: Politics, Media, and the Litigation Crisis* (Chicago: University of Chicago Press, 2004).

6. Staff Report of the Domestic Subcommittee Majority Staff, Oversight and Government Reform Committee, Chairman Dennis J. Kucinich, July 21, 2009; Staff Report, Subcommittee on Domestic Policy, Committee on Oversight and Government Reform, Jim Jordan, July 22, 2009.

7. Ibid.

8. Theodore Eisenberg, Geoffrey P. Miller, and Emily Sherwin, "Arbitration's Summer Soldiers: An Empirical Study of Arbitration Clauses in Consumer and Nonconsumer Contracts," *University of Michigan Journal of Law Reform* 41 (2008), 883. CRS Report, "Courts Continue to Recognize Validity of Mandatory Arbitration Agreements," September 5, 2013. See, too, Amalia D. Kessler, "Stuck in Arbitration," *New York Times*, March 6, 2012.

9. Alexander J. S. Colvin, "An Empirical Study of Employment Arbitration: Case Outcomes and Processes," *Journal of Empirical Legal Studies* 8 (2011), 5–6, 19.

10. "Mandatory Binding Arbitration: Is It Fair and Voluntary?," Subcommittee on Commercial and Administrative Law, House of Representatives, 111th Congress, 1st Session, September 15, 2009, at 2.

11. Ibid.

12. Ibid., at 86.

13. *AT&T Mobility LLC v. Conception*, 131 S.Ct. 1740 (2011). See also Andrew Cohen, "No Class: The Supreme Court's Arbitration Ruling," *The Atlantic*, April 27, 2011, http://www.theatlantic.com/national/archive/2011/04/no-class-the-su preme-courts-arbitration-ruling/237967/.

14. See Charles Pollack, "An American Crisis: Proprietary Schools and National Student Debt," *American University Business Law Review* 1 (2012), 157–58.

15. *Compucredit Corp. v. Greenwood*, 132 S.Ct. 665 (2012). CROA stipulates clearly and succinctly, "You have the right to sue a credit repair organization that violates the Credit Repair Organization Act."

16. *American Express Co. v. Italian Colors Restaurant*, 133 S.Ct. 2304 (2013).

17. *Compucredit Corp. v. Greenwood.*

18. "Workplace Fairness: Has the Supreme Court Been Misinterpreting Laws Designed to Protect American Workers from Discrimination?" Hearing before the Committee on the Senate Judiciary, October 7, 2009, 2.

19. The two most commonly used methods of ADR, arbitration and mediation, date back the furthest. Arbitration is a consensual process in which the opposing parties present their positions to a neutral third party or panel (agreed upon by the parties) with decision making authority, who is typically a respected expert in the subject area of a dispute. Arbitration is the ADR method that most closely resembles the process of adjudication. Arbitration clauses are typically included in contracts and, as such, are agreed upon as a means of adjudication well before a dispute arises; they also usually stipulate whether an award will be considered final and binding or whether judicial review is permissible. The most widely used court-based program, however, is mediation; a private, voluntary, informal process by which parties pick a third party neutral to assist them in reaching a mutually acceptable agreement. After listening to both sides, the mediator gives each party his or her assessment of the strengths and weaknesses of its case (and the opponent's) in hopes of facilitating settlement.

20. Regarding differences in interpretation, compare the ideologically contrasting writings of Ralph Nader, "Consumerism and Legal Services: The Merging of Movements," *Law and Society Review* 11 (1976), 247–56, and Laurence H. Tribe, "Too Much Law, Too Little Justice: An Argument for Delegalizing America," *The Atlantic Monthly*, July 1979, at 25, with the writings of Robert H. Bork, "Dealing with the Overload in Article III Courts," *Federal Rules Decisions* 70 (1976), 231–46, and Warren Burger, "Isn't There a Better Way?," *American Bar Association Journal* 68 (1982), 274–77. For a discussion of these alternative viewpoints, see Marc Galanter and John Lande, "Private Courts and Public Authority," *Law,*

Politics, and Society 12 (1992), 393–415; and Jeffrey W. Stempel, "Reflections on Judicial ADR and the Multi-Door Courthouse at Twenty: Fait Accompli, Failed Overture, or Fledgling Adulthood? *Ohio State Journal of Dispute Resolution* 11 (1996), 297–395.

21. Thomas J. Stipanowich, "ADR and the 'Vanishing Trial': The Growth and Impact of 'Alternative Dispute Resolution,' *Journal of Empirical Legal Studies* 1 (2004), 843. See also Stipanowich, "Arbitration: The 'New Litigation,'" *University of Illinois Law Review* 2010, no. 1 (2010), 1–58.

22. See American Arbitration Association, Department of Case Administration, Caseload Statistics, 2002.

23. For an overview of a range of state courts, see Stipanowich, "ADR and the 'Vanishing Trial.'" Regarding L.A., see the *Daily Journal*, December 6, 2004.

24. Marc S. Galanter, "The Vanishing Trial: An Examination of Trials and Related Matters in Federal and State Courts," *Journal of Empirical Legal Studies* 1 (2004), 459.

25. Stephen N. Subrin and Thomas O. Main, "The Fourth Era of American Civil Procedure," *University of Pennsylvania Law Review* 162 (2014), 1880.

26. Martin Shapiro, *Courts: A Comparative and Political Analysis* (Chicago: University of Chicago Press, 1986), 1.

27. Gordon Silverstein, *Law's Allure: How Law Shapes, Constrains, Saves, and Kills Politics* (New York: Cambridge University Press, 2009).

28. See Burke, *Lawyers, Lawsuits, and Legal Rights*; Haltom and McCann, *Distorting the Law*; Robert A. Kagan, *Adversarial Legalism: The American Way of Law* (Cambridge, MA: Harvard University Press, 2001).

29. Democrats during this time period also argued that there was a growing need to modernize state institutions to respond to the complexities of industrialized society, and that ADR was a novel approach.

30. See David Horton, "Arbitration as Delegation," *New York University Law Review* 86 (2011), 460–61.

31. *Gilmer v. Interstate/Johnson Lane Corp.* (500 U.S. 20 [1991], Age Discrimination in Employment Act); *Rodriquez de Quijas v. Shearson/American Express* (490 U.S. 477, [1989], Securities Act of 1933); *Shearson/American Express, Inc. v. McMahon* (482 U.S. 220 [1987], Racketeer Influenced and Corrupt Organizations Act and the Securities Act of 1934); *Perry v. Thomas* (482 U.S. 483 [1987], finding that the FAA preempts California law guaranteeing access to courts in wage collection actions).

32. See *Rent-A-Center West, Inc. v. Jackson*, 130 S.Ct. 2772 (2010).

33. See *AT&T Mobility LLC v. Concepcion*, 563 U.S. 321 (2011).

34. The quotation is from "Arbitration Proposition of Mr. Stevens in the Convention," *The True American*, August 5, 1846, 1.

35. "Legislative Acts/Legal Proceedings," *The Mail*, September 3, 1791, 3.

36. "To the Legislatures of the respective States," *National Intelligencer and Washington Advertiser*, September 5, 1804, 2. See, too, *Trenton Federalist*, February 27, 1804, 3.

37. "Constitution," *Gazette of the United States*, May 14, 1803.

38. "Constitutional Convention," *Albany Argus*, August 21, 1846, 2. It was proposed that this court be first tried in New York City, "and if it worked well there, to allow the legislature to extend it to other sections of the state." Massachusetts and Pennsylvania considered similar creations in 1855. See *Washington Review and Examiner*, February 3, 1855; "Courts of Mediation and Arbitration," *Boston Herald*, March 10, 1855.

39. Report of the Debates and Proceedings of the Convention for the Revision of the Constitution of the State of New York, 1846, 588. Quoted in Eric H. Steele, "The Historical Context of Small Claims Courts," *American Bar Foundation Research Journal* 6 (Spring 1981), 306.

40. "Courts of Arbitration," *Baltimore Sun*, August 27, 1846.

41. "Courts of Mediation and Arbitration," *Boston Herald*, March 10, 1855.

42. "A Court without Lawyers," *Massachusetts Spy*, February 23, 1859.

43. In further support of arbitration as preferable to litigation for speed, price, and common good, see "Plan for Diminishing Litigations," *The New-Yorker*, April 13, 1839, 52; "Litigation-Arbitration," *Friends' Weekly Intelligencer*, April 6, 1844, 9. With regard to Ohio, see R. W. Russell, "Reform in the Judiciary System of Ohio," *The Western Law Journal* (August 1844), 508; Speech of Mr. Pennington, "Law Reform in Ohio," *The Western Law Journal* (September 1849); "Courts of Conciliation," *Maine Farmer*, April 12, 1849, 2. On support from railroads fighting each other, "Arbitration in Railway Disputes," *American Railway Times*, October 16, 1858.

44. *Milwaukee Sentinel*, May 1, 1849, 2.

45. See, for example, Maxwell Bloomfield, "Lawyers and Public Criticism: Challenge and Response in Nineteenth-Century America," *American Journal of Legal History* 15 (October 1971), 276.

46. Morton Horwitz, *The Transformation of American Law, 1780–1860* (Cambridge, MA: Harvard University Press, 1977), 150. More generally on the early decades after the American Revolution, see chapter 5.

47. *Tobey v. County of Bristol*, 23 F. Cas. 1313, 1321, Circuit District Court of Massachusetts (May 1845).

48. Ibid.

49. Ibid., at 1321.

50. *Insurance Co. v. Morse*, 87 U.S. 445 (1874), at 451.

51. See, for example, Charles Sumner's promotion of international arbitration as an alternative to war. Mr. Sumner, "Resolutions," Senate, 43rd Congress, 1st Session, December 1, 1873.

52. Hearings before the Committee on Foreign Relations, Senate, 50th Congress, 1st Session, January 30, 1888, 6. Field also famously created the Field Code in 1850 in the state of New York, which moved the state's legal system away from common law pleading to code pleading. See Stephen N. Subrin, "David Dudley Field and

the Field Code: A Historical Analysis of an Earlier Procedural Vision," *Law and History Review* 6 (September 1988), 311–73.

53. As such, there are two separate questions regarding the administrative state and courts, only one of which is addressed in this chapter. What I am not addressing here is the constitutional fight over the "primacy between courts and administrators," one that involves questions of the delegation of power between branches of government and the scope of administrative discretion vis-à-vis judicial activism. For this, see, for example, Horwitz, *The Transformation of American Law*, 222.

54. See, for example, Karen Orren, *Belated Feudalism: Labor, the Law, and Liberal Development in the United States* (New York: Cambridge University Press, 1992); Herbert Schreiber, "The Majority Preference Provisions in Early State Labor Arbitration Statutes, 1880–1900," *Journal of American Legal History* 15 (1971), 186; John Fabian Witt, *The Accidental Republic: Crippled Workingmen, Destitute Widows, and the Remaking of American Law* (Cambridge, MA: Harvard University Press, 2004).

55. See the testimony of W. A. A. Carsey, chairman of the Anti-Monopoly League of the state of New York, before the Senate Committee on Interstate Commerce, 50th Congress, 1st Session, March 8, 1888.

56. Reports on the Industrial Commission on Labor Organizations: Labor Disputes and Arbitration, and on Railway Labor, House of Representatives, 57th Congress, 1st Session, Doc. No. 186, 1901, 423. Under the authority of the act, the president appointed a special commission to investigate the great railway strikes of 1894, but the investigation produced findings well after the dispute was settled.

57. See Stephen Skowronek, *Building a New American State: The Expansion of National Administrative Capacities 1877–1920* (New York: Cambridge University Press, 1982), 150–54, and in particular at 152, quoting Brewer.

58. *Chicago, Milwaukee and St. Paul Railway Co. v Minnesota*, 134 U.S. 418 (1980), at 457.

59. Reports on the Industrial Commission on Labor Organizations: Labor Disputes and Arbitration, and on Railway Labor, House of Representatives, 57th Congress, 1st Session, Doc. No. 186, 1901, 423–78.

60. Ibid., 428–31, 434–36, 442–44, 449–52.

61. Ibid., 455–56.

62. Schreiber, "Majority Preference Provisions," 187.

63. *Berkovitz v. Arbib and Houlberg, Inc.*, 230 NY 261 (1921), at 274–75. An editorial in the *New York Law Review* at the time pointed out that while judges are imperfect and lawyers are criticized for their self-interested promotion of litigation, arbitrators were struggling to provide a competent and fair alternative; and unlike judges who are bound by procedures and appeals, prejudicial arbitrators could issue orders against parties without recourse to counsel or appeal. "What Is the Matter with Arbitration?," *New York Law Review* 1 (September 1923), 355–63.

64. Orren, *Belated Feudalism*, 185.

65. Imre S. Szalai, "Modern Arbitration Values and the First World War," *American Journal of Legal History* 49 (October 2007), 355–91, 363–64, 376.

66. "Mediation, Conciliation, and Arbitration," House of Representatives, 62nd Congress, 2nd Session, Report No. 853, June 7, 1912.

67. George I. Lovell, *Legislative Deferrals: Statutory Ambiguity, Judicial Power, and American Democracy* (New York: Cambridge University Press, 2003), 81.

68. "Settlement of Business Disputes by Arbitration," *New York Herald*, July 30, 1881, 4; "Reform of the Judiciary," *Galveston Weekly News*, January 18, 1883, 5.

69. Jerold S. Auerbach, *Justice Without Law?* (New York: Oxford University Press, 1984), 33; Horwitz, *The Transformation of American Law*, 145.

70. See Christopher J. Cyphers, *The National Civic Federation and the Making of a New Liberalism, 1900–1915* (Westport, CT: Praeger, 2002).

71. Gompers is quoted in Christopher L. Tomlins, *The State and the Unions: Labor Relations, Law, and the Organized Labor Movement in America, 1880–1960* (Cambridge, MA: Harvard University Press, 1985), 73.

72. See Samuel Gompers, "The Limitations of Conciliation and Arbitration," *Annals of the American Academy of Political and Social Science* 20 (July 1902). See, too, Orren, *Belated Feudalism*, 186; Schreiber, "Majority Preference Provisions," 191.

73. See, for example, William F. Forbath, *Law and the Shaping of the American Labor Movement* (Cambridge, MA: Harvard University Press, 1989); Orren, *Belated Feudalism*; Tomlins, *The State and the Unions*.

74. "Address of Samuel Gompers," *Advocate of the Peace*, issue 59, April 1897, 88.

75. See Horwitz, *The Transformation of American Law*, 217. See, too, John Fabian Witt, *Patriots and Cosmopolitans: Hidden Histories of American Law* (Cambridge, MA: Harvard University Press, 2007), 221.

76. Stephen N. Subrin and Margaret Y. K. Woo, *Litigating in America: Civil Procedure in Context* (New York: Aspen, 2006), 217.

77. Horwitz, *Transformation of American Law*, 219.

78. F. R. Aumann, "The Lawyer and His Troubles," *The North American Review* (1833), 31.

79. See, for example, Charles L. Bernheimer, "The Advantages of Arbitration Procedure," *Annals of the American Academy of Political and Social Science* 124 (March 1926), 98–104.

80. Bernheimer, "Advantages of Arbitration," 98.

81. Ibid., 98–99.

82. House of Representatives, 68th Congress, 1st Session, Report No. 96, 1924.

83. Mr. Sterling, Committee on the Judiciary, "To Make Valid and Enforceable Certain Agreements for Arbitration," Senate, 68th Congress, 1st Session, Report No. 536, May 14, 1924. See Preston Douglas Wigner, "The United States Supreme Court's Expansive Approach to the Federal Arbitration Act; a Look at the Past, Present, and Future of Section 2," *University of Richmond Law Review* 29 (1995), 1499–554.

84. "Arbitration of Interstate Commercial Disputes," Joint Hearings before the Subcommittees of the Committees on the Judiciary, 68th Congress, 1st Session, January 9, 1924.

85. Ibid., at 15 and 13.

86. See Committee on Commerce, Trade, and Commercial Law, "The United States Arbitration Law and Its Application," *American Bar Association Journal* 11 (1925), 153; "Plan to Promote Industrial Peace Considered," *American Bar Association Journal* 14 (1928), 166.

87. "Arbitration of Interstate Commercial Disputes," at 15.

88. Ibid., 21–22. Quotation is from Evans Clark, "Business Arbitration Spreads Over World: New Law Gives It a Legal Standing in the United States," *New York Times*, April 12, 1925, 26. Clark writes that "to the uninitiated it might seem as if commercial arbitration were a concerted movement on the part of business men, tired of the law's delays, to take matters into their own hands and settle their disputes among themselves. Whatever it may be, commercial arbitration has the hearty support of leaders of the bench and bar" because it would free them from clogged dockets.

89. The new board was seen as essential due to the perceived failing of the prior Railroad Labor Board, which was rarely able to enforce the outcomes of its administrative hearings.

90. See "Arbitration Between Carriers and Employees, Boards of Adjustment," Hearings before the Subcommittee of the Committee on Interstate Commerce, Senate, 68th Congress, 1st Session, March 18, 28, 29, April 4, 7, 1924.

91. Evans Clark, "Industry Is Setting Up Its Own Government: American Capital and Labor Find a New Way to Avoid Disaster," *New York Times*, March 21, 1926, 25.

92. Ibid., 117.

93. Charles O. Gregory and Richard M. Orlikoff, "The Enforcement of Labor Arbitration Agreements," *University of Chicago Law Review* 17 (1950), 233–69.

94. 363 U.S. 564 (1962).

95. 363 U.S. 574 (1962).

96. 363 U.S. 593 (1962).

97. *Enterprise Wheel & Car Corp.*, at 597.

98. Ibid., at 599.

99. Report of the Special Committee on Administrative Law, *Annual Report of the ABA* 63 (1938), 331 and 339. See also Horwitz, *Transformation of American Law*, 219–22.

100. See, for example, Alan Brinkley, "The New Deal and the Idea of the State," in Steve Fraser and Gary Gerstle, eds., *The Rise and Fall of the New Deal Order, 1930–1980* (1989), 85–121; Horwitz, *Transformation of American Law*, 230–33; Theodore J. Lowi, *The End of Liberalism: Ideology, Policy, and the Crisis of Public Authority* (New York: W. W. Norton, 1967).

101. Horwitz, *Transformation of American Law*, 240–41.

102. See, for example, William B. Gould, "Labor Arbitration of Grievances Involving Racial Discrimination," *University of Pennsylvania Law Review* 118 (1969), 40–68.

103. See, for example, *Alexander v. Gardner-Denver* 415 U.S. 36 (1974).

104. See, for example, Michael J. Klarman, *From Jim Crow to Civil Rights* (Cambridge, MA: Harvard University Press, 2004); Paul Frymer, *Black and Blue: African Americans, the Labor Movement, and the Decline of the Democratic Party* (Princeton, NJ: Princeton University Press, 2008); Risa L. Goluboff, *The Lost Promise of Civil Rights* (Cambridge: Harvard University Press, 2010); Risa L. Goluboff, "We Live in a Free House Such as It Is: Class and the Creation of Modern Civil Rights," *Pennsylvania Law Review* 151 (2003), 1977–2018; Kenneth W. Mack, "Rethinking Civil Rights Lawyering and Politics in the Era Before Brown," *Yale Law Journal* 115 (2005), 256–354.

105. See, for example, Richard L. Abel, *The Politics of Informal Justice* (New York: Academic Press, 1982); Christine B. Harrington and Sally Engle Merry, "Ideological Production: The Making of Community Mediation," *Law and Society Review* 22 (1988), 709–36; Sally Engle Merry, "Disputing Without Culture: Review Essay of Dispute Resolution," *Harvard Law Review* 100 (1987), 2057; Laura Nader, "Disputing Without the Force of Law," *Yale Law Journal* 88 (1979), 998.

106. See Owen Fiss, "Against Settlement," *Yale Law Journal* 93 (1984), 1089.

107. Sean Farhang, *The Litigation State: Public Regulation and Private Lawsuits in the United States* (Princeton, NJ: Princeton University Press, 2010); Frymer, *Black and Blue*, chapter 4; R. Shep Melnick, *Between the Lines: Interpreting Welfare Rights* (Washington, DC: Brookings Institution, 1994).

108. Indeed, it is the emphasis on mediation in the Civil Rights Act that has led many public law scholars to conclude (not incorrectly) that the EEOC had strikingly weak enforcement powers that subsequently necessitated private litigation to carry out its mandate. See, for example, Farhang, *The Litigation State*; Frymer, *Black and Blue*; Nicholas Pedriana and Robin Stryker, "The Strength of a Weak Agency: Title VII of the 1964 Civil Rights Act and the Expansion of State Capacity, 1965–1971," *American Journal of Sociology* 110 (2004), 709–60; John D. Skrentny, *The Minority Rights Revolution* (Cambridge, MA: Belknap Press, 2002).

109. See Jerome T. Barrett with Joseph P. Barrett, *A History of Alternative Dispute Resolution: The Story of a Political, Cultural, and Social Movement* (San Francisco: John Wiley & Sons, 2004), 159.

110. Lawrence M. Friedman, "Legal Rules and the Process of Social Change," *Stanford Law Review* 17 (April 1967), 798–840; see the quotes on 801 and 803.

111. See, for example, *Mediating Social Conflict* (New York: Ford Foundation, 1978); Lon Fuller, "Mediation: Its Forms and Functions," *Southern California Law Review* 44 (1971), 305; James Willard Hurst, "The Functions of Courts in the United States, 1950–1980," *Law and Society Review* 15, (1980/1981), 401; Herbert M. Kritzer, "Studying Disputes: Learning from the CLRP Experience," *Law and Society Review* 15 (1980/1981), 503.

112. Tomiko Brown-Nagin, "'Broad Ownership' of the Public Schools: An Analysis of the 'T-Formation' Process Model for Achieving Educational Adequacy and

Its Implications for Contemporary School Reform Efforts," *Journal of Law and Education* 27 (1998), 343, 374. She adds, "Alternative processes create channels through which communities, together with lawyers, may use techniques of pressure and negotiation to gain the attention of those in power, and ultimately, to generate change in the inequitable social and political relations reflected in the racially stratified system of public education."

113. Alan W. Houseman, "Legal Services and Equal Justice for the Poor: Some Thoughts on Our Future," *NLADA Briefcase* 35 (1978).

114. Abel, *The Politics of Informal Justice*; Carrie Menkel-Meadow, "Toward Another View of Legal Negotiation: The Structure of Problem Solving," *UCLA Law Review* 31 (1984), 754; Martha Minow, *Making All the Difference: Inclusion, Exclusion, and American Law* (Ithaca, NY: Cornell University Press, 1990); Judith Resnik, "Many Doors? Closing Doors? Alternative Dispute Resolution and Adjudication," *Ohio State Journal on Dispute Resolution* 10 (1995), 211–66.

115. See Linda R. Singer, *Settling Disputes: Conflict Resolution in Business, Families, and the Legal System*, 2nd ed. (Boulder, CO: Westview Press, 1994); and H. Baer, "History, Process, and a Role for Judges in Mediating Their Own Cases," *New York University Annual Survey of American Law* (2002), 131–151.

116. See "The Pound Conference: Perspectives on Justice in the Future," in A. Levin and R. Wheeler, eds., *Proceedings of the National Conference on the Causes of Popular Dissatisfaction with the Administration of Justice* (New York: West, 1979), 65.

117. Thomas F. Sheehan, "The Medical Malpractice Crisis in Insurance: How It Happened and Some Proposed Solutions," *The Forum* 11 (Section of Insurance, Negligence and Compensation Law, American Bar Association, 1975), 80–128; Tom Goldstein, "A Dramatic Rise in Lawsuits and Costs Concerns Bar," *New York Times*, May 18, 1977, 1.

118. *Congressional Record*—Senate (April 7, 1975), 9103; *Congressional Record*—Senate (January 29, 1975), 1716–17.

119. Ibid., 1717.

120. Ibid., 1035–1041.

121. Statement of the Association of Trial Lawyers of America before the Subcommittee on Health of the Senate Committee on Labor and Public Welfare on S. 188, S. 215, S. 482, S. 1211, Federal Medical Malpractice Insurance Act, 1975, April 9, 1975, 303.

122. "Causes of Popular Dissatisfaction with the Administration of Justice," Subcommittee on Constitutional Rights of the Committee on the Judiciary, Senate, 94th Congress, 2nd Session, May 19, 1976.

123. "State of the Judiciary and Access to Justice Act," Subcommittee on Courts, Civil Liberties, and the Administration of Justice, House of Representatives, 95th Congress, 1st Session, June 20, 1977.

124. This was in reference to the Supreme Court's decision in *Warth v. Seldin*, 422 US 490 (1975).

125. Kastenmeier, "State of the Judiciary and Access to Justice Act," 6.

126. Ibid., 12.

127. Ibid., 47.

128. Ibid., 251.

129. "Dispute Resolution Act," Hearings before the Subcommittee on Courts, Civil Liberties, and the Administration of Justice, Committee on the Judiciary, House of Representatives, 95th Congress, 2nd Session, July 27 and August 2, 1978. See, too, "Consumer Controversies Resolution Act."

130. Senator Dennis Webster DeConcini, "Court-Annexed Arbitration Act of 1978," Committee on the Judiciary, Senate, Report No. 95-1103, August 10, 1978.

131. "Access to Justice," Hearings on the Judiciary Committee, Senate, 96th Congress, 1st Session, February 13 and 27, 1979, 1.

132. Ibid., 38.

133. Ibid., 48–49.

134. Ibid., 48–52.

135. Ibid., 9. Tate also pointed to a range of examples from the United States to England to Sweden involving small criminal and civil matters, "from a barking dog to an overhanging tree," that were best handled by small "public complaint boards." See 10–11.

136. Barrett and Barrett, *A History of Alternative Dispute Resolution*, 214.

137. Three prominent journals include the *Journal of Dispute Resolution* at Missouri/ Columbia, *Ohio State Journal of Dispute Resolution*, and the *Negotiation Journal* at Harvard.

138. Regarding the use of ADR in federal district courts, see Elizabeth Plapinger and Donna Steinstra, *ADR and Settlement in the Federal District Courts: A Sourcebook for Judges and Lawyers* (1996), http://www.fjc.gov/public/pdf.nsf/lookup/adrsr-cbk.pdf/$File/adrsrcbk.pdf.

139. See, for example, "FOIA: Alternate Dispute Resolution Proposals," Subcommittee on Government Information, Justice, and Agriculture of the Committee on Government, December 1, 1987 (the ACLU was skeptical of ADR despite its recognition that litigation was inefficient and costly, because it feared the executive branch might resist requests against its own officials, whereas the courts offer an independent and equal branch of government that could stay independent from executive affairs). See also "Mediation and Older Americans: Consider the Possibilities," Committee on the Judiciary, House of Representatives, June 23, 1988; "Fair Housing Amendments Act of 1987," Subcommittee on Civil and Constitutional Rights, Committee on the Judiciary, House of Representatives, April 22, 1987. (The NAACP stated [233], "The NAACP has grave concerns about arbitration." It tries to split the difference, and doesn't deal with situations where "rights were denied.")

140. "The Problem of Civil Case Backlogs in the Federal Judicial System in District and Appellate Courts," Hearings before the Subcommittee on Courts of the Committee on the Judiciary, 98th Congress, 1st and 2nd Sessions, November 8, 1983, and February 1, 1984.

141. Senator Mitch McConnell, "Litigation Abuse Reform Act of 1986," Hearings before the Committee on the Senate Judiciary, February 21, 1986, 1.

142. See "Alternative Dispute Resolution," Hearing before the Subcommittee on Courts and Administrative Practice of the Committee on the Judiciary, Senate, 100th Congress, 2nd Session, S. 2274, May 25, 1988; "Alternative Dispute Resolution Use by Federal Agencies," Hearing before the Subcommittee on Administrative Law and Governmental Relations of the Committee on the Judiciary, House of Representatives, 100th Congress, 2nd Session, June 16, 1988; "Alternative Dispute Resolution Act of 1989," Hearing before the Subcommittee on Oversight of Government Management of the Committee on Governmental Affairs, Senate, 101st Congress, September 19, 1989; "Administrative Dispute Resolution Act," Subcommittee on Administrative Law and Governmental Relations, Judiciary Committee, House of Representatives, 101st Congress, 2nd Session, January 31, 1990.

143. Statement of Marshall Breger, Hearings on the Administrative Dispute Resolution Act, House Judiciary Committee Subcommittee on Administrative Law and Governmental Relations, January 31, 1990.

144. William Funk, "RIP ACUS," *Administrative & Regulatory Law News*, American Bar Association, Winter 1996.

145. I discuss these developments at length in Chapter Four.

146. Testimony of William P. Barr, Hearings on the Administrative Dispute Resolution Act of 1989, Subcommittee on Oversight of Government Management of the Committee on Governmal Affairs, United States Senate, 101st Congress, 1st Session (September 19, 1989), 10.

147. Statement of the Hon. Don J. Pease, "The Negotiated Rulemaking Act," House Judiciary Subcommittee on Administrative Law, May 3, 1989.

148. Executive Order No. 12,988,61 *Federal Register* 4,729 (1996). President Bush issued a similar order in 1991; see Executive Order No. 12,278,56 *Federal Register* 55,195 (1991).

149. "Alternative Dispute Resolution: Employer's Experiences with ADR in the Workplace," U.S. General Accounting Office, Report to the Chairman, Subcommittee on Civil Service, Committee on Government Reform and Oversight, House of Representatives, 1997, 2.

150. Statement of Mitchell F. Dolin, American Bar Association, "Alternative Dispute Resolution and Settlement Encouragement Act; Federal Courts Improvement Act, and Need for Additional Federal District Court Judges," Hearing before the Subcommittee on Courts and Intellectual Property of the Committee on the Judiciary, House of Representatives, October 9, 1997, 59.

151. Statement of Hon. D. Brock Hornby, Chief Judge, U.S. District Court for the District of Maine, on behalf of the Judicial Conference, Hearings before the Subcommittee on Courts and Intellectual Property of the Committee on the Judiciary, House of Representatives, 105th Congress, 1st Session, on H.R. 2603

(Alternative Dispute Resolution and Settlement Encouragement Act) and H.R. 2294 (Federal Courts Improvement Act, and Need for Additional Federal District Court Judges), October 9, 1997, 14.

152. "The Future Direction of the EEOC," Hearing before the Subcommittee on Employer-Employee Relations of the Committee on Education and the Workforce, House of Representatives, 105th Congress, 2nd Session, March 3, 1998, 6.

153. "Examining the Use of Alternative Dispute Resolution for Medical Malpractice Claims," Hearing before the Subcommittee on Administrative Law and Governmental Relations, Committee on the Judiciary, House of Representatives, 102nd Congress, 2nd Session, June 24, 1992, 4.

154. Ibid., 16.

155. Ibid., 17.

156. Ibid., 20.

157. Ibid., 30.

158. Ibid., 137–8.

159. "Federal Employee Fairness Act," 103rd Congress, 2nd Session, House of Representatives, Report No. 103–599, Part 2, August 19, 1994.

160. See, for example, "Mandatory Arbitration Agreements in Employment Contracts in the Securities Industry," Hearings before the Committee on Banking, Housing, and Urban Affairs, Senate, 105th Congress, 2nd Session, July 31, 1998. Senators Grassley and Feingold promoted voluntary arbitration in the Motor Vehicle Franchise Contract Arbitration Fairness Act, *Congressional Record* (September 2, 1998), 19,461–19,462; Patricia Schroeder, "Mandatory Arbitration Violates Civil Rights," *Congressional Record* (August 2, 1996), 1486.

161. "Joint Oversight Hearing on Equal Employment Opportunity Commission's Proposed Reform of Federal Regulations," Subcommittee on Employment Opportunities of the Committee on Education and Labor and the Subcommittee on Civil Service of the Committee on Post Office and Civil Service, 101st Congress, 2nd Session, March 1, 1990.

162. "Federal Employee Fairness Act," 43.

163. Ibid., 20.

164. Ibid., 46–51.

165. Ibid.

166. Prepared statement of Mitchell F. Dolin, Attorney, American Bar Association, Hearings before the Subcommittee on Courts and Intellectual Property of the Committee on the Judiciary, House of Representatives, 105th Congress, 1st Session, on H.R. 2603 (Alternative Dispute Resolution and Settlement Encouragement Act) and H.R. 2294 (Federal Courts Improvement Act, and Need for Additional Federal District Court Judges), October 9, 1997, 54.

167. American Bar Association Greenbook, chapter 13, "Policy on Legislative and National Issues," 205.

168. 500 U.S. 20 (1991).

169. 513 U.S. 265 (1995).

170. 517 U.S. 681 (1996).

171. 531 U.S. 79 (2000).

172. 532 U.S. 105 (2001).

173. 552 U.S. 346 (2008).

174. 552 U.S. 576 (2008).

175. S. 2662, 111th Congress, introduced November 2, 2009.

176. The bill also directs the attorney general to: (1) certify state ADR systems that meet the requirements of this act; and (2) establish an alternative federal ADR system for any state that does not establish its own system. In addition, it directs the comptroller general to study the effectiveness of private litigation insurance markets in providing affordable access to courts, evaluating the merit of prospective claims, and ensuring that prevailing parties in "loser pays" systems are reimbursed for attorney's fees.

177. 111th Congress, 1st Session, 155 *Congressional Record*–Senate 11050 (November 3, 2009), 12,106.

178. H.R. 1283, 106th Congress, introduced July 24, 2000.

179. H.R. 2496, 106th Congress, introduced September 24, 2000.

180. See the Pregnancy and Trauma Care Access Act of 2005 (S. 367), introduced by Senator Judd Gregg on February 10, 2005.

181. See, for example, "Arbitration Fairness Act of 2007," Hearing before the Subcommittee on Commercial and Administrative Law of the Committee on the Judiciary, House of Representatives, October 25, 2007; "Automobile Arbitration Fairness Act of 2008," Hearing before the Subcommittee on Commercial and Administrative Law, Committee of the Judiciary, House of Representatives, March 6, 2008; "Arbitration: Is it Fair When Forced?," Hearing before the Committee on the Judiciary, Senate, 112th Congress, 1st Session, October 13, 2011.

182. 561 U.S. 63 (2010).

183. 563 U.S. 321 (2011).

184. P.L. 90–321, 82 Stat. 164.

185. *Compucredit Corp. v. Greenwood*, 615 F. 3d 1204, reversed and remanded.

186. 133 S. Ct. 2304 (2013).

187. Binyamin Applebaum, "Justices Support Corporate Arbitration," *New York Times*, June 21, 2013, B3.

188. *American Express Co. v. Italian Colors Restaurant*, at 2313 and 2315, respectively.

189. "Class Actions—Class Arbitration Waivers—*American Express Co. v. Italian Colors Restaurant*," *Harvard Law Review* 127, issue 1 (November 2013), 278. See also Myriam Giles and Gary Friedman, "After Class: Aggregate Litigation in the Wake of *AT&T Mobility v. Concepcion*," *University of Chicago Law Review* 79 (2012), 645–46.

190. "In Resolving Disputes, Mediation Most Favored ADR Option in District Courts," United States Courts, July 2006, http://www.uscourts.gov/news/

TheThirdBranch/06-07-01/In_Resolving_Disputes_Mediation_Most_
Favored_ADR_Option_in_District_Courts.aspx.

191. There was a moment of indecision from the Court in 2003 when it heard *Green
Tree Financial Corporation v. Bazzle* (539 U.S. 444), facing the question of
whether or not the FAA permits classwide arbitration hearings. The plurality
opinion managed to avoid speaking to the broader issue, focusing instead on a
procedural question in concluding that an arbitrator must decide whether a specific contract forbids class arbitration, not the courts. The opinion came from an
unlikely plurality, which included not only Breyer, Souter, and Ginsburg, but also
Scalia. Further, Stevens concurred only in the judgment so that they were able to
issue a controlling opinion.

CHAPTER 4

1. Adam Liptak, "Justices Void Ex-Detainee's Suit Against 2 Officials," *The New York
Times*, May 19, 2009.
2. *Ashcroft v. Iqbal*, 556 U.S. 662 (2009).
3. Adam Liptak, "9/11 Case Could Bring Broad Shift on Civil Suits," *The New York
Times*, July 21, 2009.
4. *Conley v. Gibson*, 355 U.S. 41 (1957).
5. *Ashcroft v. Iqbal*, at 681.
6. "Has the Supreme Court Limited Americans' Access to Courts?," Hearing before
the Committee on the Judiciary United States Senate, 111th Congress, 1st Session,
December 2, 2009, 14.
7. Robert G. Bone, "The Process of Making Process: Court Rulemaking, Democratic
Legitimacy, and Procedural Efficacy," *Georgetown Law Review* 87 (1999), 887;
Stephen B. Burbank, "The Rules Enabling Act of 1934," *University of Pennsylvania
Law Review* 130 (1982), 1015; Judith Resnik, "Changing Practices, Changing
Rules: Judicial and Congressional Rulemaking on Civil Juries, Civil Justice, and
Civil Judging," *Alabama Law Review* 49 (1997), 133; Stephen N. Subrin, "How
Equity Conquered Common Law: The Federal Rules of Civil Procedure in
Historical Perspective," *University of Pennsylvania Law Review* 135 (1987), 909.
8. Marc Galanter, "Why the 'Haves' Come out Ahead: Speculations on the
Outcomes of Legal Change," *Law and Society Review* 9 (1974), 95–160.
9. See Stephen B. Burbank and Sean Farhang, "Litigation Reform: An Institutional
Approach," *University of Pennsylvania Law Review* 162 (2014), 1543–1617.
10. The preexisting rules informing adjudication were known as the Field Code of
Civil Procedure, which was part of the Laws of the State of New York, Section 258
(1848).
11. Judith Resnik, "Failing Faith: Adjudicatory Procedure in Decline," *University
of Chicago Law Review* 53 (1986), 494; Subrin, "How Equity Conquered
Common Law."

12. Burbank, "The Rules Enabling Act of 1934," 1035.

13. Quoted in *Wayman v. Southard*, 23 U.S. 1 (1825), at 262.

14. Quoted in William D. Mitchell, Edgar B. Tolman, and Charles E. Clark, "'Open Forum' Discussion of Proposed Rules of Civil Procedure," *American Bar Association Journal* 23 (1937), 972.

15. The act did not speak to the issue of what law to apply to states that joined the nation after the original thirteen colonies; in 1828, however, Congress passed a law stipulating that federal courts in new states would follow the civil procedure in effect at the time the original thirteen states joined the union.

16. Quoted in Mitchell et al., "Open Forum," 972.

17. *Wayman v. Southard*, at 263.

18. Burbank, "Rules Enabling Act," 1038.

19. See "Ineffectiveness of the Conformity Act," *Yale Law Journal* 36 (1927), 853; Mitchell et al., "Open Forum," 972.

20. See, for example, *Report of the Committee on Uniformity of Procedure and Comparative Law*, ABA Report No. 19 (1896), 411, 419.

21. Thomas W. Shelton, "Will the Senate Allow the Courts to Be Saved?" *The Central Law Journal* 98 (1925), 1.

22. Thomas W. Shelton, *The Spirit of the Courts* (Baltimore, MD: John Murphy Company Publishers, 1918).

23. Quoted in "Judicial Procedure," Hearings before a Subcommittee of the Committee on the Judiciary, *Congressional Record*—Senate (January 12, 1910), 17, 26.

24. Wilson (speaking in 1915) is quoted in "Procedure in the Federal Courts," Hearing before the Committee on the Judiciary, House of Representatives, 67th Congress, 2nd Session, February 14 and March 7, 1922, 2.

25. "Judicial Procedure," 20.

26. "Procedure in the Federal Courts."

27. See Taft, (Three Needed Steps of Progress), *American Bar Association Journal* 8 (1922), 34.

28. Shelton also emphasized that courts were simply handling administrative matters, but that if any dissent occurred, Congress was entirely in control of the rules and could repeal anything it didn't like. See "Procedure in the Federal Courts," 8.

29. Thomas W. Shelton, "Will the Senate Allow the Courts to Be Saved?," 1.

30. See, for example, "Simplified Procedure," *New York Times*, August 1, 1938. Of the few examples of national newspaper attention were letters to the editor written by Shelton replying to Senator Walsh, and another letter to the editor written at the behest of Thomas Shelton. See Thomas W. Shelton, "Delayed Justice: A Reply to Senator Walsh on the Question of Judicial Procedure," *New York Times*, January 21, 1925; Charles A. Boston, "Federal Court Uniformity," *New York Herald Tribune*, October 31, 1926.

31. Shelton, *The Spirit of the Courts*; Subrin, "How Equity Conquered Common Law."

32. "Simplification of Judicial Procedure," Hearings before the Committee on the Judiciary, Senate, 64th Congress, 1st Session, November 10 and 22, 1915, 8–10, 26.

33. "Procedure in the Federal Courts," 7.

34. The Senate Judiciary Committee issued negative reports in 1916, 1924, and 1928, and issued a positive report in 1926.

35. This wariness was largely unsurprising, given that in the Lochner era, Democrats regularly found their legislative efforts thwarted by an antiregulatory Supreme Court. See Howard Gillman, *The Constitution Besieged: The Rise and Demise of Lochner Era Police Powers Jurisprudence* (Durham, NC: Duke University Press, 1992) and Karen Orren, *Belated Feudalism: Labor, the Law, and Liberal Development in the United States* (New York: Cambridge University Press, 1992).

36. Walsh never took on the job, as he died suddenly just days before the presidential inauguration in 1933.

37. "Simplification of Judicial Procedure," 27–28; T. J. Walsh, "The Law's Delays and the Remedy," *New York Times*, January 12, 1925, 14; Mr. Walsh of Montana, from the Committee on the Judiciary, "Adverse Report: Authority for Publication of Rules in Common-Law Actions," Senate, 70th Congress, 1st Session, Report No. 440, February 28, 1928. See, too, Burbank, "Rules Enabling Act," 1085–89.

38. Burbank, "Rules Enabling Act," 1095–96.

39. Charles E. Clark, "Practice and Procedure," *Annals of the American Academy of Political and Social Science* 328 (1960), 62.

40. Lori A. Johnson, "Creating Rules of Procedure for Federal Courts: Administrative Prerogative or Legislative Policymaking?" *The Justice System Journal*, 24 (2003), 23–42. See, too, Mitchell et al., "Open Forum."

41. Mitchell et al., "Open Forum," 971.

42. The rulemaking process itself was also affected by amendments to the Rules Enabling Act in 1988. However, the amendments largely codified procedures that the rules committees, for a variety of reasons (discussed below), already followed at the time, such as requiring that all committees "consist of members of the bench and professional bar, and trial and appellate judges," requiring the appointment of a standing committee, authorizing the Judicial Conference to appoint other committees to assist it, and requiring that committee meetings be open, minutes be recorded and made available to the public, and interested parties sufficiently notified of their proceedings ahead of time (28 U.S.C. Section 2073).

43. Section 2074 of the Rules Enabling Act was amended in 1988 to require that proposals be transmitted to Congress "not later than May 1 of the year in which [it] is to become effective," and that changes go into effect "no earlier than December 1." The previous extension, enacted in 1950, had extended the time frame from the Rules Enabling Act's initial sixty days to ninety days. See the act of May 10, 1950.

44. Resnik, "Changing Practices, Changing Rules," 201.

45. *Sibbach v. Wilson*, 312 U.S. 1 (1941), at 18.

46. Burbank, "The Rules Enabling Act of 1934," 1027.

47. Bone, "The Process of Making Process," 3–4.

48. Elisabeth S. Clemens and James M. Cook, "Politics and Institutionalism: Explaining Durability and Change," *Annual Review of Sociology* 25 (1999), 441–66.

49. Stephen N. Subrin and Margaret Y. K. Woo, *Litigating in America: Civil Procedure in Context* (New York: Aspen, 2006).

50. See, for example, Jack B. Weinstein, "After Fifty Years of the Federal Rules of Civil Procedure: Are the Barriers to Justice Being Raised?," *University of Pennsylvania Law Review* 137 (1989), 1901–23.

51. Rule 23(a) as amended in 1966 lists four prerequisites for all class actions, whether plaintiff or defendant (in practice, there are almost no defendant class actions): numerosity, commonality, typicality, and representativeness. These require that the class be so large that joinder of all members would be impracticable, questions of law or fact be held in common, that the claims and defenses of the representative parties are typical of all of those in the class, and that the named representatives can fairly represent the whole class (respectively). Historically speaking, class actions proliferated in the decade following the 1966 amendments, proving to be a highly effectual tool for incentivizing lawyers to represent economically disadvantaged groups in court.

52. Joinder of claims in civil law, which is governed by Rule 18(a), allows claimants to consolidate all claims that they have against an individual who is already party to a case. Joinder of parties, governed by Rule 20, allows multiple plaintiffs to join in an action if each of their claims arises from the same transaction or occurrence, and if there is a common question of law or fact relating to all plaintiffs' claims.

53. Discovery refers to the right of civil litigants to acquire, under the auspices of the judicial system, information bearing on disputes to which they are a party. Discovery rules had been severely limited prior to 1938, and the creation of Rule 26 sought to balance various factors, such as eliminating surprises at trial. Formal discovery devices include (1) interrogatories (written questions requiring answers under oath), (2) oral depositions (questioned under oath, recorded), (3) written depositions (similar), (4) requests for documents, (5) examinations of property, etc., where applicable, and (6) mental and physical examinations of opposing parties. Discovery also permits each side to demand that the other admit or deny facts and allows for mandatory disclosure, whereby some information must be disclosed to the opposing side without request. In 1993 the rules were amended to distinguish discovery from the antecedent processes of disclosure, wherein parties have a duty to disclose, without awaiting formal discovery requests, certain basic information that is needed in most cases to prepare for trial or to make an informed decision about settlement. Disclosure requirements are located in Rule 20(a).

54. See Feeley and Rubin, *Judicial Policymaking in the Modern State*. Despite their prominent role, the activities of special masters were somewhat limited by their treatment in the original 1938 rules. Drawn from equity, they seemed only to govern the use of special masters in trial functions, whereas much of the perceived need for them arises in the pretrial and posttrial phases of litigation.

55. Abram Chayes, "The Role of the Judge in Public Law Litigation," *Harvard Law Review* 89 (1976), 1281–316; Charles R. Epp, *The Rights Revolution: Lawyers, Activists, and Supreme Courts in Comparative Perspective* (Chicago: University of Chicago Press, 1998); R. Shep Melnick, *Between the Lines: Interpreting Welfare Rights* (Washington, DC: Brookings Institution Press, 1994).

56. Thomas F. Burke, *Lawyers, Lawsuits, and Legal Rights: The Struggle Over Litigation in American Society* (Berkeley: University of California Press, 2002); Howard Gillman, "Party Politics and Constitutional Change: The Political Origins of Liberal Judicial Activism," in Ronald Kahn and Ken I. Kersch, eds., *The Supreme Court and American Political Development* (Lawrence: University of Kansas Press, 2006); Melnick, *Between the Lines.*

57. Stephen B. Burbank, "Procedure and Power," *Journal of Legal Education* 46 (1996), 513.

58. 347 U.S. 483 (1954).

59. "The Class Action Fairness Act of 1999," Hearing before the Senate Subcommittee on Administrative Oversight and the Courts of the Committee on the Judiciary, Senate Hearing 106-465, 106th Congress, 1st Session (May 4, 1999), 60.

60. *Congressional Record* (January 29, 1973), 2395–96.

61. "Rules of Evidence," Hearings before the Special Subcommittee on Reform of Federal Criminal Laws of the Committee on the Judiciary, House of Representatives, 93rd Congress, 1st Session, February 7, 8, 22, 28–March 9, 15, 1973.

62. "Rules of Evidence," 142–46.

63. Ibid., 200.

64. Warren Weaver, "Whose Rules of Evidence? Courts vs. Congress," *New York Times*, February 4, 1973, 220.

65. These rulemakers, however, do not consider themselves as political. Throughout the years of House and Senate hearings, members of the Judicial Conference would continually state that their activities were purely procedural and should not be interfered with by the political branches. See, for example, Judge Keeton, Chairman of the Rules of Practice and Procedure, Judicial Conference of the United States, Hearing before the Subcommittee on Intellectual Property and Judicial Administration, House of Representatives, June 16, 1993, 6.

66. "Rules of Evidence," 189.

67. *Congressional Record* (March 19, 1973), 8345.

68. Warren Weaver, Jr., "Congress Moves to Curb Justices," *New York Times*, February 1, 1973, 9; Weaver, "Whose Rules of Evidence?," 220.

69. "Rules of Evidence," 5.

70. Ibid., 8.

71. *Congressional Record* (1973), 3739–40.

72. "Rules of Evidence," 150.

73. See, for example, Warren Weaver, Jr., "Senate Puts Off Evidence Rules," *New York Times*, February 7, 1973.

74. For a systematic account of legislation promoting private enforcement, see Sean Farhang, *The Litigation State: Public Regulation and Private Lawsuits in the United States* (Princeton, NJ: Princeton University Press, 2010).

75. Warren Weaver, Jr., "House Unit Drops Limit on Courts for Secret Data," *New York Times*, July 2, 1973, 43; Warren Weaver, Jr., "Code on Evidence Passed by House: Changes for Federal Courts to Be Submitted to Senate," *New York Times*, February 6, 1974, 40; Warren Weaver, Jr., "Federal Courts to Initiate Code for Rules of Evidence on July 1," *New York Times*, January 26, 1974, 52.

76. "Conference Report: Federal Rules of Evidence," House of Representatives, 93rd Congress, 2nd Session, Report No. 93-1597, December 14, 1974.

77. For a list of congressional actions prior to 1985, see "Rules Enabling Act of 1985," 99th Congress, 1st Session, Report No. 99-422, December 6, 1985, footnote 20.

78. See Judith Resnik, "Managerial Judges," *Harvard Law Review* 96 (1982), 380.

79. Burbank, "Procedure and Power," 515. See also Bryant Garth, "From Civil Litigation to Private Justice: Legal Practice at War with the Profession and Its Values," *Brooklyn Law Review* 59 (1993), 931.

80. To the degree that Republicans and the Reagan administration were involved, it was less from its (largely failed) efforts to defund government lawyers and prevent the Legal Services Corporation from litigating than from making critical appointments to the Supreme Court. The Court (while keeping its distance, as usual, from official rulemaking procedures), in turn began to exploit its opportunities to chip away at the vast judicial system.

81. Stephen B. Burbank, "Implementing Procedural Change: Who, How, Why, and When?," *Alabama Law Review* 49 (1997), 224.

82. Stephen N. Subrin and Thomas O. Main, "The Fourth Era of American Civil Procedure," *University of Pennsylvania Law Review* 162 (2014), 1856.

83. Roy D. Simon, Jr., "The Riddle of Rule 68," *George Washington Law Review* 1, 54 (1985), 1–89.

84. The rules enabling acts have a supersession clause that provides that "all laws in conflict with any such rules [those promulgated under the enabling acts] shall be of no further force or effect after such rules have taken effect."

85. "Rules Enabling Act of 1985," 99th Congress, 1st Session, Report No. 99-422, December 6, 1985, 13. The report referenced in particular a Supreme Court ruling that same year, *Marek v. Chesny* (473 U.S. 1), which held that Rule 68 denied a judge the discretion to award statutorily provided attorney's fees that are in conflict with the rule's stated purpose of motivating and enabling settlement between the parties.

86. Georgene Vairo, "Rule 11: A Critical Analysis," 118 *F.R.D.* 189 (1988), 191–94.

87. "Amendments to the Federal Rules of Civil Procedure," Hearings before the House Subcommittee on Intellectual Property and Judicial Administration of the Committee of the Judiciary, House of Representatives, 103rd Congress, First Session (June 16, 1993), 6.

88. Rule 11 Judge Survey and Field Study, Federal Judicial Center (1991), 6.

89. Amendments to the Federal Rules of Civil Procedure, 6 and 8.
90. Ibid., p. 27.
91. Richard L. Marcus, "Modes of Procedural Reform," *Hastings International and Comparative Law Review* 31 (2008), 157.
92. In 1979 Representative Elizabeth Holtzman proposed large-scale changes to the Federal Rules, with the goal of changing the burden from Congress needing to stop bad rules to the rulemakers needing to articulate and better explain why their proposed rules are good. *Congressional Record* (January 15, 1969), 64.
93. *Congressional Record* (December 15, 1982), 30, 929–38.
94. "Rules Enabling Act," Hearing before the House Subcommittee on Courts, Civil Liberties, and the Administration of Justice, Committee on the Judiciary, House of Representatives, 98th Congress, 1st and 2nd Sessions, April 21, 1983, and March 1, 1984, 1.
95. As Alan Morrison of the ABA stated in hearings, he was not necessarily in favor of more congressional activism: "If the process at the rules committee levels were improved, made more open, made more responsive, and the members were more balanced in their viewpoints, there would be far less of a need for Congress to be involved at all." "Rules Enabling Act," 33. In an advisory report issued by the ABA, the Criminal Justice Section of the ABA argued that the "policy did not specifically endorse Congressional action as the preferred way of bringing about all the changes necessary to implement the policy." It preferred transferring rule-making power to the Judicial Conference. "Practical Considerations in Enacting Legislation to Implement the ABA Policy on the Rules Enabling Act," Criminal Justice Section Advisory Opinion, in "Rules Enabling Act," 48–63.
96. "Rules Enabling Act," 20–21. In July 1983 the Judicial Conference headed by Gignoux wrote Kastenmeier opposing the proposal to strip the Supreme Court of its rulemaking functions, but stating that "if the Supreme Court is to be taken out of rulemaking, the Judicial Conference is the appropriate body to continue to perform this function." "Rules Enabling Act," 104.
97. "Rules Enabling Act," 19.
98. "Rules Enabling Act," 23 (noting concern from Professor Judith Resnik of USC Law School).
99. "Rules Enabling Act of 1985," 99th Congress, 1st Session, Report No. 99-422, December 6, 1985, 5.
100. Bone, "The Process of Making Process," 4; see also Burbank, "Procedure and Power," 515–16.
101. See, for example, "Court Reform and Access to Justice Act," Hearings before the Subcommittee on Courts, Civil Liberties, and the Administration of Justice of the Committee on the Judiciary, House of Representatives, 100th Congress, 1st and 2nd Sessions, September 23 and October 14, 1987, and February 24, 1988; and "The Rules Enabling Act," Subcommittee on Courts and Administrative Practice, Committee on the Judiciary, Senate, May 25, 1988.

102. The act passed without the inclusion of a "supersession clause" that would have prevented the judiciary from amending the Rules Enabling Act so as to permit rules that supersede inconsistent procedural statutes enacted by Congress. Justice William Rehnquist, in a letter to House Judiciary Committee Chairman Peter Rodino, assured him that the Judicial Conference and its committees on rules "have always been keenly aware of the special responsibility they have in the rules process and the duty incumbent upon them not to overreach their charter. The advisory committees should undertake to be circumspect in superseding procedural statutes. At the very least, we will undertake to identify such situations when they arise so that the Congress will have every opportunity to examine these instances on the merits as part of your review." William H. Rehnquist to Peter W. Rodino, Jr., published in *Congressional Record*, 134 (October 19, 1988), 10,430. For more regarding supersession, see Paul D. Carrington, "'Substance' and 'Procedure' in the Rules Enabling Act," *Duke Law Journal* (1989), 281; Stephen B. Burbank, "Hold the Corks: A Comment on Paul Carrington's 'Substance' and 'Procedure' in the Rules Enabling Act," *Duke Law Journal* (1989), 1012.

103. Both comments and testimony were on a "by invitation only" basis prior to the passage of this law, and in practice those regularly contacted included only a handful of major legal organizations, such as the ABA.

104. Johnson, "Creating Rules of Procedure for Federal Courts."

105. "The Civil Justice Reform Act of 1990 and the Judicial Improvements Act of 1990," Hearings before the Committee on the Judiciary, United States Senate, 101st Congress, 2nd Session (March 6, 1990), 3.

106. Ibid., 56.

107. Ibid., 58.

108. Ibid., 208–09.

109. See Michael S. Greve, "Why Defunding the Left Failed," *National Affairs* 89 (1987), 91–106; Susan E. Lawrence, *The Poor in Court: The Legal Services Program and Supreme Court Decision Making* (Princeton, NJ: Princeton University Press, 1990).

110. Rehnquist, as mentioned earlier, joined congressional Democrats in supporting the Judicial Improvements and Access to Justice Act; in addition to the reforms to the Rules Enabling Act, the legislation was also designed to lighten federal court litigation dockets by removing many disputes to state courts, a move fought vehemently by the ABA and ATLA. Justice Rehnquist called the legislation "the most significant legislation affecting the Federal courts since the early part of the decade." "New Law Erects Barriers to the Federal Docket," *New York Times*, May 12, 1989, B11.

111. *Celotex Corp. v. Catrett*, 477 U.S. 317 (1986); *Anderson v. Liberty* Lobby, 477 U.S. 242 (1986); *Matsushita Elec. Indus. Co. v. Zenith Radio Corp.*, 475 U.S. 574 (1986).

112. See also Subrin and Woo, *Litigating in America*.

113. For a full discussion of the trajectory of summary judgment, see Stephen B. Burbank, "Vanishing Trials and Summary Judgment in Federal Civil Cases: Drifting Toward Bethlehem or Gomorrah?," *Journal of Empirical Legal Studies* 1 (2004), 591–626.

114. *Celotex Corp. v. Catrett*, at 323.

115. Subrin and Woo, *Litigating in America*, 171.

116. Joe Cecil and George Cort, "Estimates of Summary Judgment Activity in Fiscal Year 2006," Federal Judicial Center, Report to the Advisory Committee on Civil Rules, April 12, 2007. Some of the districts with high rates of motions granted also have ADR procedures that resolve many cases before a summary judgment motion is filed; see Table 4.

117. See Burke, *Lawyers, Lawsuits, and Legal Rights.*

118. William Haltom and Michael McCann, *Distorting the Law: Politics, Media, and the Litigation Crisis* (Chicago: University of Chicago Press, 2004), 3.

119. Vicki Kemper, "Lawyers on Trial," *Common Cause Magazine*, September 22, 1993.

120. *New York Times*, August 31, 1992, A1.

121. Dan Quayle, "Civil Justice Reform," *American University Law Review* 41 (1992), 563–64.

122. Jeffrey W. Stempel, "Politics and Sociology in Federal Civil Rulemaking: Errors of Scope," *Alabama Law Review* 52, (2001), 529–637.

123. Fifteen Democrats in the Senate and forty-three in the House voted for passage of the initial legislation; thirty-five Democrats in the House voted to override the President's veto.

124. Punitive damages vary from traditional damages in an important way; while damages are usually intended to compensate plaintiffs for their losses, punitive damages are awarded to successful plaintiffs (on top of regular damages) in order to punish defendants for egregious conduct and to defer defendants and others from future offenses. Due to their nature, they are not available to redress all legal wrongs and are never awarded automatically or as a matter of right.

125. "Private Litigation Under the Federal Securities Law," Hearings before the Subcommittee on Securities of the Committee on Banking, Housing, and Urban Affairs, Senate, 103rd Congress, June 17 and July 21, 1993, 225.

126. Ibid, 5. Dunlap told the Committee how the company used the threat of Rule 11 to make two frivolous lawsuits go away, but that it still "cost us over $500,000, which, granted, Intel can take the time and money to defend these suits, but that $500,000 could have supported another, say, ten production workers. We could have had engineers designing products." Ibid., at 20.

127. David R. Sands, "Senate Vote Completes Override of Clinton Veto; White House Lobbying Effort Fails; Lawsuit-Reform Bill Passes, 68–30," *The Washington Times*, December 23, 1995, A2. Even Clinton seemed to reverse himself the following year when he told a group of Silicon Valley business leaders that he opposed a California Proposition (Proposition 211) designed to undermine the Private

Securities Litigation Reform Act. Eric Pianin, "Clinton Opposes Calif. Securities Suit Initiative," *Washington Post*, August 8, 1996, D10.

128. P.L. 104–34.

129. *Jones v. Bock*, 549 U.S. 199 (2007). See also Jamie Ayers, "To Plead or Not to Plead? Does the Prison Litigation Reform Act's Exhaustion Requirement Establish a Pleading Requirement or an Affirmative Defense?," *University of California, Davis Law Review*, 39 (2005), 247–78.

130. See Marianne Levelle, "Class Action Crackdown," *U.S. News and World Report*, February 21, 2005, 46.

131. John F. Harris, "Victory for Bush on Suits," *Washington Post*, February 18, 2005, A1.

132. John F. Harris and Jim VandeHei, "Senate Nears Revision of Class Action," *Washington Post*, February 10, 2005, A4.

133. The PSLRA has arguably played a major role in facilitating the modern financial crisis, largely by making it difficult for investors concerned with fraud to obtain information about the investment firms in question.

134. Diversity jurisdiction is a form of subject-matter jurisdiction in civil procedure in which a district court has the power to hear a civil case where the persons that are parties are "diverse" in citizenship, which generally means that they are citizens of different states or non-U.S. citizens (corporations may also be included). While most class actions require complete diversity, under the CAFA, a case may be filed directly in federal court with minimal diversity—where *any* plaintiff in the suit is a citizen of a different state from *any* defendant.

135. 41 U.S. 1 (1842) and 304 U.S. 64 (1938), respectively.

136. It is important to note that this expansion occurred in the midst of a broader debate about the value of federal diversity jurisdiction. In 1990 the congressionally appointed Federal Courts Study Committee recommended its abolition, and members of the legal community agreed, arguing that it was largely a burden on federal courts and of little practical use after *Erie*. While Congress did not act on these recommendations, it did restrict jurisdiction somewhat by raising the minimum amount in controversy from $50,000 to $75,000 in 1996 (the minimum amount has changed over time, beginning at $500 at the time of the Judiciary Act of 1789). See David Marcus, "Erie, the Class Action Fairness Act, and Some Federalism Implications of Diversity Jurisdiction," *William & Mary Law Review* 48 (2007), 1247–313.

137. Levelle, "Class Action Crackdown," p. 46.

138. Francis B. Bouchard, "Class Action Lessons Learned," *Business Insurance*, February 17, 2005, 8.

139. At the time CAFA was passed, the problem of so-called "judicial hellholes" was arguably solving itself, largely through retrenchment as a result to changes in elected state Supreme Courts. See Stephen B. Burbank, "The Class Action Fairness Act of 2005 in Historical Context: A Preliminary View," *University of Pennsylvania Law Review* 156 (2008), 1439–551.

140. The Federal Judicial Center is tracking the effect of the CAFA on class action litigation and has issued several reports on the topic. See, for example, Emery G. Lee III and Thomas E. Willging, "The Impact of the Class Action Fairness Act of 2005," Third Interim Report to the Judicial Conference Advisory Committee on Civil Rules, 2007, and the Fourth Interim Report, April 2008.

141. Erwin Chemerinsky, *The Conservative Assault on the Constitution* (New York: Simon & Schuster, 2010), 215.

142. Mid-nineteenth century pleading rules also required "great specificity" in alleging facts to support a claim. Ibid., 216.

143. *Conley v. Gibson*, 355 U.S. 41 (1957).

144. See *Leatherman v. Tarrant County Narcotics Intelligence and Coordination United*, 507 U.S. 163 (1993), which Justice Thomas wrote for a unanimous Court.

145. *Bell Atlantic Corp. v. Twombly*, 200 U.S. 321 (2007).

146. Ironically, as Chemerinsky argues, it is likely that, under this new standard of plausibility, every sample complaint given in the federal rules would have to be dismissed for a lack of adequate facts.

147. For a summary of recent studies on the effects of *Twombly* and *Iqbal*, see David Freeman Engstrom, "The Twiqbal Puzzle and Empirical Study of Civil Procedure," *Stanford Law Review* 65 (2013), 1203.

148. "Has the Supreme Court Limited Americans' Access to Courts?," Prepared Statement of Stephen B. Burbank, Hearings before the Senate Judiciary Committee, December 2, 2009. See also Patricia W. Hatamyar, "The Tao of Pleading: Do Twombly and Iqbal Matter Empirically," *American University Law Review* 59 (2010), 553–633.

149. Chemerinsky, *The Conservative Assault on the Constitution*, 216.

150. Joe Cecil, George Cort, Margaret Williams, Jared Bataillon, and Jacqueline Campbell, "Update on Resolution of Rule 12(b)(6): Motions Granted With Leave to Amend," Federal Judicial Center, Report to the Judicial Conference Advisory Committee on Civil Rules, November 2011.

151. Prepared Statement of Stephen B. Burbank. The Federal Judicial Center is tracking this as well, preliminarily finding less of an effect than others do.

152. S. 1504, 111th Congress, 1st Session, July 22, 2009, 7890–91; "Has the Supreme Court Limited Americans' Access to Courts?"

153. "Has the Supreme Court Limited Americans' Access to Courts?," 3.

154. Ibid., 8.

155. H.R. 4115, 111th Congress, 1st Session, November 19, 2009.

156. *Wal-Mart v. Dukes* 131 S.Ct. 2541 (2011).

157. "Barriers to Justice and Accountability: How the Supreme Court's Recent Rulings Will Affect Corporate Behavior," Hearings before the Committee on the Judiciary, Senate, 112th Congress, 1st Session, June 29, 2011.

158. This is not to suggest that the standing doctrine had not played a major role in the Supreme Court's jurisprudence over the course of the twentieth century, but

rather that national attention to it increased with the gay marriage cases of the 2012–2013 Supreme Court term.

159. Subrin and Main, "The Fourth Era," 1881.

160. Even their one late-breaking victory—class action reform—has been widely argued as primarily symbolic.

161. See also Daniel P. Carpenter, *The Forging of Bureaucratic Autonomy: Reputations, Networks, and Policy Innovation in Executive Agencies, 1862–1928* (Princeton, NJ: Princeton University Press, 2001).

162. See generally E. E. Schattschneider, *The Semisovereign People: A Realist's View of Democracy in America* (Boston: Wadsworth Cengage Learning, 1975).

CHAPTER 5

1. Julius C. Smith, "Totalitarianism and Administrative Absolutism," reprinted in *Congressional Record* (July 8, 1940), 4325–30.

2. "Text of Roosevelt's Veto of Walter-Logan Measure," *Congressional Record* (December 18, 1940), 13942–43.

3. Ibid.

4. Texas Representative Hatton Sumners was the lengthiest and loudest in advocating for an override to prevent "any group of appointed people or elected people for that matter, to make rules which have the force of law and to have the power to construe those and the power to enforce those rules, all the powers a king ever had, that Mussolini claims, all the powers that Hitler exercises, with no effective complete assurance of a day in court." *Congressional Record* (December 18, 1940), 13952–53.

5. There are three constitutional clauses that arguably define the jurisdiction of the judiciary. The first two are grants of powers to Congress: the "congressional powers" clause (Article I, Sec. 8, Cl. 9), which gives Congress the power to create federal courts inferior to the Supreme Court, and the "judicial vesting" clause (Article III, Sec. 1), which gives Congress the power to make exceptions to and regulations of the appellate jurisdiction of the Supreme Court. Exercised together, these two clauses put Congress at the forefront of determining and shaping judicial power. For instance, at least in theory, lawmakers retain the power to eliminate judicial review of certain legislative or executive actions. At the same time, however, the Constitution also limits the power of lawmakers by expressly granting the judiciary authority over certain types of cases (as enumerated in Article III, Sec. 2). It is the judiciary that has original jurisdiction over "all cases, in Law and Equity, arising under this Constitution," as well as over cases affecting issues such as ambassadors, maritime law, controversies that involve the United States as a party, or disputes involving one or more states.

6. George I. Lovell, *Legislative Deferrals: Statutory Ambiguity, Judicial Power, and American Democracy* (New York: Cambridge University Press, 2003), 45 and throughout.

7. *Schechter Poultry Corp. v. United States*, 295 U.S. 495 (1935).

8. See "National Labor Relations Board," Senate, Report No. 573, 74th Congress, 1st Session, May 1, 1935, 15. For examples of federal court reinforcements of this statute, see *Amalgamated Utility Workers (CIO) v. Consolidated Edison Co. of New York et al.*, 309 U.S. 261 (1940): claiming no jurisdiction over an NLRB order; *Agwilines, Inc. v. NLRB*, 87 F.2d 146, 151 (1936): "If (the statute) gives any right, it gives a new one unknown to the common law and one which in its nature does not require, indeed does not admit the arbitrament of a jury trial.. . . Such proceedings have been authoritatively declared not to be not within the Seventh Amendment"; and *Amazon Cotton Mill Co. v. Textile Workers Union*, 167 F.2d 183, 186 (1948): "Federal trial courts were without jurisdiction to redress by injunction or otherwise the unfair labor practices which it defined." The NLRA does also provide areas where judicial review is authorized, areas that—as we will see—will later be revised by both Congress and the courts to be more expansive. For instance, 29 U.S.C. Section 160 (Section 10[e] of the National Labor Relations Act of 1935) allows the Board to petition a court to enforce its orders (while at the same time insulating other types of decision making from review) and Section 10(f) ensures that "any person aggrieved by final order of the Board. . . may obtain a review of such order in any United States court of appeals."

9. Most famous among them is the Eleventh Amendment (1795) that overturned the Supreme Court's decision in *Chisholm v. Georgia* (1793) by restating the immunity of states from lawsuits in federal court. Others include the Thirteenth and Fourteenth Amendments (prohibiting slavery and ensuring that blacks had a right to citizenship, 1865 and 1868 respectively), which in effect overturned *Dred Scott v. Sandford* (1857); the Sixteenth Amendment (1913), which gave Congress the power to require an income tax, therefore overturning *Pollack v. Farmer's Loan and Trust Co.* (1895); the Twenty-sixth Amendment (1971), which overturned the portion of *Oregon v. Mitchell* (1970) that held that Congress could not require the states to set the voting age to 18 in elections for state office; and the Nineteenth and Twenty-fourth Amendments, which prohibited the denial of the right to vote for women and the poll tax (1920 and 1964 respectively) and superseded decisions upholding these practices under the Constitution. For more on congressional actions to overturn court decisions, see William Eskridge, "Overriding Supreme Court Statutory Interpretation Decisions," *Yale Law Journal* 101 (1991), 331.

10. See Edward Keynes with Randall K. Miller, *The Court v. Congress: Prayer, Busing, and Abortion* (Durham, NC: Duke University Press, 1989), 155–56.

11. A recent study by Tom Clark finds that, in aggregate, from the period between 1877 and 2008, 897 such court curbing bills were introduced in Congress. Largely dovetailing with earlier accounts of court curbing, Clark finds several "high" periods when such proposals were particularly rampant—the late 1800s, early 1900s, New Deal and Civil Rights eras, and the early 1980s—leading to a particularly strong series of proposals in the recent two decades. While these

types of bills only rarely make it out of committee, the frequency with which they are put forth appears to mirror public opposition to the Supreme Court's recent activities, particularly those in which the Court recognizes new rights claims and subsequently increases access for citizens to redress related violations. See Tom S. Clark, *The Limits of Judicial Independence* (New York: Cambridge University Press, 2010).

12. For a broader discussion of the court curbing literature, see Stephen M. Engel, *American Politicians Confront the Court: Opposition Politics and Changing Responses to Judicial Power* (New York: Cambridge University Press, 2011). See also Clark, *The Limits of Judicial Independence*; Stuart S. Nagel, "Court-Curbing Periods in American History," *Vanderbilt Law Review* 18 (1965), 925; Gerald N. Rosenberg, "Judicial Independence and the Reality of Political Power," *Review of Politics* 54 (1992), 369.

13. After exhausting the internal process, a party may have a right to appeal in state or federal court, but this depends upon the procedures for each individual agency.

14. In fact, as Dawn Chutkow notes, this form of jurisdiction stripping happens frequently and successfully; between 1943 and 2003, for example, she finds that Congress passed 248 public laws with 378 provisions expressly denying the federal courts any power of agency review. Contrary to the popular wisdom that Congress is likely to propose court curbing bills when there is a relatively greater ideological difference between the two branches, or when widespread public opposition to the Court exists, Chutkow finds instead that "jurisdictional removals primarily are designed to prevent court review of agency decisionmaking." See Dawn M. Chutkow, "Litigation, Ideology, and Congressional Control of the Courts," *Journal of Politics* 70 (2008), 1058.

15. Frank B. Fox, "What About Administrative Tribunals? Bar Not to Be Blamed for Tremendous Advance in Removing Judicial Matters from the Courts—the Matter Goes to the Never Ending Contest for Power by Legislative and Executive Departments in Their Attempt to Avoid Judicial Control—Interpretation of Certain Provisions by the Supreme Court—What the Legislature Should be Brought to Understand," *ABA Journal* 21 (1936), 376.

16. Richard A. Merrill, "Introduction to Administrative Law Symposium," *Virginia Law Review* 72 (1986), 215.

17. Richard B. Stewart, "The Reformation of American Administrative Law," *Harvard Law Review* 88 (1975), 1676.

18. Peter H. Schuck, ed., *Foundations of Administrative Law* (New York: Foundation Press 2004), 5.

19. George B. Shepherd, "Fierce Compromise: The Administrative Procedure Act Emerges from New Deal Politics," *Northwestern University Law Review* 90 (1996), 1558.

20. William H. Allen, "The Durability of the Administrative Procedure Act," *Virginia Law Review* 72 (1986), 235.

21. P.L. 79-404. These "purposes" were outlined in the *Attorney General's Manual on the Administrative Procedure Act*, published in 1947.

22. Ibid., Sections 702–04.

23. Section 706(2)(a).

24. 435 U.S. 519 (1978). For example, the Court rejected the judicial imposition of procedural requirements for informal rulemaking under the law (at 544–46).

25. *Chevron U.S.A., Inc., v. Natural Resources Defense Council*, 467 U.S. 837 (1984).

26. See Schuck, *Foundations of Administrative Law*, 5–6.

27. Shepherd, "Administrative Procedure Act," 1560.

28. See generally Schuck, *Foundations of Administrative Law*.

29. Jerry L. Mashaw, *Creating the Administrative Constitution: The Lost One Hundred Years of American Administrative Law* (New Haven, CT: Yale University Press, 2012).

30. William E. Nelson, *The Roots of American Bureaucracy, 1830–1900* (Cambridge, MA: Harvard University Press, 1982), 12–13.

31. Stephen Skowronek, *Building a New American State: The Expansion of National Administrative Capacities, 1877–1920* (New York: Cambridge University Press, 1982).

32. Ibid., 28.

33. Ibid, 42.

34. During the Progressive era, acts of Congress that constricted the scope of the judiciary often expanded it in other ways at the same time, or otherwise sought to help reduce its growing caseload. Several Progressive era pieces of legislation provided that the judgment of the Court of Appeals would be final (not available to the Supreme Court) for various types of cases, including those arising under the Bankruptcy Act and the Railroad Eighteen Hour Act. Discretion to hear such cases was ultimately left with the Supreme Court, however, as it could hear a case on the determination that a question of constitutional right was involved. Similarly, the Judges Bill of 1925 tried harder to stem the tide of business reaching the Court by restricting appeals by right and granting the Supreme Court discretion in issuing writes of certiorari to state and lower federal courts. When Congress established the Court of Appeals in 1891, for example, it not only restricted the Supreme Court's appellate jurisdiction, but also significantly relieved overcrowding of its docket.

35. For more on the significance of Norris-La Guardia in curbing judicial power, see Karen Orren, *Belated Feudalism: Labor, the Law, and Liberal Development in the United States* (New York: Cambridge University Press, 1992).

36. See Engel, *American Politicians Confront the Court*, 254–61, and Lovell, *Legislative Deferrals*, 3 (arguing that, especially in the area of labor policy, legislators caught between "powerful constituencies with incompatible demands" chose to empower courts by writing deliberately ambiguous laws).

37. Skowronek, *Building a New American State*, 165. See, too, Woodrow Wilson, "The Study of Administration," *Political Science Quarterly* 2 (June 1887), 197–222.

38. Quoted in S. Document No. 248, 79th Congress, 2nd Session, 1946, 350.

39. Paul R. Verkuil, "The Emerging Concept of Administrative Procedure," *Columbia Law Review* 78 (1978), 268.

40. Shepherd, "Administrative Procedure Act," 1568–70.

41. Morton J. Horwitz, *The Transformation of American Law, 1870–1960* (New York: Oxford University Press, 1992), 222. See also, Daniel R. Ernst, *Tocqueville's Nightmare: The Administrative State Emerges in America, 1900–1940* (New York: Oxford University Press, 2014); Joanna L. Grisinger, *The Unwieldy American State: Administrative Politics Since the New Deal* (New York: Cambridge University Press, 2012).

42. Quoted in Shepherd, "Administrative Procedure Act," 1571.

43. Ibid., 1573.

44. Walter Gellhorn, "The Administrative Procedure Act: The Beginnings," *Virginia Law Review* 72 (1986), 219. See also ABA Report No. 59 (1934), 539.

45. The 1936 bill would have created a U.S. Customs Court and a U.S. Board of Tax Appeals. See Shepherd, "Administrative Procedure Act," 1578.

46. Shepherd, "Administrative Procedure Act," 1580.

47. *West Coast Hotel Co. v. Parrish*, 300 U.S. 379 (1937).

48. 304 US 1 (1938).

49. "Address of Justice Hughes at Law Institute," quoted in Daniel R. Ernst, "The Politics of Administrative Law: New York's Anti-Bureaucracy Clause and O'Brian-Wagner Campaign of 1938," *Law and History Review* 27 (2009), 340.

50. Wallace had argued before the Court that his initial order (issued in 1933) had been issued only after reading the appellant briefs, and that he made his decision carefully. See "Judicial Control of Administrative Procedure: The Morgan Cases," *Harvard Law Review* 52 (1939), 510.

51. *New York Times*, "Murphy to Study Federal Agencies," February 24, 1839.

52. Verkuil, "Emerging Concept," 269.

53. ABA Report No. 63 (1938), at 339.

54. One such "tendency"—the tendency "to disregard jurisdictional limits and seek to extend the sphere of administrative action beyond the jurisdiction confided"—reflects a fear common among those suspicious of judicial review. As Louis Jaffe described (in response to Pound), "Extensions of jurisdiction by the Courts on constitutional and common law grounds have provided the bitterest conflicts in the law." See Louis L. Jaffe, "Invective and Investigation in Administrative Law," *Harvard Law Review* 52 (1939), 1534–35. Jaffe also retorted that "the 'ten tendencies' are tendencies not of administrative officers as a class or judges as a class but of certain types of men and mentality" (1235).

55. See Horwitz, *The Transformation of American Law*, 219–35.

56. James E. Brazier, "An Anti-New Dealer Legacy: The Administrative Procedure Act," *Journal of Policy History* 8 (1996), 206–26; Horwitz, *Transformation of American Law*, 231. See also Ernst, *Tocqueville's Nightmare*, chapter 5; Grisinger, *The Unwieldy American State*, chapters 1–2.

57. See, for example, Christopher L. Tomlins, *The State and the Unions: Labor Relations, Law, and the Organized Labor Movement in America, 1880–1960* (New York: Cambridge University Press, 1985).

58. Grisinger, *The Unwieldy American State*, chapter 1.

59. Louis Stark, "Wagner Condemns Revision of NLRA," *New York Times*, March 14, 1940.

60. Report of the Committee on Administrative Law of the Federal Bar Association, 76th Congress, 1st Session, Senate, Document No. 71, May 4, 1839, 2, 5–8.

61. Ibid.

62. Verkuil, "Emerging Concept," 271. See, too, McNollgast, "The Political Origins of the Administrative Procedure Act," *Journal of Law, Economics, & Organization* 15 (1999), 196.

63. "Administrative Law": Hearings before Subcommittee No. 4 of the Committee on the Judiciary, House of Representatives, 76th Congress, 1st Session, March 17, 1939, 14–15.

64. Ibid., 19.

65. Ibid., 22.

66. Ibid., 44.

67. Shepherd, "Administrative Procedure Act," 1602–25. See also Richard L. Strout, "Intimate Message from Washington," *Christian Science Monitor* (March 5, 1940); "In the Nation: The Political Opposition to Walter-Logan Record of Mr. Acheson," *New York Times*, April 17, 1940.

68. Labor groups themselves spilt on support of the bill, with the CIO opposing it and the AFL—which were more critical of the National Labor Relations Board—supporting it. See Shepherd, "Administrative Procedure Act," 1608.

69. McNollgast, "Political Origins of the Administrative Procedure Act," 210.

70. "To Curb Agencies," *New York Herald Tribune*, January 28, 1941.

71. Paul R. Verkuil, " Emerging Concept."

72. "To Curb Agencies," *New York Herald Tribune*, January 28, 1941. A second memorandum was issued by Chief Justice D. Lawrence Groner of the DC Appeals Court saying that neither the majority or minority went far enough in separating administrative and judicial functions in federal agencies. "New Report Asks Code for Agencies to Protect Public," *New York Times*, January 27, 1941.

73. Verkuil, "Emerging Concept," 276.

74. 320 U.S. 297 (1943).

75. "Nation's Bar Asks Fair Agency Trials," *New York Times*, February 29, 1944.

76. "Bar Is Warned Against Growth of U.S. Agencies," *New York Herald Tribune*, September 12, 1944.

77. There were seven proposed drafts of the APA in total, prominently including the 1944 McCarran-Sumners Bill (which would become the APA), as well as the Gwynne and Smith Bills (also considered in 1944). See Shepherd, "Administrative Procedure Act," 1649–57.

78. The general review provisions of the APA are located in Section 10 of the law, specifically Subsections 702–04.

79. Cass Sunstein, "Reviewing Agency Inaction After Heckler v. Chaney," *University of Chicago Law Review* 52 (1985), 655–56. Sunstein further stresses that "judicial review serves important goals in promoting fidelity to statutory requirements and, where those requirements are ambiguous or vague, in increasing the likelihood that the regulatory process will be a reasonable exercise of discretion instead of a bow in the direction of powerful private groups."

80. Max Forester, "Business Hails Procedure Act for Agencies," *New York Tribune*, June 24, 1946.

81. John P. Callahan, "Industries Hail Curb on Agencies," *New York Times*, July 21, 1946.

82. The war played an important role in leading the ABA in particular to abandon its combative approach, as an attempt to hamper executive power could have been perceived as compromising America's ability to fight the war. Accordingly, the ABA reconstituted the membership of its Committee on Administrative Law, swapping out conservatives for moderates and appointing a new chair whom had favor within the FDR administration. The new chair, McFarland, had sat on the Attorney General's committee on administrative procedure (which was commissioned by the President) and is credited with later transforming the ABA committee's approach from conservatism to compromise. See Shepherd, "Administrative Procedure Act," 1641–48.

83. Martin Shapiro, "APA: Past, Present, and Future," *Virginia Law Review* 72 (1986), 447.

84. Verkuil, "Emerging Concept," 278.

85. Statement of Representative Walter, *Congressional Record*, 92 (1946), 5654, 5649.

86. McNollgast, "Political Origins of Administrative Procedure Act," 183.

87. Kenneth Culp Davis, *Administrative Law Treatise* (San Diego: K.C. Davis, 1984), 140.

88. Paul V. Beckley, "McCarran for More Curbs on U.S. Agencies," *New York Herald Tribune*, October 31, 1946.

89. Roscoe Pound, "Annual Survey of Law—II," *American Bar Association Journal* 33 (December 1947), 1192, 94.

90. Alexander Wiley, "Administrative Law," *American Bar Association Journal* 34 (1948), 880.

91. "Test Reveals 15 NLRB Examiners Not Qualified," *Los Angeles Times*, March 13, 1949.

92. "Bureaucrats' Sins Hit as Judges Meet," *Los Angeles Times*, June 29, 1949.

93. John F. Duffy, "Administrative Common Law in Judicial Review," *Texas Law Review* 77 (1998), 119.

94. See Sidney A. Shapiro, "Symposium on the 50th Anniversary of the APA: A Delegation Theory of the APA," *Administrative Law Journal of American University* 10 (1996), 89–109.
95. 339 U.S. 33 (1950).
96. 340 U.S. 474 (1951).
97. 357 U.S. 116 (1958); 360 U.S. 474 (1959).
98. *Ludecke v. Watkins*, 335 U.S. 160 (1948).
99. Grisinger, *The Unwieldy American State*, 197–99.
100. See the Commission on the Organization of the Executive Branch of the Government, Legal Services and Procedure, Report to Congress, April 1955, 45–93 and the Report of the Conference on Administrative Procedure, called for by the president on April 29, 1953. For a comprehensive treatment of this episode, see Grisinger, *The Unwieldy American State*, chapter 5.
101. Statement of Rufus G. Poole, Chairman of the Section of Administrative Law, American Bar Association, "Proposed Establishment of Committee on Administrative Procedure and Practice," Hearings before a Special Subcommittee, Committee on Rules, House of Representatives, 84th Congress, 2nd Session, May 22–24, 1956, 4 and 8.
102. Statement of Cody Fowler, former President, American Bar Association, "Proposed Establishment of Committee on Administrative Procedure and Practice," 19.
103. Ibid.
104. See Kenneth Culp Davis, *Administrative Law Treatise*, citing a report of the ABA Special Committee.
105. "Federal Administrative Procedure," Hearings before the Subcommittee on Administrative Practice and Procedure of the Committee of the Judiciary, Senate, 86th Congress, 1st Session, November 29–December 2, 1959.
106. Ibid.
107. Ibid., 62.
108. Ibid, 65.
109. Ibid., 66.
110. Ibid., 71.
111. Mr. Dirksen, "Overhaul of the Administrative Procedure Act," *Congressional Record* (March 4, 1965), 4088.
112. The bill was an attempt to persuade agencies to abandon various admission requirements and fees for lawyers to practice before individual agencies. See "To Remove Arbitrary Limitations Upon Attorneys' Fees for Services Rendered in Proceedings before Administrative Agencies of the United States, and for Other Purposes," Subcommittee No. 2 of the Committee on the Judiciary, House of Representatives, August 11, 1966.
113. The transcript of the meeting numbers nearly 500 pages.

114. "Overhaul of the Administrative Procedure Act," *Congressional Record* (March 4, 1965), 4088.
115. Ibid., 4094.
116. Interstate Commerce Commission, Letter to the Senate Judiciary Committee, May 12, 1965.
117. "Providing for Continuous Improvement of the Administrative Procedure of Federal Agencies by Creating an Administrative Conference of the United States," 88th Congress, 1st Session, Report No. 621, October 29, 1963, 22.
118. Louis M. Kohlmeier, "Outlook for Superagency," *Wall Street Journal*, June 12, 1963.
119. "Providing for Continuous Improvement of the Administrative Procedure of Federal Agencies," 24.
120. "Message from the President of the United States Relative to the Regulatory Agencies of Our Government," 87th Congress, 1st Session, House of Representatives, Document No. 135, April 13, 1961, 9.
121. "SEC Defines, Expands Rights of Witnesses at Its Closed Hearings," *Washington Post*, March 13, 1964.
122. "Administrative Practice and Procedure," Report of the Subcommittee on Administrative Practice and Procedure of the Committee on the Judiciary of the United States Senate, 89th Congress, 1st Session, Report No. 119, March 10, 1965, 2.
123. Executive Order 10,934 (1961).
124. The six ACUS standing committees cover adjudication, administration, governmental processes, judicial review, regulation, and rulemaking.
125. "Report of the Special Committee on Revision of the Administrative Procedure Act," ABA Annual Report 95, 322–28. In total, the twelve resolutions urged (1) amending the definition of "rule" to exclude matters of particular applicability, (2) deleting exemptions from the requirement of notice and public participation in rulemaking, (3) and (4) broadening provisions of the APA to require that all proceedings required by law be decided on the record after an agency hearing, (5) greater uniformity for rules governing pleadings in informal adjudicative proceedings, (6) authorizing appeal boards and other appellate procedures, (7) requiring effective utilization of prehearing conferences, (8) giving greater significance to the decision of the hearing officer, (9) approving the concept of abridged procedures in certain (limited) cases, (10) and (11) providing minimal standards and subpoena power for informal adjudication, and (12) making sanctions available when prejudicial publicity is leaked by an agency. For more on these resolutions, please see *Administrative Law Review*, issue 4 (1972).
126. Administrative Procedure Act Amendments of 1976: Hearings on S. 796–800, S. 1210, S. 1289, S. 2407–2408, S. 2115, S. 2792, S. 3296–3297 before the Subcommittee on Practice and Procedure of the Senate Committee on the Judiciary, 94th Congress, 2nd Session, 1976, 224, specifically the statement of

Richard K. Berg. See also H.R. 10194, 94th Congress, 1st Session (Sections 1 and 2), and H.R. 10198, 94th Congress, 1st Session (Sections 1 and 2).

127. Funding for the ACUS was cut in 1995 and reinstated in 2009.

128. P.L. 94–109.

129. P.L. 89–554. See also Shapiro, "A Delegation Theory of the APA," 101.

130. See Allen, "Durability of the Administrative Procedure Act," 244, citing William Warfield Ross, chairman of the ABA Special Committee that drafted the twelve resolutions of 1970; "The Future of Administrative Procedural Reform," ABA Administrative Law Section, 20 Annual Reports of the Committees (1983), 9–10, ABA Section of Administrative Law.

131. Cass R. Sunstein, "Law and Administration after Chevron," *Columbia Law Review* 90 (1990), 2082.

132. The sections on freedom of information, rulemaking, and requiring notice of a denial of relief were excepted by the bills' language. At the same time (and despite the general presumption of reviewability inherent in the APA), Congress sometimes opted to *include* judicial review provisions explicitly in its laws. A spate of 1970 laws were constructed in this way, among them the Civil Service Commission Act (5 U.S.C. Section 1508); the Federal Power Act (16 U.S.C. Section 825L[b]); the Federal Rood, Drug, and Cosmetic Act (21 U.S.C. Section 371[f]); and the Medicare Act (42 U.S.C. Section 139ff[c]).

133. Executive Order No. 11,821, 3 C.F.R. Section 926, 1974.

134. 3 C.F.R. Section 152; see also Allen, "The Durability of the Administrative Procedure Act."

135. "Administrative Procedure Act Amendments of 1976," Hearings before the Subcommittee on Administrative Practice and Procedure of the Committee of the Judiciary, Senate, 94th Congress, 2nd Session, April 28 and May 3, 1976.

136. Ibid., 2.

137. P.L. 94–574.

138. Prepared statement of Richard K. Berg, Executive Secretary, Administrative Conference of the United States, Hearings on the Administrative Procedure Act Amendments of 1976, Hearings before the Subcommittee on Administrative Practice and Procedure, April 28, 1976, 232.

139. For Scalia's statement, see *Congressional Record* (April 28, 1976), 90–92.

140. "Administrative Procedure Act Amendments of 1976," 5.

141. Ibid., 72.

142. 387 U.S. 136 (1967), at 148.

143. 387 U.S. 136 (1967). The "hard look" doctrine is mainly applied to cases of informal rulemaking and adjudication, as there is a "substantial evidence" standard of review that applies to formal actions. Where formal rulemaking and adjudication are concerned, reviewing courts are required to uphold a rule if they find the agency's decision to be "reasonable." Given the relative lack of procedural safeguards in the realm of *informal* activity, however, the *Overton Park* approach first

requires courts to "consider whether the decision was based on a consideration of the relevant factors and whether there has been a clear error of judgment." Courts cannot inquire as to *why* agencies relied on particular information to make their rules and regulations, but they can inquire as to what data the agency reviewed and considered.

144. 397 U.S. 150 (1970).

145. Ibid., at 153.

146. At first, it was unclear whether the newly constructed "injury in fact" test was an interpretation of the judicial review provisions of the APA or of the Constitution's Article III "case or controversy" requirement (considered the basis for standing as a doctrine). In *Sierra Club v. Morton* (405 U.S. 727 [1970]), in denying standing to an environmental group on the basis that it failed to allege that any of its members suffered an actual injury, the Court treated the test as an interpretation of the APA, claiming that, in *Data Processing*, "we held more broadly that persons had standing to obtain judicial review of federal agency action under section 10 of the APA where they alleged that the challenged action had caused them 'injury in fact.'" The Court treated the analysis the same way in 1973 (granting standing to students opposed to an ICC railroad rate increase in *United States v. Students Challenging Regulatory Agency Procedures*, 412 U.S. 669) before clarifying in 1974 that the "injury in fact" test was to be considered an interpretation of the "case or controversy" requirement (making the case that the majority in *Data Processing* had established this point). See *Schlesinger v. Reservists Committee to Stop the War* (418 U.S. 208).

147. 406 U.S. 742 (1972).

148. 410 U.S. 224 (1973).

149. 435 U.S. 519 (1978).

150. Ibid., at 549.

151. Antonin Scalia, "Vermont Yankee: The APA, the DC Circuit, and the Supreme Court," *Supreme Court Review* (1978), 345.

152. Ibid., 405.

153. Horwitz, *Transformation of American Law*, 245.

154. 467 U.S. 340 (1984).

155. Ibid., at 350.

156. An earlier indication of momentum in this direction was evident in *Dunlop v. Bachowski* (421 U.S. 560) in 1975, where although the Court held the administrative action in question reviewable, it entertained arguments that the legislative history showed "a congressional meaning to prohibit judicial review."

157. 470 U.S. 821 (1985).

158. Ibid., at 1656.

159. The Court left the door open for fighting this presumption of unreviewability in cases where an agency declines to act because it believes it does not have jurisdiction and when agency action is so extreme that the action runs clearly afoul of a statute.

160. See, for example, *Webster v. Doe* 486 U.S. 592 (1988) and *Lincoln v. Vigil* 508 U.S. 182 (1993).

161. 467 U.S. 837 (1984). See also Sunstein, "Law and Administration After Chevron," 2075.

162. 467 U.S. 837 (1984), at 865.

163. Ibid., at 844–845.

164. See Thomas J. Miles and Cass R. Sunstein, "Do Judges Make Regulatory Policy? An Empirical Investigation of Chevron," *University of Chicago Law Review* 73 (2006), 823 and 826.

165. Justice Stevens authored opinions analyzing administrative action according to the standards that predated *Chevron*, and he did so both before *and* after the case was believed to have superseded this approach. He also referred to *Chevron* as a "restatement" in speeches. See Thomas W. Merrill, "The Story of Chevron: The Making of an Accidental Landmark," in Peter L. Strauss, ed., *Administrative Law Stories* (New York: Foundation Press, 2006).

166. Ibid., 402.

167. Keith Werhan, "Delegalizing Administrative Law," *University of Illinois Law Review* (1996), 457–58.

168. *Engel v. Vitale*, 370 U.S. 421 (1962); *Abington School District v. Schempp*, 374 U.S. 203 (1963).

169. *Swann v. Charlotte-Mecklenburg School of Education*, 402 U.S. 1 (1971).

170. *Roe v. Wade*, 410 U.S. 113 (1973).

171. See Max Baucus and Kenneth R. Kay, "The Court Stripping Bills: Their Impact on the Constitution, the Courts, and Congress," *Villanova Law Review* 27 (1982), 988.

172. See, for example, H.R. Report No. 435, 97th Congress, 2nd Session, 1982, 4, reporting on H.R. 746, Section 623, a provision limiting judicial review.

173. For an in-depth discussion, see Allen, "The Durability of the Administrative Procedure Act," 245.

174. See Susan J. Tolchin, "The Damage OMB Is Doing: What Happens when a Mild-Mannered Government Agency Becomes 'Super-Regulator,'" *Washington Post*, November 28, 1983.

175. Executive Order 12,291,3 C.F.R. Section 127, 1981. (Quote is from the 1982 reprint.)

176. See Robert Pear, "Congress Moves to Shift Judicial Review Standards," *New York Times*, April 4, 1982.

177. "Regulatory Reform Act," Subcommittee on Regulatory Reform, Committee on the Judiciary, 97th Congress, 1st Session, May 14, 1981, 542–43. And "ABA, Federal Rulemaking Procedures Legislative Reform," Ibid., 578–95.

178. Pear, "Congress Moves to Shift Judicial Review Standards."

179. *Congressional Record* (April 30, 1981), 7946.

180. Pear, "Congress Moves to Shift Judicial Review Standards."

181. Statement of Hon. Robert McClory of Illinois, April 30, 1981, 8094.

182. The presidential standard at the time was to require reports for those rules with an impact of 100 million; the Dole Bill proposed lowering it to 50 million. S. 343, 104th Congress, 2nd Session, primarily Sections 622, 625, 627, and 633; for an extended discussion, see also Shapiro, "A Delegation Theory of the APA," 104–06.

183. *Congressional Record* (July 17, 1995), 19065.

184. Ibid., 19065.

185. Ibid., 19060.

186. Ibid., 19061–62.

187. "Regulatory Reform," Senate Judiciary Committee Hearings, March 17, 1995, written testimony of Christopher DeMuth, President of AEI, 81–82.

188. Ibid., George Clemon Freemon, Jr., Representative of the ABA, 75.

189. Cass Sunstein, for example, has both written prominently on regulatory reform and testified against the Dole Bill in 1995. See Cass R. Sunstein, *After the Rights Revolution: Reconceiving the Regulatory State* (Cambridge: Harvard University Press, 1990). His statement on the Dole Bill appears in the record of the Senate Judiciary Committee, at 88. He criticized the bill for compelling reviews of existing rules, which he feared "could allow private cooptation of public resources, and simultaneously threaten to increase judicial control of government in a quite undemocratic way" (91). He also found difficulty with judicial review being too common, stating that it would "drown administrators in paperwork." "It is notable in this regard that Presidents Reagan, Bush, and Clinton all decided to insulate CBA from the judiciary—on the theory that judicial review would produce delay, confusion, and error, especially in light of the judges' lack of democratic accountability or factfinding competence" (92).

190. Executive Order 12,866 (1993).

191. *National R.R. Passenger Corporation v. Boston & Maine Corporation* 503 U.S. 407 (1992), at 417–418. For a full discussion of the Court's textualist turn in statutory interpretation, see Thomas W. Merrill, "Textualism and the Future of the Chevron Doctrine," *Washington University Law Quarterly* 72 (1994), 351.

192. Werhan, "Delegalizing Administrative Law," 460.

193. 529 U.S. 576 (2000).

194. 323 U.S. 134 (1944).

195. *Christensen v. Harris County*, at 10.

196. 533 U.S. 218 (2001).

197. Ibid., at 226–27.

198. 535 U.S. 212 (2002), at 222.

199. 28 U.S.C. 2244 (b)(1)(3). Under the law the federal judiciary cannot grant habeas unless the state court decision upon which a prisoner's conviction was based is "unreasonably" wrong, in direct violation of an existing Supreme Court precedent, and/or based on an unreasonable determination of the facts in light of the evidence presented in the state court proceeding. In practice, the law eliminates the Supreme Court's power to review a Court of Appeals' denial of the right to

a second or successive petition. It also limits review of death penalty cases to one year after the conviction becomes final.

200. See, for example, the Constitution Restoration Act of 2005 (H.R. 1070, S. 520); the Marriage Protection Act of 2007 (H.R. 724); the Pledge Protection Act of 2005 and 2007 (H.R. 2389); the Public Prayer Protection Act (H.R. 4364); the We the People Act (H.R. 4379); the Safeguarding Our Religious Liberties Act (H.R. 4576); and the Sanctity of Life Act of 2007 (H.R. 2597). Jurisdiction stripping proposals have even stretched to more mundane subject matter; in 2001, for example, Ron Paul proposed the Federal Water Pollution Control Act (H.R. 7245) to remove federal jurisdiction from dumping in private, nonnavigable waters, and from state dumping permit programs.

201. "Limiting Federal Court Jurisdiction to Protect Marriage for the States," Hearings before the Subcommittee on the Constitution, House Judiciary Committee, 108th Congress, 2nd Session (June 24, 2004), 136.

202. "Pledge Protection Act of 2005," *Congressional* Record 152 (July 19, 2006), H5415. Notably, however, the Supreme Court has continued to fight jurisdiction stripping legislation, even in the face of the "war on terror." In response to the Detainee Treatment Act of 2005 and the Military Commissions Act of 2006, both of which stripped federal courts of jurisdiction to consider habeas corpus petitions filed by prisoners in Guantánamo, the Supreme Court defended its authority by holding that neither an act of Congress nor the powers given to the executive in the Constitution authorized removal of jurisdiction and the subsequent creation of military tribunals in its place.

203. Specifically, the ABA recommended extending judicial review to the sections of the APA that govern what are known as "Type B" hearings; these hearings, the ABA argued, were growing at a rate of 40 percent, constituting more than half a million cases in 2000. See Eleanor D. Kinney, Chair, ABA Section of Administrative Law and Regulatory Practice, "60th Anniversary of the Administrative Procedure Act: Where Do We Go from Here?," Hearing before the Subcommittee on Commercial and Administrative Law, Committee of the Judiciary, House of Representatives, 109th Congress, 2nd Session, July 25, 2006, 6–8, 17.

204. Peter H. Schuck and E. Donald Elliot, "To the Chevron Station: An Empirical Study of Federal Administrative Law," *Duke Law Journal* (1990), 1057.

205. Interim Report on the Administrative Law, Process and Procedure Project for the 21st Century, Subcommittee on Commercial and Administrative Law of the Committee on the Judiciary, House of Representatives, 109th Congress, 2nd Session, December 2006, 12–13.

206. Congress helped to codify the courts' perspective with the Negotiated Rulemaking Act of 1990 (the provisions of which were made permanent with the Alternative Dispute Resolution Act of 1996) by establishing rulemaking/review requirements while still giving agencies latitude in implementation. This balance, known as

"negotiated rulemaking," was embraced by President Clinton, whose National Performance Review recommended its use.

207. Shapiro, "A Delegation Theory of the APA," 95.

CHAPTER 6

1. See *New Jersey v. T.L.O.*, 469 U.S. 325 (1985).
2. Quoted in Adam Liptak, "Strip-Search of Girl Tests Limit of School Policy," *The New York Times*, March 23, 2009.
3. *Safford Unified School District v. Redding*, 557 U.S. 364 (2009).
4. Liptak, "Strip-Search of Girl Tests Limit of School Policy."
5. *Marbury v. Madison*, 5 U.S. 137 (1803), at 163.
6. Peter H. Schuck, *Suing Government: Citizen Remedies for Official Wrongs* (New Haven, CT, and London: Yale University Press, 1983), 25.
7. As Pamela Karlan describes, leaving a formal right in place while constricting its "remedial machinery" is extremely problematic, in that "at best, this will dilute the value of the right, since some violations will go unremedied. At worst, it may signal potential wrongdoers that they can infringe the right with impunity." See Pamela S. Karlan, "Dismantling the Private Attorney General," *University of Illinois Law Review* (2003), 185. See also Akhil Reed Amar, "Of Sovereignty and Federalism," *Yale Law Journal* 76 (1987), 1425.
8. Some causes of action are statutory, usually taking the form of either legal provisions crafted by Congress that allow individuals to sue government agencies for enforcement of a statutory right, or in the form of a more general grant allowing individuals to sue government officials for *any* misconduct exercised while on the job. Other causes of action are based on constitutional right (as with *Bivens* challenges, discussed below, where individuals may sue government officials for alleged violation of rights under the federal Constitution). Where there is no express statutory remedy or direct constitutional claim available to a plaintiff, a question arises of whether there is arguably a cause of action *implied* by a statute that would allow an individual his or her day in court.
9. Scholars have debated this question of whether judges can oversee remedies as well. See, for example, Abram Chayes, "The Role of the Judge in Public Law Litigation," *Harvard Law Review* 89 (1976), 1281; Owen Fiss, "The Forms of Justice," *Harvard Law Review* 93 (1979), 1; Malcolm M. Feeley and Edward L. Rubin, *Judicial Policy Making and the Modern State: How the Courts Reformed America's Prisons* (New York: Cambridge University Press, 1998); Margo Schlanger, "Beyond the Hero Judge: Institutional Reform Litigation as Litigation," *Michigan Law Review* 97 (1999), 1994.
10. As Sean Farhang recently calculated, Congress included 275 such "fee-shifting" provisions in its legislation from 1887 to 2004. Of these provisions, he finds that most were often used in legislation regarding property rights (12 percent of the

total.) Civil rights, consumer protection, and labor are the next largest categories, each constituting 9 percent of the total provisions, with environmental policy following with 8 percent. See Sean Farhang, *The Litigation State: Public Regulation and Private Lawsuits in the U.S.* (Princeton, NJ: Princeton University Press, 2010). Justice William Brennan also provided a list of 120 fee-shifting statutes enacted by Congress in an appendix to his dissenting opinion in *Marek v. Chesny*, 473 U.S. 1 (1985), 43–51.

11. Farhang uses this term in *The Litigation State*.

12. Schuck, *Suing Government*, xii.

13. See Heather Elliot, "The Functions of Standing," *Stanford Law Review* 61 (2008), 459.

14. See John Harrison, "Jurisdiction, Congressional Power, and Constitutional Remedies," *Georgetown Law Journal* 86 (1988), 2513. The legal doctrine of sovereign immunity is based on the premise that because the "sovereign" (in the United States, "the people" as embodied by the government that they empowered) created the courts, the courts have no power to compel the government to be bound by the courts, as they were created by the sovereign for the protection of its interests.

15. There are four basic types of remedies that courts may provide: damages, restitution, declaratory remedies, and coercive remedies. After a plaintiff has established a claim in substantive law, damages compensate the plaintiff for losses sustained in violation of their rights. Compensatory damages can take various forms, among them common law contract damages, sale of goods contract damages, land sale contracts, equitable remedies, and tort damages. Damages are limited by various determinations, including foreseeability, certainty, avoidable consequences, and the collateral source rule. By contrast, restitution is measured by the defendant's gains rather than the plaintiff's losses; when awarded, a judge restores property to its rightful owner or disgorges unjust enrichment from a defendant that was gained by a wrong to the plaintiff. A declaratory remedy involves the declaration of the rights or legal relations between two parties to a case. This type of remedy is often used to determine the constitutionality of a statute so that the interested parties may resolve their dispute at an early stage. Finally, coercive remedies are available to plaintiffs entitled to "extraordinary relief." In such cases, a judge may issue a preventative or structural injunction, a temporary restraining order, or compel that the original agreement between parties be carried out.

16. While judges and lawyers have had civil immunity for centuries, they have historically been subject to prosecution for criminally willful deprivations of constitutional rights under 18 U.S.C.242, which is the criminal analog of 1983.

17. This is noted in Justice Joseph Bradley's decision in the 1890 case *Hans v. Louisiana*, for example.

18. See Clyde E. Jacobs, *The Eleventh Amendment and Sovereign Immunity* (New York: Doubleday, 1972), 41–43. Other scholars seem to contend that the Founders

were altogether "silent" on the matter (as did Justice Anthony Kennedy in his decision in *Alden v. Maine* in 1999); see, for example, Erwin Chemerinsky, *The Conservative Assault on the Constitution* (New York: Simon & Schuster, 2010), 223, while yet others contend that state sovereign immunity was widely acknowledged at the time of the Constitution, but that these immunities were based on common law and were therefore subject to the limitations imposed by federal law and the Constitution. See Akhil Reed Amar, "Of Sovereignty and Federalism," *Yale Law Journal* 96 (1987), 1425–520; Martha A. Field, "The Eleventh Amendment and Other Sovereign Immunity Doctrines: Part One," *University of Pennsylvania Law Review* 126 (1978), 515–49; William A. Fletcher, "A Historical Interpretation of the Eleventh Amendment: A Narrow Construction of an Affirmative Grant of Jurisdiction Rather than a Prohibition Against Jurisdiction," *Stanford Law Review* 35 (1983), 1033–1131; William A. Fletcher, "The Diversity Explanation of the Eleventh Amendment: A Reply to Critics," *University of Chicago Law Review* 56 (1989), 1261–99; Christopher Shortell, *Rights, Remedies, and the Impact of State Sovereignty* (Albany: State University of New York Press, 2009).

19. *Chisholm v. Georgia* 2 U.S. 419 (1793).
20. Fletcher, "Historical Interpretation of the Eleventh Amendment."
21. For an overview of these cases, see Jacobs, *The Eleventh Amendment and Sovereign Immunity.* The Supreme Court did, however, give mixed signals about whether citizens would be allowed to sue states, even early on. For example, while the Court clarified that the Eleventh Amendment prohibited citizens from suing states in *Hans v. Louisiana* (1890), in the same year it determined that the amendment did not grant immunity to local governments *within* the states (*Lincoln County v. Luning,* 133 U.S. 529 [1890]).
22. See *Lincoln County v. Luning* and *Ex Parte Young* 209 U.S. 123 (1908), respectively.
23. *Yaselli v. Goff,* 275 U.S. 503 (1927).
24. Schuck, *Suing Government,* 39. See *Adair v. Bank of America National Trust & Savings Association,* 303 U.S. 350 (1938).
25. *Gregoire v. Biddle,* 177 F.2d 579, 580 (2d Cir. 1949), *cert. denied,* 339 U.S. 949 (1950).
26. This logic was also embraced in a case arising under the FTCA, *Barr v. Matteo,* 360 U.S. 564 (1959).
27. The act was passed as part of the Legislative Reorganization Act, 60 Stat. 842.
28. See "Tort Claims Against the United States," H.R. Report 2245, 77th Congress, 2nd Session, 5, June 16, 1942, 6; "Tort Claims Against the United States," H.R. Report 1287, 79th Congress, 1st Session, 2, November 26, 1945; Harold G. Aron, "Federal Tort Claims Act: Comments and Questions for Practicing Lawyers," *American Bar Association Journal* 33 (1947), 226–29.
29. 28 U.S.C. Section 2672.
30. 28 U.S.C. 2680a.

31. See "Tort Claims Against the United States," H.R. Report 2245, 77th Congress, 2nd Session, 10, June 16, 1942.

32. *Rayonier Inc. v. United States*, 353 U.S. 315 (1957). See also *Dalehite v. United States*, 346 U.S. 15 (1953). The Court reiterated its position in *United States v. Muniz*, 374 U.S. 150 (1963), holding that it would not narrow the remedies provided under the Federal Tort Claims Act because such is the province of Congress, and in *Kosak v. United States*, 465 U.S. 848 (1984), arguing that Congress, not the Court, should be addressed to extend the remedies under the FTCA.

33. Edward F. Sherman, "From 'Loser Pays' to Modified Offer of Judgment Rules: Reconciling Incentives to Settle with Access to Justice," *Texas Law Review* 76 (1988), 1863–64. See, too, Comment, "Court Awarded Attorney's Fees and Equal Access to the Courts," *University of Pennsylvania Law Review* 122 (1974), 636–713.

34. Act of September 29, 1789.

35. Act of March 1, 1793.

36. 3 U.S. 306 (1796).

37. See, for example, *Day v. Woodworth*, 54 U.S. 363 (1851); *Stewart v. Sonneborn*, 98 U.S. 187 (1878). Justice Earl Warren defended the American Rule in 1967 on the grounds that "since litigation is at best uncertain one should not be penalized for merely defending or prosecuting a lawsuit, and that the poor might be unjustly discouraged from instituting actions to vindicate their rights if the penalty for losing included the fees of their opponents' counsel." *Fleischmann Distilling Corp. v. Maier Brewing Co.*, 386 U.S. 714 (1967), at 718.

38. Laws of the State of New York § 258 (1848).

39. Paul Taylor, "The Difference Between Filing Lawsuits and Selling Widgets: The Lost Understanding That Some Attorneys' Exercise of State Power Is Subject to Appropriate Regulation," *Pierce Law Review* (2006), 51.

40. Ibid., 56–58.

41. See *Gulf, Colorado, and Santa Fe Railway Company v. Ellis*, 165 U.S. 150 (1897).

42. Sherman, "From 'Loser Pays' to Modified Offer of Judgment Rules," 865–666.

43. See, for example, Amendments to Freedom of Information Act; PubPackers and Stockyards Act/Perishable Agricultural Commodities Act; Clayton Act; Unfair Competition Act; Securities Act of 1933; Trust Indenture Act; Securities Exchange Act of 1934; Truth in Lending Act; Motor Vehicle Information and Cost Savings Act; Organized Crime Control Act of 1970; Education Amendments of 1972; Norris-LaGuardia Act; Fair Labor Standards Act; Longshoremen's and Harbor Workers' Compensation Act; Federal Water Pollution Control Act; Marine Protection, Research, and Sanctuaries Act of 1972; Servicemen's Readjustment Act; Clean Air Act; Civil Rights Act of 1964; Fair Housing Act of 1968; Noise Control Act of 1972; Railway Labor Act; The Merchant Marine Act of 1936; Communications Act of 1934; Interstate Commerce Act.

44. Another exception is when litigation produces a common fund for the benefit of a group of claimants, as in a successful class action. Here, attorney's fees are drawn from the pool of damages prior to the claimants receiving their own damages.

45. For example, *Newman v. Piggie Park Enterprises, Inc.*, 390 U.S. 400 (1968), and *Christiansburg Garment Company v. EEOC*, 434 U.S. 412 (1978). See also John Leubsdorf, "Toward a History of the American Rule on Attorney Fee Recovery," *Law and Contemporary Problems* 47 (1984), 9–36.

46. Farhang, *The Litigation State*, 68.

47. Ibid., 68. See, too, R. Shep Melnick, *Between the Lines: Interpreting Welfare Rights* (Washington, DC: Brookings Institution, 1994), especially at 27.

48. Ibid., 91.

49. Ibid., 119–29.

50. "Removing Arbitrary Limitations Upon Attorneys' Fees," 90th Congress, 1st Session, S. Report No. 795, November 20, 1967, 3. They were advocating the removal of all existing provisions of law at the time that placed any form of limitation upon attorney's fees for services rendered in any administrative proceeding.

51. Attorney's fee provisions were not only a major vehicle for getting litigants representation (and subsequently access to court) during the Civil Rights era, but they also played an important role in Congress' later environmental statutes. The environmental statutes of the 1970s often contained citizen suit provisions, with which grants of attorney's fees were often considered to go hand in hand. From the perspective of those who supported the private enforcement of environmental legislation, any private citizen acting to enforce the law for the benefit of the common good should be reimbursed for his or her litigation costs—and attorney's fees provisions provided for precisely that.

52. Susan J. Stabile, "The Role of Congressional Intent in Determining the Existence of Implied Private Rights of Action," *Notre Dame Law Review* 71 (1996), 861, 864.

53. *Johnson v. Southern Pacific Company*, 196 U.S. 1 (1904), at 16–18.

54. *Texas & Pacific Railway Company v. Rigsby*, 241 U.S. 33 (1916).

55. Act of March 2, 1893, chapter 196, 27 Statute 531, codified at 45 U.S.C. 4, 1994.

56. See *Moore v. Chesapeake & Ohio Railway*, 291 U.S. 205 (1934).

57. *Erie Railroad Company v. Tompkins*, 304 U.S. 64 (1938). For further discussion of *Erie*'s effect on private rights of action, see Stabile, "The Role of Congressional Intent." See also *Switchmen's Union v. National Mediation Board*, 320 U.S. 297 (1943).

58. See, for example, *Turnstall v. Brotherhood of Locomotive Firemen and Engineermen*, 323 U.S. 210 (1944). More recently, in *Rosado v. Wyman* (397 U.S. 397 [1970]), the Court found an implied right of action in the Social Security Act of 1935, stating that it is the duty of federal courts to resolve disputes as to whether federal funds allocated to the states or welfare programs are properly expended.

59. 403 U.S. 388 (1971).

60. See Armand Derfner, "Background and Origin of the Civil Rights Attorney's Fees Awards Act of 1976," *Urban Lawyer* 37 (2005), 653.

61. See Hearings on Legal Fees before the Subcommittee on the Representation of Citizen Interests, Senate Judiciary Committee, 93rd Congress, 1st Session, 1973.

62. For a discussion of these efforts (and there successes in the early 1970s), see Frances Derfner, "One Giant Step: The Civil Rights Attorney's Fees Awards Act of 1976, *St. Louis Law Journal* 21 (1977); Farhang, *The Litigation State*, 147–71.

63. 365 U.S. 167 (1961). The Court also decided *Mapp v. Ohio* (367 U.S. 643) the same year, with similar importance for the field of criminal law. By extending the exclusionary rule for Fourth Amendment violations to all federal and state prosecutions, *Mapp v. Ohio* quickly became a landmark case for criminal procedure.

64. 42 U.S.C. 1983 (2000).

65. The Enforcement Act of 1871, 17 Statute 13.

66. See Robert J. Kaczorowski, "Revolutionary Constitutionalism in the Era of the Civil War and Reconstruction," *NYU Law Journal* 61 (1986), 863. Because blacks in the postwar South could not be expected to bear the costs of civil law suits at the time, the government took responsibility for enforcement under the new Department of Justice, which had been created at least partially for that purpose in 1870.

67. 83 U.S. 36 (1873).

68. 92 U.S. 542 (1876) and 106 U.S. 629 (1883). In total, in these cases the Court effectively began to lay the groundwork for the "state action" requirement that the Rehnquist Court would come to rely on in its own Section 1983 decisions; that is, because many constitutional amendments are phrased as prohibitions against government action ("Congress shall make no law"), it is impossible to sue private parties for their wrongdoings, and lawsuits must show that the government was responsible for the violation of their rights.

69. This was partially because of the original purpose of the Civil Rights Act of 1871 and the problems that it sought to address, namely the mistreatment of African Americans during Reconstruction. In the early part of the twentieth century, blacks successfully sought 1983 remedies in several voting rights cases, for example, *Myers v. Anderson*, 238 U.S. 368 (1915); *Nixon v. Herndon*, 273 U.S. 536 (1927); *Lane v. Wilson*, 307 U.S. 268 (1939).

70. 313 U.S. 299 (1941).

71. 321 U.S. 649 (1943). For a thorough discussion of the legal treatment of the white primary, see Michael Klarman, *From Jim Crow to Civil Rights: The Supreme Court and the Struggle for Racial Equality* (New York: Oxford University Press, 2004).

72. The outcome in *Monroe* was also in many ways made possible by the enforcement of criminal claims against government officials during Section 1983's period of disuse. In *Screws v. United States* (325 U.S. 91 [1945]), for example, Screws (a Georgia sheriff who handcuffed a black man, Robert Hall, and beat him until he was unconscious) argued that because his actions violated Georgia laws, they were

clearly not performed "under the color of law." The Court, however, rejected this argument, setting the stage for the rebirth of Section 1983.

73. Schuck, *Suing Government*, 48.

74. *Bivens v. Six Unknown Named Agents*, 403 U.S. 388 (1971), at 396–97.

75. *Tenney v. Brandhove*, 341 U.S. 367, 376 (1951).

76. 416 U.S. 232 (1974), at 238.

77. *Wood v. Strickland*, 420 U.S. 308 (1975), at 322.

78. 424 U.S. 409 (1976).

79. "Civil Rights Improvements Act of 1977," Hearings before the Subcommittee on the Constitution of the Committee on the Judiciary, United States Senate, 95th Congress, 2nd Session, February 8, 1978, 34.

80. "Civil Rights Improvements Act of 1977," 5.

81. "Civil Rights Improvements Act of 1977," February 9, 1978, 304–05.

82. "Federalism and the Federal Judiciary," Hearings before the Subcommittee on Separation of Powers of the Committee on the Judiciary, United States Senate, 98th Congress, 1st Session, March 16, 1983, 7–8.

83. See Barry Friedman, "When Rights Encounter Reality: Enforcing Federal Remedies," *Southern California Law Review* 65 (1992), 735.

84. The test was developed over the course of three cases: *Swann v. Charlotte-ecklenburg Board of Education*, 402 U.S. 1 (1971); *Milliken v. Bradley*, 418 U.S. 717 (1974); *Milliken v. Bradley*, 433 U.S. 267 (1977).

85. *Milliken v. Bradley* (1977), at 280–81.

86. Lower courts, by contrast, have been very active at different points in time in terms of issuing sweeping institutional orders whereby the courts have effectively taken control of restructuring entire institutions, such as state prisons and mental hospitals. See also Frank M. Johnson, "The Constitution and the Federal District Judge," *Texas Law Review* 54 (1976), 903.

87. *Davis v. Passman*, 442 U.S. 228 (1979), and *Carlson v. Green*, 446 U.S. 14, 1980.

88. 422 U.S. 66 (1975). The statute in question, 18 U.S.C. 610, prohibited corporations from making contributions or expenditures in connection with presidential elections.

89. See, for example, *Chrysler Corporation v. Brown*, 441 U.S. 281 (1979).

90. 441 U.S. 677 (1979).

91. 446 U.S. 14 (1980). That the Court recognized this claim under the Eighth Amendment was especially significant given that the prisoner's allegations may also have supported suit against the United States under the Federal Tort Claims Act, which has regularly been held to disallow private enforcement. The underlying premises of such rulings were that rights were predicates for remediation and that courts were therefore supposed to respond to claims of wrongdoing. Thus, absent positive indications that federal adjudication would interfere with congressional or state remedies, courts could imply causes of action on behalf of individuals seeking to enforce constitutional or statutory provisions.

92. Ibid., at 688.

93. See *Touche Ross and Co. v. Redington*, 422 U.S. 560 (1979), at 575.

94. 444 U.S. 11 (1979).

95. For example, in *Schweiker v. Chilicky* (487 U.S. 412 [1988]), the Court determined that a cause of action should not be implied for the violation of rights where Congress had already provided a remedy for the violation at issue, even if such remedy was inadequate.

96. See generally Schuck, *Suing Government*, and Appendix 1: Volume of Federal Court Litigation Against Governments and Public Officials, 199.

97. *Scheuer v. Rhodes*, 416 U.S. 232 (1974).

98. *Wood v. Strickland*, 420 U.S. 308 (1975).

99. Quote from *Butz v. Economou*, 438 U.S. 478 (1978). See also Schuck, *Suing Government*, 89. During the same time period, the Court maintained absolute immunity for officials engaged in rulemaking (see *Supreme Court of Virginia v. Consumers Union*, 446 U.S. 719 [1980]) and for judges (see *Pierson v. Ray*, 386 U.S. 547 [1967]). In the latter, however, the Court did specify that police officials enjoy only qualified immunity, noting that the question of immunities is "far more complex" for high-level officials and judges because their discretion is "virtually infinite."

100. *Monell v. Department of Social Services of the City of New York*, 436 U.S. 658 (1978).

101. *Gomez v. Toledo*, 446 U.S. 635 (1980).

102. *Lake County Estates v. Lake Tahoe Regional Planning Agency*, 440 U.S. 391 (1979).

103. 448 U.S. 1 (1980). *Congressional Record* (January 20, 1987), 1473–78. The Municipal Liability Law was proposed by Senator Orrin Hatch.

104. Schuck, *Suing Government*, 49.

105. See, for example, *Middlesex County Sewerage Authority v. National Sea Clammers Association*, 453 U.S. 1 (1981).

106. In general, beginning in the 1980s, the Court seemed to establish a precedent that a private plaintiff would have no cause of action unless a statute grants one, or unless there is clear congressional intent to grant one. Where the *Cort* test is concerned, the Court tends to use them only to find evidence of congressional intent (*Universities Research Association v. Cotu*, 450 U.S. 754 [1981], for example), or to ignore it entirely (see *Karahalios v. National Federation of Federal Employees*, 489 U.S. 527 [1989]).

107. 489 U.S. 189 (1989).

108. For a detailed treatment of this case, see Lynda Dodd, "*DeShaney v. Winnebago County*: Governmental Neglect and the 'Blessings of Liberty,'" in Myriam Giles and Risa Golubuff, eds., *Civil Rights Stories* (New York: Foundation Press, 2007), 185.

109. The Court also seemed prepared to confer absolute immunity on officials engaged in rulemaking; see *Supreme Court of Virginia v. Consumers Union*, 446 U.S. 719 (1975).

110. See Richard H. Fallon and Daniel J. Meltzer, "New Law, Non-Retroactivity, and Constitutional Remedies," *Harvard Law Review* 104 (1991), 1731; Rudovsky, "Running in Place," 1215.

111. 457 U.S. 800 (1982).

112. Ibid., at 818.

113. This standard also applies to common law cases, recognizing no remedy for common law causes of action, such as simple negligence.

114. See *Pierson v. Ray*, 386 U.S. 547 (1967).

115. David Rudovsky, "Running in Place: The Paradox of Expanding Rights and Restricted Remedies," *University of Illinois Law Review* (2005), 1217.

116. 475 U.S. 335 (1986).

117. Fletcher, "Historical Interpretation of the Eleventh Amendment."

118. See *Monaco v. Mississippi*, 292 U.S. 313 (1934).

119. *Fitzpatrick v. Bitzer*, 427 U.S. 445 (1976).

120. 440 U.S. 332 (1979).

121. See *Will v. Michigan Department of State Police*, 491 U.S. 98 (1989).

122. 421 U.S. 240 (1975).

123. See Derfner, "One Giant Step."

124. "Civil Rights Attorneys' Fees Awards Act," 94th Congress, 2nd Session, S. Report No. 94-1011, June 29, 1976. Congress also passed various statutes with fee-shifting provisions during the same timeframe (including the Toxic Substances Control Act of 1976, for example). For more on these statutes, see Derfner, "One Giant Step."

125. Sean Farhang discusses this episode, particularly in the case of Title VII litigation, in "The Political Development of Job Discrimination Litigation, 1963–1976, *Studies in American Political Development* 23 (2009), 23–60.

126. *Congressional Record*, 94th Congress, 2nd Session, September 21, 1976 (31,473–4) and September 28 (32,933–4).

127. Ibid., September 29 (33,314).

128. Ibid., October 1 (35,127).

129. Ibid., September 21 (31,472).

130. Andrew M. Siegel, "The Court Against Courts: Hostility to Litigation as an Organizing Theme in the Rehnquist Court's Jurisprudence," *Texas Law Review* 64 (2006), 1136.

131. Derfner, "One Giant Step," 448.

132. Equal Access to Justice Act, Pub. L. 96–481.

133. See John Leubsdorf, "Toward a History of the American Rule on Attorney Fee Recovery," *Law and Contemporary Problems* 47 (1984), 9–36.

134. 446 U.S. 754 (1980).

135. 461 U.S. 424 (1983).

136. 459 U.S. 460 (1987).

137. 461 U.S. 952 (1988).

138. 489 U.S. 782 (1989).

139. *Marek v. Chesny*, 473 U.S. 1 (1985).

140. *Evans v. Jeff D.*, 475 U.S. 717 (1986).

141. Farhang, *The Litigation State*.

142. Prior to this time, Congress did periodically limit attorney fee awards with the idea of protecting specific groups and individuals from unjust claims that interfered with broader public goals. See *Calhoun v. Massie*, 253 U.S. 170 (1920).

143. "Impact of Product Liability," Committee on Small Business, September 8, 1976.

144. Ibid., at 661.

145. "Product Liability Insurance," Hearings before the Subcommittee on Capital, Investment and Business Opportunities of the Committee on Small Business," H.R. 95th Congress, April 4, 6, 18, 1977, 12.

146. Ibid., 24–25.

147. Dan Quayle, "Civil Justice Reform," *American University Law Review* 41 (1992), 567.

148. *Congressional Record* (November 22, 1993), 31652.

149. *Congressional Record* (March 31, 1992), 7662.

150. Ibid.

151. H.R. 10, 104th Congress 101, 1995.

152. "Attorney Accountability Act of 1995," 104th Congress, 1st Session, H.R. Report No. 104-62, March 1, 1995; Joan Biskupic, "To Discourage Lawsuits, House GOP Would Preempt State Laws," *Washington Post*, December 15, 1994, A25.

153. The bill's proponents most likely limited its reach to diversity cases because product liability and personal injury cases, which businesses especially worry about, are often filed in federal court in this particular way.

154. House Report No. 104-481, H.R. 956, 1995.

155. Neil A. Lewis, "House Approves Measure to Limit Federal Lawsuits," *New York Times*, March 8, 1995, A1. The bill overcame an amendment from Democrat John Conyers attempting to exclude civil rights cases from sanctions placed on lawyers for frivolous litigation.

156. The final ABA report was narrowly adopted only after the House of Delegates extensively debated whether the proposal would adequately guarantee access to the courts. See the *American Bar Association Journal* (April 1996), at 34. For a full discussion of the options raised by the ABA with regard to fee-shifting, see Taylor, "The Difference Between Filing Lawsuits and Selling Widgets."

157. ABA Offer of Judgment Procedure 10(d), February 1996.

158. H.R. 2603, 105th Congress, 1997.

159. *Congressional Record* (May 19, 1998), S5099–100.

160. 532 U.S. 598 (2001), at 618.

161. See also Catherine R. Albiston and Laura Beth Nielsen, "The Procedural Attack on Civil Rights: The Empirical Reality of *Buckhannon* on Public Interest Litigation," *UCLA Law Review* 54 (2007), 1087–134.

162. Farhang, *The Litigation State*. He finds that Congress enacted 104 "damages enhancing" statutory provisions between 1887 and 2004.
163. See Chemerinsky, *The Conservative Assault on the Constitution*. Other examples include the state of Virginia, which provides that punitive damages cannot be more than three times the compensatory award; Alaska, where they cannot be greater than the larger of either 1.5 million or three times the size of the compensatory damages; and California, where voters established that punitive damages cannot be more than four times greater than compensatory damages.
164. Siegel, "The Court Against Courts," 1149.
165. Chemerinsky, *The Conservative Assault on the Constitution*, 236.
166. 486 U.S. 71 (1988). For example, the Court summarized the potential issues regarding the Eighth Amendment's excessive fines clause, the equal protection clause of the Fourteenth Amendment, the contract clause, and the guarantee of due process.
167. 499 U.S. 1 (1991). In declining to reverse the reward, the Court argued that adequate instructions had been made available to the jury to guide them in determining the award amount, and that judicial review of the award had been available at both the district court and appellate levels.
168. *Honda Motor Company, Ltd. v. Oberg*, 512 U.S. 415 (1994).
169. *TXO Production Corp. v. Alliance Resources Corp.*, 509 U.S. 443 (1993).
170. In 1996 Clinton vetoed the Product Liability Fairness Act, which would have limited the amounts that plaintiffs could receive in punitive damages in product liability cases.
171. *BMW of North American, Inc. v. Gore*, 517 U.S. 559 (1996).
172. Ibid.
173. Siegel, "The Court Against Courts," 1149.
174. H.R. 1639, 107th Congress.
175. S. 2743 and H.R. 4942 (both 2002).
176. P.L. 105–19.
177. They did so by finding that the harm in the case was physical; that the offending conduct indicated a reckless disregard for the health and safety of others; that the target was financially vulnerable; that the conduct was repeated; and that the harm resulted from intentional deceit.
178. *Suter v. Artist M.* 503 U.S. 347 (1992).
179. See Richard H. Fallon and Daniel J. Meltzer, "New Law."
180. 536 U.S. 273 (2002), at 278.
181. *Cannon v. University of Chicago* 441 U.S. 677 (1979).
182. *Alexander v. Sandoval*, 532 U.S. 275 (2001). The Court further restricted the ability of individuals to enforce federal rights through private suits in *Gonzaga v. Doe*, 536 U.S. 273 (2002), holding that a student may not sue a university for damages to enforce provisions of the Family Educational Rights and Privacy Act of 1974; and in *Barnes v. Gorman*, 536 U.S. 181 (2002), holding that punitive damages may not be awarded through an implied cause of action under the Americans With Disabilities Act of 1990 or the Rehabilitation Act of 1973.

183. In 2013, for example, the Court held that Amnesty International USA lacked standing to challenge provisions of the Foreign Intelligence Surveillance Act, which empowers the Foreign Intelligence Surveillance Court to authorize surveillance without showing probable cause that the target of the surveillance is an agent of foreign power. Justice Samuel Alito wrote in the majority opinion that "respondents cannot manufacture standing merely by inflicting harm on themselves based on their fears of hypothetical future harm that is not certainly impending," and this holding has determined both that threatened injury must be "certainly impending" to constitute an injury in fact, and that "allegations of future injury" are no sufficient to establish standing. See *Clapper v. Amnesty International USA*, 133 S.Ct. 1138 (2013).

184. See *Correctional Services Corp. v. Malesko*, 534 U.S. 61 (2001).

185. See Brianne J. Gorod, "The Sorcerer's Apprentice: Sandoval, Chevron, and Agency Power to Define Private Rights of Action," Case Comment, *Yale Law Journal* 113 (2004), 939.

186. Ibid., 946. Gorod's article also provides a thorough treatment of how this lack of clarity has played out in the circuit courts.

187. *Seminole Tribe v. Florida*, 517 U.S. 44 (1996).

188. *Florida Prepaid Postsecondary Education Board v. College Savings Bank* (1999), at 672–73.

189. *Kimel v. Florida. Board. of Regents*, 528 U.S. 62 (2000).

190. *United States v. Morrison*, 529 U.S. 598 (2000).

191. *Board of Trustees of the University of Alabama v. Garrett*, 531 U.S. 356 (2001).

192. Chemerinsky, *The Conservative Assault on the Constitution*, 223.

193. Ibid., at 755.

194. Ibid., 225.

195. 534 U.S. 61 (2001).

196. 534 U.S. 204 (2002).

197. 527 U.S. 308 (1999).

198. See Judith Resnik, "Constricting Remedies: The Rehnquist Judiciary, Congress, and Federal Power," *Indiana Law Journal* 78 (2003), 235–36.

199. 527 U.S. 308 (1999).

200. Resnik, "Constricting Remedies, 245. See also Stephen B. Burbank, "The Bitter with the Sweet: Tradition, History, and Limitations on Federal Judicial Power," *Notre Dame Law Review* 75 (2000), 1291.

201. Senator Robert Dole, *Congressional Record* (September 27, 1995), 26548.

202. See Dorothy Schrader, "Prison Litigation Reform Act: An Overview," *CRS Report for Congress* (May 30, 1996).

203. See Malcolm M. Feeley and Edward L. Rubin, *Judicial Policy Making and the Modern State: How the Courts Reformed America's Prisons* (New York: Cambridge University Press, 2000).

204. See Margo Schlanger, "Civil Rights Injunctions Over Time: A Case Study of Jail and Prison Court Orders," *New York University Law Review* 81 (2006), 550.

CHAPTER SEVEN

1. See, for example, Judith Resnik and Dennis Curtis, *Representing Justice: Invention, Controversy, and Rights in City-States and Democratic Courtrooms* (New Haven, CT: Yale University Press, 2011).

2. Mark Tushnet, *A Court Divided: The Rehnquist Court and the Future of Constitutional Law* (New York: W.W. Norton, 2005), 11.

3. E. E. Schattschneider, *The Semisovereign People: A Realist's View of Democracy in America* (Boston: Wadsworth Cengage Learning, 1975), 102.

4. Marc Galanter, "Why the 'Haves' Come Out Ahead: Speculations on the Limits of Legal Change," *Law and Society Review* 9 (1974), 95–160.

5. Schattschneider, *The Semisovereign People*, 102.

6. Given the development and persistence of both an arbitration and litigation state, it may also be fair to characterize institutional change in this realm as evidence of "layering."

7. See, for example, Robert M. Cover, "The Origins of Judicial Activism in the Protection of Minorities," *Yale Law Journal* 91 (1982), 1287–316; Mark A. Graber, "The Non-Majoritarian Difficulty: Legislative Deference to the Judiciary," *Studies in American Political Development* 7 (1993), 35–53; Kevin J. McMahon, *Reconsidering Roosevelt on Race: How the Presidency Paved the Road to Brown* (Chicago: University of Chicago Press, 2004).

8. Marc Galanter, "Access to Justice in a World of Expanding Social Capability," *Fordham Urban Law Journal* 37 (2010), 115–20.

9. Judith Resnik, "Reinventing Courts as Democratic Institutions," *Daedalus* 143 (2014), 10.

10. Linda Greenhouse, "Introduction: The Invention of Courts," *Daedalus* 143 (2014), 5.

11. Bruce Ackerman, *We the People: The Civil Rights Revolution* (Cambridge MA: Harvard University Press, 2014).

12. Stephen B. Burbank and Sean Farhang, "Reforming Civil Rights Litigation: Why the Court Succeeded Where Congress Failed," in Lynda Dodd, ed., *Revisiting the Rights Revolution* (forthcoming).

13. Together, backlash to the rights revolution and constrictions on access to courts have both eroded rights protections and made the process of expanding others complicated. See, for example, Samuel R. Bagenstos, *Law and the Contradictions of the Disability Rights Movement* (New Haven, CT: Yale University Press, 2009); Jeb Barnes and Thomas F. Burke, *How Policy Shapes Politics: Rights, Courts, Litigation, and the Struggle Over Injury Compensation* (New York: Oxford University Press, 2015); Stephen M. Engel, "Frame Spillover: Media Framing and Public Opinion of a Multifaceted LGBT Rights Agenda," *Law & Social Inquiry* 38 (2013), 403–41; Charles R. Epp, Stephen Maynard-Moody, and Donald P. Haider-Markel, *Pulled Over: How Police Stops Define Race and Citizenship* (Chicago: University

of Chicago Press, 2014); Alison Gash, *Below the Radar: How Silence Can Save Civil Rights* (New York: Oxford University Press, 2015); Thomas Keck, "Beyond Backlash: Assessing the Impact of Judicial Decisions on LGBT Rights," *Law and Society Review* 43 (2009), 151–86; Anna Kirkland, *Fat Rights: Dilemmas of Difference and Personhood* (New York: New York University Press, 2009); John D. Skrentny, *After Civil Rights: Racial Realism in the New American Workplace* (Princeton, NJ: Princeton University Press, 2014).

14. Charles R. Epp, *Making Rights Real: Activists, Bureaucrats, and the Creation of the Legalistic State* (Chicago: University of Chicago Press, 2010), 1.

15. Karen Orren and Stephen Skowronek, *The Search for American Political Development* (New York: Cambridge University Press, 2004), 108.

16. Graham Greene, *The End of the Affair* (New York: Penguin Books, 2004 [1951]).

Index